Tourism
—
Passport to Development?

Tourism
—
Passport to Development?

Perspectives on
the Social and Cultural Effects
of Tourism in Developing Countries

Emanuel de Kadt

Published for the World Bank and Unesco
Oxford University Press

Oxford University Press

NEW YORK OXFORD LONDON GLASGOW
TORONTO MELBOURNE WELLINGTON HONG KONG
TOKYO KUALA LUMPUR SINGAPORE JAKARTA
DELHI BOMBAY CALCUTTA MADRAS KARACHI
NAIROBI DAR ES SALAAM CAPE TOWN

© 1979 by Unesco and the International Bank
for Reconstruction and Development / The World Bank
1818 H Street, N.W., Washington, D.C. 20433 U.S.A.

Library of Congress Cataloging in Publication Data

Joint Unesco–World Bank Seminar on the Social and Cultural Impacts of
Tourism, Washington, D.C., 1976. Tourism—passport to development?

Includes bibliographical references and index.

1. Tourist trade—Congresses. I. de Kadt, Emanuel Jehuda. II. International Bank for Reconstruction and Development. III. United Nations
Educational, Scientific, and Cultural Organization. IV. Title.

G154.9.J64 1976   338.4'7'91   79-18116
ISBN 0-19-520149-3
ISBN 0-19-520150-7 pbk.

Foreword

I N RECENT YEARS, BOTH THE WORLD BANK AND UNESCO have been involved in tourism development. Unesco's involvement has been mostly indirect, either supporting research projects in which the impacts of tourism figured or assisting in the preservation of cultural monuments which also happened to be tourist attractions. The World Bank has lent considerable amounts specifically for tourism development, in the form of finance for infrastructure such as roads, water supplies, and telecommunications in tourist areas, as well as for hotels. In some projects—for example, in Jordan, Senegal, and Turkey—the Bank and Unesco have combined their efforts, the Bank financing preservation of archaeological monuments as components of larger tourism projects and Unesco providing the necessary specialized expertise.

Whether tourism is an appropriate activity for developing countries to encourage has been subject to controversy, partly for the reasons spelled out by Emanuel de Kadt in his preface. The controversies have been particularly great on the noneconomic consequences of tourism; unfortunately, the debate has tended to be superficial. While our organizations have attempted to take account of sociocultural impacts in individual tourism operations, we have felt the need for more systematic approaches to this question. To this end, Unesco and the Bank undertook a series of activities which led to the present volume. First, reviews of the existing literature on the social and cultural impacts of tourism were commissioned from Raymond Noronha (the English language literature) and from the Centre des Hautes Etudes Touristiques of Aix-en-Provence (the literature in other languages). These surveys indicated a substantial and growing body of work on the subject; nevertheless, there appeared to be much existing knowledge that had not been published and so was inaccessible to researchers and policymakers. Before attempting to formulate guidelines for planners, or even to refine research priorities, the Bank and Unesco felt that it would be useful to tap additional sources of information and to have the issues discussed by persons drawn from government services and the academic and business worlds. To this end, papers were invited from persons with relevant experience, and a seminar was held in Washington in December 1976. Although this book is appearing almost three years after the seminar, its contents have already been useful to our efforts in assisting developing countries to take fuller account of social and cultural impacts in planning for tourism growth. We hope its publication now will serve to widen the group of policymakers who are able to make use of its information and its suggestions. In the longer term, we hope that the volume will stimulate researchers to take an increased interest in this field, so that future policies and decisions can be based upon better concepts and more reliable information than now exist.

Emanuel de Kadt, of the Institute of Development Studies, at Sussex University, was commissioned to prepare the background paper for the seminar on the basis of the submitted papers and then to edit these for publication. From the beginning, when he provided the analytical framework for the discussion of the issues, this exercise has benefited from his dual qualifications as a sociologist and as a person deeply concerned with the problems of development. We are also grateful to David Maybury-Lewis, whose skillful chairmanship of the seminar itself brought out the insights of all participants and ensured that controversial points were thoroughly explored in a lively but orderly fashion.

Professor de Kadt and the authors of individual papers bear full responsibility for all views expressed in this publication, and these views do not, and should not be taken to, reflect the views of either Unesco or the Bank.

S. M. TOLBERT
The World Bank

Contents

Preface

I N THE 1960S, SPURRED BY JUMBO JETS, CHARTER TOURS, and the growing affluence of the middle classes in Western industrial nations, tourism erupted on a grand scale. This was seen as offering a new opportunity for Third World countries to secure foreign exchange and stimulate economic growth. Their sunny climates, sandy beaches, and exotic cultures attracted a stream of vacationers, and resorts multiplied to meet the demand. With the oil crisis and the recession of 1974–75, there was a pause in the growth of tourism. The end of the boom gave new urgency to existing concerns about whether tourism produced sufficient gains for developing countries to justify the investments required. In addition to doubts about whether tourism yielded economic returns commensurate with its economic costs, there was a general questioning of some of the basic assumptions about the relation between development and economic growth. In the case of tourism, these doubts were reinforced by the belief that it brings larger adverse social and cultural effects than does development of other sectors.

In December 1976 the World Bank, as a major development institution, and Unesco, as the UN agency concerned with cultural development, sponsored a seminar to discuss the social and cultural impacts of tourism on developing countries and to suggest ways to take account of these concerns in decisionmaking. The seminar discussions were based on several sources. First, researchers and officials concerned with tourism in developing countries were invited to submit papers, some of which after revision are now published in this book. Second, a seminar working document which was, in effect, the first draft of Chapters 1 to 5, provided a framework for the discussions. In addition, the bibliographical research done by Raymond Noronha for the World Bank and Jean-Marie Thurot and others for Unesco provided invaluable source material for those preparing papers as well as for seminar participants.[1] The

---

1. Raymond Noronha, *Social and Cultural Dimensions of Tourism: A Review of the Literature in English,* draft report (to be issued as a World Bank Working Paper, 1979);

participants came from eighteen countries, including eleven developing countries in Asia, Africa, and Latin America. Among them were top government officials—including heads of several national tourism organizations—scholars, representatives of private business, and a small number of observers from international organizations. This book is an outgrowth of the papers presented to the seminar and the discussion that followed. The conclusions of the seminar and the list of participants form appendixes of this book.

Tourism and Development

It may well be asked whether it is worth concentrating on the development of tourism as such, rather than analyzing development in general and leaving policymakers to draw appropriate conclusions for particular sectors. Several factors justify a focus on tourism. Tourism is in one important respect different from other potential export activities: the ultimate consumer of the goods and services comes to the exporting country rather than having most goods and services delivered to him at home. An analysis of the economy of tourism therefore requires more careful attention to transport and marketing arrangements than in the case of most other exports. And the very presence of foreigners in the exporting country is widely believed to generate significant social effects by demonstrating alien and, what is perhaps worse, unattainable life-styles and values. Furthermore, there is strictly speaking no such thing as a "tourism industry," analogous to industries as normally understood (construction, steel, agriculture). Instead, tourists purchase goods and services from a variety of industries, with usually rather less than two-thirds of their expenditures being in the hotels and restaurants normally identified with the tourism sector.

Despite these differences, the problems special to tourism in developing countries still need to be set in the wider context of development, and the main questions addressed for tourism must fit in with the more general considerations of policymakers. In formulating those questions, and trying to bring a measure of coherence to

---

Jean-Marie Thurot and others, *Les Effets du tourisme sur les valeurs socio-culturelles* [The effects of tourism on sociocultural values] (Aix-en-Provence: Centre des Hautes Etudes Touristiques, Université de Droit, d'Economie et des Sciences, 1976).

this book, I have therefore been guided by the current state of thinking within the heterogeneous community of development specialists. This has led to some selectivity, with certain aspects receiving rather more attention than others. But the fundamental aim was to make the volume relevant to policymakers and others who influence decisions on tourism in developing countries. In addition to government officials and politicians, these include persons in the international and bilateral development agencies, academic institutions, and the travel industry. They will want to find some answers, however tentative, to the choices they face.

These choices are necessarily determined by the issues debated today, even if these were not recognized as central yesterday and may not be seen in the same light tomorrow. Dominant development concerns have changed over the past three decades.[2] With much oversimplification, it may perhaps be said that an earlier simple faith in the merits of economic growth as such has given way to questions about the balance of that growth and the distribution of material benefits. Also, the very definition of development is being challenged, not only in its economic interpretation but in its social, political, and human dimensions as well. Since 1970 a series of Unesco-sponsored Intergovernmental Conferences on Cultural Policies has stressed the importance of cultural development as an essential component of the general development of countries. Even so, the cultural and nonmaterial aspects of development are widely neglected by those responsible for making the crucial policy decisions both nationally and internationally, in spite of often rhetorical pronouncements on such issues as human dignity or cultural identity and pride.[3] These cultural and nonmaterial aspects are central to this book. Much of the argument hinges on the assertion that

2. An important turning point was the presidential address of Dudley Seers at the eleventh World Conference of the Society for International Development in 1969. The relevant issues are covered in his "What Are We Trying to Measure?" *Communications Series 106R* (Sussex, England: Institute of Development Studies, 1972). A more sociological perspective is provided by the introduction in Henry Bernstein, ed., *Underdevelopment and Development: The Third World Today, Selected Readings* (London: Penguin, 1973). A recent overview by an economist who has lived through much of the period and contributed significantly to development thinking from a Latin American perspective is O. Sunkel, "The Development of Development Thinking," *IDS Bulletin* (Institute of Development Studies), vol. 8, no. 3 (March 1977).

3. For an interesting view on the latter issue see R. P. Dore, "The Prestige Factor in International Affairs," *International Affairs*, vol. 51, no. 2 (April 1975).

there are often nonquantifiable tradeoffs between material and sociocultural costs and benefits.

Though this is not the place for a detailed account of recent trends in development thinking, three broad areas of concern are relevant to tourism.

First is the realization that growth alone may not suffice to overcome poverty within a reasonable time, and that the distribution of the material benefits of development among the poorest countries and the poorest population groups within individual countries requires special attention. From arguments about the general effects of different development strategies[4] on distribution of income, attention has come to rest on the staggering number of people, more than 900 million of them, living in absolute poverty.[5] More than ever before, the development community is searching for means that will enable the poor to provide for their basic needs through more productive work, more widely available social services, and increased participation in political decisionmaking. It needs to be considered whether the deliberate and large-scale development of tourism, conceived as a major net earner of foreign exchange, leads to results consistent with this newly identified goal of development.

The second area of discussion deals with the supposed causes of worldwide inequality and the workings of the international economic system. The contention is that no development strategy can hope to be successful without a restructuring of North-South economic relations as regards, for example, trade, investment, and transfer of technology. The debate on this has been cast in terms of movement toward a New International Economic Order.[6] More and

4. See especially Hollis B. Chenery and others, *Redistribution with Growth* (London: Oxford University Press, 1974).

5. Robert S. McNamara, *Address to the Board of Governors* (Washington, D.C.: World Bank, 1976), pp. 5 and 15. The figures include 750 million people in the poorest countries (with per capita incomes of less than $200 in 1975) and 170 million in the middle-income countries. Absolute poverty is defined as per capita incomes of less than $75 in 1969 prices.

6. The aspirations of the developing countries for a New International Economic Order found expression in the United Nations General Assembly, Seventh Special Session on the New International Economic Order, 1975, Resolution 3362. The issues raised are discussed in a number of important publications. See particularly: Reginald Herbold Green and Hans W. Singer, "Toward a Rational and Equitable New International Economic Order: A Case for Negotiated Structural Changes," *World Development*, vol. 3, no. 6 (June 1975); Dag Hammarskjold Foundation, "What Now?" *Development Dialogue*, 1975, no. 1/2; Gerald K. Helleiner, ed., *A World Divided:*

more it is realized that major institutional and structural adjustments will be needed in the industrialized countries if the poor nations are to achieve their development goals. For example, some nonrestrictionist response will have to be found to the flow of manufactured exports from developing countries in growing competition with domestic industries in the rich world. Tourism, as an export industry that does not significantly threaten employment in industrialized countries, may find increasing favor in international discussions and negotiations.

Third, "one-world" arguments question whether the pursuit by all countries of rapidly rising mass consumption will be feasible for much longer, given the consequent environmental deterioration and looming exhaustion of nonrenewable natural resources. According to this view, further rises in the consumption of the rich will increasingly conflict with attempts to improve the living standards of the poor.[7] The consumption patterns of international tourism are a particularly conspicuous example of the consumerism that is now being challenged in the industrialized world, out of reach of the poor countries' masses but within the reach of their elites.

The study of tourism and its effects has not, on the whole, taken a great deal of account of these broad issues. The dangers of this oversight are twofold. First, such tourism as does take place may not be planned so as to generate a maximum effect on development. Second, a pro- or anti-tourism stance might be taken up without real evidence to support it.

The Less Developed Countries in the International Economy (Cambridge: Cambridge University Press, 1975); G. N. Bhagwati, ed., *The New International Economic Order: The North-South Debate* (Cambridge, Mass.: M.I.T. Press, 1977); and Unesco, *Moving Towards Change: Some Thoughts on the New International Economic Order* (Paris, 1976).

7. The basic documents in which the issues are debated with conclusions that have very different implications for the rich as well as for the poor countries are the following: Donella H. Meadows, Dennis L. Meadows, and others, *The Limits to Growth: A Report on the Club of Rome's Project on the Predicament of Mankind* (Washington, D.C.: Potomac Associates, 1972); Science Policy Research Unit, *Thinking about the Future: A Critique of "The Limits to Growth"* (London: Chatto and Windus for Sussex University Press, 1973); J. Tinbergen, ed., *Reviewing the International Order* (Rotterdam: Bouwcentrum International Education, 1975). See also the view developed by the Fundación Bariloche, Amilcar Herrera, ed., *Un Monde pour tous* [One world for everyone] (Paris: PUF, 1977). Related, though with a somewhat different emphasis, is the approach which argues that many of the problems of the rich countries themselves should not be divorced from a "development perspective." See, for example, "Britain: A Case for Development," *IDS Bulletin*, vol. 9, no. 2 (December 1977).

Sociocultural Costs and Benefits

Economists who have examined tourism development programs have tended to emphasize the benefits in terms of receipts expected and to balance these against the costs associated with the program. Specific tourism projects, when their economics have been analyzed at all, have been analyzed with the tools of social cost-benefit analysis.[8] This methodology attempts to express all important consequences of a project in monetary terms to permit comparison with alternative projects and with alternative designs for the same project. It is now understood that low or negative social benefits so calculated can coexist with quite reasonable net benefits to the individual investor, and the reverse is also true. As a result of recent refinements to the technique, different weights may be given to the benefits and costs accruing to different income groups to reflect distributional considerations, or a concern with the growth consequences of alternatives can be reflected in the different weights applied to increases in incomes which are saved rather than consumed.[9] Inevitably, however, there is a need for extensive judgment by the analyst, and in the opinion of critics, cost-benefit analysis may conceal his value judgments and political views behind a sophisticated economic facade.[10] It might be less misleading if different types of costs and benefits were measured separately and their size clearly portrayed. Decisionmakers would then have to take responsibility for assigning the relative weights to each compo-

8. A study which sensitively combines macroeconomic and cost-benefit analyses is John M. Bryden, *Tourism and Development: A Case Study of the Commonwealth Caribbean* (Cambridge: Cambridge University Press, 1973).

9. See, for example, I. M. D. Little and J. A. Mirrlees, *Project Appraisal and Planning for Developing Countries* (London: Heinemann, 1971); and Lyn Squire and Herman G. van der Tak, *Economic Analysis of Projects* (Baltimore: Johns Hopkins University Press, 1975).

10. See particularly E. J. Mishan, *Cost-Benefit Analysis: An Informal Introduction*, 2d ed. (London: Allen and Unwin, 1975); Frances Stewart, "A Note on Cost-Benefit Analysis and Class Conflict in Lesser Development Countries," *World Development*, vol. 3, no. 1 (January 1975); special issue of the *Bulletin of the Oxford Institute of Economics and Statistics*, vol. 34, no. 1 (February 1972), especially papers by Paul Streeten, Frances Stewart, and P. das Gupta. The important book by Peter Self, *Econocrats and the Policy Process: The Politics and Philosophy of Cost-Benefit Analysis* (London, New York, Melbourne: Macmillan, 1975) deals with the major issues especially cogently.

nent, *including* those of a distributional, social, and cultural nature. Moreover, and more fundamentally, the essence of social effects, as these are generally understood, may not be reducible to monetary equivalents, so that some additional data based on other modes of analysis may be needed for decisionmaking.[11]

In the past, sociocultural issues and effects on arts and crafts have been at best considered as afterthoughts by tourism planners. They have not usually been equipped to deal with such questions even if there was a lone noneconomist on the staff. Virtually never assessed nor predicted beforehand are possible changes in the social structure of tourism development areas, likely modifications in class relations, and the more general potential consequences for the local area of attracting the interest of groups with economic or political power in the national or transnational sphere.[12] These social changes, together with important material effects on employment and income, are, of course, precisely the results that determine whether the process of tourism development is judged good or bad by the people affected.

Tourism studies have turned up a formidable catalogue of effects, but this research has not had much influence on development of tourism facilities.[13] Perhaps the catalogue was too large and the approaches, theories, and frameworks too diffuse. Perhaps the situations dealt with were too different. Perhaps there were value conflicts among different actors in the decisionmaking process which it was more desirable to paper over than to resolve. This book is based on the belief that it is worth attempting to analyze the impacts of tourism in the light of the development issues mentioned above, and that such an analysis will benefit from reference to the lessons on social and cultural impacts learned from other projects or other

11. S. Herbert Frankel, "Concepts of Income and Welfare, and the Intercomparability of National Income Aggregates," *The Economic Impact on Underdeveloped Societies: Essays on International Investment and Social Change* (Oxford: Blackwell, 1959), pp. 29–55.

12. An interesting exception to this was the debate in "The Standard" on whether tourism was an appropriate activity for Tanzania to encourage. The contributions to that debate were later published in book form. See L. G. Shivji, ed., *Tourism and Socialist Development*, Tanzania Studies no. 3 (Dar es Salaam: Tanzania Publishing House, 1973).

13. Noronha's excellent review of the literature *(Social and Cultural Dimensions of Tourism)* shows the multiplicity of issues addressed.

societies.[14] It represents a first step. I hope it will make the questions asked and answered in the process of tourism development a little more coordinated with those to which development planners are currently addressing themselves.

14. The following five chapters make use of much material discussed in the papers published in the second part of this book and in the other papers prepared for the Joint Unesco–World Bank Seminar on the Social and Cultural Impacts of Tourism, Washington, D.C., December 8–10, 1976. Since in most cases the source of such material can be deduced from the text (and the table of contents), there will be only limited cross-referencing.

Acknowledgments

W HEN I SET OUT on these, for me then quite uncharted, waters of tourism, at the time of preparation of the basic conference document, I was fortunate to obtain the help of Anthony Ferner in ordering and organizing the material. His creative input in those early days went well beyond the usual contribution of a research assistant. I remember it gratefully. Later, a number of friends and colleagues kindly commented on different parts of the first draft; they include Paul Isenman, Dudley Seers, Edmundo Fuenzalida, Rita Cruise O'Brien, David Harrison, and (extensively) Reg Green. Various members of the Tourism Projects Department of the World Bank also read the manuscript at different stages. Without detracting from the contribution of others, I want to mention Stokes Tolbert, Jacomina de Regt, and particularly Augusto Odone. His insistent prodding of what he once called my "melancholy view of tourism" was most useful—even if our interpretations still remain, I think, rather distinct at the end of the road.

The discussions at the seminar and the comments of many of the participants helped to rub down the rough edges of earlier output. Pushpa Nand Schwartz wrote a helpful summary of the synthesis document for the seminar and provided a report of the seminar discussion, which I found most helpful when writing Chapter 1. To the contributors, too, I owe a special debt. They responded with forbearance to my often extensive (and not always especially diplomatic) comments on their draft papers, making my job as editor interesting and rewarding. I hope they feel it was all worthwhile.

Most of the typing of many waves of drafts was done by the staff of Tourism Projects Department, though a great deal of work, under a great deal of pressure, was also done at Sussex, especially by Audrey Hugett and Jo Stannard.

There are two persons whose input contributed substantially to whatever merit this work may now seem to have, and to them I am especially grateful. Frank Mitchell, of the Tourism Projects Department, not only commented critically and incisively on draft upon draft, but also played a major part in producing the final version. His advice on reorganizing Chapters 1 to 3 and his extensive suggestions for textual change were crucial in getting the published version into the final stage. Jane Carroll collaborated with me on the editing of the assembled papers, and she also worked over my own text. In the course of many months of transatlantic cooperation we established a close working relationship, during which I developed much admiration for her patience, insight, and immense professionalism. How fortunate I am to have been able to work with her.

Harry Einhorn read and corrected proof of the book, Margaret H. Seawell prepared the index, and Larry A. Bowring drew the maps. Typography and graphics for the book were coordinated by Joyce C. Eisen, Pensri Kimpitak, V. Clare Warren, and Joseph F. Malloy, and design and production were supervised by Brian J. Svikhart.

The usual disclaimer, that all faults remain mine and all views expressed my responsibility, is clearly more than a formality in the light of such extensive help received.

EMANUEL DE KADT

Part I

The Issues Addressed

CHAPTER 1

Introduction

T OURISM IS A MAJOR ECONOMIC ACTIVITY. In 1975 over 200 million international visitors spent around US$45 thousand million after reaching their destinations. Of these amounts, the lower- and middle-income countries secured approximately 30 million visitors and earned US$10 thousand million from them.[1] These earnings came to around 1 percent of the gross national product of the destination countries. Moreover, they were second only to foreign exchange earnings from petroleum exports and were almost double those from sugar, which was the next most important primary commodity exported from developing countries in that year.[2] In many countries, domestic travel by residents of the country is also significant, so that tourism is economically more important than the figures on international travel alone would imply.

These aggregates serve to illustrate the global importance of tourism. It is, however, impossible to generalize on the social impacts of

1. The data exclude the centrally planned economies. Lower- and middle-income countries are defined as those which in 1976 had per capita incomes of US$2,500 or less. Countries with per capita GNPs of between $1,500 and $2,500 (Hong Kong, Iran, Malta, Netherlands Antilles, Portugal, Puerto Rico, Yugoslavia, and Trinidad and Tobago) had foreign exchange earnings from tourism of around US$3 thousand million, leaving $7 thousand million for countries with incomes lower than this. These figures exclude receipts from tourists on transport account (such as international air fares). The data on tourist receipts were drawn from International Monetary Fund balance of payments tapes and national sources. Visit data were drawn from *UN Statistical Yearbooks* (annual) and the World Tourism Organization, *International Tourism Statistics* (annual). The figures refer strictly to visits rather than to visitors. The latter figure is unknown but is less than the number of visits, since particular visitors may visit more than one country, or the same country more than once, during any year.

2. World Bank, *Commodity Trade and Price Trends*, Report no. EC-166/77 (Washington, D.C., August 1977), p. 13. Sugar exports amounted to US$5.6 thousand million; the next most important export was coffee at US$3.9 thousand million.

3

tourism at this level. Tourists differ, as do societies. The familiar caricature of the man in a loud sports shirt with a lei of camera equipment slung around his neck represents only one kind of tourist, and the stereotype of the host country population being able to meet all its basic needs with a minimum of physical effort or social or psychological stress—at least until the tourist invasion—is equally untypical. The economic, social, and cultural impacts in particular cases will depend upon the type of tourism and the type of society.

Types of Tourism

No unique and comprehensive classification of tourism can adequately serve all purposes. Noronha has ably summarized the main classifications in the existing social science literature.[3] Most of them concentrate on one or two of the following dimensions: the characteristics of the tourist (his income group, his life-style, his educational background); the characteristics of the tour (its duration, the number of countries visited, whether the tour is spent at a single destination or in several ports of call); the mode of organization (individual arrangements or packaged tour); the type of facilities used (both the mode of transport and the type of accommodation, which may range from camping outdoors, through renting a room in a private home, to staying in a luxury hotel); and the motivation for the trip (whether it is taken for business, as a pilgrimage, to visit friends and relations, or for a vacation).

One of the most recent typologies is framed exclusively in terms of the tourists' attitudes toward the tourism experience and the meaning they attach to it.[4] Tourist attitudes are not directly accessible to those responsible for tourism development, although it may be possible to identify typical situations in which certain kinds of

3. Raymond Noronha, *Social and Cultural Dimensions of Tourism: A Review of the Literature in English*, draft report, 1977 (to be issued as a World Bank Working Paper, 1979), section 2.

4. Erik Cohen, "A Phenomenology of Tourist Experiences," forthcoming, suggests four modes of tourist experience, ranging from the recreational (temporary relief from workaday lives through leisure or entertainment) to the existential (a search for a spiritual center external to the mainstream of the tourist's own society and culture).

tourist motivations will predominate. This can have practical importance, as the impact of tourism on the local population will vary with the predominance of different types of tourists. Those who seek to give added meaning to their lives by temporarily identifying with another and perhaps preferred culture—such as Jews going to Israeli Kibbutzim, hippies to Indian ashrams, and descendants of emigrants visiting the "old country"—will behave differently as tourists from those who have merely responded to the identical-looking travel brochures that describe sunny places at the sea.

Some tourists do not even tour: "settler" tourists retire to a destination. Among the cases reported in this book, they are most important in Malta and Puerta Vallarta, Mexico. They are still considered to be tourists because they do not earn their livings in the destination and because they do not share the cultural background of the indigenous population.

Some authors have used stages of tourism development as an ordering principle. Noronha has summarized these into three.[5] First, a few tourists "discover" the destination; second, in response, local entrepreneurs provide facilities to accommodate the growing number of visitors; third, "institutionalization" or mass tourism follows, when the further development of tourism facilities tends to come under the control of agencies—public as well as private—rooted outside the local community and often outside the country. Attempting to characterize a particular destination within this natural history of tourism development may aid the planner in identifying feasible alternatives and in assessing their possible outcomes. The sequence is far from inevitable, however, and the last phase may overlap with the first in the case of major developments such as the Mexican Cancun project, where infrastructure and hotels were built by national public institutions in an area with no prior tourism development.

Although the papers here refer to many different types of tourism, this volume does not deal at all with tourism by nationals within their own country nor with that immensely important reason for traveling—visiting friends and relations. As defined here, tourists are essentially people who stay in hotels or guest houses, not visitors who stay as guests in private dwellings. None of the papers deals with religious pilgrimages, tourism situations that are of over-

---

5. Noronha, *Social and Cultural Dimensions of Tourism*, section 4.

whelming importance in certain places (Mecca, Lourdes, Benares) and of secondary relevance elsewhere (Jerusalem, Rome). Pilgrims create special demands and possibilities not unlike those described by Cohen for the existential mode, where tourism has a deep personal meaning for the tourist's very identity.[6]

The situation most widely referred to in this book is that of resort tourism, which consists largely of tourists seeking sun and sand, staying in relatively large hotels, and often (but not always) traveling on a group tour that includes transport, room, and board in one "package." Resort tourism has been particularly important in developing countries that have secured rapid and large-scale growth in the number of tourists from Europe and North America in recent years. Some of the reasons for this were wholly or largely outside the control of the destination country—for example, the rapid increases (at least up to 1973) in the per capita incomes of the industrialized countries and the low prices of this type of tour. Equally important, however, were economies resulting from the application of volume production and marketing techniques to tourism. By chartering whole aircraft rather than buying individual seats, and by making multiroom reservations for a whole season rather than booking one room for a week or two, the tour operator was able to secure lower prices than could a single customer. By packaging transport and accommodation into "convenience travel," analogous to convenience foods, the tour operator also reduced the time the consumer had to spend in seeking out and choosing among different travel options. At the same time, the operator increased the number of options that could be considered, a factor which was particularly important in generating tourism flows to new and smaller destinations.

Another reason for the importance of resort tourism is that its growth and scale were relatively unconstrained by the limited skills, entrepreneurship, or savings of the population of the resort area itself. If the area had good beaches and reasonable weather, and was not much farther from tourists' residences than competing destinations, the human and financial resources required to construct and operate facilities for tourists could be secured either from

6. Cohen, "A Phenomenology of Tourist Experiences." Some students traveling abroad are not dissimilar to religious pilgrims, if they are seeking identity-affirming experiences, as are American blacks who study African history and culture at special summer courses in West African universities.

national or international sources if not available locally. While this feature made resort tourism an appealing choice for the rapid stimulation of large-scale development, it also had important—and often negative—implications for the social and cultural impacts of tourism on host communities.

To be successful, package tourism, like any other "mass" consumer product, has to appeal to a large market. The common denominator has been recreational escape from the problems of everyday life, in a resort offering sun, sea, and some ration of exoticism. Although mass marketing techniques have been used, only a small fraction of international tourism has been on package tours to developing countries, in part because the prices of such tours are still high enough to make them inaccessible to the majority. Continued rises in the incomes of potential tourists plus reductions in the real costs of travel should serve to widen the market. Tours could then be packaged for those who want something beyond mere sun on their vacations, and might entice from the beach those who would not initially have thought of other options on their own. Such tours range from cruises that offer standardized and mostly fleeting encounters with the natural assets or the culture of the locality visited (especially in the Mediterranean and Caribbean), through combined seaside and safari holidays (East Africa), to resort holidays that offer brief side trips to specially created or preserved environments where the indigenous culture of the destination may be experienced. Two such destinations are described at some length in this book: the village guest houses in the Casamance region of Senegal and the cultural tourism of Bali.

In the future, there may be more scope for growth in tours to developing countries where sociocultural experiences are the main purpose of the trip, as is already the case with much transatlantic travel. Liberalization of the rules regarding the minimum size of group which can benefit from low airfares on scheduled flights will enable operators profitably to package a greater variety of special-interest tours. Such tours might cater to an interest in art, history, or archaeology through visits to museums, sites, or performances. In this case, encounters with the local people would be incidental to the visit. Or the tourist might be concerned with present-day culture and thus necessarily seek out the people who are its bearers. The mixture of ancient monuments, cultural artifacts, and contemporary events forms a potent appeal for visitors to countries as diverse as India and China. Already, specialized tour operators send a few thousand people abroad annually from each major tourist-originating country, and there may well be scope for at least some market expansion of this kind of tourism.[7]

The Issues

Many sectors may have a claim on the limited resources available for economic growth and investment in a country. Their potential for earning foreign exchange and for bringing about increases in national income, employment, and regional development may be equal to or greater than that of tourism. The logical place, therefore, for a country to begin development of the tourism sector is to determine how it fits into the national development plan—if, indeed, one exists and is taken seriously—and what priority tourism development is to receive.

Politics and planning

In Chapter 2 matters of planning, intervention, and decisionmaking on tourism are examined at the transnational, national, and local levels. A good part of the initial discussion is normative, stating what would seem desirable from the point of view of the developing countries and arguing a case. This was inevitable, as there appears to be very little documented experience of successful and sustained planning and plan implementation in the tourism sector.[8] The same normative approach dominated the Unesco–World Bank seminar discussions on these topics, and recommendations for more

7. One classification of such special-interest package tours divides them into adventure/exploration holidays, action holidays, educational and cultural tours, pilgrimages, specialist tours of communist countries, tours for the gourmet, and one-time tours for specialized groups such as museum-goers and chambers of commerce. Thirty to fifty thousand such tours were sold in the United Kingdom in 1977, compared with a total of 4,960,000 package tours sold in that year. These classifications and figures were drawn from Economist Intelligence Unit, "Special Interest Package Holidays Abroad," Special Article no. 27, *International Tourism Quarterly*, no. 1 (1978), pp. 48–56.

8. There are more examples of bad planning, and especially of poor bargaining; see John M. Bryden, *Tourism and Development: A Case Study of the Commonwealth Caribbean* (Cambridge: Cambridge University Press, 1973), which presents some fascinating evidence on the Caribbean in chapter 8 and its appendixes.

vigorous, active, and widespread planning and intervention were formulated.

In the past, sufficient attention has not been paid to ensuring that gains from tourism development go to those most in need among the local people rather than only to the better-off or outsiders. Participants in the seminar agreed that, although a more equitable distribution of the benefits of tourism is desirable, mere tinkering with projects at the margin will not accomplish this. Rather, considerations of equity have to be at the center of national politics. The tourism sector cannot by itself correct or create conditions that are normally part and parcel of overall national social and economic policies. Government policy toward tourism and the degree of government influence—whether it be labeled "control," "regulation," or "intervention"—will be determined by a country's overall approach to economic and social issues and the role of the national government in tackling them. The cases discussed by contributors suggest that without active intervention, and without planning and monitoring, the proportion of benefits of tourism development accruing to the poor will be smaller than it need be, relative to the share which goes to better-off groups, to transnational enterprises and their senior employees, or even to the tourists themselves.[9] Even *with* planning it is difficult enough to ensure that the poor share in the benefits of development. The problem is of course not unique to tourism; similar comments apply to commodity production, import-substituting manufacturing, and export-oriented processing and assembly. Ultimately, as all participants agreed, the "model" or style of development adopted by a country is of primary importance in this respect. But the desirability of different models produced less agreement and led to a lively discussion of the relative benefits of capitalist or private development on the one hand and socialist development on the other.

Local capacity to control tourism development appears to be generally weak, especially where such development is rapid and massive. This is partly owing to lack of trained personnel and effective organization at the local level, but mostly to the sheer strength of outside interests that move in. They easily ride roughshod over

9. As Bryden says (ibid., p. 2): "Whether such benefits for tourists exist is not our concern. It is not part of a developing country's responsibility to provide benefits to the wealthier inhabitants of developed countries, who make up the bulk of the tourist market."

such limited and often ill-conceived by-laws and regulations as exist; alternatively, laws are often enacted after the damage has already been done. Resentment by the local population of tourism can, and often does, result. Such problems are less likely in the early days of tourism development and where it is promoted on a small scale. Successful small-scale projects may require considerable organizational inputs, however, and the costs of promotion and implementation may be high in relation to the costs of construction and equipment. Nevertheless, the prospective gains make it worthwhile to introduce more appropriate technologies and more workable organizations, such as cooperative arrangements, to encourage small enterprises.

It is rare that the people in the local community, whether through existing structures of local government or through specially created organizations, are given a genuine chance to influence the course of events—though these events will profoundly affect their lives. The seminar recognized the importance of this issue and recommended the creation of and support for community groups to ensure such involvement. In this sphere perhaps more than in any other, however, the needs of local people with regard to tourism development cannot be isolated from wider sociopolitical considerations. Participation in tourism planning is likely to be meaningful only where popular participation in politics is acceptable to the government and is promoted as a counterweight to the power that can be mobilized by those who stand to gain most from uncontrolled development.[10]

Chapter 2 also examines the problems inherent in collaboration with foreign transnational enterprises and the possibilities for increasing national participation in the tourism sector. There is some discussion of the desirability of regional agreements on tourism development, especially among a number of small countries in competition with each other. Regional cooperation may be particularly useful in combating the market strength of large tour operators who

---

10. An interesting discussion of these issues can be found in Albert Meister, "Quelques Problèmes de la recherche sociale et sociologique appliquée au développement participationniste," *Genève-Afrique,* vol. 10, no. 2 (1971), pp. 5-67. For a case study of the impact of a changed political environment on local capacity to participate, see Emanuel de Kadt, *Catholic Radicals in Brazil* (Oxford and London: Royal Institute of International Affairs and Oxford University Press, 1970), especially chapters 10–14.

have a great influence on the choice of destination and the type and scale of tourism. Some seminar participants emphasized the difficulties foreign tour operators face in a very competitive industry. In spite of those difficulties, it was claimed, there are real opportunities for mutually beneficial collaboration with host governments.

In general it was felt that better information on the structure of the tourism industry, together with data on prices, should be made more widely available to negotiators and planners in developing countries. The complex links between tour operators, hotels, and airlines need to be fully understood if benefits to the host country are to be increased while economic, social, and cultural costs are kept low. This is equally true as regards the operation of transnational hotel chains and such multifarious arrangements between transnational tourism enterprises and local operators as operating and management contracts, franchise agreements, and hotel-leasing arrangements.[11]

Economic benefits and social welfare

The central issue of the material benefits from tourism development—the question who benefits or suffers, and how much—is addressed in Chapter 3. The most obvious and immediate benefit of tourism is the creation of jobs and the opportunity for people to increase their income and standard of living. Employment generated directly in the tourism sector, in hotels and restaurants, is generally shown to yield earnings at least as high as, and often higher than, those available in other sectors, especially agriculture. Tourism also has secondary spillover effects in other sectors. Through increased demand for food products, souvenirs, and other goods, it generates employment in agriculture, food processing, handicrafts, and light manufacturing. Jobs also will be created in construction and capital goods industries when new hotels and resort complexes are built. Special problems may arise, however, when construction booms end and unemployment results.

---

11. An important, but unfortunately not yet generally available report, *The Role of Transnational Corporations in International Tourism,* by John H. Dunning and Matthew M. McQueen of Reading University, deals extensively with many of these issues. More briefly they are discussed in Louis Turner, "The International Division of Leisure: Tourism and the Third World," *World Development,* vol. 4 (March 1976), p. 3.

The extent to which local people will benefit more or less than others from this employment generation depends on many factors. Expanding opportunities may draw in nationals from other regions of the country, and high-level jobs frequently go to expatriates. Locally, young people and women especially appear to benefit from tourism jobs, and their resulting economic independence weakens the traditional authority of the family head.

Other ways in which the local people can benefit are through the general improvement in the quality of life. Participants in the seminar were concerned that, along with the development of tourism facilities, planners should give attention to the basic needs of the local population for housing, water, sewage disposal, schools, and other services. Training and education for the local people were also considered. Special facilities or schools are one means to improve the skills of the host population for jobs in tourism. In some cases, on-the-job training could prepare local people for full management and operation of tourism facilities. Negotiations with enterprises which fully or partially own tourism facilities will have to provide for training of locals, and the agreements must carefully and methodically spell out details on how and when the objectives will be accomplished.

The ways in which the distribution of the benefits of tourism affect the social structure are only beginning to be understood. In some cases the emergence of a new entrepreneurial class leads to the strengthening of a middle-income group; elsewhere the existing power structure is simply reinforced by the growth of tourism, with those in the lower classes moving into the lowest layers of workers in the industry, while the wealthy are made even richer by the proceeds of the new development. As in other forms of modernization, rising real estate values may also skew the economic and political structure of society, depending on who profits most from the sale of land for the development of tourism enterprises. In many cases, as the local community is bound into the wider structure of the society at large, many of the benefits—and much new power—flow into the hands of people outside the immediate region or town.

The encounter

"Tourism is not a unique devil," as one participant remarked; it is but one of several modernizing influences, such as the mass media, education, and urbanization, that significantly affect the attitudes and values of people in all societies. The impact can be powerful on people who come into direct contact with tourists and particularly on those who work in tourism facilities. This is especially so in small or island countries, relatively isolated until recently.

Chapter 4 deals with changes in values and attitudes brought about at least in part by tourism, and it pays special attention to the nature and circumstances of the encounter between tourists and host population. Resort tourism is on the whole not conducive to informal interpersonal meetings and exchange. Resort tourists seem not to want such informal encounters, and it is unlikely that middlemen could arrange them for large numbers of people without destroying the nature of the exchange.[12] Resort tourists in fact seek a holiday environment that replicates the amenities and improves upon the life-styles to which they are accustomed at home. The tourist enclaves that are created thus have more to do with tourists' fantasies than with the culture of the host country.

Tourists' expectations about their destinations are generated or reinforced by the false images disseminated by tour operators, travel agents, the media, and even official tourism organizations. It would help dispel these misconceptions if the national tourism organization were to collaborate with tour operators and travel agents to publish and disseminate honest, up-to-date information that is also in good taste. National tourism organizations need to be more aggressive and imaginative in distributing this information abroad, both directly to tourists (perhaps while they are en route to the destination) and to the agencies they are likely to visit in preparation for the trip. At present, many host countries appear not to provide appropriate or adequate information on the choices they have to offer; nor are tour guides, airline and hotel personnel, and others who come in contact with the tourists properly trained to explain their country's culture, history, geography, or archaeology.

Most of the contact between resort tourists and hosts takes place in the context of service relations. Those who accuse mass tourism of demeaning the host population have such service encounters mainly in mind. But as the papers in this volume show, it is by no means necessary for the service relation to be one of servility, although in countries which have witnessed colonialism, slavery,

---

12. Tours involving home-stays do of course exist, but they are normally run by agencies that are partly motivated by considerations other than profit.

and racism, sensitivities are heightened. The general standard of living in the country, the nature of class relations, and the ability of those in service occupations to organize themselves and defend their interests (for example through trade unions) are other relevant variables.

It was generally agreed that tourism brings certain informal and traditional human relations into the area of economic activity, turning acts of once spontaneous hospitality, for example, into commercial transactions. Apart from this, it is extremely difficult to isolate the impact of tourism itself, or of tourists as such, from other forces of change.

Tourism is often grafted onto societies where the standard of living is very low indeed compared with that enjoyed by the tourists, and where extreme poverty is still widespread. In such a situation, the presence of free-spending vacationers, no longer bound by the rules of their daily routine, can be a particularly jarring phenomenon to the uninvolved observer. The gap between the life-style of the rich tourists and that of the poor inhabitants is perhaps most noticeable where large-scale resort tourism exists. Such tourists demonstrate values and behavior patterns that are now questioned even in the rich countries themselves.[13] It is not clear, however, that it is better to isolate tourists from the local population in order to secure economic gains while minimizing adverse social impacts. This type of strategy characterizes tourism in some Eastern European countries particularly. At the very least, it is obvious that excluding local residents from tourist facilities for the benefit of the tourists is widely resented.

Arts and crafts

In the area of arts, crafts, and cultural manifestations, dealt with in Chapter 5, the effects of tourism are also mixed. The frequent charge that tourism contributes to a degeneration in this field appears, however, to be an exaggeration. Even though curio production, "airport art," and performances of fake folklore are of course stimulated by tourist demand, the seminar papers and discussions brought to light that frequently arts, crafts, and local culture have

13. Apart from the basic documents mentioned in note 7 to the Preface, see the stimulating article by Johan Galtung, "Alternative Life Styles in Rich Countries," *Development Dialogue*, 1976, no. 1.

been revitalized as a direct result of tourism. A transformation of traditional forms often accompanies this development but does not necessarily lead to degeneration. To be authentic, arts and crafts must be rooted both in historical tradition and in present-day life; true' authenticity cannot be achieved by conservation alone, since that leads to stultification.

In many countries regional or local manifestations of culture have come to be newly appreciated by the local population. In some places this new interest in arts and crafts created, and in others it reinforced, a national sense of cultural identity and rediscovery. When colonies achieved statehood after World War II, this stimulated an interest in the cultural underpinnings—the roots—of the nation. This interest has found expression in new museums of history and anthropology, the revival of old cities, the celebration of festivals through dance, drama, song, and ceremony, and the creation of crafts centers. Tourist demand has given an additional economic push in these directions.

Policies to stimulate the arts and crafts often appear to be relevant only to those objects purchased directly by tourists, but the manufacture of craft objects for use in tourist facilities and by the population at large should also be encouraged. Government as well as private institutions can play an important role in giving technical assistance and vocational training and skills to people engaged in handicrafts. Similar collaboration or assistance is needed to design and produce objects to decorate hotels, tourism offices, airline offices, and airports. Marketing arrangements for local crafts are often felt to be inefficient, and distribution through government shops and cooperatives has been suggested as a way of increasing returns to the craftsmen. Unless such outlets are well run, however, they do not guarantee that the artisans will receive higher prices for their products than if they sell through private middlemen.

The preservation of simple historic buildings and traditional environments, for enjoyment by tourists and local people alike, needs to be more vigorously pursued. All too often only notable historic monuments and prominent plazas receive the attention of the authorities. Many less noteworthy examples of indigenous architecture, which are now usually left to deteriorate, could be converted to tourism use. The creation of integrated environments on a small, intimate scale could bring substantial benefits, both material and cultural. If properly planned, such environments should entice resort tourists away from the beaches to enjoy the ambience of the town. They would give added meaning to the entire tourism experience and might attract a greater variety of tourists to the area.

Host Country Situations

Faced with a considerable variety of tourists and types of tourism, a country interested in tourism development needs to ask whether, and to what extent, it can match its own resources with the requirements of different types of tourists. It also needs to ask what options it faces in developing these resources. Whatever the means chosen, the success of that development still depends at least in part on an assessment of the impacts it is likely to have. In this context a number of different host country situations may be distinguished.

Each country is unique in its geography, resources, stage of economic development, type of government, and so forth. Nevertheless, certain characteristics are relevant for making at least a preliminary assessment of the impacts tourism may have. Of particular importance are the size of the country and its general level of development. These same characteristics are important in considering the likely impacts of tourism in a destination area within a country.

Neither size nor level of development is a simple concept. Size refers not only to physical land area but also to population and its density. In small countries, especially islands, even modest tourist developments may place considerable pressure on physical resources and the environment, with immediate and dramatic consequences for the welfare of the inhabitants. Contacts between tourists and hosts can be frequent and intense, especially if population density is high in the areas visited by tourists or if a large fraction of the population is employed in the tourism industry, as is often the case in the Caribbean. Determining the level of development is yet more complicated, and gross national product per capita is only one, very imperfect, indicator of it. There also needs to be a concern with the distribution of wealth, skills, and education among the local population and the strength and resilience of local cultural traditions. If the indigenous culture and society is compatible with the values and roles needed to operate a successful tourism industry, development of this sector can draw at least in part on domestic resources rather than depending on outside skills, initiatives, and capacities for everything except sunshine and unskilled labor.

These issues are complex. Nevertheless, some generalizations and recommendations are possible. Small countries, with relatively underdeveloped production facilities and infrastructure and relatively low levels of skills among their people, are likely to experience more negative sociocultural effects as a result of tourism development than are larger, more developed countries. Resource-poor island economies with limited space are, however, precisely the ones that may have most difficulty in identifying viable development strategies which do not rely heavily on tourism.

The negative sociocultural effects are likely to be reduced if the growth of tourism facilities is neither rapid nor massive, and if there is time for local populations to adjust to this activity and for tourism to fit itself to the local society. On the whole, the seminar endorsed a gradualist approach, especially for small countries.

The notion of "tourist carrying capacity" was discussed in the seminar and seems to be worth developing. The term applies not only to the maximum number of tourists—or tourist accommodations—which seem desirable at a given time, but also to the maximum rates of growth above which the growth process itself would be unduly disruptive. If estimates of carrying capacity became a regular feature of all tourism sector and project planning, they would become a useful indicator to orient community and government discussions and decisions on this activity. From the cases described in this book, it seems highly likely that the carrying capacity of particular destinations would differ, depending on the type of tourism to be encouraged.

The few broad distinctions offered here are only a framework for discussion of the issue. Developing a comprehensive taxonomy of tourists and host societies, designed to assist predictions of impacts in particular situations and to serve as a basis for planning guidelines, is a task for the future.

At present, the data on different types of tourists are scanty. Usually, only data on the entrance, exit, and length of stay of international travelers are collected as a matter of course; most of the information that would be needed to characterize and categorize tourism development in any particular place, and hence rationally to plan for its likely effects, is simply unavailable. In the field of statistics as in any other, however, supply will often grow to meet demand. If tourism planners make continuing demands for relevant information, the data base will expand. Perhaps the issues raised in this book can help identify what information is relevant and what is not.

CHAPTER 2

Politics, Planning, and Control

B EFORE COMING TO GRIPS WITH THE VARIOUS SOCIAL and cultural impacts that tourism may have on host societies, it is necessary to examine the ways in which destination countries themselves affect tourism. Policy decisions will determine whether tourism is developed at all, what type of tourism is attracted, how fast it grows, and the size of the benefits it generates. In this chapter the discussion of the planning and control of tourism is divided into four major areas: the extent to which the basic sociopolitical structure of the society conditions policies on tourism; the success of planners in ensuring that tourism contributes to national goals; the extent to which the local destination area itself, as contrasted with the country as a whole, is able to control tourism for its own benefit; and the means at the disposal of destination countries to deal with foreign investors and transnational enterprises.

Politics and Tourism Policies

A few socialist countries, among them Burma, Albania, and—until recently—China, have actively discouraged international tourism, at least in part in order to reduce the degree of outside influence on their populations and to minimize the degree of dependence on other countries. But the majority of countries have not adopted this approach, and among those which actively promote tourism are many from both the socialist and capitalist camps. It would therefore be incorrect to assume that tourism can flourish only in right-wing, capitalist countries, and that the level of tourism serves as a sort of litmus test of a country's conservatism or its dependence on outsiders. The ways in which tourism is organized and its impacts can, however, be expected to differ considerably in countries with different political structures.

Apart from some intriguing references by Green, there is little material in this volume (or, for that matter, elsewhere), that throws light on the differences between tourism development in states which pursue a broadly socialist policy and those which do not. If the case of Spain may be of special interest to the tourism authorities of, say, Tunisia or Kenya, those planning for tourism in Tanzania or Algeria may find the experiences of Yugoslavia, Cuba, or Rumania more relevant. A comparative analysis of the social and cultural implications of the policies followed by the different Eastern European countries with respect to tourists from the West would also be illuminating. The major objective of their tourism policies is to raise the welfare of their citizens by providing appropriate recreational facilities; foreign exchange is only a secondary objective. Many of the Eastern European countries have shown themselves adept at extracting monopoly rents from Western tourists; for example, they are required to purchase minimum amounts of domestic currency at unfavorable rates of exchange and are charged higher prices for hotel rooms than are domestic tourists or tourists from other Eastern countries.[1] The "ghetto" resort tourism promoted by Bulgaria and Rumania, the more varied tourist menus offered by Poland, Hungary, and Czechoslovakia, and the *sui generis* approach of Yugoslavia, visited every year by millions of Western tourists by sea, land, and air, surely offer contrasts and experiences relevant for assessing the returns from tourism and the impacts of different types of encounter between host and tourist populations.

In most of the countries discussed here, the private sector has been given a predominant role in tourism development. During the 1960s Spain established strict regulations on the nature and quality of services and prices, but within these limits real estate operators, foreign entrepreneurs in the tourism business, tour operators, and foreign travel agencies were given great freedom of action. In its quest for foreign currency Spain reduced restrictions on the acquisition of real estate by foreigners, on the setting up or operation of foreign enterprises in Spain, and on the remittance of profits; it made available large amounts of official credit for hotels and vacation houses at interest rates that were little higher than the rate of

---

1. See, for example, Denise Cambau, "Travel by Westerners in Eastern Europe," *ITA Bulletin,* no. 40 (November 1976), pp. 883–99.

inflation during the 1960s. Moreover, the state itself took an active role in the tourism industry, running a network of reasonably priced *paradores,* state-owned hotels of high quality, usually built and furnished in harmony with the historical environment. Cyprus offers an interesting comparison, with less formal control over the tourism industry and less active state participation than in Spain. Foreign participation in Cyprus appears to have been kept intentionally to a minimum. In spite of these nuances, the ideological context of tourism development has been similar in both countries, while the sociopolitical structure has clearly leaned heavily toward individualism, free enterprise, and capitalism. In Tunisia, the state actively stimulated the emergence of a private enterprise tourism sector by giving entrepreneurs substantial aid and incentives, after assuming the risks of developing the first major tourism facilities. Between 1960 and 1965, 40 percent of the bed capacity was constructed by the state itself, but since the end of the 1960s virtually all construction has been by the private sector or by mixed private and government enterprises.

In such economies as these, an important component of tourism policy is to reconcile any conflict between the pursuit of private profit and the desire for social gains. Where the state is determined to maximize social benefits, investors will tend to find its regulations onerous, and they will probably exert themselves considerably to avoid those regulations. They may bargain with the state on particular projects or even attempt to influence legislation and regulations. Beyond that, it becomes a question of finding loopholes in the law or of corrupting officials to bend the rules. Where enforcement machinery is weak, the rules and regulations may simply be ignored. Central as they are to determining the impacts of planning, such issues as these are often hidden from sight and not infrequently obscured by ideological interpretations of reality. In the following section, we examine some of the experiences of tourism authorities in planning for this sector.

Tourism Planning

Most governments of developing countries that promote tourism do so in order to earn more foreign exchange, to increase national income and employment, and, sometimes, to achieve regional development of backward areas. Some small economies that are poor in natural resources may have few alternatives to the promotion of tourism in aiming for these goals. In others there may be plentiful alternatives to tourism. In most, there will be alternatives as to the scale and speed with which tourism is developed.

The main emphasis of tourism plans and policies has been upon increasing the gross returns from this activity in terms of higher foreign exchange earnings or more visitors. Less attention has been given to maximizing *net* returns, let alone ensuring that those returns are distributed in a fashion which corresponds to stated objectives regarding income distribution. In fact, I am aware of no evidence that any government has deliberately set out to assess the overall effects of alternative types of tourism in order to promote those that appear to promise the greatest net social benefits. Nor has any country been cited as having secured higher returns from this activity through appropriate taxation or other policies, although there is some advice on how countries could secure larger returns in dealing with the transnationals (taken up in the section after next). Instead, it would appear that tourism projects are often developed without being tested within the framework of a sectoral plan, while their costs and benefits may not even be compared with those of alternative projects in the same sector. Most seriously, although the sectoral plan should establish the place of tourism within the development strategy for the whole economy, in many cases such a plan is nonexistent or not decisively implemented.

Where tourism planning has been undertaken it has often been remedial, attempting to intervene after much development had already taken place. As in other fields, many countries have exhibited limited ability to learn from mistakes made elsewhere, and much planning may be characterized as "shutting the stable door after the horse has bolted."

Take, for example, the question of land transfers. In the Seychelles, restrictions were placed upon the sale of land to foreigners only after they had acquired almost a quarter of the land area of the islands, including much of the best land for development on the coastal plateau. After Mexican and foreign corporations and private individuals had illegally purchased communal land in Puerto Vallarta, regularization of those purchases in essence confirmed the new dominance of nonlocal groups in the town. Similarly, planning controls were not adopted in Cyprus until after private enterprise had been allowed to create utter chaos in Famagusta. As a final example, Malta introduced measures to curb land speculation after the boom had run most of its course, though in this case the steps were taken by a new government, elected after a campaign in which this issue had been stressed.

With the exception of Mexico, all these examples refer to small developing countries. In general, most small countries have only limited planning capacity, in part because they lack experts with the appropriate training. But in addition, planning techniques and approaches to planning are not particularly well adapted to the problems of small countries, where physical and social constraints to development possibilities may be much more acute than in larger economies. In the Seychelles, for example, the boom associated with building the airport and the new hotels, plus the opening of those hotels, placed unprecedented demands on the local labor supply and drew many persons out of the agricultural sector. With the end of the construction boom, labor did not flow back into agriculture and unemployment rose. This chain of events is similar to that in many other small island economies and in small areas of larger countries which have enjoyed tourism booms. When planners determine the pace of development, they apparently give little weight to the social impacts of such discontinuities in the employment market. In this, of course, tourism planning is no different from planning for other activities.

Another issue which appears to have received little attention from tourism planners, perhaps because little experience with it has accumulated in developing countries, concerns the likely life-cycle of a tourism product, or even a tourism destination. Many traditional European resorts have had their ups and downs, and some have seen their function and their clientele change completely. For example, the Côte d'Azur started as a winter resort, although now the heaviest traffic is in the summer. From catering almost exclusively to the rich, it now serves tourists representing a cross-section of Western European societies, excluding only the poorest groups. The history of tourism in Bermuda as reported by Manning is a similar case. Although it is impossible to predict the future with accuracy, planners do need to devote more explicit attention to the possible implications of market changes—for example, by consciously promoting diversity in tourism facilities. An awareness of possible future shifts in market tastes might also lead to restricting the total size of the tourism industry relative to the economy, at least where there are viable investment opportunities in addition to tourism.

Managing Impacts at the Level of the Community

The people who enjoy, or suffer, the main impacts of tourism are those who live in the communities in the tourist destination areas. The defense of community interests demands that those interests be formulated, and then that they be defended with the right kinds of executive instruments. These tasks would seem to be best carried out by those who have an intimate knowledge of local conditions, needs, and wishes, together with an interest in seeing those wishes implemented. Experience from the cases presented here suggests, however, that even where local authorities are endowed with the legal powers to regulate the effects of tourism through planning controls and responsibilities for municipal services, they often lack the human resources to grasp the issues involved. Usually, they have not established a clear framework to determine which questions need to be considered and what factors should enter into their decisionmaking. Their ability to enforce the laws and regulations ostensibly under their control is also diminished when such enforcement would hamper the activities of important interest groups outside the community. In other cases, the community, as such, has little or no legal authority to deal with development, such powers being vested in central or provincial governments.

Famagusta was, even before the development boom, one of the three largest towns in Cyprus. As such, it was presumably better equipped with a governmental structure than are most small localities where tourism gets under way. Yet it had neither the technical expertise nor the legislative powers needed to deal with the new problems created by tourism development. Even in areas where it could act—such as the control of building heights and densities—it was apparently tardy in issuing appropriate regulations and incapable of enforcing them against the weight of those who believed those controls were against their interests.

In Spain, tourism development in Fuenterrabia was much more gradual than in Famagusta. But in spite of this, local government was unable to act in a number of vitally important areas. It was beyond the powers of the local authority to resist sales of land to outsiders, to stem the outflow of profits accruing to them, to control outside investors, to make room for local initiatives, or to improve the job chances for local labor. Nor was it able to use the tourism-generated resources to diversify the local economy. Even where it did have the right to make decisions, as on matters of land use and infrastructural investment zoning, the Fuenterrabia municipal council failed to act.[2]

In Bali, the decrees implementing the tourism development plan are "statements of intention without teeth—they cannot be enforced." The profusion of uncoordinated regulatory agencies makes it easy to circumvent the few rules that exist, and the tourism industry has now largely fallen under the control of non-Balinese interests. In Puerto Vallarta, where the local authorities were equally impotent in the face of the activities of economically powerful groups from Mexico's large cities, there is a term for this lack of local control: internal neocolonialism.[3] Not only were local representatives on the local planning authority thought by some middle-class businessmen to be "too intimidated by the power, status, and presumed expertise of outside officials to be forceful in presenting their views," but the investments made by the authority were aimed at benefiting outside elites.

In two of the cases discussed in this volume, the interests of the local community seem to have been better safeguarded and promoted. They are at the opposite ends of the tourism spectrum. One is the Senegalese village guest houses built by the local people themselves and run by community cooperatives for tourists seeking a modicum of adventure during their basic sun and sand resort vacations.[4] In their limited scale and essential links with the local community, these isolated projects differ fundamentally from the resort tourism developments reported on elsewhere. To what extent their success could be transferred to the more usual kinds of tourism projects is difficult to assess. While the capital cost of these guest houses was low in monetary terms, the inputs of local labor and time were quite high, and receipts were modest. An essential ingredient of these projects was foreign technical assistance provided by an anthropologist. In innumerable meetings with government officials as well as villagers, he assisted them to understand the nature of the

2. Davydd J. Greenwood, "Tourism Employment and the Local Community," paper presented to the Joint Unesco–World Bank Seminar on the Social and Cultural Impacts of Tourism, Washington, D.C., December 8–10, 1976.

3. The term was first given currency by Pablo González Casanova, in "Internal Colonialism and National Development," *Studies in Comparative International Development*, vol, 1, no. 4 (1965).

4. See Chapter 18.

facilities required and to work out viable social arrangements for their construction and management. Many private entrepreneurs became interested in imitating this type of facility once its feasibility had been established in principle, and it will be interesting to see whether such schemes can be replicated without undermining their very nature and their close link with the local community.

The other example is Bermuda.[5] Tourism has been a major industry since the 1860s, and the main industry since the 1930s when depression-era protectionism closed the U.S. market to Bermuda's agricultural exports. Over this extended period, the economy, society, and way of life of Bermuda have apparently established a symbiosis with tourism. I shall return in Chapter 4 to the unusual adjustment of this small country. At this point, however, it needs to be noted that tourism development in Bermuda has apparently not been at the expense of the local inhabitants. Moreover, most of the planning problems endemic to small countries (the island is only eighteen miles square) appear to have been overcome, with planning having been aimed largely at ensuring that the environment remains attractive to tourists and that the island offers a contrast to other competitive destinations. This objective seems to be quite widely accepted in the society; although there are sharp political and social divisions, there is a high degree of consensus on the importance of tourism and how it may best be promoted. But it is of course hard to say how deep the consensus really runs, especially after the riots at the end of 1977.

Most communities have been substantially less successful than Bermuda or the Senegalese villages in incorporating tourism into their lives, and it must be asked what measures might be taken in order to improve that situation. Of importance is the legal allocation of responsibilities to community or local institutions for issuing various permits connected with development. At an early stage, local voluntary efforts could be enlisted, particularly in promoting the resort or in securing the interest of outside investors, but substantive local participation in planning requires well-defined local powers. Given appropriate powers, local institutions need appropriately trained people to formulate plans and implement them. Both of these points argue for strengthening the local government.

For community interests to be taken into account in tourism (or any other) development, it is essential that those interests be articu-

5. See Chapter 11.

lated from the moment potential projects are identified. That usually means that somehow local people have to be helped to grasp the issues from *their* point of view, by a process of education and increasing self-awareness that Latin Americans have come to call *conscientisación*. The mass of local community members would then need to be mobilized in active defense of their interests as they had come to see them. This is far from easy, especially if the wider sociopolitical context is unfavorable to popular demands. The important attempt in this direction by the Community Development team in the Ixtapa-Zihuatanejo project described in this volume highlights some of the problems.[6]

Efforts may also be made to build up the capacity of local individuals to participate in development and to ensure that they are given a fair opportunity to compete. In a different context McClelland has suggested a program to train and motivate local people to run small businesses that cater to the needs of tourists—shops, cafes, taxi services, agencies to organize local excursions.[7] Training could be supplemented by access to technical assistance and credit. To the extent that such measures were successful, the economic power of community members—and hence their participation in decisions on, and benefits of, tourism—would be increased. Even in resort developments that depend heavily on outside capital and skills, the outside promoters could be required to provide opportunities for local entrepreneurs to lease facilities or otherwise gain access to the tourist market. The terms would be subject to negotiation with the appropriate governmental authorities approving the project.

The issue of local community interests cannot, by itself, determine the desirability of a tourism project. But if social impacts are taken into account and undue weight is not given to economic considerations, then local community interests are probably better promoted by slower development of widely dispersed, small-scale facilities than by massive integrated and concentrated ones. In a small project community members can more easily develop and keep an interest, and the project is less likely to attract the attention of powerful outsiders who could use their influence with national or regional authorities to override local preferences or controls. In addition, it takes time for people to acquire new skills or perfect the

6. See Chapter 8.
7. David C. McClelland, "Developing Local Business in the Promotion of Tourism," paper presented to the Joint Unesco–World Bank Seminar.

skills they have, and gradualism would be less disruptive of the local society. Securing local participation in planning decisions is bound to be more time-consuming than an approach which relies heavily upon the exercise of national powers to expropriate land or make exceptions to general rules. A community-based approach therefore may cut severely into the profits that promoters might otherwise expect.

There are, of course, cases where gradualism is not a viable option. For example, at a destination where a major new airport is needed to give tourists access, only rapid and large-scale development will earn a reasonable rate of return on the airport. Rather than choosing between slower and faster or dispersed and concentrated tourism, the choice may have to be between tourism and no tourism. If the likely long-term social effects are judged to be negative, economic considerations of a good rate of return on the airport may no longer be given priority.

Evidence of the weakness of local authority is so overwhelming that the national authorities are frequently seen as having to take on the role of protecting local interests. This happened in Cyprus and Mexico, for example. In most places, it is up to the central authority to decide whether to introduce land development taxes, betterment charges, or capital gains taxes, potentially powerful and important weapons in the hands of those who wish to prevent the benefits of tourism growth from falling solely into the hands of the propertied classes. As Greenwood puts it: "The people must ultimately be able to find a powerful ally in the state or national government or their agencies, or they will have no allies at all."[8] Whether such an alliance can really safeguard local interests against the designs of outsiders depends upon factors beyond the control of planners. As noted earlier, government policies, decisions, and plans reflect both the broad balance of power in the society and the development strategy which that balance implies. Many governments are likely to be concerned about problems posed by unrestrained physical development, as in Famagusta, and willing to think of zoning or building regulations. Rather fewer will interfere when nationally powerful groups bend such regulations to their own advantage and in doing so reinforce existing inequalities and widen the gap between rich and poor, national elite and "peripheral" mass.

8. "Tourism Employment and the Local Community."

National versus Foreign Interests

Most of the poorer nations hoping to derive developmental benefits from tourism have neither a strong nationally owned private sector, nor a vigorous national entrepreneurial class, nor indeed much spare managerial capacity in the public sector. Such countries will necessarily have to place considerable reliance upon foreign skills and finance if there is to be tourism development. Introducing the options open to the governments of developing countries in promoting tourism, Green says: "Some believe that there is a standard, unalterable tourist contract package that involves ceding full control to external firms and then subsidizing the sector. This is not accurate."[9] While careful to analyze the constraints under which the recipient governments have to operate, Green leaves no doubt that a great deal can be gained by first examining just what services are required from foreign firms, and then by carefully negotiating for those services. In addition, general policies on taxation of the sector, employment of local citizens, and investment promotion may have an important role to play.

Knowledge, communication, and organization are the basic assets and sources of power of foreign enterprises for promoting and developing tourism. But those resources may not be equally necessary for all parts of tourism. At one end of the spectrum, most tourist destinations—even in developed countries—must rely heavily on foreign operators to package and market tours. Some local inputs are useful even in this function, and Spain, Bulgaria, and Yugoslavia have actually entered into tour operating, albeit with limited success. Where a country has a national airline, it may play an important part in arranging transport for tourists. At the other end of the spectrum is the provision of facilities in the destination country, including not only hotels but also handicrafts, excursions, and so on. In these areas the need for foreign partners is not so evident, although there may be benefits from foreign expertise and organizational abilities at the start. This is true even for handicraft promotion, where technical assistance, including that from private organi-

---

9. Chapter 6; Green adds: "Neither is the subsidiary belief that this package was designed and promoted by the World Bank."

zations, has played an important role in its development in some countries.

In the case of hotels, foreign expertise may be needed in hotel design and management, but hotels do not have to be foreign owned. The transnational hotel chains may be useful from the point of view of marketing, since they are well known and they help establish standards of service. They will generally fill key positions with expatriates who know from experience with the company how such a complex organization operates.[10] The replacement of expatriates and the training of local staff to make this possible is a policy which should be vigorously pursued; it is also an issue which should be taken up in negotiations, particularly on large projects. That legislation can work on this question is shown in Cyprus, where even tour operators and travel agencies are obliged to employ local staff unless persons with the required skills are not locally available. As for training, hotel schools at postsecondary level are being used in Tunisia. Countries with smaller tourism sectors may not find that feasible and may have to rely on overseas training combined with on-the-job training. Elkan supports a plan for on-the-job training in existing hotels.[11] He points to the paradox that these hotels stand to benefit from training staff for their future competitors, since this would reduce the likelihood of their own experienced staff being poached.

Empirical data from the seminar papers add some useful nuances to these general prescriptions and observations. The case of Bermuda shows some of the possible complexities. Between the two World Wars, when the island specialized in elite tourism from the United States, the local merchant aristocracy joined in the building of hotels as well as the provision of ancillary tourism services. After World War II, however, foreign interests came into prominence, first when they took over some existing large hotels that local owners were unwilling or unable to renovate, and then when international chains constructed large new luxury hotels. Nine of the ten large hotels (accommodating 64 percent of the tourists in 1975) are under foreign control and the tenth is in the hands of resident ex-

10. Doreen Calvo, *Caribbean Regional Study*, vol. 6, *Tourism* (Washington, D.C.: World Bank, 1974; restricted circulation document), mentions that it is usual practice to keep locals out of the higher echelons of hotel management in the Caribbean.

11. Walter Elkan, "The Impact of Tourism on Employment," paper presented to the Joint Unesco–World Bank Seminar.

patriates. This foreign take-over has been possible because the hotel industry is exempt from the general rule that there be 60 percent Bermudian ownership of all firms. The exemption may have been due to a simple lack of finance, though perhaps local investors decided that they could earn higher returns on their capital in fields other than hotels, especially since full employment exerted substantial upward pressure on wages and international competition exerted downward pressure on prices.

Gaviria notes significant differences in foreign penetration of different regions of Spain.[12] Catalonia, Valencia, and Alicante had a commercial and industrial tradition before the great expansion of tourism and therefore maintained local control of facilities to a much greater extent than did the less developed areas of the country, such as Andalucia and the Canary Islands, where the multinational enterprises appeared in strength. Gaviria also throws light on the way in which the tour operator relates to the local hotel and restaurant facilities in Spain. Seldom, he writes, do tour operators become involved in the actual hotel business. This they leave to specialized chains and particularly to local entrepreneurs, who compete savagely for cheap foodstuffs and labor to offer lower prices to the tour operators and indirectly to the tourists. Perhaps this is no more than a typical buyer's market, a situation in which there was overinvestment because of state incentives and a rapid growth in demand. It is a matter of judgment just how the state can best manage such situations and ensure that an optimal fraction of the gains from tourism flow to the destination rather than to tourists and market intermediaries. In the case of countries with a very strong tourism sector, such as Spain, the most effective means are probably to reduce incentives to investors and to increase taxes on tourist services. These measures would not increase the profitability of individual tourism firms, which would continue to compete with each other; they would, however, raise prices paid by tour operators and tourists and raise receipts to the country.

Such measures may be more difficult to implement in small destinations with many close competitors. There may even be fears that the country will attract no trade if it offers less favorable terms than its competitors. The issue of the sensitivity of tourism flows to prices requires more attention, as does the ease with which major

12. Mario Gaviria, "The Mass Tourism Industry in Spain," paper presented to the Joint Unesco–World Bank Seminar.

tour operators in fact switch their clients among different destinations in response to price changes. Where they have pulled out, were the reasons economic or political? Are there cases where operators have reduced their demands for bed allocations as a bargaining tactic?

In other fields, there have been campaigns for international cartels or price-maintenance arrangements. Green correctly notes that because of the heterogeneity of services involved, tourism is not an appropriate field for a seller's cartel on OPEC lines. Nevertheless, as Villamil has pointed out, competitors may stand to gain from getting together on a regional basis to develop coherent and common strategies to deal with the transnational firms.[13] Such strategies could include agreement on desirable levels of tourism taxes, the extent of concessions offered to investors, the basic terms which governments could approve for standard management on franchise agreements, and policies on training local staff. A first step in such action would be the collection and diffusion of information on these issues, which has already commenced.[14] Apart from affecting the overall balance of benefits between host country and foreign enterprise, the specific policies adopted on these issues can have more subtle social and economic effects. For example, incentives to investment may stimulate capital intensity and dependence on imported equipment and discourage employment creation.

Another alternative worth considering is for governments of the tourists' home countries to take a more active interest in the well-being of many of the poorest countries in the world. The terms of trade of tourism and its transnational organization may have to be scrutinized as closely as those of other sectors of the international economic order. The nature of packaging arrangements, the terms of management contracts, transfer pricing, policies on expatriate personnel, and use of imported inputs are only some of the issues that strong transnational companies may resolve to their own advantage when faced with weak or nonexistent bargaining partners. Negotiation requires destination countries to have specialized knowledge of the world tourism industry and of the firm negotiated

13. José Villamil, "Tourism in the Caribbean," paper presented to the Joint Unesco–World Bank Seminar.

14. Caribbean Tourism Research Centre, *Caribbean Tourism*, vol. 1, *Tourism (Hotel) Incentive Legislation* (Barbados, no date; processed), is a compilation of relevant legislation for several countries in the Caribbean region. The World Tourism Organization also collects and disseminates tourism-related legislation.

with, and such expertise is hard and expensive to acquire. Yet the trouble and expense are worthwhile, because those costs are small compared with what is to be gained. Unfortunately, too little attention is paid to the importance of data collection for negotiation, in tourism as well as in other sectors involving foreign partners. A kind of vicious circle exists because of the lack of data to indicate just how much is lost. Technical cooperation on these matters, or more direct regulation of the activities of the transnationals in their home countries, might have a more positive effect than some of the aid currently provided for tourism development—for example, funds to build large tourism complexes with donor technology and using donor consultant engineers.

Conclusion

Though governments may have some impact on the configuration of social forces, they inevitably represent the interests of certain groups more than others and operate within limits that are fairly narrow at any one time. To the extent that policies in any sector, such as tourism, reflect the existing socioeconomic situation, the development of the sector is likely to reinforce the position of the more powerful classes, confirming existing social patterns. As we shall see in the next chapter, however, this last proposition need not always be true, and the employment distribution of tourism may generate some shifts in the social position of particular groups.

The ways in which tourism is organized, and its impacts, can be expected to differ considerably in countries with different political structures. A whole range of policies and political outcomes determines in a broad sense how the benefits of tourism development will be divided: how nationals and the national economy will benefit on the one hand, and foreigners or transnational operators on the other; how the local inhabitants of tourism areas will fare in comparison with those coming in from other parts of the country; how the poor will do as compared with the better off. In these respects the tourism sector cannot be isolated from the rest of the economy, and sectoral policies regarding tourism are likely to reflect the wider social and economic policies of the government. Planners of tourism can do little to promote greater equality in the distribution of the benefits of that industry, if the forces making for inequality are left a free rein in their society and if policies aimed at the eradication of poverty are not vigorously pursued. It is a nation's overall political economy that will, in effect, largely determine the eventual social outcome, if not the initial economic shape, of projects. "Planning" can do little to alter this fundamental fact.

CHAPTER 3

Effects of Tourism on Life Chances and Welfare

T HIS CHAPTER EXPLORES SOME OF THE WAYS in which tourism may affect the life chances of the population of tourist destination areas. The term "life chances," first used by the German sociologist Max Weber more than half a century ago, denotes the probability of individuals' achieving during their lifetime an array of goals (long life, good health, a desirable job, recognition from their fellow citizens) and a range of benefits and resources (income, education for their children, housing, social security). Social classes are distinguished by their members' sharing different patterns of life chances.

The ways in which tourism development affects life chances are closely related to its effects on incomes and the distribution of incomes. The discussion here concentrates mainly on the nature of those impacts and the identity of the affected groups rather than on the exact amount of the changes in income.

Writing of Fuenterrabia, Greenwood states: "The major impact of tourism on local people over the past twenty-five years can be summarized in one word: jobs."[1] Questions to be considered are how much employment is generated by tourism, what types of skills are required, and what type of worker is most in demand (whether young or experienced, male or female, and so on). Tourism also generates incomes for others—investors, landowners, and banks, for example. The government is also a major beneficiary; even in capitalist developing countries it typically secures at least 20 percent of tourism receipts through taxation (indirect taxes on goods and

---

1. Davydd J. Greenwood, "Tourism Employment and the Local Community," paper presented to the Joint Unesco–World Bank Seminar on the Social and Cultural Impacts of Tourism, Washington, D.C., December 8–10, 1976.

services purchased by tourists as well as direct taxes on income generated in the sector) and may make additional returns if it also invests in this activity.[2] In many destinations, landowners also stand to secure substantial gains from selling their land to developers, and speculative land booms have been a feature in many countries which have experienced rapid growth of tourism.

The incremental gains to the society from transferring land and labor into tourism are rarely equal to the price or wages paid. These resources are typically drawn from other productive activities, and this shift in the use of resources may mean changes in the availability and prices of some goods. It may thus have repercussions on the welfare of people who are not directly involved in the tourism sector. Tourists also consume some of the same goods and services that are used by residents. If tourism tends to increase the availability of desired goods this will bring benefits to the local people, but if tourists compete with residents for a limited supply then the outcome will tend to be negative for the local population as consumers, if not as producers.

Employment Generation

The employment generated by tourism varies widely from place to place. In the larger and economically more diversified Caribbean

2. In Tunisia, the *net* budgetary impact (that is, budgetary receipts less budgetary costs such as promotion, interest subsidies, and the like) came to 15 to 20 percent of receipts, depending upon occupancy rates and the type of hotel and tourist. Indirect tax receipts alone came to over 10 percent of tourist receipts. (Tunisian National Tourism Office, *Etude de l'aide de l'Etat au secteur touristique* [Study on state aid to the tourism sector], prepared by Francis H. Mitchell, SETEC Economie, and SOTUETEC, Report no. 3, August 1975, p. 1.17.) In Kenya in 1966–67, total budget receipts were estimated at 28 percent of tourist receipts, and budgetary outlays at 8 percent, leaving a net return to the budget of 20 percent (Francis H. Mitchell, "The Economic Value of Tourism in Kenya," Ph.D. dissertation, University of California, Los Angeles, 1971, pp. 81–82). World Bank estimates, made when examining the justification for tourism projects, show that budget receipts generated by tourist expenditures normally range between one-fifth and one-third of tourist receipts. On the other hand, John M. Bryden, *Tourism and Development: A Case Study of the Commonwealth Caribbean* (Cambridge: Cambridge University Press, 1973), p. 178, finds that government receipts as a percentage of tourism receipts come to only 10 to 13 percent in the Caribbean, depending on occupancy rate. This is presumably due to the widespread tax exemptions allowed to tourist firms in that area.

islands, such as Jamaica and Puerto Rico, tourism provides perhaps 5 percent of total employment. In some of the smaller islands, this proportion can go up to one-half, and in Bermuda employment created directly and indirectly by tourism keeps three-quarters of the labor force busy. Elsewhere, the figures are not so spectacular: in Cyprus, the total lies between 5 and 10 percent, for Malta, hotel employment alone accounts for 3.5 percent of the labor force, and Noronha reports 5 percent for Fiji, 3 percent for Tahiti, and less than 1 percent for Bali.[3]

For planning purposes, the absolute amount of employment generated by a certain level of tourism is of even greater interest than its percentage in the total. The data on this question are incomplete, and intercountry comparisons are risky because the definitions of tourism-generated employment differ from one place to another. Smaoui has provided a useful classification of such employment:

1. Direct employment in businesses that sell goods and services directly to tourists, such as hotels, restaurants, transport operators, and shops
2. Indirect employment stimulated by tourists' expenditures in activities, such as manufacturing and wholesale distribution, that supply goods and services to tourism businesses
3. Investment-related employment in construction and other capital goods industries.[4]

Direct employment

The statistics on direct employment in hotels are usually the best available, with information becoming increasingly sketchy on other direct employment, indirect employment, and capital goods employment. In Tunisia and Malta, hotels employ around 0.4 persons per bed, whereas they employ twice as many in East Africa and the Seychelles. The amount of employment generated by a hotel varies according to its location, size, category of price, and standard of service, and may also reflect country-related characteristics such as wage rates and policies regarding investment. Work done at the Caribbean Tourism Research Center suggests that larger hotels, and particularly those of higher category, create more jobs per bed than

3. Raymond Noronha, *Social and Cultural Dimensions of Tourism: A Review of the Literature in English,* draft report to the World Bank, 1977, para. 6.08.
4. See Chapter 7.

smaller hotels of lower category. Employment in the larger hotels is more stable seasonally, perhaps because large Caribbean hotels can attract off-season convention and conference business.[5] The extent of family labor in smaller hotels may also influence the statistics, since family members are often not counted as employees. This area would justify more research attention; the possibility of trading off savings on investment costs by employing more workers needs to be examined as well as the extent to which employment per bed rises or falls with hotel size for each category of accommodation.

The wages of hotel employees everywhere compare favorably with wages in agriculture, and even more so with earnings in subsistence agriculture. In Cyprus, unskilled hotel employees earned between half and three-quarters more than other unskilled workers in 1973, and those in managerial positions earned around one-fifth more than those in other sectors. But Tunisian figures suggest that on average industrial workers earn some 12.5 percent more than hotel employees (before tips), and Gaviria, comparing the thriving new tourism center of Benidorm, Spain, with nearby industrial towns, finds few differences in living standards, although wages in industry are somewhat higher, on average, than in tourism.[6]

Information is more sparse on employment in direct tourism activities outside hotels. In Tunisia for 1972, Smaoui estimates this at only 0.08 jobs per bed, or approximately one-quarter of a job per hotel employee. (This is, however, an underestimate since it excludes employment in tourist shops, which he includes with indirect employment.) Nonhotel direct employment in Kenya in 1966–67, at 1.3 per hotel job, was rather higher.[7] The difference results only in part from the incompleteness of the Tunisian figure; more important are the differences in types of tourism in these destinations. For example, most tourists to Kenya travel around the country in small groups in seven-seater Volkswagen Combis; when tourists in Tunisia go on excursion, they travel in buses that carry forty to sixty people. Each tourist in Tunisia thus generates one-sixth (or less) of the driving jobs generated by a Kenya excursionist. Moreover, tourists to Kenya spend much of their time touring,

5. José Villamil, "Tourism in the Caribbean," paper presented to the Joint Unesco–World Bank Seminar.

6. Mario Gaviria, "The Mass Tourism Industry in Spain," paper presented to the Joint Unesco–World Bank Seminar.

7. Francis H. Mitchell, "The Economic Value of Tourism in Kenya," p. 58.

whereas in Tunisia, as Groupe Huit points out, they rarely leave their beach hotels.[8]

There are widely divergent views as to whether direct tourism activities are more or less capital intensive than other industries and hence create fewer or more jobs than other sectors per unit of capital invested. For example, Bouhdiba argues that a job in the tourism sector may cost as little to create as 5 percent of a job in "the classical industrial sector."[9] Green, on the contrary, believes that the weight of evidence is on the side of those who think it is expensive to create a job in tourism. In the second half of the 1960s, the investment cost per job in hotels in Tunisia, at $13,300 to $20,300, was somewhat higher than the $12,700 average for all manufacturing. Unpublished estimates by the World Bank indicate that in hotels costs of $20,000 to $40,000 per job at 1977 prices are quite normal. These costs are lower than those for such heavy industries as chemicals and steel, but are higher than those for small-scale industrial and repair activities in many developing countries. But if account is taken of the relatively low-cost nonhotel employment which goes together with hotel expansion, tourism can be a relatively cheap way of creating jobs, especially in middle- and higher-income countries. Thus, in Yugoslavia, hotels and catering together had investment costs per job of less than half the figure for industry, including mining and quarrying.[10]

Indirect employment

Tourism can generate considerable indirect employment, especially in agriculture, food processing, and handicrafts, as well as transport and distribution, and a range of local light manufacturing industries. In Tunisia, for each hotel employee, there are three to four persons in employment indirectly generated by tourism. For every hotel job around three-quarters of a job is generated in agriculture, more than one in shops and production of goods such as handicrafts purchased by tourists, and a little more than one in other manufacturing and distribution activities supplying hotels,

8. Chapter 16.

9. Abdelwahab Bouhdiba, "The Impact of Tourism on Traditional Values and Beliefs in Tunisia," paper presented to the Joint Unesco–World Bank Seminar.

10. Robert Erbes, *International Tourism and the Economy of Developing Countries* (Paris: Organisation for Economic Co-operation and Development, June 1973), pp. 49–52.

ground transport, and the like. In Kenya, indirect employment is less, at around one and three-quarters for each hotel job; of these, three-quarters of a job is in shops, and a half job each in agriculture and miscellaneous manufacturing and distribution activities. Specifically, the ratios of indirect employees to hotel jobs were[11]:

Employment	Tunisia (1972)	Kenya (1966–67)
Direct		
Hotels	1.00	1.00
Other	1.57–1.96	1.31
Subtotal	2.57–2.96	2.31
Indirect		
Agriculture	0.72–0.90	0.56
Tourist purchases	1.35–1.71	0.72
Miscellaneous	1.01–1.17	0.46
Subtotal	3.08–3.78	1.74
Total	5.65–6.74	4.05

The extent to which tourism generates employment in agriculture depends on many factors, including natural conditions, potential for local production of the types of foodstuffs demanded by hotels, availability and price of imports, efficiency of distributive mechanisms, and government policies affecting these matters. In East and North Africa most food requirements can be procured locally, even by luxury hotels, while in West Africa different patterns of agricultural output make such targets unrealistic. The Canary Islands, though perfectly capable of producing much of the necessary foodstuffs themselves and actually exporting bananas and tomatoes, appear to import a large part of the tourists' food needs from Europe, presumably in part because such imports are duty free. In the case of Majorca, Gaviria reports that hoteliers have banded together in purchasing cooperatives to by-pass domestic distribution networks and agricultural producers and to deal directly with overseas exporters. In Sousse, on the other hand, most agricultural and horticultural goods for hotels are supplied by local producers.

11. Tunisian data are drawn from Chapter 7, and the range of estimates refers to different occupancy rates; the Kenyan data are drawn from Mitchell, "The Economic Value of Tourism in Kenya," p. 58. Tourist purchases include jobs in producing handicrafts, souvenirs, clothing, cosmetics, and the like. In the case of Tunisia, direct employment in shops is also included. The miscellaneous category includes mainly jobs in agricultural processing, wholesale marketing, transport, and a variety of light industries and repair services.

The Senegalese villages' profits from tourism were, among other things, invested in agricultural improvements, giving new employment to youths who would otherwise have migrated to the towns and increasing the availability of local supplies for the guests. Shopping by tourists provides a market for many items, from imported cosmetics to clothing and local handicrafts. Handicraft production is discussed in more detail in Chapter 5. As for other purchases by tourists as well as by hotel and catering establishments, from cleaning materials to repair services, rather less evidence is available than in the case of agriculture. Nevertheless, it seems clear that the indirect employment stimulated by tourism will depend upon much the same type of factors as enumerated above for agriculture.

It is not known how much employment is generated by tourists' expenditures in the informal sector. Direct informal sector employment would include occupations such as shoe-shine boys, street vendors, the unregistered guides mentioned by Groupe Huit in Tunisia, beach boys, and beggars. Although tourists' perceptions of these occupations loom large in some destinations, little is known of their quantitative significance. In most destinations indirect informal sector employment in production of handicrafts and other items such as clothing purchased by tourists is probably more important than direct informal sector employment. The importance of informal sector employment in the supply of goods and services to hotels, restaurants, ground transport operators, and other direct activities is also unknown. It is possible that larger hotels or restaurants deal less with relatively small informal sector suppliers than do smaller ones. This is a topic which would justify research.

Investment-related employment

Tourism development creates jobs not only in the running of establishments but also in the construction and capital goods industries. In Tunisia, Smaoui estimates that for each new hotel bed a total of 2.7 man years of employment are needed for construction and such investment items as furniture. The production of household utensils, glass products, porcelain, earthenware, plastic tableware, or sanitation products will be stimulated, as it was in Spain, more or less in proportion to the size of the industry, once demand has expanded beyond certain thresholds. A few isolated and modest hotel projects will not, of themselves, be enough to spur the growth of such manufactures, although there may be opportunities opened up for various small-scale enterprises as discussed by McClelland.[12]

The timing and rate of the tourism sector's expansion may have social effects at least as important as the amount of employment and the income generated. Green reminds us that "a building boom in tourism causes serious problems in the construction sector. Initial demand strains capacity and pushes up prices; then after the tourism sector enters a period of moderate growth there are major adjustments as the construction industry contracts." Perhaps for small economies the main message of Wilson's case study of the Seychelles lies precisely in the problems caused by the rapid creation of the airport, other general infrastructure, and hotels in that small country.[13] Between March 1970 and May 1971, the number of workers in the construction industry rose from around 1,500, or just over 10 percent of the labor force, to a little over 4,000, as much as one-quarter of the labor force. The figure stayed at that level for about three years and then started to drop, reaching about 2,750 by August 1975. Once a small country has allowed itself to get into this type of situation, it may be faced with a serious dilemma. Either it accepts the unemployment which will result from a slowdown in construction and the failure of the hotels to employ most ex-construction workers, or it postpones the day of reckoning by seeking to retain high investment levels. If that investment is in tourism, its continued expansion could, as Wilson states, "increase the density of tourists to levels which would place an intolerable strain on both public and social services as well as on the social fabric of local community life."

The changes in social relations and in sociopsychological expectations which have resulted from boom conditions cannot be reversed without major traumas of an individual or social kind. The work of Force in the Pacific is relevant here, even though it deals with slightly different circumstances. As Noronha summarizes it: "Tourism cycles can mean unemployment of many who have been attracted to urban areas by tourism. The unemployed would then find themselves living in tropical slums, frustrated and unable to return to a substandard lifestyle." In Force's words: "Such individuals and their family members are prime candidates for malnutrition, psy-

12. David C. McClelland, "Developing Local Business in the Promotion of Tourism," paper presented to the Joint Unesco–World Bank Seminar.
13. Chapter 13.

chological and neurological disorders, and temptations and 'retaliative' behavior."[14] The life chances of such people, temporarily improved by tourism development, deteriorate once the boom has run its course. As was noted previously, this aspect of longer term development needs to be taken into account in planning. It is especially important in small economies. While the development of some sectors, such as petrochemicals, is possible only by promoting large projects that cause major upheavals in the labor market, for tourism there is at least a choice. In the light of other social impacts, to be discussed in a later section, modest and particularly gradual initiatives may be preferable in small countries.

This phasing problem is less acute in large economies: the vast Mexican Ixtapa-Zihuatanejo project was constructed mainly by migrant laborers who lived in temporary camps and moved on once the infrastructure and buildings were completed. The flux of people involved also may have important social impacts on the welfare of members of the local community, positively by generating temporary jobs in activities serving the construction workers, and negatively by straining the capacity of community services.

Who Benefits from Tourism Employment?

When tourism development takes place gradually, most jobs in the early days are taken by people from the immediate area. If, before tourism development in a rural area, people had been leaving for the towns, whether pushed by lack of work or land or pulled by the presumed employment opportunities in the cities, the jobs which tourism brings can slow down such urban drift. When tourism flows grow, when facilities increase, and especially if institutionalized or mass tourism develops, migrants may constitute an increasing proportion of the local labor force. This occurs acutely when large resort projects are implanted in sparsely populated areas, where little or no tourist activity had taken place before.[15]

14. Noronha, *Social and Cultural Dimensions of Tourism*, Annex I, p. 117; and Roland W. Force, "Pacific Urban Centres in Perspective," in R.W. Force and B. Bishop, eds., *The Impact of Urban Centres in the Pacific* (Honolulu: Pacific Science Association, 1975), p. 360.

15. E. W. Blake, "Stranger in Paradise," *Caribbean Review*, vol. 6 (1974), pp. 9–12, discusses the social problems and tensions in the Virgin Islands between the native labor force and immigrant workers imported because of a tourism-induced labor scarcity.

Tunisia's coastal zone, which saw booming tourism development, attracted a good deal of migration as employment opportunities grew. The local population also responded to the new chances for work. In Sousse, farmers and farm workers were drawn into tourism and were replaced by migrants from elsewhere. Similarly, in Spain, where tourism has been occurring on a massive scale, jobs are frequently filled by migrants. This is by no means a simple uniform process. In Fuenterrabia, where sustained but gradual tourism development has taken place since the early 1950s, large outside investors brought in their own labor force, apparently to the detriment of the local population. Here, as in Catalonia and the Costa Blanca, migrants from Spain's less developed areas took some of the more menial jobs which no longer interested the local population as living standards rose. The other side of the picture is that in less developed regions, in Spain as in Bali, the more responsible posts frequently are filled by outsiders. There is widespread agreement that top management posts, and also jobs at the intermediate supervisory levels in hotels, tend to be filled by nonlocals, often expatriates—though not in the earliest stages of tourism development.

Two categories of people appear to benefit particularly from the employment opportunities provided by tourism: young people and women. Statistical evidence on the age question comes exclusively from Tunisia. A national survey of hotels and similar establishments in 1975 showed that one-third of those employed were under twenty-three years old. In most traditional societies, relations between the generations are governed by strict authority patterns, underpinned by the financial dependence of youth on the older generation. The widening of employment and of earning opportunities decreases that dependence and cannot but strain intrafamilial relations. In Malta, for example, youths have experienced considerable social mobility as a direct result of tourism, while family ties have loosened and intergenerational conflicts have emerged.

About 16 percent of jobs in Tunisian tourism establishments are held by women. In contrast to the relative stability of female hotel employment in Tunisia, Maltese women are employed in the more marginal and temporary jobs. In 1974 a bill was passed to encourage male employment and reduce rising male unemployment; partly as a result, female workers in tourism fell from 38 percent of the total in 1970 to 32 percent in 1975.

The jobs provided by tourism for women have liberating effects similar to those seen for young people in some destinations, but not all. In the Seychelles, where females seem to have received preference over males in a number of hotel and restaurant jobs, the result has been that women lead less restricted lives than was previously the case. According to Wilson, "If a young girl lands a good job, she can earn more money than her father and is better able to dictate her own life-style." In Cyprus, the new earning opportunities helped young women to acquire more of the necessities for setting up their own households, and thus gave them more independence from their families; in Malta, they have helped unmarried women to move out from their traditional, mother-controlled, housebound existence. In Tunisia, on the other hand, Groupe Huit reports that employers in the tourism industry have been prevailed upon to pay girls' wages to their fathers rather than directly to the employee. The girls are dependent on tips for what financial independence they have, and the authoritarian family structure and social subordination of women are maintained, at least for the time being.

Effects of Tourism on Local Consumption

In addition to its impacts on incomes, tourism affects welfare through changing the range, prices, and quality of the goods and services available for consumption. Shifting resources to tourism from alternative activities may decrease the supply of those goods to local people and raise their prices. Thus, the outflow of labor from agriculture into high-paying construction and tourism jobs in the Seychelles may have had some influence on rising food prices in that area during the tourism boom. In Sousse, also, food prices rose, partly as a result of declining agricultural productivity as the original farmers were drawn into high-paying tourism jobs and were replaced by less-skilled migrants. In both cases, presumably, the total welfare gains from more employment offset the welfare loss from rises in food prices, though the effects on the poorer population groups may well have been negative. In addition, the seasonal fluctuations in tourism may generate seasonal cycles in food prices.

On the more positive side, tourists' demands to view artistic performances, historical treasures, and natural wonders and to purchase the products of local artists and artisans may provide a basis for the survival of these artifacts, sights, and activities for the benefit of local resident consumers as well as the tourists and producers. These effects receive more discussion in Chapter 5.

Green, describing other shifts in the use of resources, writes that "extending game parks, banning hunting by savanna and forest peoples, relocating fishermen away from home and markets, and clearing out unsightly evidence of poverty (such as squatter villages) near tourist sites are not only common to the development of tourism complexes in Africa but also highly damaging, even in narrow economic terms, to the poorest and weakest of the initial residents." Another resource for which tourists and residents may compete is access to the beaches and parks. A common complaint is that such environmental facilities are closed off to local residents in favor of tourists and richer residents. Some reserved areas, such as private clubs and swimming pools, are inevitable, but it is impossible to justify depriving the local population of access to its natural or cultural heritage.

Although the present discussion does not deal with the physical environment (a subject all of its own), it is relevant to note that over-extended tourism development has clearly had serious environmental impacts in some places. There is now a growing awareness of these problems, and preservation and even enhancement of the environment has of late increasingly become an important component of the tourism product. As noted in the previous chapter, there is also usually some scope for modifying these impacts in desirable directions through planning.

Government Services

An increasing proportion of resources is now allocated to individuals, families, and population groups through administrative mechanisms. Some of the main services involved are health care, education, and housing. There is not much evidence on the effects of tourism on these services, and few generalizations can be made safely, except that rapid, unplanned migration in response to tourism growth can place a heavy strain on the social services that do exist.

As for health facilities, the income from one of the village guest houses in the Casamance area of Senegal was used to establish a health post and maternity clinic. Tourism development has also brought Puerto Vallarta a social security hospital "complete with ambulance, clinics, and specialists."[16] Its services are available to

16. Chapter 17.

government employees and unionized labor, but what proportion of the population in fact has access to this hospital is not known. It could be argued that the necessity to cater to tourist health needs would bring positive benefits to local inhabitants, but this may be only partly the case. Tourists need mainly curative facilities for emergencies and the diseases of middle-aged and older people—a place that copes with coronaries and accidents, for example. Local populations need preventive health care above all, especially for their children.

Except for foreign students taking courses in destination country universities, tourists do not make direct demands on schools. The main impact of tourism in this area is indirect, through a demand for certain types of training to prepare youngsters for jobs in the industry. In Gaviria's opinion, jobs in tourism require only limited intellectual and technical ability that can be easily absorbed. He suggests that 98 percent of those employed in tourism in Spain have been trained on the job, "learning by imitation." Green, on the other hand, believes that a higher proportion of tourism workers are semiskilled, managerial, or professional than in many other sectors, including manufacturing. "The image of a handful of managers and an unskilled army of waiters and chambermaids is totally erroneous," he asserts. Many countries have established special hotel schools, some with the assistance of Unesco and the International Labour Organisation, as in Lebanon, for example. The experience of these agencies suggests that it is preferable to provide formal training in tourism, since on-the-job training is likely to be at the expense of the tourists, and if service is poor it would discourage a return visit.

The establishment of hotel-training institutions of course has little effect on the general level of education in a country. But when tourism brings increased prosperity, demand for better schooling for the children is likely to increase and educational levels are likely to improve. This was seen in Puerto Vallarta as well as in the Seychelles, but it is impossible to ascribe these changes conclusively to the growth of tourism alone.

Tourism seems to have no predictable impacts on housing, whether for better or worse. The influx of settler tourists in Malta aggravated the existing housing shortage, with particularly serious effects on the poorest classes, who competed in the market for the properties which were being snapped up as "old houses of character" by settlers and by nonresident foreigners in search of investment opportunities. Tourism development has sometimes led to public housing specifically for the local population. In Puerto Vallarta a government housing project was set up in one of the suburbs, with 400 low-cost houses being made available at a subsidized rate.

Another, more indirect effect of tourism on the distribution of welfare relates to the impact of tourism on the national budget. Initially, governments may face considerable outlays for tourism infrastructure and superstructure, the latter either directly in the form of government ownership or indirectly through lending to hotels by public sector financial institutions. Once tourism facilities are operational, however, and provided that public policies on taxation and user charges for public facilities are sound, governments stand to make more than enough from tourism to repay any debt on the initial investments. This tourism "surplus" may lead them either to expand expenditures or to reduce the tax burden on other activities or both.[17] The ultimate distributional consequences of this will depend on their incidence in the budget, as is the case for other development activities.

Class Structure and the Distribution of the Benefits of Tourism

As already indicated, tourism may provide relatively more benefits to young people and to women than did traditional activities. But to what extent do these gains go to other groups in the society as defined by ethnicity, income, or social class? Is the distribution of gains related more to the nature of tourism or the society concerned?

The ways in which development of different types of tourism affect different types of social structure are only beginning to be understood. New employment opportunities and increased economic benefits do not necessarily lead to changes in the class structure.

---

17. There have been a number of studies on the impact of tourism on the budgets of state and local governments of Hawaii, which show substantial positive impacts in this respect. See Mathematica, *The Visitor Industry and Hawaii's Economy: A Cost-Benefit Analysis,* prepared for State of Hawaii Department of Planning and Economic Development, Princeton, N.J., 1970; and Karen Ah Mai and others, *The Impact of Hawaii's Visitor Industry on Public Sector Revenues and Costs* (forthcoming).

Even when all classes benefit, tourism development, especially through large projects, may serve to reinforce the divisions among social strata and the existing inequalities in the community. Hotel condominiums, expensive restaurants, and exclusive residential areas may become the focus for rich and status-conscious people, residents as well as tourists, who appropriate to themselves the community's most desirable spaces such as the beaches.

Patterns of tourism employment reflect those of the existing system of stratification. Waiters, busboys, gardeners, room maids, and kitchen helpers tend to be locals whose prospects for upward social mobility are usually low—not because of anything inherent in the nature of tourism jobs but because the chance for upward mobility by unskilled workers are low in most countries. In ethnically stratified, often ex-colonial societies, the employment hierarchy may closely follow the ethnic one. In such Pacific tourism destinations as Fiji, Tahiti, Hawaii, and Guam indigenous groups, whose general position in society is subordinate, also make up the lowest layers of workers in the tourism industry.[18]

For those with more education or training, including often children of poorer parents, tourism can provide new opportunities in employment and in entrepreneurship. One common result seems to be the growth of a middle-level income group where previously there were only the rich and the poor. In the Seychelles, census data and special surveys show that over the ten years preceding the take-off of tourism (but including most of the tourism-linked construction boom) the number of skilled working-class and white-collar jobs increased as a proportion of the total. The size of the local middle class also rose considerably in Fuenterrabia as a result of tourism development. Greenwood hints, however, that at the lower levels improvements were smaller than they might have been because of a lack of collective organization and the failure to pursue collective demands. Gaviria, in comparing Spanish industrial towns with similar-sized towns based on tourism, finds that the middle classes in the tourism towns are more important (and also that the tourism towns tend to be more conservative politically). In a more complex process, new strata can challenge the economic or political power which has underpinned existing inequalities. Moore's classic study of a Canary Island village shows that a class of new entrepreneurs emerging as a result of modest tourism development meant a

18. Noronha, *Social and Cultural Dimensions of Tourism*, paras. 6.05–6.07.

considerable challenge to existing social relations and especially to the power of *caciques*, the local political bosses.[19]

In Tunisia during the late 1960s, tourism was the only sector of the economy where large-scale private investment, as contrasted with cooperative or government investment, was encouraged. A new entrepreneurial class emerged, "catapulted into the position of heads of large-scale business" by readily available credit at subsidized interest rates, new facilities for acquisition of land, and state aid in general. Bouhdiba refers to the new class of property owners who emerged as a result of real estate speculation as being "all the more greedy because they became rich too quickly." In Malta, too, the building boom led to a "truly wealthy class" of property owners, businessmen in construction and real estate, lawyers, and notaries. The same road to riches through land deals was opened up by the tourist boom in Famagusta, where prices for tourist seaside land rose by almost 600 percent in the span of three years (1970 to 1973). Rising real estate prices occur in many contexts other than tourism development, of course, as does real estate speculation with its attendant impacts on the distribution of income and wealth. While these repercussions are not exclusive to tourism, tourism makes them likely, at least where there is a well-developed private market for land. Speculative gains of this kind are not conducive to reducing inequalities in wealth, notwithstanding the occasional peasant who becomes rich, and in spite of the speculative losses (even bankruptcies) which occur when the economic tide turns at the time of recession.

19. Kenneth Moore, "Modernization in a Canary Island Village: An Indicator of Social Change in Spain," *Journal of the Steward Anthropological Society*, vol. 2 (1970), pp. 19–34.

CHAPTER 4

The Encounter: Changing Values and Attitudes

T OURIST-HOST ENCOUNTERS OCCUR in three main contexts: where the tourist is purchasing some good or service from the host, where the tourist and host find themselves side by side, for example, on a sandy beach or at a nightclub performance, and where the two parties come face to face with the object of exchanging information or ideas. When its promoters claim that tourism is an important mechanism for increasing international understanding, it is normally the third type of contact they have in mind. As we shall see, however, the first two are quantitatively more common, at least for resort tourism. Other types of contact—for example, when tourists treat local persons as objects of curiosity—can usually be assimilated into the first type of relationship, except that the local person may receive little remuneration for the service of exoticism he provides. Thus, tourists often "take" photos of local people, although in some destinations (for example, East Africa) the tourist can be expected to reciprocate with a cash payment.

Encounters between tourists and the local inhabitants must be differentiated according to the stage of tourism development in which they occur and the type of tourist involved. Nettekoven notes that intercultural encounters occur less during touristic travel than is often assumed and that intense encounters are less desired by tourists than is often suggested.[1] These observations refer to mass or institutionalized tourism, with its predictable and standardized situations. They do not fit the much smaller numbers of

---

1. Chapter 9.

explorer or drifter tourists, who may be especially interested in visiting places in the early stages of tourism development.[2]

Although the papers in this volume do not contain much empirical material on what tourists actually want, or even on what they say they want, the study on tourist attitudes in Sousse reported on by Groupe Huit seems to confirm Nettekoven's points.[3] The sample interviewed was a small one, and since Tunisia's climate and beaches are its primary tourist attractions, results might have been different for a sample of tourists visiting, say, Egypt or Morocco. Almost nine-tenths of the tourists interviewed said they came exclusively for the setting (especially the sun, the beach, the palm trees, and the sea); the country's civilization, history, people, or present-day society together constituted attractions for only one-tenth of the tourists. Some three-quarters of the respondents might just as well have gone to another resort or country. A similar response was given by two-thirds of the tourists whom Nettekoven surveyed in Tunisia in 1969; to a query about whether they were interested in the country, they replied "Yes, but it must not interfere with the vacation." The search for sunshine and sandy beaches is of course not the only motivation for travel abroad, as indicated by the large number of tourists generated by countries such as the United States, France, and Italy which have sun and beaches of their own. Nevertheless, for most tourists a trip is a chance to "get away from it all," and the last thing they want is to be confronted with anything problematic during this short period of the year when they can be essentially pleasure-seekers.

The tourists interviewed in Sousse had been recruited by tour operators and flown in by charter plane. They were transferred collectively by bus to the hotel complex where they spent on average twenty-two out of the twenty-four hours of the day during their vacation, leaving two hours a day for visits to Sousse and else-

---

2. These terms are taken from the typology of tourism formulated by Erik Cohen, "Toward a Sociology of International Tourism," *Social Research*, vol. 39 (1972), pp. 164–82. He classifies tourists along a continuum according to the degree to which the tourist searches for the familiar or the strange during his travels, and classifies tours by the extent to which they are organized by others (institutionalized as opposed to noninstitutionalized tourism). The range of tourist types is from the organized mass tourist, through the individual mass tourist, to the explorer and the drifter.

3. Chapter 16.

where. But that was an average—65 percent of the tourists made no such visit at all. Although about one-fifth of the tourists visited the house of a Tunisian family (which seems quite a high proportion), the overall impression from the enquiry was that the tourists kept to themselves. Similarly, Boissevain and Inglott write that most tourists to Malta remain relatively or totally ignorant about the customs, life-styles, political aspirations, and social problems of their hosts, with whom they have had no contact beyond perfunctory service relations.[4]

Both Bouhdiba and Saglio point out that, in fact, the mass tourist really wants to be confirmed in his prejudices and to be left alone in a milieu as similar as possible to his own familiar background.[5] He prefers to stay in his air-conditioned bus rather than to walk around, like the irritated German whom Bouhdiba overheard to say, "I know, I know, I read all about it in the guidebook." Resorts become enclaves that isolate the tourist from the host environment, creating a kind of "total institution," to use the term first coined by Goffman for his analysis of asylums and prisons.[6] Enclaves minimize the adjustments the tourist has to make, but they increase the difficulties of adaptation for the local people who serve them. In the extreme, the process turns the resort area into "an annex of the countries providing the tourists."[7]

But why should the tourist want or expect anything beyond the pleasures of the resort and superficial service relations with the host people? This is precisely what he has been offered and sold by the tour operator, what he has seen in the glossy brochures he studied before deciding where to go. Bouhdiba looked at the material tourist agencies distribute to "sell" Tunisia, and he found that the imagery reinforces the potential client's expectations about the land and its

4. Chapter 15.
5. See Abdelwahab Bouhdiba, "The Impact of Tourism on Traditional Values and Beliefs in Tunisia," paper presented to the Joint Unesco–World Bank Seminar on the Social and Cultural Impacts of Tourism, Washington, D.C., December 8–10, 1976; and Chapter 18.
6. Erving Goffman, *Asylums* (New York: Doubleday, 1961).
7. The quote is from Robineau's interesting paper on Tahiti in the volume reporting on the 1974 workshop on tourism in the Pacific (Ben R. Finney and Karen A. Watson, eds., *A New Kind of Sugar: Tourism in the Pacific*, 2d ed. [Honolulu: East-West Center, 1977]). On the encounter generally, see W. A. Sutton, Jr., "Travel and Understanding: Notes on the Social Structure of Touring," *International Journal of Comparative Sociology*, vol. 8 (1967), pp. 217–23.

tourist facilities. Nettekoven notes that agencies and operators present a partial picture to promote sales: "beach, sun, palms, untouched landscape, art, monuments of the past, friendly population, amusement potential, quality of the hotel beds, number of courses of meals, and measurements of the hotel swimming pool." The brochures produced by the national tourism offices may depict the country more in line with reality, but they are on the whole not widely distributed abroad.[8]

In the case of Cyprus, tour operators' brochures are apparently based on texts provided by the Cyprus Tourism Organization, and commercial publicity is carried out in close collaboration with the authorities. That case might be worth studying more closely. The processes of imagemaking and of building up expectations certainly influence tourists' behavior patterns and probably determine at least in part whether such behavior will leave the host country nationals and the tourists dissatisfied with the whole experience. The national tourism organizations can play a major role in developing appropriate promotional material. Bouhdiba suggests that hotels or travel agencies should be required to spend a small percentage of their profits on improving the quality of tourist reception and on better information for and education of tourists as well as the host population. Attempts are being made in some rich countries to produce more "valid" information on less developed destination countries for prospective tourists. In Germany, for example, the Studienkreis für Tourismus has produced booklets which describe certain African countries—their people, culture, and customs—accurately, objectively, and realistically. These booklets are handed out to tourists going to these countries by the tour operators. The Studienkreis proposes to do research on how this information changes the tourists' perception of the host country and the experiences they look for and report to their friends back home. Such efforts could be replicated elsewhere, possibly with financial assistance from official agencies.

The presentation of information, however, often stems directly from the fact that private tour operators, agencies, even guides are in the tourism business for commercial reasons and are propelled essentially by the profit motive. In pursuing their profits they may

---

8. Boissevain and Inglott write that in Malta, however, the officially produced brochures promote mainly the seaside image and add local culture no more and no less than the brochures or guidebooks put out by private agencies (Chapter 15).

act in ways considered undesirable by host governments, tourism planners, sociologists, even by tourists themselves. To a limited extent incentives, disincentives, and controls can be used to turn them in preferred directions. But rather than concentrating on controls or legislation, countries might analyze their own attractions and make it possible for tour operators and tourists to choose something more than just the resort holiday. With more varied possibilities, governments could introduce incentives to encourage additions to the standard packaged tour.

Little is likely to change, however, without some organizational effort. A country may present much of potential interest to outsiders, but creative action is necessary to translate this potential into some form of offering to tourists. Famous places, monuments, and buildings, or renowned markets, festivals, and other folkloric manifestations should have no problem in attracting visitors away from the beaches—at least for a brief excusion. But they probably already figure in the brochures and are included in many of the packaged tours. The real difficulty is, of course, that most tourist resorts do not offer the equivalent of the Mona Lisa or the Taj Mahal, a spectacular carnival, or a notable celebration of the town's patron saint. Often they do not even have a well-organized handicrafts center or an interesting fair in the vicinity, which might be discovered by tour operators looking for something to add to their package. Much less do circumstances exist in which easy and relatively spontaneous noncommercial encounters between tourists and hosts are likely to arise. To organize the latter using commercial agencies is by no means easy, and may be impossible, except in the rather unusual circumstances of tourism arranged through professional, trade union, or other special interest associations, where common interests bind tourist and host together.

Ellis calls for small-scale projects which would aim for a sense of unity, integrating the local population, the tourists, the physical environment—buildings and urban spaces—and local handicrafts or popular arts.[9] Even in such schemes the successful inclusion of the human dimension remains the most difficult. The Senegalese project in Casamance faced that issue squarely by building village guest houses. Their simple comfort reduces the standard-of-

---

9. Eduardo J. Ellis, "Tourism and the Unity of the Sociocultural Environment," paper presented to the Joint Unesco–World Bank Seminar.

living gap that usually separates tourists and local population; their authentic reflection of local architecture brings tourists and villagers closer together; their use of local food, furnishings, and methods of transport approximates the village life-style; and, as members of a cooperative, the villagers are directly involved in running the guest houses. Many opportunities are thus created for guests and hosts to interact outside stereotyped service roles.

Saglio relates some of the difficulties of a social and cultural nature (beyond the sheer hard work of organization and construction) which were encountered in Senegal. The administrative authorities were far from enthusiastic at the beginning. They criticized the small scale of the projects, doubted whether tourists would want to stay in simple traditional buildings, and even worried about troubles and disturbances at the village level. Beneath these doubts Saglio sensed "a deep-seated reluctance to show visitors some of the traditional ways of life, which many of the elite tend to hold in contempt under cover of an official attitude of 'overvaluation.'" Happily, in Senegal that reluctance has been overcome. The task was not easy, nor would it be easy elsewhere.

In this connection, too, the dynamics of nationwide social structures and the ideologies underpinning them (sometimes differences of class, sometimes of ethnic groups) are likely to determine what can be achieved locally. In some periods and places these conditions prove particularly favorable. After the Mexican Revolution, for example, when inequality was being reduced in Mexico, the *indigenista* movement vigorously promoted a revival of the indigenous Mexican culture previously despised by the ruling classes with their Hispanic traditions. An interest developed not only in Mexico's ancient civilizations but also in the contemporary peasantry and its arts and crafts. The situation is less favorable in societies where the life-styles and living standards differ greatly between classes or ethnic groups and where the general configuration of social relations is inegalitarian and elitist. In such societies governments, tour operators, or local agencies are unlikely to find something "worthwhile" for tourists to see or do that would bring them in touch with local populations in any but totally stylized situations.

If the Casamance example is to be followed, it will take not only dedication but also understanding of and sympathy for the day-to-day life and culture of the common people. Perhaps there are lessons in the facts that Saglio is by training an anthropologist and that all his expenses were defrayed by French technical cooperation and were not borne by the village guest houses themselves. The Casamance projects are still too new for a proper evaluation to be possible. Can they, in the long run, avoid some of the problems that have often plagued more conventional projects—the undermining of the village social structure, for example? By their very nature, such projects cannot provide the major contribution to national economic development which is (correctly or incorrectly) expected from conventional tourism projects. But what they can contribute at the village level may be more than any conventional project ever does. They would, on present evidence, appear to be well worth pursuing, certainly where spin-off traffic from resort tourism can be expected.

Mediation Between Tourists and Hosts: Setting up the Encounter

Tour operators, travel agencies, and other providers of tourism services are important intermediaries between the tourists and the host country because they select and distribute information. Some employees of these agencies act as couriers or tour leaders to groups of tourists, accompanying them abroad or receiving them at their destination. They fulfill this function in a personal way by providing a perspective on the vacation at its beginning and incidental advice during the rest of the stay. Unfortunately, they usually appear to be culturally ill prepared for their mediating function and are mainly oriented toward commercialism. They often receive no more than a middling salary, which they eke out by commissions on the sale of excursions or souvenirs to members of their group. For Nettekoven the widespread payment of commissions is a crucial stumbling block to a more positive and genuine mediating role. Whether his proposal—raising basic wages—would eliminate the practice is by no means certain. But it might be a step in the right direction and worth a try.

The most familiar function of local guides is to interpret to the tourists the more prominent examples of material culture and the major points about the history of the place, its religion, or its national pride. Guides need to have an appropriate education in order to present the national or regional sights in an acceptable way to visitors. In Cyprus all guides have to be licensed, and during their training they acquire a good knowledge of Cyprus history, archaeology, art, and culture.

Guides may serve as direct mediators between the tourists and the local population if they interpret religious ceremonies or popular or folkloric cultural manifestations that directly involve the people, their culture, and their way of life. Ideally, as McKean writes, guides would act as culture brokers, persons who are familiar with "two cultural traditions or [with] the ethnic and social features which separate groups or persons, and spend a good deal of their time attempting to bridge these differences."[10] But, in places where regulations are lax, guides—like tour leaders—often fall far short of the ideal. The result, in Nettekoven's phrase, can be "an inexhaustible source of misunderstandings and false information."

Culturally mediating guides play an important role on the island of Bali, which is celebrated for its temple services and religious ceremonies, for the artistic performances derived from them, and in general for the appealing life-style of its people. Bali's people are renowned for their friendliness and for living simple, contented, and intrinsically satisfying lives, very different from those led by the tourists from urban industrial environments. Tourists want to meet those people and experience their society, in addition to seeing performances or sharing in ceremonies.[11] The guides try to ensure that the human encounter conforms to the tourists' expectations, that Balinese are not discovered to be materialistic or interested in making a profit off the visitors. Since the guides share the tourists' culture as well as that of the local population, it is acceptable that they make a living out of guiding and charge for their services. But part of those charges surreptitiously find their way to the people of Bali, when tourists come as "guests" to temples or ceremonies. McKean cites a lecture of one of Bali's most famous and senior guides, Nyoman Oka:

Many Balinese are not as friendly and hospitable as in the old days. Then no-one was asked to donate when one entered a temple. Today this has become a general practice. No-one was asked to give something if they visited a compound where a ceremony was going on. Now you find a donation in more and more places is expected. You

10. Philip F. McKean, "The Culture Brokers of Bali," paper presented to the Joint Unesco–World Bank Seminar.
11. Erik Cohen, "A Phenomenology of Tourist Experiences" (forthcoming) describes this type of tourism in his discussion of the "experiential mode."

have to expect this today, so be prepared. The foreigner need not know this. If you can avoid it, you should, to keep the image of Balinese being friendly and hospitable. You should pay the donation yourself, without the tourist noticing it.

Here, then, is a remarkable example of a stage-managed encounter, which deliberately tries to reconcile the expectations of tourists and local hosts.[12] In the past, the values of hospitality made the encounter between visitor and host a human experience, without ulterior motives. Now the encounter has been commercialized, while appearances are preserved. Balinese society is clearly not the paradise that tourists are meant to experience, but neither McKean nor Noronha suggests that the impact of tourism has been destructive of the more important aspects of traditional culture. It appears to be sufficiently resilient to find a positive adaptation to this and other forms of modernization impinging on the society.

Friendliness, Service, and Servility

The friendliness of the Balinese, and the fact that they willingly accept the rather lowly jobs that can go with serving tourists (and do so without loss of dignity) are cultural characteristics underpinned by basic values and beliefs, partly secular, partly religious (Hindu). Another place that appears to be rather like Bali in this respect (but without the religious element) is Bermuda. There, too, people serve the tourists without being subservient to them, and Manning holds that this is at least in part because the traditional values of the islanders have easily accommodated tourism. He argues that in the small, isolated, and close community of Bermuda, the colonial and racist structure of society, rooted in slavery, was mediated by a personalistic patronage system and a widely accepted folk concept of Bermuda as a large extended family. In spite of racial segregation which lasted into the 1960s, structural socioeconomic inequality, and a profound division between whites and blacks along cultural lines, "there has been mannered politeness and external warmth between the races, a spirit kindled by the ideal of family closeness as

12. See D. MacCannell, "Staged Authenticity: Arrangements of Social Space in Tourist Settings," *American Journal of Sociology*, vol. 79 (1973), pp. 589–603, for a general discussion of this phenomenon.

well as by the practical considerations of patronage. Social relations have masked and tranquilized social organization." The rich and elitist tourists who helped to set the patterns of interaction and encounter in Bermuda before World War II slipped "easily into the role of the Bermudian gentry." The black population responded with courtesy and hospitality, and the custom evolved of "recognizing every tourist on the street with a smile, a wave, or a word of greeting." For many years this custom has been reinforced by their political leaders, including those of the black, strongly anticolonial, and moderately socialist opposition, the Progressive Labor party. Newspapers frequently remind the people that "tourists rank friendliness as Bermuda's chief asset," attributing tourism slumps elsewhere to "sullen attitudes and bad manners."[13]

Bermudians' continued capacity to serve without rancor cannot be derived only from historical sources, however. The explanation may well be more directly related to the extraordinarily high standard of living of all classes in Bermuda. To be a waiter, or even a beach attendant, is acceptable, above all, if earnings compare reasonably well with the current incomes of others, as well as with one's own income in the past. In addition, it helps if the money can be spent in ways that are psychologically meaningful.

This particular issue is a major theme in Manning's analysis of the black workmen's clubs, which have spread over the island during the postwar period of expansion of the tourism industry and rising standards of living. Bermudians do not focus their response to the tourists on the actual encounters, but outside it. The club world, where money is spent easily and often lavishly, "is a reflection of the tourist world, a native imitation of the free-spending, pleasure-seeking orientation of visiting vacationers." It embodies the tourists' values of consumerism without, however, destroying or denigrating the indigenous value system. Having emerged as the blacks' response to racial segregation, the clubs came to embody and glamorize their members' racial identity and cultural tradition,

---

13. See Chapter 11. Manning's view of Bermuda's sociohistorical experience is interesting in that it attempts to reconcile the undeniable structural inequalities—the subservience, exploitation, caste or class elements—of the society with the lack of interpersonal antagonism or race-focused conflict. Others would no doubt wish to interpret the situation differently (Marxists would call it "false consciousness," for example). Yet it would be hard to fault Manning on his careful setting out of the unusal combination of factors in this most unusual society.

stressing Afro-American and Afro-Caribbean cultural expressions and infusing the whole of life (including race relations) with a sense of sporting rivalry and competition. Even so, it can be asked whether the club-focused response, with its overtones of sporting competitiveness, does not distract attention from real conflicts of interest that may be generated by mass tourism.[14]

Most tourism societies do not have the traditional values that justify the performance of duties in occupations of low rank, and much of the controversy that rages over tourism concerns the supposedly demeaning nature of the work. At issue is the fact that tourism, as opposed to other sectors, provides personal service in which the lower level employee is at the direct beck and call of the tourist. Compared with other types of work, there is a massive multiplication of bosses, of people who give orders in person-to-person contact and whose whims have to be indulged.

Furthermore, employee-tourist contacts may occur in a sociopsychological and sociohistorical context that colors employees' perceptions. In certain ex-colonial societies, for example, the memories of the colonizers' expressions of superiority and disdain in personal relations, perhaps in racial or ethnic terms, is still alive among the population. In such societies, the personal service encounter with tourists may evoke resentment based on feelings arising from those memories. Similar conditions may exist in societies with profound class divisions. Resentment may arise even if the tourists are radically different, in terms of language and class, from the colonizers, as is often the case.

These issues are related to the question whether the phenomenon of tourism is experienced as similar to past (or present) oppression or dependence. Noronha stresses that the loss of local control, which tends to accompany the growth of institutionalized tourism, causes resentment—which is conveniently focused on the tourists.[15] The Basques' long history of conflict with the Spaniards

14. Manning notes certain significant economic achievements of the clubs as such; he does not, however, tell us to what extent the chances of success are loaded against the blacks in their competition with the whites.

15. See Doreen Calvo, *Caribbean Regional Study,* vol. 6, *Tourism* (Washington, D.C.: World Bank, 1974), on the possibility that in the Caribbean tourism is experienced as a continuation of the plantation system; and Raymond Noronha, *Social and Cultural Dimensions of Tourism: A Review of the Literature,* draft report to the World Bank, 1977, paras. 5.19–5.28.

rubs off on tourism in Fuenterrabia, in part because of the way in which the Spaniards have moved in to dominate the industry locally.[16]

This is not to say, of course, that serving tourists will inevitably be experienced as servility and create resentment. Proper training of tourism personnel may have a role to play in this respect by conferring status on acquiring skills and on performing them with professional pride, thereby breaking the possible associations with inferiority and imposed deference. Trade union organization of tourism personnel could well be another factor of much importance.

The conclusion, though hardly simple, is certainly clear in broad lines. Whether the encounter with tourists, and especially the service relationship, is experienced as demeaning and an expression of servility, and thus whether it provokes hostility, depends at least in part on the sociohistorical context, especially on the elements of slavery and colonialism. The nature of the socioreligious system (such as Hinduism in Bali) also may have an influence. The gap in living standards between tourists and local population and whether or not local living standards are rising, and how fast, seem to be of considerable importance. In prosperous Switzerland the problem of servility seems not to arise; nor does it at the other end of the scale, in the villages of Casamance. In Malta, however, the growing number of less affluent tourists who compete more directly with the average Maltese citizen for goods and services has led to some resentment.

The Impact of Tourism on Local Values

The most notable impact of tourism on traditional values is that certain social and human relations are brought into the economic sphere; they become part of making a living. The seminar papers and most other writings on the subject suggest that tourism's most serious effect on values is in this area of commercializing relations, and that specifically noneconomic encounters account for only a marginal part of the entire experience.

Even in Bali, where the outward forms of traditional hospitality are maintained by means of payments or donations hidden from the

16. Davydd J. Greenwood, "Tourism Employment and the Local Community," paper presented to the Joint Unesco–World Bank Seminar.

tourists, the arrival of large-scale tourism has meant that goods or services that used to be part and parcel of people's personal and social lives have now been commercialized and are offered as commodities. Whether the Balinese can continue to stage-manage the way they make a living, so that it appears that material benefits are of no consequence to them, would seem to be an open question.

Noronha documents both the original enthusiasm of locals for the tourists and the warmth of the interpersonal encounter in the early stages of tourism development, and the increased impersonalism, resentment, and commercialization later on.[17] Those contributors who discuss the matter are agreed that commercialization is a basic change which, if not brought about entirely by tourism development, is at least accelerated by it. In Cyprus most people not directly engaged in the tourism industry are said to see the encounter not as "a cash-generating activity, but as an opportunity for genuine human rapport," but this is probably true only of the interior of the island.[18] Off the beaten track, where tourists are still rare, and in a country in which strangers have from time immemorial been received with warmth and ritual, the people will give visitors the traditional reception. But where there are hordes of tourists the situation is presumably different. Tourists may be seen as "cashing in" on traditional attitudes of hospitality, which in the host society were firmly embedded in patterns of reciprocal behavior. As John Peterson writes about Hawaii, tourists effectively convert such a system of social exchange into unwilling altruism, by stepping "into and out of the Hawaiian community without fulfilling expected obligations."[19] If this does not create resentment, it brings about commercialization, and in this respect Bouhdiba's description of Tunisia (another Mediterranean country with an age-old tradition of hospitality) is very much to the point:

> The tourist is not only a transient, but, above all, he is a client. There is a contract on both sides for a package of services which must be provided in the best way possible. A certain reserve is felt to be good manners. What would once have been regarded as unpardonable coldness, unworthy of the Tunisian character and tradition, becomes

17. Chapter 12.
18. Chapter 14.
19. John Peterson, "If You Can't Join Them—Do Something Else: Hawaiian Alternatives to Progress," in Sandra Wallman, ed., *Perceptions of Development* (Cambridge: Cambridge University Press, 1977), p. 66.

a necessity . . . Hospitality has become just another technique of selling a set of standardized goods and services for the best price.[20]

If some people are prepared to pay for goods and services and other people can provide them, a market and commercial relations will inevitably develop. Tourism, in this respect, produces changes that are no different from other forms of "modernization." Yet, once again, the contrast between small-scale, gradual tourism promotion and mass tourism development is worth noting. Remember in this context the Senegalese village guest house projects, which attempt to maintain a sense of the traditional values of hospitality and of the immediacy of arts and crafts: they seek to bring about a gradual change and "harmonious" commercial relations with tourists.

Certain changes in sexual morality or patterns of behavior are also attributed to tourism in some of the papers. It has at times been said that prostitution flourishes in tourism resorts,[21] but on this not much evidence is adduced in this volume. In the Seychelles girls seek contacts with tourists (and with white people working on the island), perhaps in the hope of a prestigious wedding to a white foreigner, perhaps because of the "rather more basic attraction of being taken to nightclubs, bought drinks, given money and presents, and, at least for a while, taken away from the hard realities of day-to-day life." Wilson emphasizes that these behavior patterns are part of "a system of male-female relations rooted in historical traditions, the prestige of a lighter skin, and the economic exigencies of island life."[22] In Bermuda a government commission of enquiry observed in 1951 that the high rates of illegitimacy were "attributable to the 'holiday atmosphere' generated by large-scale tourism," but again the impression is that tourism merely confirmed patterns and values already present in the culture.

Tunisia appears to have been rather more directly affected. Both Bouhdiba and Groupe Huit report on the activities of young Tuni-

20. Bouhdiba, "The Impact of Tourism on Traditional Values and Beliefs of Tunisia."

21. Vijay Joshi and Michael Sharpston ("Tourism and Development: A Study of Antigua," a restricted circulation report prepared for the World Bank, 1973) make mention of the problem for Antigua; and a paragraph or so reports on the topic in Jean-Marie Thurot and others, *Les Effets du tourisme sur les valeurs socio-culturelles* [The effects of tourism on sociocultural values] (Aix-en-Provence: Centre des Hautes Etudes Touristiques, Université de Droit, d'Economie et des Sciences, 1976), p. 18.

22. Chapter 13.

sian males, who make themselves available to women tourists (at a price to the older ones) and, to a lesser extent, to tourist homosexuals. In a country where the majority of the local female population is still mostly kept out of view and where the veil has not entirely disappeared, the simple presence of many scantily dressed young women on the beach is bound to attract attention from the local males. In the nightclubs, where the local population is always welcome, shows and behavior depart from the traditional strict sexual morality. Bouhdiba concludes that the role of tourism in changing sexual values is undeniable, a view shared by Boissevain and Inglott, who report on the increased aggressiveness of Maltese youths toward unaccompanied female tourists with more permissive moral standards than those of Maltese girls. But Bouhdiba also warns against the tendency to impute directly to tourism all undesirable changes: it merely accelerates changes that are brought about by other forces. In relation to sexual behavior this is, no doubt, the wisest conclusion to reach.

In the realm of values and attitudes tourism has not, it seems, led to a great deal of change that has been particularly highly valued. Two instances of positive change have been mentioned already: the easing of authoritarian intergenerational relations and the widening of acceptable activities for women. Local values have also "benefited" where tourists have placed a high value on elements in the local environment which were previously taken for granted by the local population. In the Seychelles, for example, the need to conserve the natural environment as a major tourism asset, as well as the tourists' admiration for the island's rare species, have obviously stirred local pride. Similarly, in Malta, under the influence of tourists, "there is a greater awareness and appreciation of things Maltese, not only historical monuments, but also arts, crafts, and even locally produced wine." Some of these changes have, no doubt, come about because of direct contact with tourists. Some are more the results of the "modernizing" influence of national and local opinion leaders, or perhaps of resident foreigners. Some changes, finally, may have been the result of "demonstration effects."

Demonstration Effects

The changes in behavior and values referred to in the preceding section were, on the whole, attributable to the direct interaction of local population and tourists. Demonstration effects are best regarded as something a little different: changes in attitudes, values, or behavior which can result from merely observing tourists.[23] The effect is most easily and frequently seen in the local patterns of consumption which change to imitate those of the tourists. Bouhdiba puts it graphically when he writes that "a beach ball or a beach towel, a lipstick or a pair of sunglasses represent a temptation and an invitation to taste the indiscreet, but as yet forbidden, charms of the consumer society."[24]

Greenwood has seen it happen in Fuenterrabia: "Over time, local people have come to adopt a style of life markedly similar to that of the middle-class tourists they have seen." More than that, young Basques react to the "rude, rich, and idle" outsiders they see around them with a "combination of defensiveness, hostility, and attempted social invisibility. They mimic the consumption patterns of the tourists, dropping all external signs of their Basque culture."[25] Wilson tells of the adoption of imported tastes in the Seychelles. In Malta the demonstrative impact of tourist behavior has perhaps been of greater importance than elsewhere because of the permanent tourists, or settlers. They constitute a visible 1 percent of the population and demonstrate foreign patterns of consumption all the year round. After seeing and visiting the luxurious villas built by the settlers, the Maltese have come to aspire to housing better than their own relatively simple terraced dwellings and have taken over the custom of eating out in restaurants on special occasions. Tourism is also credited with the boom in the popularity of sailing among the Maltese. A clearly negative consequence of the demonstration effect, according to a survey cited by Bouhdiba, is that the desire to satisfy certain secondary needs, taken over from the tourists, has led to juvenile delinquency in Tunisia.

Expectations and values are changed not only by the presence of tourists but also by the facilities built to receive them. Though there appears to be much excellent local architecture in Tunisia, the hotels ("large tourist cages") designed in a nondescript international beach style, introduce aesthetic values which in fact represent the worst of

---

23. Raymond Noronha (*Social and Cultural Dimensions of Tourism: A Review of the Literature in English*, para. 5.29) applies the term to all changes in values and attitudes of the host population attributed (or attributable) to tourism.
24. "The Impact of Tourism on Traditional Values and Beliefs of Tunisia."
25. Davydd J. Greenwood, "Tourism Employment and the Local Community."

"modern" culture. According to Groupe Huit, they are, "in the eyes of the local people who have no other basis for comparison, true symbols of the life-style of the highly industrialized developed countries. Thus they regard as 'most beautiful' the hotel that is most conspicuous, the tallest, and the most monstrous of all." And many of the houses being built, often by hotel personnel, behind the big tourist complexes have fallen prey to the same imitation of what tourism brought.

In this connection it must be said again that tourism is but one factor among many making for change. In most places other forces such as radio, television, the press, or commercial advertising, which have usually been identified with demonstration effects or with cultural dependence, are present alongside the tourists. Noronha, Andronicou, Nettekoven, and Green all draw attention to these factors and join Bouhdiba in putting the demonstration effects of tourism in proper perspective.[26]

Nevertheless, tourists on vacation usually demonstrate a standard of living that is considerably higher than their average level of consumption during the rest of the year. The image they project of their home society is thus distorted and further magnifies the great gap between their living standards and those of the majority of the host country's population.

Tourism: The Rich and the Poor

When tourism development is grafted onto a society where poverty is still widespread and where many inhabitants do not share in the benefits brought by tourism, negative attitudes toward the tourists and resentment of their wealth and well-being should cause no surprise. The unemployed Seychellois youths "staring with faint aggression at the . . . tourists bustling happily about the handicraft shops" are, so Wilson tells us, not only bored but also suffering from "a feeling that they have been demeaned"—in part, apparently, because many of the jobs created by tourism have gone to the girls rather than to them. Similarly, the many poor in Sousse have developed "a disturbing sense of frustration" because they

26. In reference to some African countries, Green adds (Chapter 6) that a substantial expatriate community may be a more permanent hub of demonstration effects than even a large number of transient tourists.

have had few chances of satisfying the new desires aroused in them by the tourists and their richer compatriots.

Forster remarked that "A tourist region . . . must possess natural advantages and a slightly lower standard of living than the region from which it draws its tourists."[27] But in many tourism resorts today the difference is not "slight." On the contrary, it is overwhelming. Tourists now often go to places "where many people live a marginal existence," and where "the subsistence requirement is drastically below the limit which, in industrial societies, is viewed as an acceptable minimum."[28] The ethical and human problems which this raises, and which admit of no easy solutions, are movingly stated by Bouhdiba:

> Tourism injects the behavior of a wasteful society in the midst of a society of want. What the average tourist consumes in Tunisia in a week in the way of meat, butter, dairy products, fruits, and pastries is equivalent to what two out of three Tunisians eat in an entire year. The rift between rich and poor societies at this point is no longer an academic issue but an everyday reality.

27. See J. Forster, "The Sociological Consequences of Tourism," *International Journal of Comparative Sociology,* vol. 5 (1964), pp. 217–27.

28. Lothar Nettekoven, Chapter 9.

CHAPTER 5

Arts, Crafts, and Cultural Manifestations

T OURISTS' DEMAND FOR SOUVENIRS AND THEIR uncritical stance toward the performances which they observe in their search for local color have often been mentioned as causes of a decline in cultural and artistic standards.[1] In this vein, Gaviria argues that once craft production comes under the impact of the demands of mass tourism, it becomes the manufacture of mere souvenirs, which are not necessarily objects of traditional craftsmanship.[2] In Tunisia, where traditional artifacts are being bought by tourists for uses which have no relation to their original function (camel muzzles become handbags, for example), craftsmen have responded by changing the design and execution of these products to bring them more in line with the taste of the new customers. The same kind of adaptation has happened in the case of Mexican bark paintings. Their gaudy luminous colors, apparently preferred by North American tourists (or thought to be preferred), are, most would agree, an aesthetic step backward.

Examples of "degeneration" in the area of the performing arts are found among the ubiquitous nightclub acts based on local or national performing traditions (the flamencos in Spain, for example), and competition for custom can lead to a lowering of standards among more serious groups. The intermediaries who bring tourists and local performers together may develop a greater say in what is

1. For an early expression of this view, see J. Forster, "The Sociological Consequences of Tourism," *International Journal of Comparative Sociology*, vol. 5 (1964), p. 226.
2. Mario Gaviria, "The Mass Tourism Industry in Spain," paper presented to the Joint Unesco–World Bank Seminar on the Social and Cultural Impacts of Tourism, Washington, D.C., December 8–10, 1976.

68

to be presented, and how, than the performers themselves (as in Bali, where travel bureaus may influence even the dancers' choice of costume).[3]

Preservation or Transformation?

In other examples reported by the contributors, tourism, far from leading to a degeneration of arts and crafts, has contributed to their preservation and revival.[4] Andronicou speaks of the impetus given to the revitalization of certain crafts, "some of which were moribund," and adds that "without tourist development some of these would have become completely extinct."[5] He mentions pottery, weaving, embroidery, jewelry, and leather work; these same crafts are mentioned by Groupe Huit as having been revived by tourist demand in Sousse and elsewhere in Tunisia. In Malta tourism has led to flourishing industries in knitwear, textiles, and glass among other handicrafts. Schädler suggests piquantly that the demand for counterfeits may help preserve craftsmanship, since these "make heavy demands on the abilities of carvers and casters," although counterfeiting is not mainly stimulated by the tourists who visit Africa.[6]

Tourist interest has led to an upsurge of the performing arts and folklore in Cyprus, where the authorities have encouraged and supported performances, shows, and festivals. In Malta, too, tourists have helped stimulate existing local ceremonies and carnivals, and their interest in local music and folk dance has made these acceptable to young middle-class Maltese. In the Seychelles the tourists have kindled local pride in traditional Creole folk music, song, and dance, "which were beginning to disappear in favor of Western-style music and dance," although Wilson also mentions that their performance for tourist audiences can be seen as "devaluing" the originally spontaneous cultural expression.[7] A similar devaluation

---

3. In Chapter 4, I mentioned the unfortunate influence of international styles of architecture in Tunisia; this may have a "degenerative" effect on authentic local craftsmanship.

4. See also Forster, "Sociological Consequences of Tourism."

5. Chapter 14.

6. Chapter 10.

7. Chapter 13. Forster, "Sociological Consequences of Tourism," mentions this for the Pacific Islands he studied.

of community ritual through its transformation into a tourist attraction has been discussed by Greenwood for Fuenterrabia.[8]

In Bali ceremonies previously imbued with religious meaning have been made more available and enacted on schedule in standardized form for successive groups of tourists. But Noronha indicates that creativity and quality are usually not impaired in this secularization of ancient rituals. He links this to the fact that the Balinese distinguish clearly between the meaning of a performance for themselves and its meaning for the tourists. The income from the performance is "channeled back to strengthen the religious and temporal bonds that are the sources of strength for the Balinese," and which they express in those ceremonies attended by tourists. More generally, Noronha argues that the capacity of any local population to maintain this duality of meanings is a necessary condition for the painless integration of tourism development into their lives.[9]

The impact of tourism on the *meaning* of cultural manifestations is discussed at some length by Schädler, though in the context of artifacts rather than of activities or performances. In his detailed analysis of the changes that have been taking place in African arts and crafts, he is at pains to point out that such changes are not necessarily owing to tourism at all. They result primarily from an erosion of the religious beliefs or social customs that have always been the mainspring of African artistic expression. Objects such as carvings were created for use in the cult; with the demise of traditional religious beliefs and their associated rituals, the objects to which craftsmen devote themselves become "meaningless fragmentary husks of a cult or religion." Because the original meaning invested in craftsmanship has disappeared, Schädler regards the objects, by definition, as degenerate.

Crafts can, however, acquire new meanings. A craftsman can produce objects of beauty without their being invested with ritual significance either for him or for his clientele, and even in Africa there has always been traditional craftsmanship *not* linked to

8. Davydd J. Greenwood, "Culture by the Pound: An Anthropological Perspective on Tourism as Cultural Commoditization," in *Hosts and Guests*, Valene L. Smith, ed. (Philadelphia: University of Pennsylvania Press, 1977).

9. Chapter 12; see also Raymond Noronha, *Social and Cultural Dimensions of Tourism: A Review of the Literature in English*, draft report to the World Bank, 1977, p. 29.

religion.[10] The satisfaction of having made a "good"—that is, an appropriate—cult object can be replaced by pride in having matched or surpassed certain standards of workmanship or creativity and in sharing a craft tradition with others. The performances of the Balinese dancers are another notable example in which an activity of originally religious or ritual significance can be carried out in a secular context and acquire a new meaning. The process is better termed transformation than degeneration.

The demand created by tourists can, if appropriately channeled, be the force in such a transformation, as shown by Schädler, who discusses at length how African craftsmen have responded to tourist demand with new forms and styles based on traditional models. He mentions the new cult figures and animals invented in the Upper Volta; the new examples of brass casting in the tradition of the Ivory Coast and Ghana gold weights; and generally the extension of the casting tradition into hitherto untried areas. Increased demand and increased production mean greater problems of quality control; to overcome these, and to satisfy tourist tastes, these castings have grown in size—traditionally they were often very small figures indeed. In Latin America similar innovations, in which traditional quality is maintained, can be found in countries of the Andean region and in Central America and Mexico. In Bali, too, new styles emerged in arts and crafts after World War II. Painting and design as well as weaving and jewelry were stimulated by the influx of tourists, though some traditional crafts are dying out.

Craft Production: For Souvenirs and for Use

Tourists probably buy local products more as souvenirs, to evoke the visited places for themselves or for friends, than as objects of

10. Schädler's emphasis on the link between religion (the cult) and traditional art would appear to understate the importance of secular tribal activities. For example, much artistic expression was (and continues to be) linked to the institutions of chieftancy, which have secular functions in addition to any links they may have (had) with the cult. May's definition is less problematic: traditional art comprises works "made within a traditional society for use—religious or secular—within that society or for trade with traditional trading partners." (R. J. May, "Tourism and the Artifact Industry in Papua, New Guinea," in Ben R. Finney and Karen A. Watson, eds., *A New Kind of Sugar: Tourism in the Pacific*, 2d ed. [Honolulu: East-West Center, 1977], p. 125.)

aesthetic, cultural, or utilitarian value. Such souvenirs do not necessarily have a close relation to the traditional arts and crafts of a locality, although official promotion of good quality craftsmanship rooted in local traditions may play a role in ensuring that they do. But the discussion of arts and crafts should not be confined to those objects or activities which tourists themselves buy to take away or performances they go and see. There may also be opportunities for the production of crafts for *use*, both by local populations and in the hotels, restaurants, and recreation facilities visited by tourists.

Provided tourist comfort is safeguarded, these crafts make unusual and decorative furnishings for tourist rooms. Together with craft-based manufacturing that conforms to local styles and traditions, they can help create an atmosphere which will educate the tourist and give an appreciation of local culture. The networks of state inns in Spain and Portugal are notable examples of this approach; there, from the moment of arrival, tourists encounter expressions of the local culture.[11] After all, craft products have always been made primarily for use: pots for cooking, tables to eat from, rugs to walk on, or blankets to sleep under.

Since the Industrial Revolution, craftsmanship has retreated before manufacturing industry, as people have switched from craft products to mass-produced goods. This was due primarily to price, but also to the poor quality of craft production for popular use: pots that break easily and are awkwardly shaped, shoes that do not fit, chairs or stools that wobble and are uncomfortable. Now handmade goods produced for the wealthy may be the last stronghold of craftsmanship in many places. If demands of the tourist industry are added, this may provide the basis for a vigorous sector and a revival of interest in indigenous crafts among the local and national population. It may even lead to exports.[12]

Quite a few countries have now instituted training and assistance schemes for traditional crafts: the contributors mention them for Africa, Curaçao, Cyprus, and Tunisia. These training programs at times operate in conjunction with official retail outlets or museums, or, in the case of song and dance, with national dance theaters, espe-

---

11. See also Belt, Collins, and Associates, Ltd., *Tourism Development Programme for Fiji* (Honolulu, 1973), for similar views on tourism development in Fiji.

12. The poorest groups may not be much affected by this: they will continue to buy what is cheapest—be it earthenware, plastic, or aluminium!

cially in West Africa. The aim is to preserve local cultural and craft traditions, to train new generations of craftsmen and performers, and to maintain quality. But the training programs must also prepare craftsmen for creativity, so that new designs can be produced and traditional patterns do not rigidify into repetitive derivations. Artisan centers or villages specializing in certain types of craft production will help keep creativity alive. Such schemes seem, however, to have a tendency to emphasize crafts for tourists and give insufficient attention to the integration of crafts and tourist environment, or to possibilities for meeting the demands of local residents. In addition to activities aimed at increasing the supply of handcrafted goods, there must also be efforts devoted to ensuring that architects and designers fully explore the possibility of using local designs and motifs in their buildings.

Marketing

The income-generating effect of tourism-stimulated demand for arts and crafts is confirmed in many ways. It is seen in the revival of a traditional craft; a "degenerate" form of curio production; a voluntary association that helps people, as in Bali, supplement their income by performing traditional dances for the tourists; or even in an entirely new cottage industry, such as that in the Seychelles, to cater to the "rapidly expanding market for locally produced trinkets such as shell necklaces, coral artifacts, hats and bags." But little is known about the distribution of income earned in these ways. The craftsman's or performer's share of the final price differs greatly from one place to another, and marketing arrangements may have a considerable influence on the outcome.

Only for Bali do we have some detailed information.[13] Tourists there tend to come on package tours which include visits to certain performances and to craft shops, or they join such tours once on the island. The guide or the tour agency makes arrangements with certain shops and dance associations and receives a certain commission on purchases made or entrance tickets sold. Recently the competition for contracts has grown fiercer, and the earnings of the per-

13. This paragraph draws on I. Gusti Ngurah Bagus, "The Impact of Tourism upon the Culture of the Balinese People," paper presented to the Joint Unesco–World Bank Seminar; see also Chapter 12.

formers have suffered.[14] Craft shops tend to have their regular suppliers, the majority of whom appear to be wage laborers producing on the instructions of the owner of the shop; a minority are free artisans who sell their products to the craft shops, having bought the raw materials personally.[15] The latter are estimated to receive about 40 percent of the sales price; the employed carvers 20 percent. Alternative arrangements, such as cooperatives, appear not to exist.

The few other contributors to this volume who discuss the issue of marketing, even if only in passing, suggest that cooperative sales organizations of the craftsmen and state-run crafts centers are preferable to private craft shops and market stalls of middlemen. Schädler is most explicit in this respect, explaining that tourists who go to government-promoted or approved artisan centers "need not waste time bargaining with street vendors; here shopping seems thrifty, quick, and without problems." In Tunisia, Curaçao, and Cyprus government or cooperative marketing arrangements exist which appear to be working well.

Intuitively one is inclined to agree with those who wish to see cooperative or state-run organizations take a major role in the marketing and promotion of handicrafts. And yet, knowledge of the effects of these arrangements is scanty. There are official craft shops in Africa, Asia, and especially in Latin America where goods are certainly of excellent quality, but in at least some of these, prices are considerably higher than those which a discerning buyer could bargain for at market stalls or in private retail outlets. The cost of running such official organizations can be very high, and the craftsman-producer may receive no more for his product than he would from a private middleman. Apart from tourists, who are at least assured of quality, the main beneficiaries have been known to be the organization's officials, whose middle-class living standards are supported by the enterprise.[16] Cooperatives in developing countries have had at least as great a share of problems and failures as of successes, and organizationally they are far from easy to keep afloat.

---

14. Between 1971 and 1973 the total fee for the elaborate monkey dance, performed by a troupe of some 100 members, dropped from US$21 to between US$14 and US$17, presumably as a result of increasing competition.

15. According to a survey conducted by Udayana University in Bali in 1972, some 55 percent were wage laborers, while 45 percent were free artisans.

16. This was true for two large Latin American organizations with which I had personal contact in the early 1970s.

Distribution to the local market—to hotels, cafes, and bars, for example—is another area in which there are questions galore but where answers are hard to come by. It should not require a great deal of research to get some hard data on the actual mechanics of these different marketing arrangements.

The Integrated Environment

In many tourism areas the authorities are aware of the importance of preserving the urban environment and its local characteristics, especially where these are seen as part of the locality's attractiveness to tourists. In Bermuda, for example, rigid planning codes keep new buildings consistent with the island's unique architectural style; no family may own more than one car, and the speed limit remains at twenty miles an hour. Bermuda is thus kept as a place of "insular quaintness and peculiar charm." In Spain, too, much attention is now paid to this important asset for tourism, after earlier neglect led to severe environmental deterioration. As Ellis stresses repeatedly, however, the urban environment is in considerable danger of change and deterioration if it does not contain significant monuments or noble spaces.[17] The more humble manifestations of material culture, especially popular architecture as expressed in simple dwellings, shops, and minor squares, are frequently allowed to decay, if they are not unceremoniously removed for the sake of urban development. The Casamance experience is a notable exception in this respect, reviving a nearly forgotten form of architecture, the great round house with impluvium, for tourist guest houses. It is through the simple and popular elements of material culture and the urban environment, and not through the cathedrals, mosques, or palaces, that Ellis would seek a genuine integration of the tourists with the peoples and places they visit.

Local craft products sold in local shops or markets, with a training school nearby; centers where tourists can learn about the local culture in all its aspects;[18] didactic, cultural, and educational en-

17. Eduardo J. Ellis, "Tourism and the Unity of the Sociocultural Environment," paper presented to the Joint Unesco–World Bank Seminar.

18. Adelwahab Bouhdiba ("The Impact of Tourism on Traditional Values and Beliefs in Tunisia," paper presented to the Joint Unesco–World Bank Seminar) similarly suggests transforming tourism into a cultural sector by organizing talks, round tables, artistic manifestations, and guided tours with well-qualified guides.

terprises on a small and intimate scale; harmonization of urban renewal with the traditional local culture; hotels that reflect local crafts and architectural style, possibly as demonstration models with aid from the authorities—according to Ellis, such ventures aim "to establish proper relations between the local inhabitants—their traditional and their new ways of life—and the urban environment and tourism." Since little is known about the ways in which these relations can best be set up, Ellis calls for research into the perceptions of tourists and local inhabitants. He is concerned to limit the number of tourists encouraged to visit small-scale environments, and in general he calls for caution, believing that ambitious, expensive, and large-scale projects have tended to fail because the plans were not based on successful pilot projects and realizations at the micro level.

The integrated tourist environments sought by Ellis may best be seen as part of touristic *circuits*, perhaps added to resort holidays. Ellis himself pleads for this kind of approach, giving the examples of Salvador de Bahia in Brazil and Cuzco/Macchu Pichu in Peru. In Tunisia some discovery circuits appear to have been instituted in recent years, leading to the preservation of certain types of traditional habitat which were in the process of disappearing, and drawing people away from the beaches for at least a short while.

That there are problems in such an approach no one would deny. Groupe Huit, for example, queries the reaction of the local population to the transformation of the fortified grain stores of Ksar Tathouine into hotel rooms and in general seems to worry about local peoples' reactions to the tourists' interest in their everyday activities and traditional objects. But that is querying the very process of social change. If tourism can help to stem the tide of increasing uniformity and cultural homogeneity in the world, through preserving (albeit in a different form and with different functions) cultural and craft traditions that would otherwise disappear, that would seem to be a positive result. But the difficulties should not be underestimated, and success should not be taken for granted.

Part II
The Papers

T HE PAPERS ASSEMBLED HERE CONSTITUTE an unusual contribution to the North-South dialogue. Some represent the work of people from industrialized countries of the North who have studied the phenomenon of tourism among the developing countries of the South; others are written from the point of view of the developing countries themselves. The authors represent a wide range of disciplines—such as sociologists, anthropologists, economists, and geographers—and administrators directly concerned with the development of tourism. Some are scholars, who have used the tools of their trade to research the subject. Other authors have written out of their own practical experience with tourism as an instrument of change. Where the papers repeat each other they serve to reinforce the arguments; where they differ, or even contradict each other, they indicate the complexity of the subject and the diversity of situations and perspectives.

The papers have been grouped into three categories: studies that concentrate on the planning and policy decisions of tourism, particularly in the economic realm; papers that emphasize the effects of tourism on the art and culture of the societies and on the people themselves; and case studies of tourism development in specific localities (see table of contents). Inevitably a few papers could fit into two or even all three categories; their placement is based on an assessment of the main contribution of the material to this volume.

CHAPTER 6

Toward Planning Tourism in African Countries

Reginald Herbold Green
INSTITUTE OF DEVELOPMENT STUDIES
UNIVERSITY OF SUSSEX

D ISCUSSION AND ANALYSIS OF THE NATURE, effects, and role of tourism in developing countries is hampered by inadequate data, concepts, and communication. Proponents and opponents tend to pursue such different issues that they talk past rather than to each other. Analysis from the vantage points of different disciplines is rarely welded into a coherent whole. Varying types of tourism and tourism sectors in countries with radically different levels of productive forces and with divergent sociopolitical and economic systems are conflated into a simplistic unity. All too often the result is not even exemplified by the fable of the blind men, each of whom touched one part of an elephant and tried to describe the whole; it is as if each man had touched a different part of a different animal.

These notes are limited. They relate to foreign tourism from high-income countries to medium-sized, low-income African states. The emphasis is on political and economic issues with special reference to the organization and planning of the tourism sector in the context of the overall goals of national decisionmakers. Many of these goals (and therefore some of the costs and benefits flowing from tourism) are not economic, but within limits the political-economic analysis of tourism and its planning can treat the social and political elements either as externally given constraints or as costs to be offset against more narrowly economic gains.[1]

1. This treatment is not fully satisfactory. Ends and means cannot be separated so simplistically, especially at the level of national strategy. The approach is more practicable for tourism than for many other sectors, however, because no convincing case can be made for the development of tourism in Africa except on narrowly economic

Analysis of the more narrowly economic aspects of tourism is not irrelevant to broader social, cultural, and political considerations. The gains—if any—from tourism are primarily economic. Therefore it is critical to determine which economic gains of what orders of magnitude can be secured, subject to which conditions. Only then can one contrast these gains to social, cultural, and political costs, or attempt to identify means of limiting noneconomic costs without major erosion of economic gains.

Tourism is a peculiar product, a luxury export consumed by non-citizens in the exporting (not the importing) country. Many of the social, cultural, and political consequences of tourism flow from its being an internally consumed export. So do certain of its economic potentials, such as earning foreign exchange, and its problems, such as the need for external partners.

It is agreed by critics and proponents alike that tourism was a growth sector from 1960 to 1973 and, with somewhat less unanimity, that the rapid growth trend will continue until the year 2000. These generalizations apply in general to the continent of Africa. It is equally agreed that the growth of tourism has been highly uneven among individual countries and is closely linked to state policies and resource allocations. Again, African examples bear out this view. The natural assets of Tanzania and Kenya offer similar attractions for tourists, but Kenya's greater resource allocations to, and policy support for, tourism has resulted in growth that is both absolutely and relatively much more rapid. A similar comparison can be made between Tunisia and Algeria.

On the achieved and achievable gains from tourism, however, there is no general agreement among commentators or analysts, even if the discussion is limited to political and economic gains. Relatively large and, on the face of it, economically beneficial tourism sectors like those of Morocco and Tunisia have been argued to be net consumers, not providers, of investible surplus and very marginal net contributors of foreign exchange. In contrast, weak sectors, like that of Tanzania, have been perceived by some writers as major contributors to the national product and external receipts. When

---

grounds. An analysis of economic gains does provide a benchmark against which decisionmakers can measure social and political costs. At project level, basic goals and their implications must be taken as given parameters, and actual analysis centers on maximizing political-economic net gains within these constraints.

prospects are considered, even less agreement can be found—in the extreme, the same type of tourism development in the same country is presented as both a gift of the gods and the work of the devil. This conflict does not turn solely on sociological or political judgments. Economic estimates—especially of indirect costs and benefits and of net as opposed to gross foreign exchange earnings—vary tremendously. Fragmentary methodology leaves such a wide margin for guesstimation that each observer tends to back his own judgment and very often his own personal feelings about tourism. As a result, studies done by those involved in tourism (including independent analysts as well as promoters) tend to be remarkably positive, and those carried out by academicians (who often react negatively to mass tourism for personal and noneconomic reasons) tend to be dominantly negative.

Quite unrealistic expectations and attributions surround the tourism sector. Some may have validity in microeconomies or regions where tourism is, or can be, the dominant economic sector, but they are much less relevant in most African states because the tourism sector will of necessity be relatively small. Others appear to arise as a result of attributing to tourism responsibility for all events taking place at the same time as the rise of the tourism sector. For example, in the context of dependence on foreign firms and of highly unequal distribution of domestic income, the argument that tourism will benefit foreign and domestic elites is no doubt valid, but it seems somewhat fanciful to transpose this argument into a claim that tourism *as such* causes, or is critical to the dominance of, a domestic elite and dependence on foreign firms.

Less sweeping analytical efforts usually identify specific gains and costs associated with ongoing or proposed tourism projects. But evaluation of individual projects, even in the context of careful negotiations, is not adequate by itself because many factors can be evaluated and acted on only sectorally. Tourism is an area in which sectoral planning is particularly critical; nevertheless it is relatively incomplete and inadequate even in countries like Tunisia and Kenya with large tourism sectors backed by substantial state support.

The opportunity costs of developing a given sector, and the alternatives to it, cannot be estimated on the basis of that sector alone. This must be done in the context of a consistent set of exercises in sectoral planning within a national plan. This is particularly true of tourism, which is usually perceived as meeting basic developmental goals only indirectly. Foreign exchange, investible surplus, and the generation of tax revenue are its products, rather than direct provision of critical domestic goods and services.

Objectives and Limitations

The usual political and economic goals of a tourism sector are: foreign exchange, government revenue and other investible surplus, employment, and general or regional economic growth.

Foreign exchange

By definition, tourism generates gross foreign exchange earnings. In Kenya and Tunisia it is the largest gross export, and even in Tanzania it ranks seventh. But serious problems can arise with respect to gross earnings because of the very low ratio of gross foreign exchange inflow to the total cost of package tours that are made up, sold, transported, staffed, and supplied by foreign firms and personnel, as in the case of Club Méditerranée.

Estimates of net to gross foreign earnings range from 10 percent in one study of Mauritius, through 40 to 50 percent in the working notes for planning in Tanzania, to 60 to 70 percent in similar material for Kenya and Tunisia.[2] Part of the problem is in identifying outflows consistently and comprehensively. Direct operating imports are a clear case but far from the only one. Other major categories are management fees, expatriate salaries, capital goods not financed from foreign funds, loan redemption as well as interest and dividends, the import content of local purchases (for example, domestically manufactured cement and gasoline in East Africa have an import content of 60 to 70 percent), and the import content of government infrastructure and supporting services.[3] If gross earnings

2. See G. Young, *Tourism: Blessing or Blight?* (New York: Penguin, 1971); and I. Shivje, ed., *Tourism and Socialist Development* (Dar es Salaam: Tanzania Publishing House, 1973). See also A. Smaoui, "Développement touristique en Tunisie" [Tourism development in Tunisia]; H. Sebbar, "Tourisme et développement: Cas du Maroc" [Tourism and development: The case of Morocco]; and R. H. Green, "Tourism and African Development," papers presented at the Tunis Seminar on Tourism, Environment, and Development (Dakar: United Nations Environmental Programme and Institut de Développement Economique et de Planification [African institute of planning and economic development], 1974).

3. Imports paid for out of citizen income, government revenue, and the profits of domestic enterprise are not directly relevant at the sectoral or project level, and they

from tourism are estimated from samples and not counted from currency received, a further deduction must be made for illicit currency exchange that ends in capital flight, and not in the central bank.

Major net gains from foreign exchange are taxes collected on imported and local purchases, citizen wages and salaries, the domestic content of local purchases, and a share of operating surpluses. To raise taxes on imports, special tax concessions (all too frequently made, especially in West Africa) should be avoided, and imports should be channeled through locally based commercial houses (instead of being imported direct) to take advantage of the markup and limit transfer pricing.[4] To raise operating surpluses requires systematic identification and perhaps improvement of local services and goods suitable for the tourism sector and then an effort to have them purchased. Food and furnishings are usually among the broad areas in which action is possible, but real difficulties arise because it is the tourist, not the indigenous decisionmaker, who must be satisfied by the product or service. The tourism entrepreneur genuinely does know tourists' requirements better but may have other reasons to "buy foreign."

Hiring nationals for middle- and high-level posts is critical because upper wages and salaries are normally far larger in the aggregate than the total payment of low-level wages. Because expatriates are expensive in Africa there is a common interest in replacing them with local people, especially at the managerial level, and in the provision of training facilities (and allocation of their costs), but the timetable for these innovations poses major problems. This is probably especially true in the case of foreign management contractors, who are usually paid on the basis of cost plus or gross turnover. Local management is relevant to the degree of domestic control, which explains why foreign firms tend to resist it.

The domestic share of gross operating surplus depends only in part on ownership of facilities in Africa. Equally critical are man-

---

are unlikely to differ radically among sectors or projects. Only at the level of national foreign exchange do they become critical for planning, and measures to reduce them are unlikely to be specific to tourism.

4. Transfer pricing in the technical sense arises if a foreign-owned or foreign-managed unit imports from companies in the same group at artificial prices. More generally, it covers transactions in which overpricing is accepted whether because of more distant linkages, balancing transactions, some form of tax, or avoidance of exchange control. Experience in Tanzania suggests that, in the latter sense, it is common in tourism.

agement and fees (an area of amazing variations), the rate of interest on the ubiquitous state loans to major hotels, the allocation of infrastructure costs, and tax rates, including deductions, such as for depreciation and concessions.[5] The inverse of transfer pricing on purchases can arise on sales. The obvious case is transactions within a group, but lack of information on what *can* be charged apparently often leads to rates to tour operators well below what could be secured.

Employment

Tourism generates employment as does any economic activity. How much is harder to say. Even for hotels and internal transport estimates are shaky, though 1 to 1.5 employees per bed in these subsectors seems the most probable range. Secondary employment is even harder to guess and depends primarily on the extent of local services (including government) and goods (including crafts) purchased by the sector and by individual tourists. A total of two to three jobs per bed is not unreasonable in East and North Africa. Because more food is imported for tourists in West Africa the amount of employment generated is probably lower, and that for microstates like Mauritius lower still. Gross employment tends to vary inversely with wage levels; a very low minimum wage may maximize jobs but not the amount of wages paid.

The quality of employment varies widely. Much is seasonal, although less so in Africa than in the Caribbean. Governments and hotels share a common interest in seeking to extend the peak season and shorten the empty season. A seasonal labor force tends to be rel-

---

5. For a profitable enterprise the difference between standard or "give away" tax terms—5 percent as against 9 percent construction loans, 5 percent of gross turnover as against 10 percent of net profit for management fees, and lavish as against minimal state provision of associated infrastructure—can easily be 50 percent of operating surplus and 20 percent of gross receipts. Except for a central city hotel using existing services and paying normal property taxes and utility bills, infrastructure will always be significant. A suburban beach hotel forty kilometers out of town could easily eat up US$3 million to US$8 million of link roads, water-power-telephone extensions, and beach bulkheading or US$10 to US$15 per bed night for 300 beds at 60 percent annual occupancy. The cost per tourist of international airports is very high if a 10 percent opportunity cost of capital is used. For the new Nairobi and Mombasa airports alone it would come to US$15 to US$20 per tourist assuming (optimistically) that direct charges cover 80 percent of total operating costs (including civil aviation and meteorology) and that there are 500,000 tourists a year.

atively unskilled and transient. But hotels require a high proportion of workers at the semiskilled, skilled, or managerial and professional level—probably a higher proportion than to most other lines of activity, including much manufacturing. The image of a handful of managers and an unskilled army of waiters and chambermaids is totally erroneous, as demonstrated by the training schools—often operated at government expense—that are needed to supply the skills required of even lower level employees. Encouraging, or requiring, the tourism industry to employ citizens in middle and higher level posts may be at the expense of creating (or aggravating) scarcities of manpower in other, perhaps more basic, sectors of the economy. Managers, accountants, technicians, and repairmen are scarce, as are really competent drivers and telephone operators. With training comparable to that needed to be a cook, a dining room manager, a receptionist, a supervisor, or a booking clerk, many other abilities could be mastered for semiskilled through junior professional jobs.

Employment in construction related to the tourism sector poses special problems because demand tends to be lumpy and unstable. In smaller economies such as Seychelles a building boom in tourism causes serious problems in the construction sector. Initial demand strains capacity and pushes up prices; then after the tourism sector enters a period of moderate growth there are major adjustments as the construction industry contracts.

Investible surplus

Net investible surplus is harder to generate than either net foreign exchange earnings or employment. It is probable that the tourism sector was a net user of investible surplus in Tunisia from 1960 to 1970, in Morocco almost continuously for two decades, and in Kenya since the major upgrading of airports began at the end of the 1960s.[6] A curious and vicious circle develops. An unsuccessful sector has few surpluses; a successful one is expanded and uses more surplus than it generates. For example, Kenya's Diani Complex scheme is estimated to cost about US$900 million or two and a half times the current total annual gross fixed capital formation of the economy and six times the directly productive annual investment

6. See Sebbar, "Tourisme et développement" and papers on Tunisia presented at the Tunis seminar. The Kenyan case turns on the massive investment in airports.

of Kenya. For the purposes of enterprise management this may be acceptable, but because tourism does not provide goods and services that meet basic domestic needs and, indeed, is used domestically by only a tiny elite, problems arise for national development.[7] It may be true that the tourist "product cycle" requires expansion to stay in one place,[8] but this belief can be used both to justify continued growth and to argue against major initial commitments to tourism.

Tourism is sometimes expected to become a leading sector, generating rapid overall economic growth as a variant of the export enclave. The objective is rarely likely to be attained, however, unless tourism is one of a package of export industries. In most African economies tourism is not a large enough sector to become a dynamic force for growth. But limited areas that are initially at very low levels of productivity, such as African game parks, offer better prospects for growth. Among a number of basic problems with such developments, one merits special mention here: The local gains are not necessarily—or even usually—concentrated among the initial residents of the area. Frequently these people suffer from dislocation of their existing patterns of production, lack of attention to their direct needs, and loss of land. Certainly extending game parks, banning hunting by savanna and forest peoples, relocating fishermen away from homes and markets, and clearing out unsightly evidence of poverty (such as squatter villages) near tourist sites are not only common to the development of tourism complexes in Africa but also highly damaging, even in narrow economic terms, to the poorest and weakest of the initial residents.[9]

The appropriateness of tourism for attaining any stated objective cannot be determined simply by studying existing and potential

7. This will be perceived differently by different states. If decisionmakers respond primarily to elites and social groups with large stakes in the tourism industry as owners, high-level employees, and consumers, then it will be found acceptable for a permanently expanding tourism sector to make net calls on government resources and investible surplus. A state would take a less favorable view of such a situation if it were committed to a transition to socialism, if it gives priority to meeting the basic needs of workers and peasants, and if it is severely constrained by the inadequacy of its surplus and government revenue.

8. See J. M. Miossec, "L'Espace touristique africain" [African tourist space] and "Réflexion sur les rapports entre transport aérien et tourisme en Tunisie: Conséquences spatiales et économiques" [The relation between air transport and tourism in Tunisia: Spatial and economic consequences], Tunis seminar.

9. Young, *Tourism: Blessing or Blight?* Similar Kenyan, Tunisian, Ivory Coast, and Senegalese cases were outlined at the Tunis seminar.

tourism projects or even sectoral patterns. Because tourism projects and sector development use scarce resources and because other means of attaining each objective exist, it is critical to assess opportunity costs and benefits.[10] Tourism has a relatively high ratio of capital to labor. Recent East African data suggest a cost of at least US$15,000 for each hotel bed or about US$10,000 for each direct job created. Adding indirect capital expenditure and employment may well merely double the figures for both capital and employment, leaving the cost per job at US$10,000. This is higher than the job cost in plantation agriculture or textiles. In Tunisia the estimated capital cost per job in tourism is about in the middle of the range for manufacturing subsectors.[11] Similar questions of alternatives and their cost-benefit ratios pertain to other objectives. In East or North Africa even a luxury hotel can procure up to 80 to 90 percent of its food requirements locally; in West Africa the patterns of agricultural output make such a target unrealistic.

It is artificial to abstract specific objectives from the overall goals of decisionmakers. Certainly for some analytical purposes the approach is useful, but rarely is it sufficient by itself. For example, it is perfectly true that both Kenya and Tanzania include in their tourism policies the objectives of earning foreign exchange and establishing a degree of local control. But Tanzania sees export development primarily as a means of meeting the import requirements of its nationally oriented political-economic development, while Kenya counts on exports to lead its overall development strategy. Tanzanian decisionmakers perceive local control in the context of a transition to socialism and reduced dependence on large external economic units. In Kenya local control relates to state and private capitalists and enterprises in the context of closer—but less unequal—integration into the present capitalist international economic order. Even the purely economic aspects of tourism development

10. Costs and benefits for purposes of decisionmaking include social, political, and cultural costs and benefits as much as economic. There is little problem in ensuring that decisionmakers are aware that noneconomic concerns are real; the difficulties lie in identifying them clearly and indicating their order of magnitude to facilitate informed decisions.

11. See A. Smaoui, "Développement touristique en Tunisie" [Tourism development in Tunisia]; H. Couchane, "Système d'aide de l'Etat aux investissements touristiques en Tunisie" [System of state aid to tourism investments in Tunisia]; and M. Boughezala, "Impact du tourisme sur l'emploi" [Impact of tourism on employment], Tunis seminar.

must be placed in the context of national ideologies and strategies if applicable results are to emerge.

Foreign Partners: Needs, Uses, Costs

Tourism is not a sector in which an autarkic approach is feasible. At one level this is a truism—foreign tourism requires foreigners—but the need for foreign involvement is deeper than that. Local production, processing, and marketing of primary raw materials need foreign partners less and are less directly influenced by the nature of the ultimate users.

The need for external partners—whether true transnational corporations or smaller, less agglomerated enterprises—is not primarily financial. If it were and if external capital transfers were needed, they could be borrowed abroad and channeled to domestic enterprise. In fact, such borrowing is rather common but is very often paralleled by relending to a foreign-owned or foreign-managed enterprise with a small external equity. Financing transportation to Africa could pose quantitatively greater financial problems, but few African airlines are really constrained primarily by an inability to raise external loans to finance equipment; on the contrary, a number have been gravely injured by the ease of securing them.

The basic needs are for knowledge, communication, and organization both in Africa and in the tourists' home countries. Knowledge, communication, and organization are the transnationals' primary assets and sources of power, especially when they must be deployed in a coordinated way in several very different and dispersed countries. Tourism is a sector that requires such deployment.

In looking at the reasons for seeking external partners it may be useful to divide tourism into six segments: designing salable tour packages, selling them, moving tourists to and from host territories, providing local facilities, coordinating local elements of the package tour, and ensuring adequate local performance as perceived by the tourists. The first three necessarily take place outside Africa, while the first two and perhaps the last turn far more on knowledge of individual preferences in the context of industrial economies than on familiarity with Africa. Unless all segments work relatively effectively and interact smoothly, each will be unsuccessful. The quality requirements of manufacturers are easier to learn than how to keep tourists happy. It is easier to sell directly to a few manufacturers than to a host of tourist agents, let alone to swarms of distant individuals. Few problems result if coffee is delayed in transit for a few days or there is a major disturbance in an adjacent country, but the effect of delay and disturbance on tourism is traumatic.

Designing package tours

The design of salable packages requires information on tourist preferences—at least a little more articulated than the obvious quest for sun, sand, and sea or rum, rooms, and recreation—and knowledge of available facilities and costs. The mass tourist market, as demonstrated in 1973–75 in the United Kingdom, is one in which errors in packaging and pricing can be very costly. In Africa governments, let alone private firms, do not have the requisite knowledge. Unlike industrial economies, they cannot afford the data base or the high-level personnel to build up an ongoing system to collect and analyze information. Some African participation is possible in designing tours and side trips geared to local facilities and attractions and in seeking to promote these with agencies handling specialized types of tourism. But in the final design of packages for the mass tour market it is unlikely that African states or firms can act on their own as senior partners.

Selling the packages

Still less within present or likely future African capacity is the selling of package tours. Most tourists do not have clear preferences as to destinations but merely a desire to be on a beach or climb hills or see wild animals.[12] Therefore a network of retail outlets linked via main agents or wholesalers to packagers is needed in the tourists' home countries. Organizing a network of independent travel agents is theoretically possible for African states, but it would require expensive promotion, skilled market research, and extensive commercial structures in industrial economies. No mass tourist

12. The high proportion of Swedes traveling to Gambia, Sri Lanka, and southern Tunisia is explained historically by regulations for charter flights which forced packagers to design and promote tours to the handful of main airports not covered by the restrictions.

destination in a Third World country or in socialist Europe has been able to build up a major outlet for direct sales.

This is not to say that there are no areas in which African states can promote sales, although most present publicity is probably nugatory. Some background publicity may create useful awareness. Programs aimed at independent agents can tap the small but lucrative market for the individual tailor-made trip. Publicity aimed at packagers can interest them in a new destination or in putting together a new package. But these promotional efforts take place at the secondary level, not at the point of direct sales.

Transport

African participation in the long-distance transport of tourists to and from the continent is limited by three factors: airline capacity, traffic to make routes economically viable, and negotiating muscle. On the whole, African airlines have relatively weak divisions operating charter flights. Scheduled services appear to be limited mainly by route viability. These weaknesses are compounded by governmental failure to demand fifty-fifty sharing of traffic, including fifty-fifty division of charter business. African tourist firms and their sectoral ministries have usually been reluctant to get tough in negotiations with foreign airlines, fearing it would reduce service, alienate packagers (especially those with their own fleets of planes), and lose business.

Providing local facilities

There is less need for foreign partners—as opposed to foreign personnel or specialist consulting firms hired by an African enterprise or state—in the provision of local facilities. A good deal of the knowledge needed is of African situations and potentials. Further knowledge of the design, construction, and pricing of facilities to conform to actual demand can be secured fairly readily on the open market. There are consultants specializing in tourism, and some foreign tourist sector operators such as international airlines are eager to help states locate data because it is to their mutual benefit to build marketable facilities.

Financing for facilities is usually provided locally or, if from foreign borrowing, is relent by the state; a foreign financial partner is therefore rarely critical. Admittedly, if a state encourages foreign private investment in general, as in Ivory Coast, Kenya, and Ghana, there is no good reason to exclude tourism. Conversely, a general strategy of domestic ownership need not make exceptions for tourist facilities.

Designing and coordinating local components

Greater knowledge is required for designing and coordinating the local components of tour packages than for providing local facilities. A ministry or a sectoral corporation or a joint marketing body for individual enterprises can build up a capacity fairly rapidly. Some foreign personnel will be needed but can be hired directly.

Africanization in this field is risky because learning through serious mistakes is expensive. Attracting a greater array of interested overseas packagers would reduce risks and uncertainties and increase bargaining power. Domestic capacity can be built up parallel to, and in gradual replacement of, foreign-based or partnership capacity, and the risk can be held to fairly low levels by phased Africanization.

Ensuring adequate performance

If facilities are not acceptable to tourists and tour packagers, there will be few tourists in Africa and goals cannot be met. To gain this acceptance certain standards of performance must be maintained, but there is more than one way of ensuring the adequacy of service and facilities. Some successful units are either managed or controlled entirely by Africans, using some expatriates hired directly. The scope for expanding the number of such units relatively rapidly is real and large. For a large number of other units, however, whether foreign owned or not, the use of foreign managing agents is justified on the basis of efficiency of operation. As an interim measure with provision for building African capacity, and if undertaken in a framework of carefully negotiated contracts, this is no more (and no less) unsound than the use of foreign managers for new complex technology units in manufacturing. The ideal managing agent is usually one who is not a tour packager and therefore does not have a conflict of interest over prices charged. The managing agent is a direct source of business, but this is desirable only if his other operations do not benefit from undercharging for the African facility.

The structure of the tourism industry precludes full African control in the foreseeable future. As a result, foreign partners or close contractual arrangements are necessary. It can be argued that much the same is true in the case of primary products that are taken from initial production through international trade and manufacturing to the final consumer. Tourism, however, has a less homogeneous and accessible set of markets and requires close coordination among its six functions; the foreign presence is therefore more ubiquitous.

The costs are loss of control, instability, and unequal division of gains. A weak African sector, even if 100 percent locally owned, may be dominated by overseas operators. Even a strong one will be less able to make decisions on its own than will a comparable sector in the domestic market or other export sectors.[13] The experience of, say, Bulgaria, Rumania, Hungary, and Poland, however, suggests that a medium-sized tourism sector (relative to the economy as a whole) need not lead to general loss of control or to an inability to lay down and enforce a framework for the tourism sector.

Instability in tourism is high. Because the growth trend is also high, there are at the global level rare and limited absolute falls in demand or price but wide variations in growth. For individual countries, absolute loss of business as well as loss of anticipated growth is a real danger, especially if one or two packagers or one or two countries provide the bulk of the tourists. Ultimately packagers decide where mass tourist flows go, and they can afford to reduce or cut out any one African destination.

Under these circumstances the division of gains can be most unfavorable to African states. Because of cutthroat competition for volume, much of the charter flight industry was in financial trouble in the early and mid-1970s. Its desperate efforts to regain solvency have put further pressure on African tourism. A small country is not in a strong position, especially if it also lacks data on alternative sources of tourists. Joint action might help, but a tourist OPEC is an unreal goal, given the heterogeneity and number of the tourist-receiving countries in the Third World. Tourism cannot be easily incorporated into the Manila Declaration or UNCTAD Common Fund proposals, though its incorporation in compensatory finance stabilization schemes is possible and desirable.

13. The degree of domestic control over tourism can be greater than that over component fabrication or subassembly units linked to a single transnational corporation. In the latter case, conversion to new markets may be impossible and is always difficult and expensive.

Negotiation: Needs and Parameters

The combination of the need for external partners and the need to maintain control over the domestic impact of the tourism sector leads directly to the need for a strategy of negotiated agreements and for the negotiating capacity to implement it. Without negotiations based on both knowledge and skill, it is unlikely that substantial gains can be achieved. Neither carte blanche nor take-it-or-leave-it orders to partners is likely to be economically satisfactory.

Given negotiation, some tourism projects can be made to yield some economic gains. It is critical to identify those which cannot do so before, not after, resources have been used on them. Some believe that there is a standard, unalterable tourism contract package that involves ceding full control to external firms and then subsidizing the sector. This is not accurate. Neither is the subsidiary belief that this package was designed and promoted by the World Bank. On the contrary, a wide variety of possibilities exists, depending on local inputs, the degree to which nationals are employed, domestic charges, foreign exchange flows, management fees, control, taxation, and the like.

The myth of uniform terms is dangerous. It usually leads not to a rejection of tourism but to a fatalistic failure to analyze proposals, to build African capacity for project identification and analysis, and to negotiate effectively and tenaciously.[14] A tourism sector or a tourism project is desirable only if there are net political and economic gains. As a secondary sector with enclave properties, tourism cannot logically be subsidized for purposes of overall development. Not all projects or partners have the same potential for net gains. Almost any foreign partner will negotiate better terms than his initial offer if faced by informed, forceful negotiations.

If negotiation is limited to querying clauses in someone else's proposal it is deficient in three respects. It lacks a clear definition of

14. The misconception that all foreign partners in all projects are evil and the resulting failure to select and negotiate are problems not unique to tourism. In Tanzania many of the worst foreign-initiated manufacturing proposals—including some with negative Tanzanian value added—were backed by decisionmakers who vehemently detested transnationals but saw them as inevitable partners. As a result they failed to concentrate on selective use of transnationals or on negotiation.

African targets and of minimum acceptable results; it allows the would-be external partner to set the parameters of negotiation; and it usually proceeds with the African side lacking adequate information to evaluate or to make counterproposals. An effective negotiation process requires identifying why, what, who, when, and how.

"Why" must be answered in terms of objectives. Those for tourism have been sketched earlier, but a need to involve a partner presupposes objectives that cannot be achieved alone.

What is sought in negotiation relates to the means for achieving the objectives that have been defined. For example, Africanization of middle and senior personnel may be sought to gain foreign exchange, ease external control over operations, and possibly to increase flexibility for selecting among partners. "What" is not a simple question—many negotiations are on side issues, especially if one party sets the parameters and directs attention to minor issues on which he is willing to make concessions.

"Who" asks which partners can provide the inputs needed to achieve African objectives and are willing to do so at a price that is reasonable from the African perspective. A small firm with no capacity for packaging or promoting tours may be able to operate a hotel in Africa, but that is the limit of its potential contribution. In contrast, Hilton can ensure a flow of tourists as well as manage local units in a way acceptable to their clientele. The negotiating problems turn on achieving a total package of fees, conditions, and procedures that provide an acceptable division of surplus and an adequate degree of African control.[15] A firm unable to purchase and promote cannot be satisfactory, no matter how low its fees.

When to negotiate is partly a matter of sequences and partly one of tactics. Both counsel early initiatives, that is, before significant resources have been spent on a project. A completed hotel with no clients is not merely evidence of inadequate planning; it is in a weak negotiating position and more at the mercy of external partners than one not yet built.

How to negotiate is a matter of immediate and future tactics. It is critical to make clear (to the African negotiators themselves, as well as to the prospective partner) what issues are not negotiable and

---

15. Hilton International prefers to manage hotels rather than have a substantial stake in ownership. Its total charges vary tremendously; those for the Nairobi Hilton are less than half the share of turnover proposed for the (rejected) Dar es Salaam Hilton.

what objectives must be met. It is equally important to avoid creating obstacles to future progress in order to win short-term gains. Africanization—both of personnel and of detailed control over a managing agent—is an area in which such mistakes are particularly easy to make. Over time, development of the tourism sector requires growing use of African knowledge, personnel, institutions, finance, goods, and associated services. Properly conducted negotiations should center on getting growth in the short as well as the long run.

Successful negotiation requires knowledge and personnel capable of making good use of it. Experts in law and economic analysis, for example, may be the backbone of a negotiating team for general purposes, but they need to be joined by specialists in the subject under negotiation. In the present case they must be specialists in tourism.[16]

Knowledge of more than the African territory and its present tourism sector is required. Equally critical is information about the world tourism industry, the subsectors relevant to a proposed project, and the firm with which one is negotiating. In addition, it is necessary to be informed about other competitive tourist destinations, both in Africa and elsewhere, and the nature and main provisions of their relations with foreign tourism units. Such information is not easy or cheap to acquire, but if a state questions its cost it should also reassess the worth of the tourism sector or of a project. Marginal gains on investment in negotiation are usually far above costs. Indeed, the lack of adequate attention to data collection and negotiation, both in tourism and in other sectors involving foreign partners, can itself be explained only by a lack of data to indicate how much is lost.[17]

From Negotiation to Planning

Microproject analysis and negotiation cannot encompass the whole tourism sector. Policies and infrastructure are by their nature

16. A general applied political economist—like the author—can advise on a tourism project to some purpose but is more useful if a tourism specialist is also involved. It is not trivial to point out that tourism projects are like other export sector projects in certain respects but different in others, even on the purely economic front and more so on the socioeconomic or sociopolitical.

17. No matter what the aims of African decisionmakers might be—even if they were to seek benefits for a narrow elite or bribes for themselves—good data skillfully deployed would increase the chances of achieving those ends.

general. Sequences among projects and infrastructure cannot be analyzed without aggregation. To compare alternative tourism projects with each other requires a sectoral framework for evaluating each in relation to sectoral objectives. Any African state concerned with developing or regulating a tourism sector of more than minute proportions should therefore engage in the sectoral planning of tourism. In this context, planning includes implementation, supervision, and review as well as the formulation of plans and covers private as well as governmental and public enterprise.[18]

Sectoral planning starts with a statement of the contributions the sector is expected to make to national objectives—whether foreign exchange, employment, diversification of exports, or income distribution—and of the possible negative contributions to be avoided—whether a drain on public revenue, increasing foreign control over the economy, or the erosion of national culture. Planning requires information on the existing sector, its past evolution, ongoing trends, and readily identifiable potential changes. From this data base it is possible to identify additional contributions or reductions in negative contributions that will be needed over a given period and to indicate in a preliminary way what policies, infrastructures, projects, and regulations might lead to them.

Microanalysis of projects and policies, infrastructure and regulations is then possible to determine what gains could be derived and at what real resource costs. The next step is the formulation of a plan that identifies major gains and costs and that is then modified and eventually implemented. In practice, the formulation process is more iterative than this schema suggests. The initial availability of goods and resources is rarely precisely known and does not readily match identified potential. The process must be repeated with sharpened goals and more data.

Sectoral planning also involves implementation (by several units, including public and private enterprises), supervision (by one or more governmental or parastatal bodies), and a review of successes

---

18. Sectoral planning includes policies as well as projects. Incentives, penalties, and regulations to induce and control private actions are therefore integral to the planning, especially if private enterprise has a large share in the sector. This suggests a need for government involvement in negotiations between African and foreign enterprises. This may take the form of setting parameters, but given the economies of scale of negotiation and the weakness of most African firms a more active state role would appear advisable.

and failures (so that the existing formulation can be modified or a new one constructed). Negotiation is relevant primarily at these stages and within the frame set by the sectoral plan. Like negotiation, sectoral planning requires inputs of knowledge, analysis, and personnel. Planning for tourism is usually very weak in African states compared with that for other sectors. Those directly involved in the tourism industry (including the relevant ministry) are often too optimistic and too little self-critical, while ministries of planning and finance and the central banks are apt to view tourism as too specialized and peripheral to deserve much of their time.[19]

Sectoral planning for tourism cannot be given top priority because tourism is not the most important sector, but, as with negotiation, increasing the amount of attention given appears to have a high benefit-cost ratio. This is particularly true because the large sums often expended on infrastructure—notably jumbo jet airports—seem to be in excess of the needs of the existing or any probable expanded tourism sector.[20]

Sectoral planning is inadequate by itself and in no sector more so than in tourism where realistic objectives are more development supporting than developmental. The special costs—whether sociopolitical or political-economic—cannot be defined or evaluated

19. Sectoral planning in Tunisia is elaborate but appears to be dominated by those directly involved in the sector and inadequately analyzed and controlled by central ministries. Kenya's sectoral planning for tourism is weak, in marked contrast to its negotiating ability, which is good, and its strategic ambitions for the sector, which are high. In countries with less experience with tourism, such as Ghana and the Ivory Coast, there is still no serious sectoral planning. In those such as Tanzania, which place quite secondary emphasis on the industry, shortages of analytical capacity result in weak initial sectoral plans that are somewhat more effectively monitored at the implementation stage.

20. In East Africa from 1965 to 1980 on the order of US$150 million has been or will be spent on tourist-oriented airport construction or extension at Nairobi, Mombasa, Kisumu, Kilimanjaro, Dar es Salaam, Entebbe, and Gulu. At a 10 percent opportunity cost of capital plus operating deficits, this represents a US$20 million to US$25 million a year subsectoral drain from public revenue to tourism or US$20 to US$25 per tourist even if the number of visitors were to rise to a million a year. On the order of 80 percent of this drain will represent foreign exchange, not local cost. It is doubtful whether governmental revenue from tourism exceeds US$20 million today. Even if other costs are ignored the amount of government finance available for other sectors and services appears to be eroding. In proportion to revenue this deficit is largest in Uganda and smallest in Kenya; in absolute terms it appears to be largest in Kenya and smallest in Tanzania.

for the sector except in reference to the broader setting.[21] Therefore sectoral planning logically requires a national framework to set parameters for it. Tourism is a complement to or a substitute for other economic activities. Its opportunity costs and gains need to be considered in relation to those of the complements and substitutes. If the main objective for tourism is to earn net foreign exchange (the most realistic objective in most African states), then comparisons need to be made with new or expanded primary exports, pre-export processing, component manufacturing for export, and import substitution, and these comparisons should be made in the context of some planning of the sources and uses of national foreign exchange. It is unlikely that the appropriate decision will be to opt 100 percent for one sector and 0 percent for another, but to be even approximately efficient at gaining foreign exchange the sectoral balance requires intersectoral comparison. The case for such an approach is strengthened by the fact that several objectives, costs, and benefits are involved, including such issues as the degree of national control over enterprises, flexibility in resource use, national cultural identity, and the individual African's self-image.

Most African states do have national plans, though not necessarily nationwide planning beyond the formulation stage. Relatively few, however, engage in systematic comparison of sectoral sizes in relation to the sectoral contributions, direct or supporting, to national objectives. Tourism is not unique in requiring sectoral planning that is closely linked to overall development plans, but the need is especially urgent because of the supportive (or perhaps the erosive) nature of the sector.

Conclusion

A few generalizations arise from even a cursory study of the African tourist experience and the global tourism industry:

—Except in microeconomies, tourism in Africa can rarely be a major leader of growth or source of employment; adequate size is unattainable.

---

21. The demonstration effect of tourism, for example, cannot be estimated or evaluated without an analysis of other aspects of openness. If the press, films, universities, and advertising are Western oriented and there are 10,000 resident expatriates (equivalent in total contact to about 300,000 to 500,000 transient tourists), it is very doubtful that the problem—if so perceived—can be tackled primarily in the tourist context.

—Even less can it be a major contributor to integrated national development; tourism is inherently a luxury export.

—Under certain conditions, however, significant contributions to net foreign exchange earnings and more modest ones to net government revenue (after sector-related costs) and net national investible surplus (available for investment outside tourism) can be secured.

—Foreign tourism involves both foreigners in Africa and tourism enterprises in foreign countries. Foreign partners are therefore inevitable, although the degree of their control over and involvement in tourism activities in Africa can be reduced.

—To achieve positive results in a partnership sector requires skilled negotiation.

—To build up a tourism sector that contributes directly or indirectly to African goals requires sectoral planning in the context of national planning.

—No rational evaluation of a tourism strategy can be made without knowledge of the goals it is intended to further and of alternative ways of furthering them.

These generalizations must be adapted to circumstances in a particular country. For example, if a state places a high value on internal economic integration and wishes to avoid external control over domestic institutions and enterprises, it is likely to perceive tourism negatively. If, however, the state also places a high value on increasing exports in order to reduce foreign borrowing or hold it constant, the decisionmakers may wish to negotiate for some type of tourism. If tourism has a low ratio of net to gross foreign exchange and a high ratio of capital to net foreign earnings, the decision may be to consolidate use of existing facilities but not to engage in much expansion. This sketch is not radically dissimilar to the political-economic position of Tanzania. A state with less willingness to control imports, more concern to create opportunities for African capitalists, a greater belief in the developmental potential of export-oriented sectors managed by foreign senior partners, and fewer natural resources might decide to promote growth through tourism and export-oriented manufacturing based on imported materials and knowledge. Kenya, Tunisia, and Mauritius have made such choices on the basis of similar values and considerations.

It is not useful to describe the Tanzanian strategy as right and the Kenyan as wrong or, on the contrary, to call the Kenyan policy efficient and the Tanzanian inefficient. The political-economic and other national goals of the two countries differ so that, even if the narrowly economic options were identical, what is right and efficient for meeting Kenya's goals could be wrong and inefficient in the Tanzanian context. This is not to argue that tourism has a one-to-one correlation (whether casual or consequential) with attempts to integrate more closely with the world of transnational corporations. The Bulgarian, Rumanian, Hungarian, and Czechoslovak sectors should serve to refute that idea. Tourism sectors in socialist Europe are different from those in Africa, however, in large measure because of requirements and prohibitions flowing from broad objectives determined at the national level.

Even with identical goals, two appropriate tourism sector strategies might well diverge because of different 'constraints and potentials. This is most dramatically true of ministates such as Gambia, Mauritius, and Seychelles. The degree to which their national economies can be integrated is limited; so is their natural resource base. The only real ways to sustained development of net foreign earnings do appear to be export-oriented manufacturing and tourism. If the economies are small enough tourism could become a leading sector in terms of growth and employment as well as foreign exchange. The problems of foreign control and instability are less critical if tourism is only one of a number of significant exports and a small economic sector. The Caribbean demonstrates only too clearly that if few options other than tourism are perceived and acted on, then the tourism sector is likely to have high political-economic, sociopolitical, and socioeconomic costs.

Among other countries the differences in location, climate, existing infrastructure, and scenic attractions are relevant; these conditions in Ghana, the Ivory Coast, and Zambia appear less favorable to mass tourism than those in Kenya, Madagascar, and Egypt. The alternative means of attaining foreign exchange and employment open to Algeria and Angola seem broader and more economically attractive than those for Somalia and Lesotho. In any African country its specific conditions must be evaluated in conjunction with its actual goals before an appropriate sectoral strategy, set of projects, or pattern of relations with external tourism enterprises can be formulated and implemented.

CHAPTER 7

Tourism and Employment in Tunisia

Ahmed Smaoui
TUNISIAN NATIONAL TOURISM OFFICE

T HE DEVELOPMENT OF INTERNATIONAL TOURISM over the past two decades and its prospects for expansion make it one of the key economic sectors in many developing countries. In Tunisia tourism is already an important export industry and one of the major sources of foreign exchange. Gross earnings rose from US$20 million in 1961 to nearly US$300 million in 1975.[1]

These earnings are particularly significant for an overall economic expansion that requires the mobilization of substantial foreign exchange resources to meet the cost of imports of plant and equipment. Tourism also generates employment and thereby stimulates social change, both directly through the expansion of education and vocational training to meet its needs as a service industry and indirectly by introducing different styles of social behavior. The concentration of tourism in certain regions of Tunisia and the absolute as well as relative importance of its various activities in the regional and local economy have given rise to certain problems. Among them are the migration of workers attracted by jobs in the tourism industry and the impact of tourism on the development of urban and coastal areas where it has been established. The social changes that tourism engenders and the characteristic rapidity with which they occur create friction that, if not checked, can easily give rise to attitudes of distrust and even rejection of the tourists themselves.

---

1. Net foreign exchange comes to around 80 percent of gross earnings, depending on rates of capacity utilization in tourism. See Tunisian National Tourism Office (ONTT), *Etude de l'aide de l'Etat au secteur touristique* [Study on state aid to the tourism sector], prepared by Francis H. Mitchell, SETEC Economie, and SOTUETEC, three reports in 6 vols., March 1974, December 1974, and August 1975.

Jobs Created by Tourism

A survey of tourism jobs in Tunisia was made as part of a study to evaluate the overall profitability of the sector and the returns on state aid to tourism.[2] Tourist expenditure creates jobs directly in enterprises such as hotels and restaurants that serve tourists, and it creates jobs indirectly in activities that supply goods and services to the tourism sector. Indirect employment is divided between activities that contribute to the operation of tourism enterprises (as agriculture provides food for hotels) and activities such as construction and furniture manufacturing that provide investment inputs.

Jobs created directly in tourism

The study estimated the number of directly created jobs at between 0.88 and 1.12 per hotel bed, depending upon occupancy rates. These jobs are divided among tourism activities as shown in Table 7.1. Because good data were unavailable on the split between direct and indirect employment in handicrafts, the table includes both the retailers who sell crafts to tourists (whose jobs could be regarded as direct employment in the tourism industry) as well as the producers of crafts, whose jobs should, strictly speaking, be classified as indirect employment in relation to tourism. Classified as "indirect," however, was general retail employment generated by tourists' purchases of sundries (tobacco, newspapers, clothing, film, and the like), and this may partly counterbalance the overestimate from including craftsmen among the direct employees.

The number of employees per bed rises with higher occupancy rates, as shown in Table 7.1, because the amount of goods and services purchased increases with the number of tourists accommodated. Employment rises less than proportionally with output in service industries if the increase in output is owing to higher rates of capacity utilization, but employment in the production of goods (such as handicrafts) may be expected to rise more or less proportionally with sales. The increase shown for handicrafts is not proportional with the increase in occupancy rates, however, because of rounding. And sales of different items do not vary proportionally

2. Ibid.

Table 7.1. *Jobs Created Directly by Tourism*
(person years of employment per hotel bed per year)

Activity	Occupancy rate	
	40 percent	*56 percent*
Hotels	0.34	0.38
International transportation	0.02	0.02
Domestic transportation	0.03	0.04
Restaurants	0.01	0.01
Government	0.02	0.02
Production and sale of handicrafts	0.46	0.65
Total	0.88	1.12

Source: ONTT study.

with rates of capacity utilization because the seasonal distribution of demand varies at different occupancy rates.

Indirect employment

A figure for indirect employment generated by tourism operations was arrived at by first estimating the wage bill generated in each indirect activity in the Tunisian economy (with the help of the inverse matrix of the sixteen-sector 1968 input-output table) and then dividing this by the average wage per worker found in that sector. Since the estimates were made over the life of an average

Table 7.2. *Jobs Created Indirectly by Tourism,*
at Different Occupancy Rates
(person years of employment per hotel bed per year)

Activity	Hotel operation		Other direct activities		Total	
	40 percent	*56 percent*	*40 percent*	*56 percent*	*40 percent*	*56 percent*
Agriculture	0.19	0.26	0.06	0.08	0.25	0.34
Other indirect activities	0.16	0.19	0.18	0.25	0.34	0.44
Total	0.35	0.45	0.24	0.33	0.59	0.78

Source: ONTT study.

Table 7.3. Jobs Created by Investment in Tourism
(person years of employment per hotel bed)

Category of investment	Con-struction	Other sectors	Total
Hotels	1.0	1.1	2.0
Initial investment	0.9	0.8	1.6
Renovations	0.1	0.3	0.4
Infrastructure and other tourism activities	0.3	0.4	0.7
Total	1.3	1.5	2.7

Source: ONTT study.

hotel, an allowance was made for a 2 percent annual rise in productivity.

Table 7.2 presents the annual number of indirect jobs in agriculture and other activities per bed available. The table also records indirect employment generated by tourist expenditures in hotels and in other tourist activities for the two occupancy rates.

Table 7.3 shows the number of person years of employment generated by investment in hotels and other tourist activities, per hotel bed constructed. These figures include the jobs created by the initial investment, and by replacements over the course of the twenty-five-year life assumed for a typical three-star hotel.

Recapitulation on amount of tourism employment

To render the figures on investment and employment comparable with those of direct and indirect employment in tourism operations, it is necessary to add up all person years of employment during the life of the investment.[3] It is then possible to derive the ratio of employee years relative to person years of employment in hotels, which are set equal to one for this analysis (see Table 7.4). In brief, this analysis indicates that tourist expenditure in Tunisia generates as many as four jobs outside hotels for each job within hotels.

3. Future employment was given less weight than present employment. Specifically, the present value of future man years of employment was reduced by 10 percent compounded for each year between the year that employment was expected and the present. For example, employment of 100 persons six years from the present would be counted as $100/(1.1)^6 = 56.45$ man years of employment.

Table 7.4. *Direct and Indirect Employment Relative to Employment in Hotels*

Employment	Occupancy rate	
	40 percent	*56 percent*
Direct (operations)		
Hotels	1.0	1.0
Other	1.57	1.96
Subtotal	2.57	2.96
Indirect (operations)		
Agriculture	0.72	0.90
Other	1.01	1.17
Subtotal	1.73	2.07
Subtotal for operations (direct and indirect)	4.30	5.03
Indirect (investment and renovations)		
Construction	0.15	0.14
Other	0.17	0.16
Subtotal	0.32	0.33
Grand total	4.62	5.33

Source: ONTT study.

A large proportion of these jobs are in relatively low-paying activities, as shown in Table 7.5. Although tourists spend on "luxuries," their expenditures have a significant impact on employment in agriculture and crafts and thus have a favorable effect on the income of some of the poorer classes of Tunisians.

Characteristics of Jobs Generated by Tourism

The following information on the composition of tourism employment was taken from an unpublished survey carried out by the Tunisian National Tourism Office (ONTT) from August 20 to September 18, 1975. The survey covered 213 hotels with a total of 56,848 beds, 36 travel agencies, 12 tourism organizations, and 5 car rental companies. Some 50 city hotels that date back to before independence were excluded because their contribution to tourism is negligible; retail establishments selling to tourists were also excluded. The figures for "other" activities exclude the government and Tunis Air. The number of jobs counted was 20,306. This com-

Table 7.5. *Average Annual Wages*

Sector	Dinars[a]
Agriculture	120
Construction	410
Textiles	450
Hotels	480
Food industry	540
Construction materials	580
Mining	590
Trade	620
Electricity	1,000

Source: ONTT study.
a. In 1974 the exchange rate was about 0.4 dinars to the U.S. dollar.

prehensive survey gives a clear idea of the job structure of the direct tourism activities covered. The percentage distribution of jobs according to level of responsibility is shown in Table 7.6.

Hotel personnel in Tunisia were typically young: 33 percent of the employees were less than twenty-three years old, and only 5 percent will reach retirement age by 1985. Females accounted for 16 percent of all tourism personnel surveyed. In the main, women were employed in hotels (room service, linens, and reception), travel agencies, and administrative services.

Table 7.6. *Percentage Distribution of Tourism Employment by Level of Responsibility*

Level	Hotels	Other activities
Managers	1.4	3.9
Heads of departments	4.5	14.7
Middle-level supervisors	16.7	28.9
Regular personnel	46.3	24.0
Apprentices	6.7	—
Service staff	24.3	28.5
Total	99.9	100.0

— Zero or negligible.
Source: ONTT.

Foreigners accounted for only 2 percent of the total. Most of these jobs were supervisory staff and organizers of recreational activities at vacation villages (such as the Club Méditerranée) and representatives of foreign tour operators.

Seasonal variation of job supply in the hotels cannot be taken as a fixed parameter. For all hotels together, this variation was 30 percent (of peak employment) in 1973 and 24 percent in 1975. The extent of seasonal fluctuation differs according to the region and size of the hotel, however. It also varies among the different departments of the hotel. The biggest fluctuations were noted in kitchen and restaurant jobs. The typical women's jobs are relatively more stable than those occupied by men.

The mobility of hotel personnel is high. The cumulative effect of job changes results in a turnover rate of 29 percent of the staff every three years. Although this proportion is high, turnover is not a serious sectoral problem because in most cases it consists of movement between hotels; the drop-out rate from the industry is low. Job changes tend to occur in the second or third year of employment. After that there is a relatively stable period of three straight years, followed by another wave of job-changing in the seventh year. The first changes can be attributed to the effect of the creation of new openings for personnel with some experience. Job-changing in the later years, particularly during the seventh year, may reflect a lack of promotion opportunities within the company. The situation seems to have stabilized somewhat following a collective agreement signed by the entrepreneurs and the unions that established wage rates and uniform social benefits. The lower rate of growth of Tunisian hotel capacity in recent years may also be a cause of reduced turnover.

Vocational Training

The findings of the ONTT survey on the educational background of tourism employees indicate that 21 percent had no formal education, 45 percent had some primary education, 32 percent had attended secondary school, and 2 percent had attended a university. Before 1970 hotel personnel were trained on the job under a system of short courses, though some supervisory staff were trained abroad. Since then, recognizing that service is a basic element of the tourism product, the Tunisian government has undertaken a national vocational training program. Six hotel schools have been built which can provide training for 2,000 employees a year, and two new hotel schools and an advanced institute of hotel management and tourism were expected to open in 1978. The expansion of vocational training through refresher courses and advanced programs also fosters social change by equipping employees with the skills necessary for promotion to a higher level job.

Urban and Coastal Development

The geographical distribution of tourism jobs closely follows that of tourist facilities: 96 percent of the jobs are on the coast, which is hardly surprising since the basic attraction of tourism in Tunisia is the beach resorts.

The coastal concentration of tourism jobs has aggravated the shift of the Tunisian population away from the interior. This shift began with the development of export-oriented manufacturing industries, a major element in Tunisia's economic development, and the proliferation of large urban complexes. Ten of Tunisia's nineteen major cities are on the coast, and forty-seven of the 100 largest towns, with 75 percent of Tunisia's urban population, are less than ten kilometers from the coast.

The movement of people into urban and coastal areas is becoming more marked and is one of the major problems of regional development. It results in steeply rising prices for land in the towns, higher costs of urbanization, and more urgent need for plant and equipment.

The tourism industry may place considerable strain on the services of the local community. Often a resort is located in an urban area that lacks sufficient infrastructure and is ill prepared to accommodate a large flow of tourists. The introduction of tourism often provides ample economic justification for introducing, expanding, or upgrading the basic infrastructure such as airports, roads, electricity and drinking water, and the sewerage system. In certain cases, however, these infrastructure works are undertaken and tailored exclusively to meet the needs of the tourism sector. In Hammamet, for example, a sewerage system is being installed in the tourist zone without taking account of the needs of the old town, which is still using cesspools or discharging its effluents into the sea, obviously endangering health conditions in the entire area.

Efforts should be made to see that infrastructure built for tourism benefits as many inhabitants as possible without jeopardizing the profitability of specific projects.

Social Mobility

Success in obtaining a job in a country where there is chronic underemployment represents definite social advancement. In this sense, tourism may be regarded as an agent of social progress. But who really benefits from tourism development?

Because of the considerable investment required and the size of the turnover and profits, tourism in Tunisia has helped to create and strengthen a clearly defined class of entrepreneurs. Many of these were originally merchants, farmers, or owners of small handicraft factories who have initiated tourism projects. They had a little capital to start with, but, thanks to the system of credit and state aid and the facilities granted for land purchase, they have found themselves catapulted into the position of heads of large-scale businesses. Without much technical knowledge at the beginning, they learned their trade on the job. Many of them have proved excellent businessmen who can evaluate very precisely the return on their new projects and manage their affairs successfully, with a firm hand. The tax laws and the state aid system have, in most cases, encouraged them to plow back their profits into the sector so that their businesses have grown larger.

Currently emerging is a new group of young businessmen with proven technical competence (degrees in economics or tourism, or experience in hotel management), who are anxious to leave the ranks of employees and set up their own businesses. The state is encouraging this trend and is trying to work out specific programs for granting assistance to them.

Conclusion

The development of tourism has political, economic, and social implications. Tourism has no doubt helped to solve some of Tunisia's urgent problems by earning foreign exchange and providing opportunities for employment. It does, however, tend to foster social change that, unless kept in check, could result in serious confrontations. Before deciding to develop tourism the authorities must therefore assess its economic returns in precise terms, with a thorough knowledge and an objective evaluation of its advantages and disadvantages.

CHAPTER 8

Growing Pains: Planned Tourism Development in Ixtapa-Zihuatanejo

Agustin Reynoso y Valle
COMMUNITY DEVELOPMENT SERVICES, FONATUR

Jacomina P. de Regt
TOURISM PROJECTS DEPARTMENT, THE WORLD BANK

I N 1972, UNDER THE DIRECTION OF THE GOVERNMENT of Mexico, workers broke ground for a tourist resort near Zihuatanejo, a fishing village on the Pacific coast of the state of Guerrero. Except for the natural beauty of the area, which had long attracted a limited number of visitors, the barren and mountainous region could claim few resources. Its economy depended mainly on farming in the narrow coastal plain and on fishing. The development of tourism was expected to provide a major source of income and employment and to curb migration to the cities.

Beginning with a population of less than 5,000 in 1970, Zihuatanejo was caught up in a swirl of conflicting forces, some introduced by the tourism project itself, others the result of larger social, economic, and political changes in the region. The proximity of Acapulco, the increased accessibility of Mexico City, the construction of an iron and steel complex in the nearby town of Lazaro Cardenas, and the complex problems of land tenure exacerbated the effects of the new resort and the influx of construction workers and tourists.

Some of the consequences of rapid social change had been foreseen, and a unique component was built into the project to deal with them. A Community Development team was formed to ease the personal and social stresses related to the rapid growth of Zihuatanejo. It works directly with the people, assisting them in the intricacies of the expropriation of land and the resettlement process and is responsible for developing training facilities, small industries, and health and educational programs.

This paper deals with the reaction of the people of Zihuatanejo to the changes introduced by the development of their community. There is special emphasis on the major problem of land regularization and on the work of the Community Development team in dealing with the disruptions that occurred as a result of growth. The cumulative effects on education, employment, the political scene, and the special impact on the role of women are analyzed in the final section.

The Background

In the remote and barren state of Guerrero the chief sources of income have always been products found only along the sliver of coast—copra and sesame seeds, some livestock, and fish. The mountain range that claims most of the area is totally unworked because of unfavorable topography and climatic conditions. During the 1960s the inequities and frailties of the economy gave rise to guerrilla disturbances that in turn may have deterred private investment in the region.

Guerrero's main asset is its spectacular scenery, and when the Mexican government sought ways to develop the region, tourism seemed a likely prospect. At the southern end of the coastline Acapulco has long been a major resort attracting international visitors. A new tourist complex was therefore planned for Zihuatanejo, a site farther north with a setting of beaches, bay, and mountains similar to that of Acapulco.

By careful planning the government hoped to avoid the mistakes of Acapulco, where the haphazard growth of tourism has led to the pollution of the beautiful bay, the erosion of the surrounding hills, and squatter settlements without water and sewerage services or electricity. A site for the tourist resort was selected in Ixtapa, a virtually unpopulated tract of land on the ocean, about five kilometers from the village of Zihuatanejo. In addition to tourist facilities, the project included the development of housing, education, and health services, and training for the population of Zihuatanejo, and an effort was made to encourage local participation in tourism.

A secluded fishing village, Zihuatanejo was accessible only by sea until the 1950s, when a small airstrip and a new highway to Acapulco, 200 kilometers to the south, opened up the town to outside influences. Its urban development and its business activity

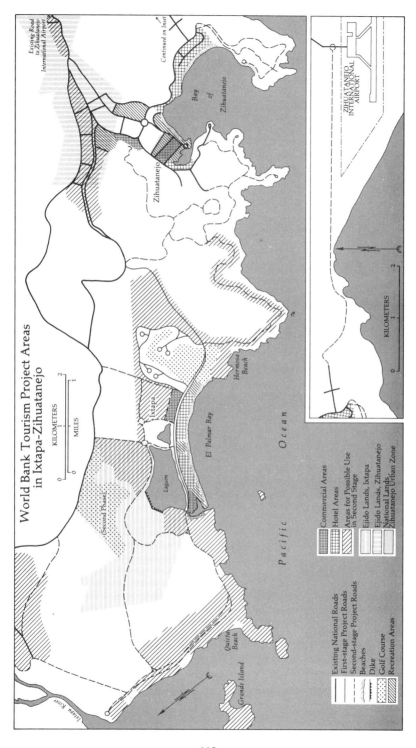

World Bank Tourism Project Areas
in Ixtapa-Zihuatanejo

KILOMETERS

MILES

Existing Road
to Zihuatanejo
International Airport

Continued on Inset

Bay
of
Zihuatanejo

Zihuatanejo

Ixtapa

El Palmar Bay

Hermosa
Beach

Lagoon

(Second Phase)

Pacific   Ocean

Quieta Beach

Grande Island

Ixtapa River

ZIHUATANEJO
INTERNATIONAL
AIRPORT

KILOMETERS

Existing National Roads
First-stage Project Roads
Second-stage Project Roads
Beaches
Dike
Golf Course
Recreation Areas

Commercial Areas
Hotel Areas
Areas for Possible Use
in Second Stage
Ejido Lands, Ixtapa
Ejido Lands, Zihuatanejo
National Lands,
Zihuatanejo Urban Zone

were limited, however, except for the few tourist shops, which inexorably appeared. Part of the town's attraction at that time was its primitiveness. Even today the streets are filled with beasts of burden, cows, and goats, which threaten the incipient gardens of the new town.

Despite its relative isolation, travelers from Mexico City and elsewhere were attracted by the quiet and the beauty of the place. In 1970, the year before the tourism project was begun at Ixtapa, Zihuatanejo received just under 15,000 tourists, a third of whom were foreigners. Half a dozen hotels offered a total of 158 rooms.

The Project

The tourism project included many elements, divided between Zihuatanejo and Ixtapa. This resulted in a well-defined duality, which the population was quick to sense.

Ixtapa—a tract of nothing but marshes, stands of coconut and plantains, mangroves and scrubland—was to be transformed into a modern tourist resort. This entailed reclaiming land and draining marshes; providing water, electricity, telephone service, and sewerage; constructing a boulevard and road system; and developing lots for hotels and villas, with parks, tennis courts, an eighteen-hole golf course, and a commercial center. Ixtapa was planned to house only a very few permanent inhabitants to support the resort itself.

The master plan for Zihuatanejo projected a population of 80,000, and a complete urban renewal was planned. The plan included provision of water, sewerage, and power for all households; construction of a marina for the fishermen; paving the long winding streets in the hills and lining them with coconut stumps and benches; installation of public laundry areas; and construction of schools and health facilities. A stagnant pool used by the inhabitants for swimming, washing, and household consumption was to be eliminated because it was contaminated by sewerage effluent and was a breeding ground for malaria-carrying mosquitoes. In addition, the Zihuatanejo airport was to be enlarged to accommodate an international jet service. The project also included training programs for hotel personnel and construction of a hotel training school. An important component of the project was the Community Development team, formed and staffed to assist in the transformation of a quiet fishing village into a busy tourist center and to help the inhabitants make the necessary social adjustments. Its work is discussed in detail in a later section, but one important function was to assist in relocating people, moving them from homes that lay in the path of new roads and bringing families in from the outskirts to densify the center of the urban area.

The decision in 1971 to make Zihuatanejo a tourism development center had immediate consequences for the local inhabitants. Technical teams preparing the project began to disrupt local tranquility, and negotiations with the federal government brought additional changes to the village along with visits by the top-ranking leaders of the country and state. The people were understandably on guard since their participation in this preliminary work was very limited. Although plans were known and discussed with municipal and state authorities, the overwhelming majority of the residents had only hearsay knowledge about the plans and did not grasp the magnitude of the project. The scale seemed too large for tiny Zihuatanejo. The villagers knew that their resources would be tapped and tried to prepare themselves mentally for the future, but the consequences were difficult to foresee.

Construction work on the project in Ixtapa began in September 1972. Because of problems in regularizing land tenure, work in Zihuatanejo started two years later. As a result, the local people observed the transformation of Ixtapa and participated in the construction of the new resort while their own living space was in fact deteriorating because of the influx of newcomers. The contrast between Ixtapa and Zihuatanejo was immediately evident. Thus, even before the Ixtapa development became a physical reality, the local people were confronted with the project, and they reacted with a feeling that "something different" was being created, subject to unfamiliar and uncontrollable forces.

The process of social comparison resulted in confusion, hostility to what was different, and reinforcement of a sense of communal identity. In a manner without local precedent, the inhabitants of Zihuatanejo formed a collective self-awareness. They referred to Ixtapa as the "new" Zihuatanejo and called their own town the place of the "poor" and Ixtapa—even though empty—the town of the "rich." With their newly created awareness of being an in-group, the people were heard to say that "if we *ourselves* do not join together *they* (that is, the developers of the project) will harm us," "they want to get rid of those living here."

A form of social control was clearly operating to affect those who were believed to be on the side of the developers (though not necessarily those working at Ixtapa). They were described as "selling out," "being in their pay," "a harmful person." In most cases, the reaction of those so regarded has been to demonstrate the opposite behavior and to act against the project or its officials. Social control, therefore, made for a greater degree of cohesion among the population. During this same period, 1972-74, land regularization for Zihuatanejo was in dispute, and tension arose from those negotiations.

The Regional Context

Just as work was getting under way in Zihuatanejo, construction was also begun on an iron and steel complex in Lazaro Cardenas, only 120 kilometers from the project site. The Lazaro Cardenas project was of such magnitude that it had a clear-cut effect on the entire national economy and, naturally, on Zihuatanejo. The construction of the plant boosted the price of basic commodities and caused a rise in wages paid to unskilled workers. Higher wages attracted laborers into the region, especially poor farmers from Oaxaca. Because of a shortage of manpower, especially of skilled labor, the workers stood at the center of supply and demand forces and were paid in excess of the legal minimum wage. The construction work at its peak provided over 75,000 jobs in Lazaro Cardenas and over 6,000 in Zihuatanejo. After the boom most unskilled workers left and returned to their part-time agricultural pursuits or moved on to find other construction jobs. The wage levels also dropped back to the minimum legal rural wage, which in fact is inadequate in the urban situation of Zihuatanejo with its high cost of living.

Another effect of the steel plant is that many of its professional staff spend their weekends at hotels in Zihuatanejo. Furthermore, the Zihuatanejo airport is frequently used by plant personnel so that fewer plane seats are available for tourists who wish to vacation in Zihuatanejo.

Different government agencies are in charge of each project. The Fondo National de Turismo (FONATUR), the agency in charge of the tourism sector throughout Mexico, is directly responsible for the development of the Ixtapa-Zihuatanejo project area; it created a trust, Fideicomisco Bahia de Zihuatanejo (FIBAZI) to regulate land tenure in Zihuatanejo. Although the tourism project was originally intended as a regional development pole, development of the rest of the region was left to the Comision de Rio Balsas, the agency responsible for the development of the iron and steel complex in Lazaro Cardenas. Coordination between these two agencies and the two states in which these developments were taking place was lacking. Only in 1976 was a commission established to look into the problems of the municipalities affected by these two big developments. The new developments in both towns require consumer goods in greater abundance than and of a different quality from those in demand before 1970. And each project requires workers with different backgrounds, different types of training, different salary expectations, and varying degrees of vertical mobility.

The proximity of Acapulco has had a clear-cut influence on the life-style of the inhabitants of Zihuatanejo. For a great many years Acapulco served as the gateway to Zihuatanejo. It was the point of arrival for visitors coming by land, sea, and air, and it supplied the goods and services that could not be found in Zihuatanejo: doctors, medicine, consumer goods, repairs of machinery and automobiles, and the like.

The greatest influence of Acapulco stems from its role as a model for Zihuatanejo's infant hotel industry. It was in Acapulco that the people of Zihuatanejo got their first vivid impression of a hotel, a tourist resort, a market, and a department store, and first learned the art of serving and pleasing tourists. Acapulco served—not only for the government, but also for the population of Zihuatanejo—as a first-hand lesson in the dangers of haphazard tourism development. Once Zihuatanejo had been selected as the site for a tourism development project of national and international scope, many of the inhabitants used Acapulco as a point of reference. People often speak about what is or is not in Acapulco and whether or not it is wanted in Zihuatanejo—for example, invasions of land, urban disorder, tourist facilities. Because the Acapulco plan[1] was implemented before the Ixtapa-Zihuatanejo project was begun, everything undertaken in Zihuatanejo was compared with what had been done in Acapulco for urbanization, regularization of land tenure, and so on. This explains in part why people in Zihuatanejo

1. The plan was designed to improve the situation that had arisen from uncontrolled tourism development in Acapulco. It included provisions for urban renewal, pollution control, and squatter resettlement.

are more than willing to accept the project's endeavor to make
Zihuatanejo into a planned tourist resort.
A new road will soon connect Zihuatanejo directly with Mexico
City. Like Acapulco, the project zone will then be only about 400
kilometers from the enormous population of the capital. The opening of the road will thus greatly expand the development
possibilities of Zihuatanejo.

Land Alienation

One of the underlying concepts of planned tourism development
was that one agency should possess all the land in order to control
the development and to limit the speculative gains accruing to individuals or groups. Therefore, all 4,382 hectares designated for the
project in Ixtapa and Zihuatanejo were brought under the jurisdic-
tion of a trust fund, the Fideicomiso Bahia de Zihuatanejo (FIBAZI).

Land ownership and the regularization process

Acquisition of the land by FIBAZI was a complex process because
ownership was in various forms. About a third of the project site
was owned privately by two individuals and was simply purchased
outright. A little over 60 percent of the land belonged to three *ejidos;*
the rest included a few small tracts under federal control[2] and
twenty-two hectares of nationally owned land. The ejido land and
the nationally owned hectares presented the major difficulties.
An ejido is a communal form of land tenure, based on pre-Colum-
bian social structures, in which a group of families was given joint
and inalienable rights to certain lands. The three ejidos in the
vicinity of Zihuatanejo had received these rights by a 1938 decree. A
member (*ejidatario*) cannot sell, divide, or lease his portion of the
land, and only one heir can inherit his right to the land. Nevertheless, over the years other people were frequently allowed to settle
and build on ejido land, either with an informal agreement or a formal transfer of the property that was in fact illegal. These occupants
considered themselves, not the ejido, as the rightful owners,

---

2. The Federal Maritime Land Zone and other land under the authority of the Secretariat for Hydraulic Resources and the Secretariat for Public Works.

however, and the basic misunderstanding was often further compounded by subsequent resale.

About 7 percent of the population in 1972 was ejidatarios, which means that, including family members, approximately 30 percent of the population was dependent on incomes obtained from the ejidos. All other community members are called *avecindados* (settlers) and are thus defined by their status as nonmembers of the ejidos. Many of these people occupied nationally owned land to which they had no legal claim, although they had lived there all their lives.

The ejido land necessary for the tourism project had to be expropriated, which the government had the legal right to do for purposes of national development, including tourism development. Under the Echeverria administration, however, there was a resurgence of concern for the ejidos and an attempt to make up for decades of neglect. Therefore, no development could take place without integration of the ejidos in the development process and appropriate compensation. The ejidatarios were aware of these national political issues, and they sought the maximum compensation to which they felt entitled. The ejido assemblies voted in favor of expropriation, thereby improving their claims for proper compensation.

It took two years to complete the negotiations with the ejidos on the exact package of compensation for their land. In the end, every member received two large urban lots, each 600 meters square, located in the center of Zihuatanejo on prime commercial land. Since the minimum allowed lot size was 200 square meters, many ejidatarios divided their lots into smaller ones and built several houses on them for rent. The ejidos received cash compensation for the value of their land in excess of the value of the urban lots, of which 20 percent was retained by the national ejido fund (FONAFE) and invested in local income- and employment-generating activities for the benefit of the ejidatarios. The individual ejidatarios also received cash compensation for improvements they had made on the land. In addition, the ejidos are represented on the board of FIBAZI and will receive 20 percent of any future profits on the sale or development of the land held in trust by FIBAZI.

In some cases the ejido member was compensated for land which he had "sold," while the "buyer" received nothing despite having paid for it. Many ejidatarios were not affected at all by the project, since their land was not expropriated, and most ejidatarios continue to hold large tracts of grazing land for their cattle. Nevertheless, because the national laws gave preferential treatment to the ejido members, as individuals and as a group, they benefited most from land regularization.

The twenty-two hectares of national land in the center of Zihuatanejo were occupied for the most part by avecindados. Their "possession" had taken many forms. In some cases taxes were being paid on the property as though it were privately owned, and the title was listed in the public registry at Chilpancingo, the capital of the state of Guerrero. In other cases contracts of sale notarized by a notary public were offered as "proof" of ownership. A few ejidatarios claimed rights to some of this land as though it belonged to the ejido when in fact it did not. Some avecindados had invalidly been given possession of land by the ejido, others had private contracts without any legal form of sale or had simply occupied land with or without the oral permission of the municipality or a federal authority. Some were recognized as occupants of the land by the Agrarian Reform Law, but others had not received any occupancy papers.

These twenty-two hectares of national land were transferred to the trust by presidential decree of September 1975. Although this decree regularized ownership, it did not automatically solve the specific problems inherent in the irregular and complicated occupancy of the land. Even today some cases have not been finally resolved.

The avecindados were allowed by FIBAZI to establish clear title to the land they occupied by paying a standard fee per square meter, which included the purchase price and urbanization costs. If unable to raise the money, they were forced to move. Unlike the ejidatarios, they were not entitled to receive any compensation for "their" land, although there was some compensation for their house and other improvements. Avecindados were at a further disadvantage in having no representative to protect their interests. Their reaction was often to band together to press their claims, organizing in groups such as the Children of Ejido Members. In addition, each barrio (district) formed its own association with the help of the Community Development team for the purpose of getting the best possible solution for the development of that barrio, which in some cases meant confronting FONATUR.

Many dissatisfied avecindados modeled their interests and values on those of the ejidatarios. Almost all the claims brought before FONATUR/FIBAZI were made in reference to the ejido members and were based on arguments such as "I was an ejido member, but I was arbitrarily stripped of my land" or "I am more deserving than some on the list of ejido members who don't even farm." Other claimants tried to shift the blame for the original illegal purchase of the land and make the trust responsible for correcting the error. Such statements as "I already paid," "I don't have to pay for what is mine," ".'We all did it this way," "They took advantage of us," implied that the trust, an abstract entity, was at fault and not the swindlers. When tenure was regularized, however, the claimants made no formal complaint to the legal authorities against those who allegedly swindled them.

Social consequences of land regularization

The land regularization took control of all the project land away from the ejidos, the municipality, or individuals and gave it to FIBAZI. This had a decisive effect on the life of the occupants, touching not only their emotional relation to the land but also a range of economic and social relations. Private ownership of the urban lots has meant that many people are now paying taxes for the first time; ejidatarios had been exempt from taxation on ejido land, and most avecindados had not legally owned their land and had therefore not paid taxes either. Collective decisionmaking by the ejido came to an end with respect to the land itself, and such decisions now rest with the individual. Land has been transformed into a negotiable object; perhaps it always was, but everyone recognized the limits and dangers of the transactions. Use of the land is now dependent on tourism activity and urban needs and no longer serves agricultural purposes. The project, the law, and rising costs have imposed limitations on the area of land held; when a lot changes hands its size must now be approved by the authorities. For some—especially the aged and early settlers who are now required to legitimize their possession of land they have held all their lives without question—their personal sense of security has been threatened.

The position of the ejidatarios as a group was a curious one. They were a minority of the population and were not a homogeneous group. Before the expropriation ejidatarios belonged to different classes; rich ejido leaders belonging to the elite of the village, poor ejido members with no regular sources of income belonging to the lower classes. During the expropriation procedures the group became stronger and more cohesive, but still the divisions between rich and poor, powerful and weak were apparent. The powerful tried to use their position to gain more than others in the process of fighting for a good compensation package. For example, when the ejidatarios of Zihuatanejo had finally been granted lots in the center of town, the ejido leaders undertook to allocate them. They designated the best lots for themselves and assigned lots with less economic potential to the less powerful. FIBAZI declared that process illegal and unethical. The Community Development team then stepped in to ensure a fair distribution of the compensation by holding a raffle and assigning lots randomly.

Government action, based on national laws favoring the ejidatarios, created a new structure of inequality that cut across class boundaries of the *old* Zihuatanejo. Despite being favored by compensation, the ejidatarios as a group are not an elite now. Some of those who were previously well-off remain members of the local elite. They invested wisely, built impressive houses with rooms to let to tourists, and they go on with their agricultural pursuits and local political intrigues. Many squandered the money without thinking about it; others did build a house on their lot but do not know how to manage it; and some have already lost out—sold the lot, lost the money, and returned to poverty. In general, they were ill prepared to handle these sums of money

It is theoretically possible that the ejidatarios as a group will receive dividends, employment, and income from the small cement block factory started with part of the funds received for indemnification. In addition, they are entitled to share in any profits resulting from decisions made by the Technical Committee of FIBAZI, which includes representatives of the ejidos.

The poor members of the community among the avecindados are definitely worse off than before. Many of them could not afford to purchase all of the land they occupied, although whenever possible ingenious individual solutions were worked out by the Community Development team to enable people to stay where they were. In addition, the monthly cash payments for utilities and taxes are further burdening these families, which have in general not benefited from the additional employment that was created by the project.

As a result of the pressure for compensation and the inequities inherent in the system, the entire population was in conflict with FIBAZI, while the avecindados were in conflict with the ejido members. In both cases the conflict was intense (though not necessarily violent) because the participants attached great importance to it and invested a good deal of energy in it.

Another consequence of FIBAZI's control of the land was the implementation of the carefully conceived land-use plan and regulations. When houses were in the way of planned roads the inhabitants were supposed to be relocated; and those living beyond a certain altitude in the hills were supposed to move to the center, because it would be too costly to bring urban services to these few people. Some parts of the original plan were renegotiated during the actual execution, and fewer families than originally foreseen were in fact moved. FIBAZI and the Community Development team were extremely responsive to personal and local situations and tried to accommodate the special needs of as many families as possible. In the end about 120 families were displaced by urban development, and about fifteen families have moved down from the hills. Because of strict codes for land use, the reverse process is taking place now. Poorer families move out to the hills, beyond the reach of utilities they cannot afford, where they can keep goats and grow subsistence crops to eke out a living.

Community Development

Only when all the expropriation decrees had finally become effective and FIBAZI had been established could FONATUR start its work in Zihuatanejo and the Community Development team enter the scene. It was December 1974, construction in Ixtapa was in full swing, and Zihuatanejo had already experienced many changes. The atmosphere was tense and emotional as a result of the process of land regularization.

Financed through FIBAZI by FONATUR, the Community Development team was given a broad mandate to minimize the problems of development, but its specific role was left ill defined. The team has tried to interpret its role to be that of helping people adjust to the rapid transition from a rural to an urban way of life in such a way that they may take full advantage of the social, cultural, and economic benefits that living in a tourist center may bring. Of necessity, however, the team was caught up in the difficulties of land tenure. On the one hand, it helped the ejidatarios establish eligibility for indemnification and helped avecindados establish clear titles to the land they occupied. On the other hand, the team helped the authorities execute the urban plan, relocating people, negotiating compensation, and enforcing the new regulations. The inherent danger was that the team would be perceived as "pushing" the people into certain positions rather than serving their needs, but this has been skillfully avoided.

The team members worked with each case individually, which usually involved lengthy discussions with the owners or occupants, engineers, and architects. The boundaries of the lots had to be restaked several times, plans drawn up, documents filled in, individual settlements reached, and down payments collected. With the actual distribution of lots, the team helped to move families to new sites, gave technical assistance in constructing houses, worked with surveyors, and explained regulations. In February 1977 the Community Development workers started the paperwork of processing purchase and sale agreements and registering titles. All these activities were larded with emotion and conflict, and the Community Development team felt like "the filling in a sandwich," serving as an intermediary between the people and the institutions, of which the engineers and construction workers were the most visible and menacing representatives.

It has created conflicts for the team to be made executing agency for FIBAZI. Although the Community Development workers sided with the avecindados and helped them organize, they also had to explain and carry out FIBAZI/FONATUR's policies and decisions. On various occasions the team has supported members of the community against authorities in an attempt to reverse earlier decisions. The team members resented the time spent on the claims of the ejidatarios, who grossly overstated their assets in many cases. The process of verifying these claims left less time for the other community members who were less privileged.

The team consists of a director and ten young professionals—sociologists, lawyers, psychologists, social workers, and others trained in tourism development. This young and enthusiastic team has grown into the work and has devised its own organizational structure. The community is divided into seven geographical areas that include the ejido settlements, the center of the town, and the new neighborhoods created in the urban plan. A team member is responsible for each geographical unit and coordinates all activities in that area. Two to four staff members who are responsible for adjacent geographical areas sometimes form small teams to coordinate their work and assist each other in planning and executing all activities. The size of these teams is determined by the similarity of problems and the proximity of the various geographical units. The whole team is responsible for the center of Zihuatanejo, the area which is furthest developed. The team at large is thus exposed to problems which are likely to arise at later stages in the areas assigned to individual members. This organizational setup assures a common philosophy and integrated actions. In addition, each team member is able to follow up more easily on cases from his or her assigned area.

In addition to a geographical area, each member is also assigned an activity, such as camps for construction workers, health services, tourist-host encounters, and housing. Three members of the team have no geographical assignment but only a functional responsibility: organization of producers' and consumers' cooperatives, organization of formal and informal education, and regularization of land tenure in places where no team member is assigned, such as the hotel area in Zihuatanejo itself.

The team also tried to be active in more traditional community activities. They helped to organize neighborhood clubs for special interests such as sports or sewing and conducted classes for adult literacy. They opened a small employment office to help people find jobs in construction work and in the hotels, and assisted in forming cooperatives. A consumers' food cooperative has been so successful that it now operates six stores and has expanded into the manufacture of furniture; another cooperative operates a quarry. In the field of education the Community Development team was instrumental in persuading the authorities to build several new schools, including the new college preparatory school. Although the team occasionally contributed small amounts of money to get a project started, they usually helped the people find the necessary funds from an appropriate agency, or—as in the case of the cooperatives—the people would invest their own money.

To prepare the community to take full advantage of the development of tourism, the Community Development team sponsored courses to train taxi drivers and waiters, develop construction and maintenance skills, teach the English language, and instruct fishermen in navigation. Tourism courses were also given in the secondary school with practice sessions in hotels on Saturdays. To prepare the people in a sociopsychological sense, so that tourists and hosts could experience a true encounter and form less prejudices, various activities have been organized. The whole community participates in an annual tourism week that includes events such as a contest for the best local dish and open house in certain neighborhoods on certain days when all tourists are invited for a meal. Boys aged six to twelve are trained to be "host-informants"; there are clean-up activities, painting sessions for local and tourist children, and similar events.

Because of the work involved in the land regularization processes, the amount of time that could be spent on social and community programs was seriously curtailed. Only when all the paperwork related to land questions is completed will the team be able to reactivate its community programs and start new ones, including some related to tourism.

The questions that remain are: Has tourism development been more beneficial to Zihuatanejo because of the Community Development team? How long should such an organization be maintained by a tourism development project? Will the community eventually take over these activities? Is it possible to pinpoint the quantitative costs and qualitative benefits? How should these be judged and analyzed? Can this Mexican experience be useful to other countries? What are some of the conditions that will guarantee success? So far the major contribution of the Community Development team has been to ward off a potentially explosive situation caused by the rapid, financially painful, and seemingly arbitrary imposition of urban restrictions and changes in land tenure on the people of a small community. The team has not yet been able to accomplish a great deal in the way of establishing social infrastructure programs or training the people in basic skills.

Social Consequences

To date, the effects of the tourism project in Zihuatanejo do not differ from those that would have been generated by the construction of some other project. Economic development of any sort would have brought about rapid urbanization and modernization of the community and an increase in the population. The specific effects of mass tourism as such have not yet been felt. Only when large numbers of tourists begin to flock to the new hotels, filling the beaches and streets and actively demonstrating a different life-style, and when a service structure has evolved to meet the special needs of these visitors, will it be possible to determine the long-term social consequences that are attributable to tourism alone. The discussion in this section is therefore limited to the immediate effects of the project that are now discernible.

Changes in population structure

The project has already had a substantial impact on the population structure. Within the short span of four years the population doubled, and the age pyramid underwent appreciable change. Normally in Mexico, the age distribution of the population is such that young children are the predominant group. In Zihuatanejo, the number of people in the age group of fifteen to thirty-four years has been increasing as labor has moved into the area to supply the manpower for tourism development programs.

The occupational structure is also being transformed. With the opening of the 227-room Aristos Hotel, which doubled the hotel capacity in Zihuatanejo, and the 300-room Presidente Hotel, which tripled it, employment in the service sector is expanding rapidly. But the major difference is the enormous increase in the number of construction workers.

In 1970, in Zihuatanejo and the surrounding rural area there were 4,462 economically active people; more than half were farmers, cattlemen, and fishermen, while only 113 were in construction. By 1975 the number of farmers, stockmen, and fishermen had not changed, but at times there were as many as thirty-five construction companies on site with at least 4,000 unskilled laborers and perhaps 1,000 skilled workers and professionals. The labor force was thus doubled by those working in construction alone.

The influx of workers had many repercussions. The Mexican construction industry depends largely on transient workers who move from one construction project to another in order to supplement meager agricultural incomes. Their presence in the community was often disruptive, and the situation deteriorated further when construction began in Zihuatanejo and drew additional laborers. At the peak of building activity more than 6,000 workers at the low end of the company wage scale were living in temporary camps set up close to the construction sites. Living conditions within these camps were extremely poor, and housing, food, and the water supply were inadequate. The men were often bored from lack of anything to do, and this resulted in a high consumption of alcohol and fights. Although these conditions had only a negligible influence on the village population, they should be taken into consideration when planning future projects.

The different customs these workers introduced brought about a deterioration in the traditional values and commonly respected customs of Zihuatanejo. On Saturday afternoons and Sundays, for example, the original inhabitants abandoned their streets and recreation facilities to the newcomers (it is debatable whether they left by choice or were forced to leave). Relations between the sexes were also affected by the influx of workers inasmuch as there were many more men than young unmarried women. There was an increase in prostitution and in the number of bars.

Although little information is available, the majority of workers in the camps seem to have come from areas adjacent to Zihuatanejo, primarily from the mountains. The rest came from more distant parts of the country and were usually hired in groups by the contractors. Very few workers sent for their families or married and began a family, with a view toward settling permanently in the area. The fact that these laborers were working sporadically or temporarily on something that they themselves would never use or benefit from gave rise to certain emotional reactions, such as envy, apathy, ànd resentment.

The educational level is also changing in this small village. Formerly it had few professionals, but now it is receiving an influx of highly educated people to fulfill new work requirements. Although the professionals and high-level employees in the newly created jobs have not formed what could strictly be called a class, they exhibit certain social characteristics of a new elite without eliminating the old. For instance, they were active in forming a new school that operates on educational principles advocated by Carl Rogers. They have become a new reference group for the village, even for the elite of predevelopment Zihuatanejo. A business structure—boutiques selling high-fashion apparel, for example—has sprung up, catering to the well-educated and high-income new elite. For their leisure activities the new elite use tourism and hotel facilities, such as tennis courts, golf courses, swimming pools, and restaurants.

The changes in the population structure have, in turn, affected the functioning of the village itself. The project equipped the area with new infrastructure, a new market, schools, and clinics, and an urban transportation system has sprung up. But municipal services and infrastructure have been severely strained by the new demands made upon them, and many deficiencies have resulted:

—a shortage of schools for about one year

—a shortage of clinics in the first years

—a chronic problem of a weak municipal administration without a budget adequate to provide community services

—growing delinquency, at least in absolute terms

—a shortage of drinking water because the old water supply network is obsolete, while the new one is not yet functioning

—inadequate sewers

—a critical housing shortage with a disproportionate rise in rents

—crumbling pavements that make it increasingly difficult to navigate the narrow streets

—a serious parking problem, which will only become worse in the future.

For the most part these inconveniences were or are likely to be temporary, but they are nonetheless annoying to the people who encounter them daily.

Political changes

Zihuatanejo has attracted the attention of politicians on both the state and national levels. The deputy and senator representing this area hardly ever used to visit the village, but within three months in 1976 they came on more occasions than during the previous three years. President Echeverria himself made several visits to Zihuatanejo and personally intervened in the indemnification for the ejidos, sometimes upsetting the normal machinery of the land regularization.[3]

The people are now much more interested in local politics, and there is more political activity and fervor than in the past. It used to be that the election of the president of the municipality was cut-and-dried. The only political party would appoint a single candidate and there would be no opposition. Now several groups put

---

3. For example, a religious group whose properties were about to be affected by public works convinced the president that they should be given new housing and a church in order to continue with their work of caring for the sick in their barrio. It was thought that the entire community would benefit from the president's intervention, but as it turned out the new buildings are used only by the religious group. The houses are much better constructed than any others in the neighborhood and have caused considerable dissension.

forth candidates, with the original residents and ejidatarios aligned against the new elites.

Impact on women

In 1977 a special study was done to ascertain how the project has affected the position of women in Zihuatanejo.[4] Both urbanization and increased employment opportunities have modified the role of women.

Urbanization, which brought water, electricity, and other services to the houses, has created new cash demands. For the first time families have to meet monthly payments for mortgage, utilities, and land taxes, and many families now need a second or third wage earner to meet these demands. Women, especially in the lower class, are thus pushed to look for work outside the home, thereby challenging the traditional machismo of the Mexican male. In addition, new zoning regulations for the urban plan have unintentionally curtailed income from traditionally female activities by placing restrictions on raising gardens and livestock and on conducting commercial activities (including the long-term rental of rooms) in residential areas. In both instances the single mother, who has no additional reserves to draw on, is hit the hardest.

Women made up about 10 percent of the ejidatarios and have benefited in equal terms from the indemnification given to the ejidos. The Community Development team, more than half of whom are women, has helped them through the transition, discovered and supported female leadership in the poor neighborhoods, and initiated programs for women. Women have not been accorded special treatment, however; but the new health, educational, and housing facilities are as open to them as to anyone.

The study found significant changes in the traditional employment of women. As a result of alternative job opportunities in new hotels, working conditions and salaries for domestics have improved sharply. Opportunities have increased in the informal labor market for such activities as washing clothes, renting rooms (in defiance of regulations), selling food, and petty vending. Some women have been able to formalize their businesses by opening hotels,

---

4. Janet Kennedy, Antoinette Russin, and Amalfi Martinez, "The Impact of Tourism Development on Women: A Case Study of Ixtapa-Zihuatanejo, Mexico," a restricted circulation report to the World Bank, July 1977.

restaurants, and shops. Since the construction boom ended in January 1977, however, many of these small businesses have been suffering from a lack of customers just as the municipality has begun to charge higher taxes.

The new hotels in Ixtapa have created many jobs for women, but a smaller percentage of the total number of jobs is held by them than was the case in the old hotels in Zihuatanejo. According to the study, women hold 23 to 29 percent of the jobs in the Aristos and El Presidente hotels respectively, whereas in Zihuatanejo they hold over 50 percent of the jobs in most hotels. Women are more likely to be owners or managers of the older hotels and to work as chambermaids, secretaries, and, in one case, waitresses in the new. Female managers are more likely to hire women for a wider range of hotel positions. In the new hotels women receive the same basic salary as men, the minimum wage for most positions.

In other tourism-related enterprises, the rate of female employment varies. Women comprise 64 percent of the personnel in the restaurants surveyed, but in first-class restaurants only men wait on tables, and employment opportunities for women may therefore decrease as restaurants are upgraded.

Nontourist-related sectors do not provide a large number of jobs for women. Women represent 10 percent of all employees in government offices, 36 percent of the primary-school teachers, and between 6 and 30 percent in other new businesses. The one "old" industry, the fish-processing plant, hires women for 19 percent of the positions, but industries recently established in the industrial zone have no work for women, except as secretaries. Increasingly, workers need to acquire new skills for jobs in other fields. Basic literacy is necessary even for chambermaids and waitresses in the luxury hotels, and secretarial skills are needed for work in the offices.

The hotel training school, one of the components of the project, has yet to be opened; other training programs have already been a failure. A secretarial school, the one program aimed directly at women, was only temporary. Women still need literacy programs and training in basic skills, as well as access to other courses which will prepare them for new, high-level positions.

Impact of tourism activities

With the opening of the new airport, air service to Zihuatanejo increased from 315 to 1,500 seats weekly, or nearly 500 percent. A constant stream of buses also connects Zihuatanejo with other areas. The town is no longer isolated but has close ties with the capital city and is fully integrated into the mainstream of the nation's political life. Many more villagers now are able to travel outside Zihuatanejo and are becoming increasingly interested in events in other areas, in how other people live, what they have and what they lack. At present, their awareness of these other people makes the inhabitants of Zihuatanejo aware of their own identity as "villagers" and thus helps affirm their social identity, though in the future this same awareness may tend to have just the opposite effect of metropolitanizing the people of Zihuatanejo.

Two hotels have already been constructed in Ixtapa, each with more rooms than the total accommodation currently available in all of Zihuatanejo. The first effect these hotels had on the area was to attract skilled workers to what they considerd the "promised land"—a new hotel with higher wages and better working conditions—leaving hotels in Zihuatanejo with a serious labor shortage. Even those who stayed wanted the same salaries and working conditions as those who changed jobs. This situation had a cohesive effect on the hotels in Zihuatanejo and set them even further apart from those in Ixtapa.

The construction of 530 hotel rooms (compared with the 220 rooms available previously) created a new market for services. Boatmen and taxi drivers, threatened by the appearance of competitors anxious to cash in on new business, attempted to strengthen their position by unionizing. The unions gave new perspectives to the population, particularly to those who had lived there before 1970, but they could not keep outsiders from entering the local labor market. The fast-growing demand for service workers, especially for people skilled in providing tourism services, could not be filled by local people, and workers from Acapulco took the best jobs available. A division sprang up in the unions between the villagers and the outsiders, but no real clashes occurred because there was sufficient work for everybody. The situation had one positive effect: it encouraged some local people to get the necessary training to qualify for the better-paying jobs.

The new tourist environment accelerated the process of change. Business people, for example, began to assimilate new trends and in turn helped to modernize the style of dress, eating habits, and customs of the villagers. The community of people who lived in

Zihuatanejo when the project began in 1970 has undergone much transformation. The government's intervention, by legal means, disturbed the old social and class structure and provided opportunities for some to rise socially while others did not. This created conflicts in the community which are now subsiding. In fact, the original 1970 Zihuatanejo community is being drawn together again by some of the strong, still existing characteristics of preference for personal social relationships, importance of family institutions, and a certain cultural homogeneity. They are reaffirming their ways in relation to the newer groups.

Superimposed on the original community is an increasingly urban society. It consists of an imperfectly integrated combination of elements bound together by the road network of Ixtapa, Zihuatanejo, and low-income satellite areas. At present the city has only approximately 10,000 inhabitants, but a population of 80,000 is projected. On the basis of this projection, work is being done to widen streets, expand services, and increase facilities. As urbanization proceeds, new demands are being made on the inhabitants. The behavior of the semirural people is changing, and they are beginning to act like "urbanites." With the new street and road system, for example, taxi drivers now behave more like their counterparts in a large city.

No systematic study of the impact of tourism and tourists has yet been undertaken. But even without such a study some general observations are possible. For example, the middle-aged international tourist who came to Zihuatanejo in the past, especially before the construction of the road, adapted to the life-style of the villagers and had relatively little effect. More recent tourists, however, have made an obvious impression, especially among youths, because young foreign visitors, whether hippies or adventurers, who tend to remain apart from the established population, do seek involvement with the village youths. This has made the latter less traditional in their way of thinking.

For any analysis of the social impact of tourism a further distinction must be made between the different components of tourism: tourism infrastructure during the construction phase and in actual operation, the economic activity known as "tourism," and the provision of tourism services. Experience to date with tourism and with monitoring social change in Zihuatanejo suggests certain conclusions:

1. It is important to conduct base-line studies of population characteristics and values if one wishes to monitor the changes taking place.

2. The activities generated by the construction of a tourism project will have a significant effect on the community long before tourists begin to arrive in numbers.

3. The people who come to build the infrastructure, and the installations that result, will bring about such far-reaching social changes that it may be almost impossible to observe the specific impact of tourism thereafter, much less to measure it.

4. Although the original inhabitants of Zihuatanejo were not initially involved in the project, they have gradually adjusted to the changes introduced by tourism and have become integrated into the new social setup. It is therefore likely that tourism itself will eventually become an integrating force rather than a disruptive one.

CHAPTER 9

Mechanisms of Intercultural Interaction

Lothar Nettekoven
AFRICA-ASIA BUREAU
SOCIETY FOR DEVELOPMENT PLANNING

H OW DOES TOURISM AFFECT HOST SOCIETIES? In any discussion of the social and cultural implications of
tourism, the intercultural relations of the indigenous population
with the foreign tourists are undoubtedly of the greatest importance. Also significant are the relations among tourists themselves,
because many stereotypes of the indigenous population are formed
by tourists and disseminated through intertourist communication.

Intertourist relations are of two kinds: those among people from
the same country—whether among strangers who meet during the
trip or among friends and relatives who are traveling together—and
relations among tourists of different nationalities who encounter
each other en route. Intercultural relations of foreign tourists with
the indigenous population consist of encounters with hotel personnel (the professional "hosts"), with residents indirectly employed in
the tourism industry but not in the hotel business proper, and with
people who have no professional connection with the tourism industry. Further differentiation of intercultural relations is necessary
only in the case of tourists who make repeat visits to the same country or locality.

Misconceptions about Intercultural Encounters

Three widespread misconceptions about intercultural encounters
need to be dispelled.

1. Foreign tourists have fewer and less intensive encounters with
   residents of the host country than is often assumed.

2. In most African and Asian developing countries, interaction with tourists is one of the least important influences on the indigenous cultures, especially in view of the discrepancy between the total population of the host country and the small number of people who have direct and regular contact with foreign visitors.

3. Tourists have considerably less desire for intense intercultural encounters than is alleged.

Tourists tend to be highly concentrated in a local or regional center of attraction rather than spread throughout the total area of the host country. This is true in the traditional vacation countries such as Italy and Spain and to a much larger extent in the new vacation countries of the Third World, where tourist resorts have frequently been created in the form of semi-isolated ghettos.[1] This local or regional concentration of tourism limits the opportunities for intercultural encounters to a relatively small area of the country. Furthermore, only a small part of the local population has an opportunity for active interaction with foreign visitors. Tourists encounter primarily those directly and indirectly employed in the tourism industry and, secondarily, those residing in the immediate vicinity of the resort or near special points of interest visited on excursions.

Opportunities for intercultural interaction are further limited by the fact that tourists are less interested in such encounters than they themselves pretend. They are on a vacation, which is, by definition, supposed to be free from problems. Coming to grips with the problems of a developing country is in itself difficult and thus interferes with the desired pleasures of the vacation. Only 28 percent of the German, British, and French tourists questioned in 1969 in Tunisia wanted as much information as possible about Tunisia and the Tunisians, whereas 63 percent expressed only limited desire for information ("Yes, but it must not interfere with the vacation").[2] The normal tourist is not to be compared with an anthropologist or

---

1. With the possible exception of small islands with mass tourism, particularly in the Caribbean and increasingly in the Pacific.

2. Lothar Nettekoven, *Massentourismus in Tunesien: Soziologische Untersuchungen an Touristen aus hoch industrialisierten Gesellschaften* [Mass tourism in Tunisia: Sociological investigations of tourists from highly industrialized societies] (Starnberg, 1972), pp. 325 ff.

other researcher. Tourists are pleasure-seekers, temporarily unemployed, and above all consumers; they are taking their trip to get away from everyday cares.

Many of the developing countries were formerly under a more or less oppressive colonial rule and have suffered a corresponding loss of national authenticity. Certain elements inherited from the colonial powers, such as language, school systems, mass communication (particularly foreign films, books, and radios) are still dominant in the postcolonial present. Like these earlier foreign influences tourism is often considered to have an important cultural impact. Unlike the colonial foreigners, however, the tourists are only temporary visitors and do not hold positions of political or economic power to which the entire population is subjected. As far as the majority of the population is concerned, tourists are "invisible" in that they have no direct effect on laws, taxes, and other regulations. The traditional cultural influences remain dominant, and tourism has only a subordinate role. Its negative as well as positive implications for the values and behavior patterns of the entire population of the target countries in Africa and Asia should not be overestimated.

Intercultural Interaction

When mass tourism from highly industrialized societies is introduced into an economically underdeveloped country, the contrast between the two societies is apt to be stark and the consequences often great. The tourists' usual patterns of consumption are altered while on vacation and may exceed the normal level of their spending at home. Among their fellow countrymen some extravagance is not unusual during the relatively short vacation period. But this temporarily lavish expenditure takes place within an economically underdeveloped society, where many people live a marginal existence. The subsistence requirement is drastically below the limit which, in industrial societies, is viewed as an acceptable minimum. The difference between the consumer habits of the tourists and the living conditions of the indigenous population is thus accentuated and the differences between the two societies emphasized.

The foreign tourists are not aware of this problem or else push it aside so that their social conscience does not interfere with their vacation pleasures and their escape from problems. The tourists see nothing wrong with their consumer-oriented behavior because it is considered proper to lead a "better" life while on vacation.

The reactions of the residents depend largely on their consciousness of the problem, which is in turn dependent on the amount of information they have and the specific character of their direct contacts with the foreigners. As already indicated, by far the largest part of the indigenous population is informed only indirectly about the foreign tourists. Because of the ghetto-like isolation of the tourist centers there is almost no opportunity for direct interactions unless the two groups meet accidentally in the capital or at regional marketplaces.

The starting point for understanding the relation between tourists and the indigenous population lies in the foreign characteristics and behavior of the tourists. They have no clear or realistic perception of the country they are in. And because of the relative briefness of their stay they have little chance to become familiar with and adapt to indigenous customs and thereby lose their alien characteristics. At best they adapt to tourist conditions; they remain strangers and, as such, insecure, finding security only in their role of tourist.

The insecurity of the strangers produces problems, and during a vacation problems are highly undesirable. Tourists therefore cling together as a defense against the unfamiliar and perhaps disturbing environment. They form a protective society of their own which they leave only very seldom. Within the safety of the tourist ghetto it is possible to maintain a self-assurance which may elude the individual foreigner outside the enclave. One of the reasons for the popularity of group travel is that in purchasing a group trip the buyer acquires the right to the company of fellow travelers.

Indigenous Groups Most Frequently Encountered

Hotel employees

Those directly employed in hotels undoubtedly have the greatest amount of contact with foreign tourists. Their relations with tourists are linked with their job, which is to increase the pleasure and the well-being of the tourists. The hotel employees may try to imitate the consumer behavior of the tourists to a certain extent, although it is of course impossible for them to succeed completely because they lack the financial means. This necessarily leads to frustration, especially among young people, who are not yet able to see how unusual the tourist situation is.

To be sure, this frustration and the latent feeling of inferiority begin to diminish after prolonged employment in tourism. The young people then discover the human weaknesses and insecurities of their tourist customers and thus free themselves from the myth of the superior foreigners. The envious admiration is neutralized, and they may develop a tendency to try and benefit personally from these weaknesses. The foreign tourists are then transformed into a commercial opportunity; by creating business they help to stimulate heretofore unknown economic behavior. This change in attitude is especially characteristic of those indirectly employed in the tourism sector outside the hotel area.

After the hotel employee's initial unlimited admiration of tourists and subsequent critical distance, a third behavior pattern may emerge. As their personal advantages increase, experienced hotel employees can develop a defense mechanism against their latent, persistent inferiority complex. They adopt a recognizable pattern of trying to impress others, to demonstrate their superiority to the initially insecure tourists in a specific situation. Their attitudes range from excessive snobbism to a pervasive arrogance, in part provoked by the fact that through their professional training they may speak several foreign languages or have traveled abroad. This manner of impressing others is especially hard on tourists without knowledge of the language and with little travel experience. Only when such hotel employees finally become more self-aware is their arrogance subdued, and they are able to develop a more objective attitude toward their foreign customers.

The peripheral tourism area

The peripheral tourism area includes those businesses and services which lie outside the hotel operation and which are patronized in part by tourists and in part by residents. This area is of great importance because, on the one hand, it permits the indigenous population not directly employed in the hotel field to share in the economic benefits of tourism. On the other hand, it permits the tourist to experience a small measure of indigenous life. The peripheral sector is not entirely directed toward foreign tourists, nor does it demand from the tourist a total adaptation to a strange environment. Shopping in a local market, going to the barber, changing money at a bank, eating in a local restaurant, and similar activities offer a large number of possibilities for meeting semiprofessional indigenous people. In the process there develops an intercultural interaction on neutral ground, such as the immediate area around the hotel, which permits both groups to gain reciprocal and largely objective insights.

Unfortunately this peripheral tourism area is not very extensive, especially in many developing countries. The national or international managers of tourism frequently seek to achieve maximum profits by creating self-contained hotel complexes which offer all the goods and services sought by tourists. Thus the tourist is deprived of the rare opportunity to participate in the indigenous life and make appropriate intercultural contacts, and—even more important—the indigenous population loses the opportunity to profit from tourism, apart from simple wage-related services.

Young people

In many countries around half the population is less than twenty years old. A potentially large number of young people may thus be affected by the alienating acculturation processes of pleasure-oriented tourism. They visualize life within the tourist resort as a paradise where tourists lead an enviable existence without work but with abundance. The situation is similar to that of the cargo cults of Samoa and other Pacific islands, where the indigenous population never observed the white man at work and therefore believed that the desirable goods of Western civilization were a generous gift of the gods, of which they were unjustly deprived. The young people may also develop a disastrous misconception of the idyllic life in the countries of origin of foreign tourists and may be tempted to emigrate. They remain largely ignorant of the fact that these strangers have to work and save for a whole year for their two weeks of completely carefree pleasure. This truth is apparently not publicized by the tourists in the contacts which do arise.

The upper class

Westernized members of the lower part of the upper class are often familiar with the tourists' countries of origin through travel or study abroad. In principle they are pleased to renew their bonds with Western culture through sporadic contacts with foreign visitors at tourist centers. A genuine cultural exchange can evolve from such encounters between interested tourists and interested members of the educated class if the tourists understand the specific societal situation and problems of the host country and if the hosts have some knowledge of their visitors' own country.

Nationalistic, conservative members of the upper class for the most part remain aloof from the tourist centers, but nevertheless during personal contacts with foreigners they extend the obligatory and traditional hospitality. Otherwise they regard the behavior of the foreign tourist as excessive and disapprove of the foreign element introduced into their country by tourism.

The Role of the Professional Intermediary

If tourism serves or is supposed to serve as a medium for objective cultural exchange, the question arises as to the role of the professional cultural intermediaries (guides and the personnel of airlines, hotel chains, travel agencies, and the like). These people serve a primarily economic function—as employees of commercial enterprises they sell a product called "tourism" or they belong to the customer service sector. The profit motive is thus the key to understanding the potentials and limits of their ability to serve as cultural intermediaries.

In the commercial sector, cultural activities can be offered only if they prove profitable. If the consumer explicitly desires cultural mediation the seller will include it in his package of services. At present, however, the travel professionals advertise and promote only those aspects of a target country that will appeal to tourists; cultural activities, and particularly matters of potential interest in the contemporary social, economic, or political fields, are ignored. In an attempt to increase sales a partial picture is presented, limited to the rose-colored tourist world: beach, sun, palms, untouched landscape, art monuments of the past, friendly population, amusement potential, quality of the hotel beds, number of courses for meals, and the measurements of the hotel swimming pool.

Only in the case of the educational trip is this type of promotion replaced, for example, by an emphasis on the classical past. Participants in educational trips to Italy, Greece, Egypt, and the like travel into an ancient period and return as experts in the respective mythologies. But they learn remarkably little about the contemporary society of their target country.

What are needed are educational tours into modern reality, analogous to the trips into the past. This suggestion is based on the assumption that tourists could be motivated to establish contact with residents of the target country, to take an interest in the characteristic features of their society, and to participate in reciprocal cultural exchange. The professionals in the field of travel could achieve financial success by organizing such tours and serving as cultural intermediaries. This type of tour need not be offered as an entirely separate package but could be combined with other kinds of travel. It should, however, avoid a pedagogic character that would be incompatible with the idea of fun and relaxation. If the serious academic and educational elements come to the fore, the vacation will lose its appeal of being free from everyday concerns.

Tour Guides

Tour guides, both foreign and indigenous, function primarily in an administrative capacity in the host country. They are intermediaries between the foreign tour organizer and the indigenous tourism sector; for the tourist they are the agents of the travel bureau. In addition, professional tour guides are, especially at the beginning of the vacation stay, the most important informants about touristic as well as social conditions of the destination. They play a dominant role in intercultural encounters; potentially they can motivate the tourists to make contact with others and create opportunities which can lead to cultural exchange. This is a difficult task for which the tour guides are mostly inadequately prepared and trained.

Financial considerations will often prevent guides from creating authentic extratouristic opportunities for cultural exchange. Most tour guides receive a moderate basic salary, which is supplemented considerably by sales commissions for excursions, services, and souvenirs. The danger, therefore, is that the tourists will not be encouraged to go beyond the peripheral tourism area from which the guides can profit financially. This economic factor determines the interests and behavior patterns of indigenous and foreign tour guides alike.

In the nineteenth century guides had the task of escorting travelers during their journey; today they still fulfill this role but in rudimentary form. They temporarily accompany tourists on short-term excursions and transmit cultural information through their explanations of the tourist sights. Here the difference between indigenous and foreign tourist guides becomes apparent. The indigenous guides generally lack a profound knowledge of the societies of the foreign tourists, while the foreign guides often know little about the wider host society. The result is an inexhaustible flow of misunderstandings and false information.

To solve this contradiction and take advantage of the many possibilities for far-reaching, objective cultural exchange, a first step would be to reduce the payment of sales commissions by assuring guides a higher basic salary. In addition, the professional level of guides should be upgraded, and they should receive not only sufficient preparatory training for the job but also continuing education and motivation.

Some Results of Intercultural Interaction

Although intercultural interaction occurs less frequently and less intensively than is generally supposed, it does have certain effects on the host country, especially in the case of mass tourism. When tourism is limited locally or regionally it affects a relatively small segment of the indigenous population, but in the course of several years a large number of results are possible, only a few of which are mentioned here.

Accelerated acculturation

Like industrial projects, tourist resorts are frequently located in heretofore "untouched" regions, usually in less favored parts of a developing country, where the local population has been cut off from socioeconomic development and may have sought recourse in migration to the nearest principal city.

Apart from the fact that tourism may slow down the flight from the land and attract population into the area, the presence of strangers from foreign countries may weaken the conservative traditions and help to break down provincial patterns of thought. These changes are greeted favorably by the young people who heretofore wanted to emigrate. Because of the changes brought by tourism their horizons are expanded and their regional isolation is broken down.

These processes of acculturation are accelerated by the constantly changing tourist population, which provides at least some of the indigenous people with new opportunities for learning. Acculturation depends on the amount of exposure to the tourists and is reinforced by the collective experience with each group of new arrivals. The extent to which the indigenous population is given jobs in the tourist sector and allowed to share in the economic success of tourism thus determines the nature and extent of acculturation processes.

Positive aspects of acculturation

The many negative aspects of acculturation are frequently discussed; the positive aspects will be briefly mentioned here, without any attempt to give a balanced evaluation.

A basic factor of the acculturation process stimulated by tourism is socioeconomic change. Economically this means—as already indicated—a possibility for wider participation of the local population in the economic processes induced by tourism. In the cultural field, tourism deregionalizes the area, breaks down provincial conservatism, and stimulates multilingualism. For the enlightened youth especially, their image of the outside world is thus expanded.

In the case of young nations which were formerly colonies, the socioeconomic changes can reduce the postcolonial neurosis of dependence on a cultural superpower. In addition, when tourists are seen as insecure strangers, this revelation of their weaknesses can lead to a dissolution of the erroneous myth of the superpowerful foreigner and can ultimately provide an insight into the basic similarity of human problems. Thus tourism could, as one of many factors of social change, help remove the feelings of inferiority among the people in developing countries by divorcing human and cultural development from the economic sphere. Through its socioeconomic impulses toward development tourism also could help diminish the real differences in economic levels.

In its current state the tourism industry can hardly be expected to motivate the tourist to make contacts with the indigenous population. Nor can foreign tourists be expected to take part in any extensive and lasting learning experiences during their pleasure-oriented travel into the underdeveloped world. It would be enough of a success if their negative prejudices were not further enhanced and if the gap between the illusory world of the tourist and the socioeconomic reality of an economically underdeveloped country were not widened.

Revitalization of indigenous traditions

One of the few attempts of the tourism industry to present the traditional values, objects, and behavior patterns of a foreign culture revolves around the display of arts and crafts, folklore, and cultural monuments of the past. These may once have been characteristic of the visited culture, but often they have been neglected, primarily because of the Westernizing process of acculturation during the colonial period. Frequently these almost lost relics are transformed into consumable form and presented as characteristic of the contemporary culture. Not only does this practice further distort the tourists' view of the realities of the country, but it also deepens existing misunderstandings. The renewed interest in past cultural greatness may, however, compensate somewhat for the lack of authenticity observed in the modern forms.

The interest of foreign tourists in cultural artifacts has in many instances led directly to the revival of handicrafts or a cultural tradition or produced an often extraordinary combination of modernity and tradition. This cultural renewal is accepted only after the fact by the indigenous society and requires the prior approval of the foreigner from abroad. Nevertheless, this revitalization of traditional culture can help support the movement toward self-identity of many developing countries.

CHAPTER 10

African Arts and Crafts in a World of Changing Values

Karl-Ferdinand Schädler
ECONOMIST AND MASTER CRAFTSMAN

M OST ARTISTIC EXPRESSION IN BLACK AFRICA was and, in many parts, still is closely related to continuing religious practices. With rare exceptions, the European[1] attitude of art for art's sake is completely foreign to African ways of thinking. That which is art for the European is function for the African and is justified by its use in religious and tribal ceremonies.[2]

If the seductive simplicity of form was for the avant garde artists—who "discovered" African art early in the twentieth century—the grounds for admiration and imitation, for the Africans it is simply the embodiment of a soul, or a force, lending value and purpose to the object created. It therefore seems reasonable to believe that traditional arts and crafts will continue for as long as the ritual or religion that serves as a basis for them.

Traditional art, as it is understood here, comprises only objects that are produced for use in the cult or for other tribal purposes. Tourist art is defined as any artistic object produced not for ritual or tribal purposes but for sale to traders or directly to tourists. Models and patterns for this tourist art are taken mainly from traditional objects but have their origins in Euro-American concepts of a naturalistic art expression, inculcated in many cases by missionaries or government-sponsored carving schools.

1. The word "European" is used in the West African sense,of Western, that is, both European and American.
2. See Karl-Ferdinand Schädler, *African Art in Private German Collections* (Munich: Münchner Buchgewerbehaus, 1973), p. 7.

The Impact of Tourism on the Production of Arts and Crafts

When avant garde artists first encountered African art in the anthropological collections of European museums, they saw in it a freedom from the narrow tradition of naturalism or realism against which they themselves were rebelling. They and the art critics of the period attributed to African artists a degree of creativity and freedom from conventional rules and stylistic limitations which they themselves had been attempting to achieve. With a more complete knowledge of African arts—now that larger collections can be compared and more artistically creative tribes are known—it is evident that, although the conventions differed, African artists were and are still creating within stylistic limitations comparable in scope to those of Europe. Among the many local styles in Africa there are distinct differences, but within each of these clearly delineated styles there is usually considerable uniformity and far less creative freedom than was originally believed.[3]

In reaction to the earlier view, African artists came to be regarded by some as rigidly repeating and monotonously copying the tribal styles, which were believed to derive from the creative abilities of some unknown artists in the past and to have remained unchanged ever since. In reality, African art has always been subject to change, but at a very slow pace, and knowledge is still too sketchy to allow reliable assessments of these changes.[4]

There is clear evidence that some tribes have altered their products to conform to the aesthetic values of their customers. One of the most striking examples of this is the tourist art or "airport art" made by the Senufo who live in the northern and southern parts of the Ivory Coast and the Republic of Mali. The Senufo have traditionally made a variety of sculptures and masks, many of them fine exam-

---

3. See William Bascom, "Creativity and Style in African Art," in *Tradition and Creativity in Tribal Art*, Daniel Biebuyck, ed. (Los Angeles, Calif.: University of California Press, 1973) pp. 100 f.

4. See ibid., and also Frank Willet, *African Art* (London: Thames and Hudson, 1971), p. 239.

ples of the purely sculptural form which artists and critics admire in African art. But their *deblé* rhythm figures and the *kpelié* masks in particular have been subject to artistic "refinements," and the characteristic Senufo style has been exaggerated to accentuate both the expressive remoteness and the elegance of their sculpture. Other examples are found among the Bambara and Dogon of the Republic of Mali, the ethnical groups of the Cameroon grasslands, and, to a lesser degree, the Baule of the Ivory Coast.

Modification of wood carving, brass casting, and weaving to meet tourist demand

Whereas European aesthetics have been adopted in the production of masks and sculptures by a relatively small number of tribes, new compositions, new models, and new dimensions are encountered wherever tourist art is based upon traditional art. Many alert carvers and casters seek new ways of suiting their customers' tastes. They freely combine masks of different styles, different purposes, and even different tribes; they add to ancestor or magical figures symbols and attributes borrowed from other cultures, which they often know only from art books or other publications.

Apart from artifacts in the single or combined traditional styles reproduced again and again for the tourist market, there is no limit to the imagination of African artists in creating new models to attract the potential customer—perhaps a transient tourist or an uninitiated collector of African art. Most ingenuity is shown by brass casters. Mossi, Bwa, and Bobo craftsmen in Upper Volta invent new cult figures and animals; in the Ivory Coast and especially in Ghana the figures used until the beginning of this century for weighing gold dust (then the only currency) are now sometimes represented as cowboys, either standing with legs apart and sixshooters half drawn or riding a scrawny horse and clutching a furled lasso.[5] Other new models of these weights include couples posed in an erotic manner. In the Cameroon grasslands and the country of the Kirdi in northern Cameroon, the lost wax method of brass casting, which is common throughout black Africa, permits the artist to give expression to his fantasies. There are statues which look as though they came from outer space or have been inspired by

5. See Daniel J. Crowley, "The West African Art Market Revisited," *African Arts*, vol. 7, no. 4, pp. 54–59.

science fiction. There are all sorts of tools—"ceremonial" of course—chairs, masks, and ancestor figures of a kind that had never before existed in brass and only rarely in wood.

Senufo weavers, especially those from Korhogo, also have shown great ingenuity in satisfying the ever increasing demand for their work. They recognize that the customer wants something decorative to show off at home and indicate that the owner has been far away in Africa, and the object must be the right size to decorate a small wall or cover a normal table.

Many tourist art products are oversized compared with their original dimensions. Quality standards are easier to meet when the products are relatively large, and tourist demand tends more toward bigger models than originally was expected. This is especially true for all kinds of brass castings but also to a certain extent for wooden objects, although packing requirements impose certain limits.

Apart from the manufacture of items specifically for tourist consumption, the impact that tourism has had on the shape, color, and aesthetic appearance of traditional arts and crafts is negligible and, where it can be demonstrated at all, confined to a few exceptions. New materials such as oil paint, plastics, aluminum, and waste rubber from tires are used simply because they have become accessible, like other new materials in earlier times. Nor does the introduction of new techniques necessarily lead to a degeneration of traditional forms. Among the Malanggan of New Ireland, for example, when European tools replaced their stone implements their sculpture and craftsmanship were not impoverished but enriched.

The counterfeit industry

To avoid misinterpretation of the terms "counterfeit" and "genuine" as applied to African art, I need to explain what I mean by this, since the use of these terms differs widely.[6] In other fields of art the origin of an art object and the time of its creation play a decisive role in determining whether it is false. In African art it is neither time nor age that is important, but the reason for producing it and its actual function. For example, in some areas where the traditional religion is still practiced, woodcarvers may produce pieces of high

6. See also Karl-Ferdinand Schädler, *Afrikanische Kunst* [African art] (Munich: Heyne Verlag, 1975), pp. 27 ff.

artistic quality, and there may be a shortage of pieces in the art market because of an increasing demand for them. The woodcarver may
then produce identical pieces for two different clients: one is the
tribal priest or chief who uses it in the cult, the other is the art dealer
who sells it. Both pieces are equally authentic. As soon as one of the
objects is used by the cult, however, it becomes "genuine"; the other
is for the time being nothing but a copy—and may become a counterfeit if it is provided with false traces of use.

Whether an object of African art has been used in the cult and
merits the designation "genuine" depends on the evidence of accumulated marks of use and storage: soot, wear, damage, indigenous
repairs, sweat, dirt, and sacrificial libations. Generally such evidence is honored in the price of the object, independent of its other
qualities. Of course, the proven and even very distinctly manifested
genuineness by itself does not determine the ultimate value. A well-
carved decorative object may be more expensive than a mediocre
object that has been used in the cult for a long time.

West African art centers practice the full range of counterfeiting,
and in the course of the last two decades a flourishing industry has
become established. The process of producing counterfeits for
museums and collectors does not differ from that of making copies
for the ordinary tourist market except that another stage is added to
the production line. It is relatively more profitable to counterfeit objects of high aesthetic value, and these make heavy demands on the
abilities of carvers and casters. The number of craftsmen who are
able to meet such demand is limited, and the prices they command
for their work are therefore quite high. The high profits induce investment in this area, including investment in human capital; this
sector is definitely a growth area.

Local tradesmen of course benefit from the production of cheap
imitations for the tourist trade, and those craftsmen possessing the
required skills profit from making the more demanding counterfeits. Although the economic impact is limited, it is on balance
almost entirely favorable because growth in this area does not
detract from other sectors. Perhaps the principal economic effect
overall would be the modest contribution of the counterfeit industry
to a more favorable balance of payments.

A considerable share of the West African counterfeit art trade is
in the hands of Hausa and Diula traders who buy the merchandise
from local craftsmen mainly in the major centers of production,
such as Korhogo, Bouaké, and Abidjan in the Ivory Coast or

Bamako in Mali. As in other parts of the world, the less-skilled craftsman often gets paid a very low price or wage for his product, which is then sometimes sold at a great profit by the private trader or even by government-sponsored institutions. Knowledge of these matters is still very limited, however, and little or no research work has yet been done in this field.

Modification of arts and crafts produced for traditional purposes

The slow changes in African art that have occurred over the centuries are difficult to assess, because with rare exceptions historical records are lacking and more recent studies are confined to a limited period or a given point in time. A comparison of objects collected at the beginning of this century with objects carved or cast today shows that only in some cases is there a distinct change in shape or aesthetic appearance. This change is largely in response to Islam, Christianity, and syncretic religions and, to a lesser degree, to Euro-American influence.

Collectors and admirers often tend to compare very old pieces of high quality with inferior modern objects to prove the decadence of contemporary African art. Yet they overlook the thousands of pieces of poor quality which are equally old or which have been subject to decay because no dealer or collector happened to rescue them. Many of the objects collected early in this century could have been carved yesterday for the tourist market. It is hardly likely that the craftsmen who produced these objects carved intentionally inferior pieces because they were ordered by Europeans and not destined for the sacred ceremonies. A glorification of the past tends to obscure the ugliness of some antiquities and mistakes age for beauty.

Changes in the Traditional Values and Significance of Arts and Crafts

As in other societies of the world, in Africa the adoption of new beliefs does not completely eradicate the traditional faith. Although usually many items and objects of the old religion are ostentatiously destroyed when conversions take place, remnants of the familiar sacred forces persist and are often strangely metamorphosed to become an active part of the new religion. In contrast to earlier centuries when new religions such as Islam or Christianity were introduced by force, modern conversions are brought about by more subtle forms of persuasion. There is therefore greater moderation in replacing old religious objects with those of the new faith. Often, especially in religions with elaborate rituals, tokens of the new religions are attached to the old ritual objects, thus combining the forces of the new and the old.

Many of the Yoruba of western Nigeria still adhere to their own sophisticated religion despite the encroachments of Christianity and Islam. In Brazil, where many of this tribe were deported as slaves, they were able to subvert their forced conversion to Catholicism by identifying their gods with Catholic saints. In Yorubaland, where Islam has pressed from the north for more than 170 years and Christianity has impinged from the south since the times of colonization, there are sculptures, *ere ibeji*, that betray signs of syncretism. These traditional religious figures represent deceased twins and are carved at the order of the mother who has to care for them (wash, nourish, and anoint them). Among the Yoruba who have been converted to Islam or Christianity, most will not admit that they still believe in the necessity of twin ritual and the carving of ere ibeji because of the proscription against retaining any sculpture related to traditional Yoruba practice. There are, however, a substantial number who have merged the most meaningful aspects of their traditional faith with the new religion. Especially in northern Yorubaland, ibeji figures are often encountered with the Muslim triangular amulet, called *tirah*, whereas in the southern parts, although very seldom, such figures may be found with crosses around their necks. In recent times ere ibeji in a simplified abstract form have been ordered occasionally by second generation converts. Even plastic dolls have been encountered which replace the old twin figures.[7]

Another example is provided by the Fan of Gabon, some of whom have been Christians for several generations. During their *bwiti* ceremonies, one of which I attended, some of their priests wear pieces of Catholic ceremonial attire, and all participants hold burning candles while proceeding to the graves of their ancestors to invoke their help and blessing.

7. See Marilyn Hammersley Houlberg, "Ibeji Images of the Yoruba," *African Arts*, vol. 7, no. 1, pp. 20–27.

It becomes evident that the influence of tourism, if any, on the traditional values and significance of arts and crafts can hardly be isolated from the effects of other forces. Changes in belief occur in black Africa almost constantly. This is not surprising in view of its some 250 million people, a fast-growing communications network, and permanent missionary activity, mainly by the Muslims.[8] There is a steady amalgamation of beliefs in many parts of the continent and a constant conversion either to Islam or, to a lesser degree, Christianity, or to one of the many new syncretic religions such as Massa, Alakora, and Harrists. All these conversions and amalgamations have of course a strong impact on the traditional values of arts and crafts, wherever in African eyes these are identical with the underlying cult.

Many people believe that the cults are dying out, a trend that is of course more intense in the cities than in isolated villages. In the foreseeable future the identity between cult and art is expected to disappear almost completely—that is, art embodied in objects of worship or objects used in religious rituals (African art as commonly understood by European collectors) will cease to exist. No doubt the cult will survive in some decadent form such as superstition or traditional and customary ritual, just as in Europe remnants of paganism still survive some 1,300 years after pagan cults have disappeared. But there will no longer be a union of cult, life, and religious ritual. This unity makes possible the creation of arts and crafts that are indivisibly bound up with the cult and embody a transcendental force.

Tourism alone can hardly affect a religion as long as people adhere to it seriously; consequently, tourism alone can do little harm to traditional values and significance of arts and crafts. Any change in this area, I believe, is due only to changing beliefs and growing secularization in general—a development parallel to the trend in industrialized countries.

One of the most famous masked dances, that of the *dama* by the Dogon of the Republic of Mali, continues basically unchanged where people still adhere to their traditional religion, despite having been executed in front of tourists for a long time. The dance was

8. In contrast to Christian activities, where professional missionaries try to convert people of other faiths, every Muslim is charged with the task of converting non-Muslims.

minutely described by Marcel Griaule in 1938 and was again witnessed thirty years later by Pascal James Imperato, who was able to compare both performances.[9] His findings reveal that during tourist performances some especially sacred parts are now omitted in villages where the religion is still alive, but in those places where the cult has been given up the dance performances have also been abandoned.

The Development and Protection of Traditional Arts and Crafts

In most African countries some effort has been made to establish a center where local craftsmen may work together and sell their products, or to set up a government shop—typically in the center of the town near the main hotel or at the airport—where local crafts are sold. Most of these centers are attractive, and hasty tourists need not waste time bargaining with street vendors; here shopping seems thrifty, quick, and without problems. Products are chosen to appeal to tourist taste, but every item is somehow characteristic of the region or country. They consist mainly of tablecloths, chess sets, letter openers, stylized masks as pendants in ivory or brass, filigree jewelry, wooden statues and masks, drums, stools, and the like.

In some countries, mainly in East and Central Africa, which have a weak tradition in sculpturing, carving schools have been established, often with the aid of Christian missionaries. Elsewhere pottery has been developed and other small-scale projects or cottage industries set up. Craftsmen of different trades work together in commonly leased facilities provided by the government, sometimes combined with a sales office to foster overseas trade.[10] Thus new job possibilities based on tourism have been created, which generally seem to have proved successful.

Museums have been established where traditional arts and crafts are exhibited. It is to be regretted, however, that so few of the art treasures of West and Central Africa are left to be seen in the na-

9. Marcel Griaule, *Masques Dogons* [Dogon masks] (Paris: Institut d'Ethnologie, 1938); and Pascal James Imperato, "Contemporary Adapted Dances of the Dogon," *African Arts*, vol. 5, no. 1, pp. 28–33, 68–72.

10. See Karl-Ferdinand Schädler, *Crafts, Small-scale Industries, and Industrial Education in Tanzania* (Munich: Weltforum Verlag, 1968), pp. 169 f.

tional or anthropological museums of these countries. Most museums, although they were well endowed following independence, have deplorable collections of a quality which any average private collector of African art overseas can easily match. Noteworthy exceptions are the highly important museums in Nigeria and perhaps Angola.

Dance troupes from Benin, Guinea, Madagascar, the Ivory Coast, Niger, and Cameroon have traveled all over the world, mostly with direct or indirect assistance from the respective government. Sometimes different ethnic groups have been put together, such as the Mali national troupe, which is a synthesis of the Peulh, Senufo, Dogon, Songhai, and Bambara tribes.[11]

In many countries the national holidays provide a welcome occasion to have artisans exhibit their traditional products and to organize artistic competitions in various fields.[12] In Nigeria the government sponsors an All-Nigeria Festival of the Arts where people of different religions, customs, and languages (about 1,200 competed in the festival of 1972) meet to perform their traditional dances and music. A major goal of the federal government since the end of the Biafra war has been the unification of the country; therefore it was decided to locate the festival in a different state each year so that the diverse peoples of the country could become better acquainted with each other's art. Competitions in traditional choral music, traditional dance, traditional instrumental music, and English language drama go on for several days. In addition, painting and sculpture are displayed, as well as examples of pottery, weaving, calabash carving, and leather, metal, and woodwork.[13]

All these activities provide important stimuli for the tourism industry. Apart from palm beaches and photo safaris, traditional folk entertainment is one of the main attractions of most holiday countries. But these activities cannot preserve or protect traditional arts and crafts, insofar as these depend on the vital link with religious or other tribal practices.

Minority religions everywhere face hard psychological pressure from mass religious and ideological movements or from religious ig-

---

11. See Jean Decock, "Pré-Théâtre et Rituel" [Pretheater and ritual], *African Arts,* vol. 1, no. 3, pp. 31–37.

12. See, for example, *Arts d'Afrique Noire* [Art of black Africa], no. 10, 1974, p. 3.

13. See Lee Warren, "The Third All-Nigeria Festival of the Arts," *African Arts,* vol. 7, no. 1, pp. 44–46.

norance. As was pointed out earlier, for the African who still belongs to one of these societies, all arts and crafts created by him are the palpable expression of his belief in the magical world, and as such they are indispensable for the survival of his tradition and hence his culture.[14] Ritual instrument and belief are inseparable. As long as the underlying religion exists and people still adhere to it there is no need for any assistance in preserving it, nor is there any danger from tourism. But as soon as this religion or cult has perished, all activities to develop, protect, or preserve it must be in vain. What is developed and protected are meaningless fragmentary husks of a cult or religion.

These remnants are recognized as being an important attraction for tourists, who generally do not care whether dances, masks, and magical or ancestor figures still have any significance. The preservation of such "traditional" arts and crafts is therefore meaningful as a stimulus to the economy. But it should be understood that, whether undertaken in the hope of preserving the cultural heritage or of developing tourism, no action will protect or revive a cult or religion that is already fading away or has even perished. All efforts in this direction would be as senseless as trying to revive Catholicism, in a society where faith has disappeared, by an endless production of ritual instruments such as monstrances, ciboria, and rosaries or by staging annual Corpus Christi processions.

14. See Boris de Rachewiltz, *Afrikanische Kunst* [African art] (Zurich: Artemis, 1960), p. 189.

CHAPTER 11

Tourism and Bermuda's
Black Clubs: A Case
of Cultural Revitalization

Frank E. Manning
DEPARTMENT OF ANTHROPOLOGY,
MEMORIAL UNIVERSITY OF NEWFOUNDLAND

A S IS OFTEN OBSERVED, TWO POLARIZED POSITIONS emerge
from the growing body of literature on the effects that
tourism has on host populations. On the one side, economists tend
to depict the obvious benefits of tourism in the way of creating jobs,
providing foreign currency exchange, and generating an inflow of
capital and expertise, all of them badly needed in many of the
societies that have attempted to develop substantial tourism industries since World War II. On the other side, social scientists generally focus on the deleterious consequences of tourism, ranging from
the introduction of drugs, prostitution, and gambling to forms of
subtle racism, psychological colonialism, and cultural imperialism.
Summarizing the negative perspective, Bryden observes: "The implication of this style of criticism is that, whatever the economic
benefits, these largely unquantifiable (social) costs are of sufficient
weight to argue against further expansion of tourism."[1]

Is the dilemma between economic gain and social cost inherent in
the nature of tourism, or are there examples of societies that have
dealt creatively and constructively with tourist influences? In the

Note: Field research in Bermuda was conducted in 1969-70 with a grant from the
National Science Foundation and in 1976 with support from the Institute of Social
and Economic Research, Memorial University of Newfoundland. I am grateful to
Deforest Trimingham of the Bermuda Department of Tourism for furnishing information on his department.

1. John M. Bryden, *Tourism and Development: A Case Study of the Commonwealth
Caribbean* (Cambridge: Cambridge University Press, 1973), p. 1.

case of Bermuda, a society that has known tourism for more than a century and built its economy on it since the 1920s, I propose to show that tourism has yielded sociocultural as well as material benefits. Three main points will be covered: the evolution of Bermudian tourism; the indigenous sociocultural response to mass tourism; and aspects of the tourism industry and the tourist-native encounter that bear on the impact of tourism.

A Century of Tourism

Bermuda, a mid-Atlantic British colony of 57,000 people, has a tourism industry that has evolved in three historical periods. The first period, dating from the mid-1860s to about 1920, saw the rise of tourism on a seasonal and small-scale basis. The close of the American Civil War had ended the island's lucrative blockade-running trade, itself the final phase of a maritime economy that began with Bermuda's settlement in the early seventeenth century. The search for alternatives to seafaring yielded two answers: the export of fruits and vegetables to the United States and the "import" of wealthy Americans to Bermuda's subtropical shores. The first major breakthrough came when in 1873 the Quebec Steamship Company agreed to make a trip between the island and New York at least once every three weeks.[2] By the following decade there were two major hotels in Bermuda, and by 1907 the volume of tourists was seven times greater than it had been at the commencement of regular steamship service. The most celebrated of Bermuda's early visitors were Princess Louise, Queen Victoria's daughter, and the American author Mark Twain. Twain memorialized his Bermuda adventures with humorous encomiums that have been used since in travel publicity.

The second period of tourism, dating from 1920 until the outbreak of World War II in 1939, was ushered in when the Furness Withy Company took over steamship operations and invested heavily in building hotels and creating in Tucker's Town a fashionable resort-residential area aimed principally at attracting the social elite of the United States. Bermuda's own merchant aristocracy, which had

---

2. William Zuill, *The Story of Bermuda and Her People* (New York: Macmillan, 1973), p. 156.

come to be known as the Forty Thieves for their role in monopoliz-
ing agricultural exports, joined in the building of hotels and in the
development of such tourist amenities as ferry services, retail shops,
and the liquor outlets that earned Bermuda's reputation as the
nearest place to New York where one could legally buy a drink during American Prohibition. This period also saw a general shift of interest from farming to tourism, the result of dwindling land resources and the passage of severe tariff restrictions in the United
States. By 1930 Bermuda was almost totally reliant on its tourism industry, which had achieved an annual volume of more than 54,000
visitors.[3]

Tourism continued to grow in the following decade, despite the
worldwide depression. Steamship services expanded until there
were six lines plying the New York–Bermuda route in 1937. In the
same year, a million-dollar marine airport complex was built to accommodate the seaplanes that offered the first regular passenger
flights from the United States. In 1938 Bermuda hosted nearly
85,000 tourists, three times the resident population. The income
generated by tourism at that time accounted for four-fifths of the
national revenue.

World War II temporarily halted the tourist trade but also paved
the way for its future development. An Anglo-American agreement
gave the United States the right to establish two defense bases in
Bermuda. The Americans built an airfield on reclaimed sea land and
contributed to such development as motor transport, paved roads,
and pest-control techniques. Consequently, when the war ended in
1946 Bermuda was a modernized vacation center and tech-
nologically ready for commercial air traffic.

The third period of tourism, running from the late 1940s through
the present, exhibits three distinctive features. First, there has been a
gradual transition from selective to mass tourism. Although the established elite have continued to patronize Bermuda, the newly
affluent middle classes have gradually come to represent the bulk of
the tourist trade. This process was hastened in the late 1950s by the
racial desegregation of hotels and restaurants and by the curtail-
ment of subtle techniques aimed at keeping out Jews. It was carried
further in the next two decades by the popularization of package
tours. Second, the vacation habits of the middle classes together

3.   Ibid., p. 158.

with the expansion of air services changed Bermuda from a winter to a summer resort. The high season now runs from March through November, while the winter months constitute a shoulder season. Third, the large hotels have become foreign-owned, in part because the capital resources needed to renovate and expand them in the late 1940s and 1950s came primarily from established investors abroad and in part because new luxury hotels, which more than doubled the number of tourist beds between 1960 and 1972, were built by international hotel chains. Consequently, of the ten hotels classified by the Department of Tourism as "large" (minimum 250 beds), nine are under predominately foreign ownership, while controlling interest in the tenth, a single-entity company, is held by nonnatives normally resident in Bermuda. These ten hotels accommodated 64 percent of Bermuda's tourists in 1975, with the remainder staying at small hotels, cottage colonies, private clubs, housekeeping complexes, guest houses, owner-run small facilities, and private homes.

The transition to mass tourism is demonstrated by the geometric rates of growth in the boom period of the 1960s. The 110,000 tourists at the beginning of the decade doubled by 1966 and nearly doubled again to more than 400,000 by 1971. Growth rates leveled off after the freeze on hotel building in 1973 and in the wake of the U.S. economic slump of the same period, but more recently they have begun to climb again. In 1976 Bermuda entertained 558,874 tourists, about one-fifth of whom were cruise-ship passengers and the rest regular visitors. The 1976 tourist volume represents an impressive 9 percent increase over 1975, a rate of growth comparable to that realized in the previous decade.[4]

The economic impact of tourism on Bermuda is staggering. The industry provides, directly or indirectly, three-quarters of all jobs; one in six workers is employed by the hotels alone.[5] The abundance of jobs results in "overemployment"—the widespread practice of working more than one job—coupled with the lowest unemployment rate and the highest labor force participation rate in the

4. Figures on tourist volume and lodging patterns are from the Bermuda Department of Tourism.

5. The preliminary report of a 1976 multiplier study conducted by the Institute of Economic Research in Wales indicates that there are 7,000 jobs directly dependent on the tourist trade, while another 14,000 jobs are indirectly provided by tourism. The Bermuda labor force recorded in the 1970 census was 27,075 persons.

world.[6] Tourist spending amounts to nearly $170 million,[7] more than twice the national budget and two-thirds of all foreign dollars received. The industry contributes 45 percent of the gross national product,[8] which itself averages $3,800 on a per capita basis—a figure astronomically high in comparison with the Caribbean.[9] Wages generally approximate North American standards. For example, the 5,000 blue-collar workers organized by the largest trade union average $10,000[10] annually on full-time jobs, while some hotel workers regularly report weekly incomes exceeding $300, tips included.

It is equally apparent that tourism in Bermuda is a phenomenological as well as an economic reality. During the eight-month peak season, for instance, one in five persons in Bermuda is a tourist. Hotels, nightclubs, restaurants, boutiques, and other physical symbols of tourist life extend into every part of the island's minuscule land area of eighteen square miles, confronting the Bermudian no matter where he turns in his isolated, insular homeland. In human terms, what does this confrontation mean?

The Black Club World

Like most subjects of anthropological investigation, the sociocultural consequence of tourism is as hard to find as it is to

6. Dorothy Newman, *The Population Dynamics of Bermuda* (Hamilton, Bermuda: Government Publication, 1972), p. 9. Newman's study, an analysis of 1970 census data, puts the unemployment rate at 1 percent and the labor force participation rate—the ratio of the economically active population to the total population over age sixteen—at nearly 100 percent for men and 60 percent for women. Unemployment climbed as a result of recession in the middle 1970s and now stands at an estimated 2.5 percent.

7. The multiplier study (see footnote 5) set the figure at $166,766,000 for 1975. Dollar amounts are all in U.S. dollars.

8. Cambridge Research Institute, "The Contribution of International Business to the Economy of Bermuda" (Cambridge, Mass., 1972).

9. The $3,800 per capita GNP is an estimate made by the World Bank for 1971. Other per capita GNPs in the Commonwealth Caribbean for the same year, also estimated by the World Bank, are as follows: Antigua, $410; Grenada, $330; Bahamas, $2,400; Jamaica, $720; Barbados, $670. All figures reported in the *Royal Gazette*, February 27, 1974, p. 3.

10. This figure is based on mean salaries reported in the *Census of Establishments 1971* (Hamilton, Bermuda: Government Publication, 1973), with adjustments made for average wage hikes between 1970 and 1977.

analyze. In Bermuda the search led to an impressive network of indigenous recreational clubs developed by blacks, who account for three-fifths of the resident population and nearly four-fifths of the native-born population.[11] Their club life-style centers on sociability, sport, entertainment, and hedonistic indulgence. On weekdays an active member spends most of his free time at the club bar, fraternizing with male companions and occasionally making a sexual overture to an available woman. On weekend afternoons the scope of activities is broadened by cricket and soccer games as well as a variety of other sports, all sponsored by the clubs. At night the clubs hold dances, parties, and live shows. In the summer the pace is further accelerated by about ten major sports festivals, all one- or two-day holidays and occasions of communal license.

This brief description is enough to suggest that the club world is a reflection of the tourist world, a native imitation of the free-spending, pleasure-seeking orientation of visiting vacationers. Indeed, the Bermudian-tourist parallel in life-styles has not gone unnoticed. It was officially propagated in 1951—the beginning of what I have called the period of mass tourism—when a government commission of inquiry observed that Bermuda's high rates of illegitimacy were attributable to the "holiday atmosphere" generated by large-scale tourism, specifically the tourists' conspicuous consumption of alcohol and indecent standards of dress and conduct.[12] This proposition was partially restated by the commission that investigated the 1968 riots[13] and is regularly put forth by editorialists, ministers of church and cabinet, magistrates and schoolteachers.

The popular view of the clubs has a measure of historical support. In the century before World War II the major black secular organizations in Bermuda were the lodges or "friendly societies." Their primary purpose was the sponsorship of beneficial programs—savings projects, gift clubs, credit unions, sickness and death benefits, scholarships, and the like. A secondary purpose was recreational; the lodges ran picnics, concerts, theatrical productions,

11. Data presented in this section are drawn largely from my study, *Black Clubs in Bermuda* (Ithaca and London: Cornell University Press, 1973), and from my observations made during fieldwork in 1976.

12. *Report of Commission of Enquiry into the Growth of Population and Illegitimacy* (Hamilton, Bermuda: Government Publication, 1951).

13. Hugh Wooding and others, *Bermuda Civil Disorders: 1968 Report of Commission* (Hamilton, Bermuda: Government Publication, 1969), p. 79.

and occasional sports events. The clubs, most of which originated during the first four decades of the twentieth century, had the same purposes as the lodges but in reversed priority. Two of the earliest clubs, in fact, were started when a cricket rivalry grew too big for the lodges to promote. And unlike the lodges the clubs have bars, which average more than $100,000 a year in sales and which support the sporting and beneficial programs.

In the 1940s there were about fifty active lodges. Today there are a half dozen, all with small and elderly memberships. Conversely, the clubs have realized their greatest growth in the period of the lodges' decline. Since 1960 most clubs have at least doubled their memberships, acquired additional properties and playing fields, established ladies' auxiliaries, and diversified their role as sports organizations by building lounges, cabarets, and cocktail bars to accommodate entertainment productions. The clubs have also grown in number from fourteen in 1970 to eighteen today. They claim an average membership of 400 men and a combined membership that is an estimated half of the adult male black population. In brief, the three decades of mass tourism in Bermuda have seen the virtual disappearance of the lodges—organizations devoted to temperance and saving—and the corresponding rise of the clubs—organizations devoted to sport, entertainment, and indulgence.

Although the club world reflects the hedonism of the tourist world, it developed as a response by blacks to racial segregation, which prevailed in Bermuda into the mid-1960s. Denied access to white clubs, blacks developed their own to sponsor cricket, soccer, and other team sports. As a consequence, sport is suffused with racial-cultural meaning in Bermuda. The outstanding illustration is Cup Match, a club-sponsored cricket competition and festival that commemorates emancipation from slavery and that has become—like many other club-centered sports festivals—a secular ritual for the stylization and political expression of black identity.[14]

In a broader sense sport has become a paradigm of racial strategy, as indicated by the club vice-president who told me:

> When I was a kid you not only felt that nothing could be done businesswise unless you were white, but sportswise unless you were white. But quite a number of blacks didn't believe this. The clubs are

14. Frank Manning, "Cup Match and Carnival," paper presented to the Burg Wartenstein Symposium on Secular Ritual, Gloggnitz, Austria, 1974.

a means of getting the boys playing cricket, playing soccer. As the boys began to get local dominance and then international recognition, I think there was some carry-over into other spheres.

The carry-over from sport has many dimensions. Individual clubgoers typically pursue occupational objectives through "game plan" strategies based on the club proverb, "You've got to speculate to accumulate." Collectively they see race relations as a sporting contest for economic power in which blacks are challenging whites for a coveted prize. The notion of competition is exemplified by independent business activity. In 1969–70 my informal survey of active clubgoers revealed that 20 percent were business owners,[15] compared with 11 percent of the black male population as a whole as reported in the 1970 census. Another 13 percent had invested in businesses, usually black-controlled, while 12 percent expressed the ambition to acquire businesses in the near future. While most of this business activity remains small scale, the club system furnishes a strong inducement for blacks to see themselves as competitors rather than clients in the white-dominated economic order. This type of reorientation of thought is surely a necessary precondition of any systematic change.

The clubs themselves have engaged directly in economic competition. At least four clubs have moved against established real estate interest by acquiring housing accommodations which they rent at reasonable rates. But the most significant commercial development has been the formation of the Bermuda Clubs' Association, a company owned and managed by the subscribing clubs. Previously tried without lasting success, it was revived in the mid-1970s. The association imports its own brands of liquor to supply the clubs, as well as regular shipments of meat, which are put on sale to individual club members. Looking ahead, the association has acquired a charter that allows it to run hotels, organize tours abroad, and develop a variety of local business ventures.

The influences of sport are complemented by those of entertainment—dances, parties, "cocktail sips," fashion shows, and similar events. Two themes prevail. The first is black racial-cultural identity expressed in music, dance, dress, and performances drawn from

---

15. The survey population consisted of fifty-five men in three clubs, chosen after several months of fieldwork, because they were deemed generally representative of the club following.

Afro-American and Afro-Caribbean genres and evoking the social experience and aesthetic sensitivities of black Bermudians. The second is stylistic glamour—elegance, sexuality, and cosmopolitan sophistication—drawn primarily from the Bermudian tourist environment. In the context of entertainment the two themes are interchanged in a symbolic process[16] that enhances black identity with the material allurements of the tourist world, while conversely relating a glamorous style to a setting that is recognized as black and native.

The classic Durkheimean proposition that ritualized symbolic action makes the obligatory desirable is exemplified here. What for black Bermudians was once obligatory—withdrawal from white society and retreat into the clubs—is rendered desirable by glamorizing the racial identity and cultural tradition which the clubs embody. This helps explain why the clubs not only have persisted since the end of legalized segregation but actually have achieved their greatest growth. Having carried the black struggle through its hardest times, the clubs have become a powerful symbol of racial and cultural pride.

Like the motivation to compete economically, the motivation to develop a positive black identity has important implications. Empathy with Afro-American and Afro-Caribbean genres of entertainment encourages the clubgoer to shift from his traditional insular folk identity as a "coloured Bermudian" to a far broader racial solidarity and common cultural experience. He is also influenced by the close relation between Antillean entertainment forms, notably calypso and reggae music, and political movements.[17] The embellishment of political purpose with popular Afro-American and Afro-Caribbean styles has become a prominent trend in Bermuda. To cite one of numerous examples, the black Progressive Labour party eschewed Western dress in its 1976 parliamentary campaign in favor of shirt-jacs and kareba suits, made fashionable in Bermuda through the medium of club entertainment.

More easily recognized political influences emanate from the club bar, the principal center of fraternal sociability for thousands of Ber-

16. Discussed theoretically in Victor Turner, *The Forest of Symbols* (Ithaca and London: Cornell University Press, 1967), pp. 28–30, 54–55.
17. See A. W. Singham, *The Hero and the Crowd in a Colonial Polity* (New Haven and London: Yale University Press, 1968), pp. 276–82; and Gordon Rohlehr, "Calypso and Politics," *Moko* (Port of Spain, Trinidad), October 28, 1971.

mudian men. The club bar projects an image of swank sophistication consistent with the ambience of Bermuda's hotels, restaurants, and commercial bars. But unlike these establishments the club bar is commonly viewed as a second home, and those who gather there are a cross-section of native society. Accordingly, what is learned in club conversations tends to resonate with an emotional fervor and a sense of authority that greatly enhance both its impact and its credibility.

In bar conversations the macaronic argumentation, joking, gossip, and storytelling typical of black speech reach a high level of verbal performance. But public issues are also discussed in a mixed comical-serious vein, often at the coaxing of black politicians and labor leaders who have become increasingly aware of the clubs' political potential. Roughly three-quarters of the respondents in my 1969–70 survey revealed that the club had influenced their understanding of issues and problems in Bermuda, most of them tracing the influence to informal conversations at the club bar.

The political role of the clubs has been extensive. They were a meeting place for the embryonic labor movement in the 1940s, for the desegregation movement in the late 1950s, and for the universal suffrage movement in the early 1960s. The Progressive Labour party (PLP), formed in 1963, held many of its organizational meetings in clubs, and the international Black Power Conference which convened in Bermuda in 1969 used a club stadium for its public events. In the 1976 parliamentary election officials of two clubs publicly endorsed the PLP (the first time an official endorsement was made by a club), three clubs let the party use their premises for campaign rallies, and four clubs provided polling day headquarters for PLP candidates.

On another level, club sport, entertainment, and sociability can be seen to have a primal cultural significance. In the Bermudian context (as well as the broader Afro-American and Afro-Caribbean contexts) there are two basic types of popular heroes: sportsmen and entertainers. Both are players who both compete and perform. The appeal of sportsmen depends not only on their athletic talents but also on their ability to entertain the public with flamboyant displays of personal style, on and off the field. Conversely, entertainers not only perform for their audience but also vie against other entertainers for rank, title, and prestige.

The cultural interrelation between competitive encounter and dramatic performance throws light on the significance of the figure who holds sway at the club bar—the "good talker" or "man of words."[18] As I have shown with respect to Bermuda and as others have argued on a broader scale, oral communication among blacks is not merely a means of conveying information in the rational or technical sense.[19] It is also an expressive device commonly used in contests of verbal fluency and to impress, amuse, or persuade an audience. The good talker, then, also is both competitor and performer. His latent role is that of generating and sustaining popular appreciation for the qualities that are demonstrated more glamorously by sportsmen and entertainers.

In sum, the club world embodies diverse influences and symbolic orientations. Each sphere of club activity—sport, entertainment, and sociability—reflects to a certain extent the image of tourism, particularly its affluence, sophistication, elegance, and hedonism. But this reflection or imitation is only one level of the sociocultural reality that the club world incorporates. On a second level the clubs are monuments to the black experience under segregation as well as centers of economic, cultural, and political influences that relate the clubgoer to conditions and processes in the wider contemporary society. And on a third level the clubs perpetuate and popularize the competition-performance orientation that is expressive of black Bermudian culture. Thus the club world not only revitalizes the native cultural identity but also harnesses that identity to economic and political objectives related to native interests.

If nothing else, the proposition that tourism can stimulate cultural revitalization rather than cultural deterioration should serve to counterbalance the pejorative slant of some sociologists toward tourism. McKean's description of revitalization in Bali probably comes closest to the case presented here.[20] Tourist patronage of artistic productions, he contends, not only provides revenue that enables the performers to perfect and develop their techniques but also generates an overall sense of pride among the Balinese in seeing the

18. Roger Abrahams, "Patterns of Performance in the British West Indies," in Norman Whitten, Jr., and John Swed, eds., *Afro-American Anthropology* (New York: Free Press, 1970), pp. 163–79.

19. See Manning, *Black Clubs in Bermuda*, pp. 61–63; and Thomas Kochman, *Rappin and Stylin Out* (Urbana and London: University of Illinois Press, 1973).

20. Philip McKean, "Tourism, Culture Change, and Culture Conservation in Bali," paper delivered at the International Union of Anthropological and Ethnological Sciences, Chicago, 1973.

products of their culture appreciated by a foreign audience. My own contention, though, has a broader view of tourism as a source of symbols and images that resonate with opulence, elegance, and indulgence. These symbols are absorbed into indigenous cultural expressions and suggest that the material glamour of tourism can be part of a black frame of reference.

The association of indigenous culture with metropolitan style invites a provocative analogy between the Bermudian clubs and revitalization movements such as the "cargo cult."[21] As an extensive anthropological literature indicates, colonized peoples have frequently responded to the presence of metropolitan wealth and power by reasserting their cultural traditions in guises drawn from metropolitan imagery. On the surface this response passes as an imitation of the metropolitan life-style, but on a deeper level it can be read as a symbolic statement that metropolitan status and goods (the cargo) will pass into native hands. This type of revitalization has broad political significance and has often supported the movement toward national independence.[22]

This analogy between the club world and the cargo cult has an important theoretical implication. Although the colonial aspects of tourism are widely recognized, especially in the Caribbean, tourism has not been systematically investigated within the framework of social theory on colonialism. A revitalization model moves the study of tourism in this direction, relating it to a field of inquiry that is rich in both comparative data and conceptual insight.

There are, of course, obvious and important differences between the response of the black Bermudian clubs and that of the classic cargo cults. Cargo cult mythology typically refers to an incipient millenium in which native destroys colonial, appropriating the superior position and overturning the social order. In contrast, the black Bermudian sees his adversary as the native white elite rather than the foreigner and aspires to compete economically and politically rather than to create a new society. This difference suggests a look not only at the native response to a metropolitan experience but also at the broader context within which a particular response is

---

21. Anthony Wallace, "Revitalization Movements," *American Anthropologist*, vol. 58 (1956), pp. 264–81.
22. See Peter Worsley, *The Trumpet Shall Sound* (London: Macgibbon and Kee, 1957).

evoked and sustained. The next section will therefore discuss Bermuda's distinctive form of tourism and its intersection with native life.[23]

Impact and Encounter

Tourism has had a less bothersome and disruptive impact in Bermuda than in many other countries, notably the islands of the Caribbean, for several reasons. As a maritime-oriented society from the early seventeenth to the mid-nineteenth century, Bermuda has had long exposure to outside cultures and influences, especially those of the eastern United States and Atlantic Canada. Tourism itself has existed for over a hundred years, making the present generation of adult Bermudians the third to have known it and the second to have experienced it as the most important sector of their economy. This long-term exposure to the outside world contrasts with the situation in the eastern Caribbean, where isolated peasant societies have been assaulted in the past two decades with sudden, urgent appeals to retool themselves to the demands of mass tourism.

The traditional character of the Bermudian environment has been carefully preserved. Rigid planning codes stipulate the new buildings — residential as well as commercial — must be consistent with the island's distinctive architectural style. Driving remains on the left and at twenty miles an hour. Rental cars and billboards are

23. Although I have argued that the clubs sustain black culture and support political and economic influences consistent with black interest, I realize that this is only one perspective. Within Bermuda the clubs are criticized by two large black groups. First, the evangelical Protestant churches, which, like the clubs, have a predominately working-class constituency, condemn club activity as sinful and hold the clubs strictly off-limits. Second, the middle class views the club life-style as socially inappropriate from the standards of bourgeois respectability.

Social scientists are sometimes skeptical about the clubs for other reasons. They question whether the economic competition, cultural pride, and political participation encouraged by the clubs are really effective against the established order controlled by whites. In response, I can only suggest three considerations: (1) Blacks have recently made significant gains in Bermuda, some of them partly traceable to club influences. (2) Insofar as the cargo cult analogy holds, there is a sizable body of work which shows that cultural revitalization often generates subsequent sociopolitical movements. (3) Without the vision of a better life and the motivation to seek it, no democratic change is possible.

prohibited so that the roads retain the charm of the winding horse-paths they were until 1946 when motor traffic was begrudgingly allowed. Interestingly, environmental conservation is done because of, not in spite of, tourism. It is believed that tourists do not want another Miami Beach or San Juan but a resort that preserves its insular quaintness and peculiar charm. Hence Bermuda is kept "another world," to appropriate the title of the island's best-known native song.

The economic benefits of tourism are distributed widely enough that deprivation relative to either the native elite or the tourists themselves is minimized. The cost of living is high, of course, as customs duties are the chief source of public revenue and virtually all food, clothing, and manufactured goods are imported. But because there is no income tax, take-home pay is close to gross pay. There is an absence of poverty and its manifestations such as slums and malnutrition, the national level of consumerism and material ownership ranks among the highest in the world, and the overall standard of living (literacy, educational level, health, life expectation) surpasses that of most Western industrialized countries.[24] The general problem in Bermuda is not of providing the physical means of modern comfort but of restricting their use; for example, no household can have more than one car, a ruling to control the high density and congestion of motor traffic. In short, Bermuda, sustained by tourism, exemplifies the affluent society.

The abundance of moderately well-paying jobs accounts in part for the conspicuous absence of hustling. There is no begging, no trinket selling on the streets or beaches, and no offers of sight-seeing assistance from self-styled guides. Taxi drivers wait till they are hailed instead of imposing themselves on the tourist, and all cabs are metered. Selling is restricted to licensed premises, prices are standardized and nonnegotiable, and merchants who do not have what a customer is looking for will typically refer him elsewhere rather than try to sell an unwanted item. No brothels exist, and there is no public solicitation of either female prostitutes or the well-known beach boys of the Caribbean; if "tourism is whorism" as some of its critics contend, Bermuda is literally exempt.

Finally, the economy, like the environment, is carefully controlled. Aside from the hotels all businesses operating in Bermuda

24. Newman, *The Population Dynamics of Bermuda.*

are required to be at least 60 percent Bermudian-owned. This includes banks, insurance companies, real estate developers, and all other commercial enterprises that in the Caribbean are typically owned by metropolitan interests. The exemption of hotels from this requirement seems at first to compromise the integrity of local control, but there is a strong argument that the profitability of large luxury hotels—the only ones that are foreign-owned—is marginal in a society where labor costs are high but prices must remain internationally competitive. This contention is supported by the recent heavy losses sustained by private as well as nationalized hotels in the Caribbean, despite their considerably lower expenses for wages.

Foreign ownership of large hotels accords with cultural as well as pragmatic considerations. The economic elite of Bermuda have always been middlemen rather than primary producers. They were privateers, pirates, wreckers, and merchant transporters throughout the maritime period, import-export agents during the era of high agricultural production from 1870 to about 1920, and have been merchants, bankers, real estate dealers, and importers under the economy of tourism and international finance. With the gradual democratization of economic opportunity during the past two decades these same middle positions have attracted blacks, Portuguese, and other whites who were traditionally excluded from the ascriptive elite. Given this business culture, foreign ownership of large hotels was not a major issue until the labor union used it in 1976 as a means of gaining public support for a threatened hotel strike. The campaign failed and the strike was not called. A few months later a stratified random sample of public opinion revealed that a mere 8 percent of whites and 47 percent of blacks agreed with the proposition that "the amount of foreign ownership in Bermuda is a threat to the economic and social well-being of the island."[25]

Apart from the issue of foreign ownership, these statistics suggest the extent to which race remains a basic division in Bermudian society. Race is also a fundmental aspect of the encounter between resident and visitor. Although the Bermudian population is two-fifths white, service positions are filled overwhelmingly by blacks. And although black Americans have become a visible element in the tourist trade in recent years, the great majority of tourists are white.

25. The survey, which I conceived and administered, interviewed 301 persons in August 1976.

To understand the relation between Bermudian and tourist one must therefore look carefully at Bermuda's distinctive racial system. Historically, black Bermudians were cast as seafarers, artisans, and domestics, positions in which they experienced a physical and personal closeness to whites that was unknown in the plantation societies of the Caribbean.[26] Legalized segregation institutionally separated the races, but biracial ties, often affective and intimate, developed in the margins and interstices of the social structure. The transactional context of race relations was the patronage system, the central principle of social organization in Bermuda. Through the distribution of jobs, mortages, credit, charity, and other forms of largesse, the white elite established themselves as a "benevolent oligarchy," securing the economic clientage, political allegiance, and general subordination of the black majority.

The personalism of the patronage system coupled with the stereotyped roles of white paternal benefactors and black filial dependents facilitated the folk concept of Bermuda as a large, extended family—a metaphor that is also invoked in the Caribbean, where it serves as an antistructural counterpoint to the structural divisions of class and color. The Bermudian experience of living in a small, isolated, and extremely close community has contributed further to the family metaphor, as have kinship ties that extend across racial lines. The proverbial statement "We (Bermudians) are all one family" has, then, several levels of meaning, and, despite the institutional separation of the races and the disparities associated with it, racial divisions are in part overcome on an informal level.

Race is, then, a paradox. It has been the basis of complete institutional segregation, considerable socioeconomic disparity, and radical cultural and ideological bifurcation. Bermuda is, after all, one of the Western hemisphere's outstanding examples of a thoroughgoing race society. But in the realm of personal interaction there has been mannered politeness and external warmth between the races, a spirit kindled by the ideal of family closeness as well as by the practical considerations of patronage. Social relations have masked and tranquilized social organization.

The elitist social background of most pre-World War II tourists enabled them to slip easily into the role of the Bermudian gentry.

---

26. Elsie Parsons, "Bermuda Folklore," *Journal of American Folklore*, vol. 38 (1925), pp. 239–66.

Blacks responded to their presence with a display of extraordinary courtesy and ebullient hospitality, not only in the service encounter but in all types of spontaneous interaction. The custom evolved of recognizing every tourist on the street with a smile, a wave, or a word of greeting. Longer exchanges easily followed, the Bermudian typically taking time to explain his country and to converse (astutely, in many cases) on any subject the tourist cared to raise. This pattern of warmth and civility was reinforced throughout the socialization process. A middle-aged informant recalled that when he was in school the only acceptable excuse for being late was to tell the teacher that he had stopped to help a tourist. Newspapers frequently remind their readers that tourists rank native friendliness as Bermuda's chief asset, and editorials attribute tourism slumps elsewhere to sullen attitudes and bad manners. Laudatory letters to the editor written by tourists are given conspicuous play in the press and are often cited in political speeches. Determined to be personally convinced about tourist impressions of Bermudian behavior, a hotel night-watchman once took it upon himself to read all the postcards that were deposited in the mail chute each day; he concluded that 90 percent of the guests mentioned the friendliness of the people, a finding which he has orally publicized for years.

In this type of culture Bermudians came to present themselves to visitors as a society not of waiters and bellhops but of social directors and public relations artists. The ritual that Bermudians term "meeting and greeting" is what Singer calls a "cultural performance": a dramatized behavior pattern through which a people demonstrate—to themselves and their observers—the core meanings of their self-image.[27] The economic success of tourism has bolstered the value of the performance, as has the positive response of tourists. Hence, unlike other societies—notably those of the Caribbean—where the encounter has become associated with colonial servitude and racial subordination, Bermuda has evolved a set of symbols that define amiable interaction with tourists as an essential expression of social identity and cultural character.

It is problematic whether the meaning of the resident-tourist encounter will be transformed by the strains that Bermuda has undergone in recent years. First, there are the depersonalizing effects of

---

27. Milton Singer, "The Cultural Pattern of Indian Civilization," *Far Eastern Quarterly*, vol. 15 (1955), pp. 23–36.

mass tourism itself—high numbers, tour packaging, and rigid organization of holiday time. While volume continues to rise, average length of stay has declined from nearly seven to about five nights in the past decade. The modern resort hotels tend to restrict the encounter by sheltering the tourist in a kind of "total institution."[28] Without leaving the grounds of the hotel a tourist can take all his meals, shop in twenty different stores, play golf and tennis, have the use of several swimming pools or a private beach with full cabana facilities, and enjoy a varied program of nightclub entertainment. Such tourists encounter the hotel staff, of course, but their exposure to the wider society is clearly limited.

The more obvious strain, however, comes from the process of political change. As indicated by the discussion of club activity, Bermuda has been intensely politicized in the past two decades by the achievement of universal suffrage, the emergence of party politics, and the constitutional establishment of representative government. Political control remains in the hands of the United Bermuda party (UBP), no longer a front for the merchant aristocracy but still a guardian of the colonial system and the interests of white capital, both local and foreign. Its opposition is the Progressive Labour party (PLP), entirely black, moderately socialist, and strongly anticolonial. Though numerically insignificant in Parliament from 1963 to 1976, the PLP forced important concessions with regard to civil rights, social services, and constitutional change. Its substantial gain of seats in the 1976 election put it within striking distance of a parliamentary majority, a prospect that would almost surely lead to national independence, widespread tax reforms, and electoral changes that would make it difficult for the UBP to regain power, at least as presently constituted and ideologically situated. In short, the politicization of Bermuda has crystallized racial division and posed what a good number of white Bermudians consider a catastrophic threat.

Yet, with a few striking exceptions, black agitation has been confined to the level of formal political action. The race system remains a coincidence of opposites, a juxtaposition of structural confrontation and interpersonal civility. Race relations, both between Bermudians and with foreign visitors, retain their cordial and indeed ingratiating style. The tourist is still convinced that he has come to the

---

28. Erving Goffman, *Asylums* (New York: Doubleday, 1961).

travel agent's promised "paradise," not to the midst of a polarized and precipitous political situation.

The separation of the political from the personal is exemplified by black Bermudian attitudes toward the West Indies. Politically, the West Indies are widely admired for making greater progress toward decolonization than Bermuda has. But the personal relations of West Indians with tourists are strongly criticized by blacks familiar with the Caribbean. The following comments, both made by ardent PLP supporters and confessed admirers of West Indian nationalism, are rather typical: "Down South (the Caribbean), Departments of Tourism promote tourism. Here (Bermuda), everyone promotes tourism." And "What makes us different is that we can serve you without being subservient to you. They (West Indians) can't."

Such attitudes help to explain why tourism in Bermuda has never been severely attacked, not even during the height of black radicalism in the late 1960s. In partisan politics tourism is like the church and the family—an unquestioned moral and cultural good. Debate is concerned only with making it better or extending its benefits. Consider the remarkable similarity between the tourism planks of the two political parties in the 1976 election campaign:

> The United Bermuda Party is committed to increasing participation by Bermudians in our most important industry, and policies which are directed towards improving services to our visitors.
> Visitors come because we are a friendly people in a socially and politically stable community. This has been the key to our success in the past, and is the foundation on which to continue to build in the future.

The PLP's plank differed little:

> In the specific area of tourism every effort will be made to increase productivity, and to reshape this industry so that investments will realize more profits. Moreover, increased attention will be given to the further development of activities that will extend the season.

It is apparent that the wide ideological and racial gap between the parties virtually disappears on the subject of tourism.

Conclusion

In sum, Bermuda reveals three distinctive features: (1) a process of culture revitalization achieved through the fusion of black racial and cultural consciousness with glamour, opulence, and stylistic sophistication; (2) a system of planning and control that has developed tourism without destroying the natural or social environment and that has distributed the material benefits of tourism throughout society; (3) a tourist-native encounter that evolved easily from indigenous patterns of race relations and that has persisted in its essential form by becoming a positive symbol of cultural identity and national pride.

What impresses me most about Bermuda is not the achievement of a revitalizing cultural synthesis but the extent to which the synthesis has been institutionalized and implemented in the club milieu. The synthesis itself—the association of the indigenous culture with the material wealth of tourism—is approximated in many Caribbean festivals, notably the Antigua Carnival.[29] Yet the revitalizing thrust of Carnival does not appear to have moved beyond the festival context; in day-to-day life tourism remains a bothersome presence.[30] Not only are there no clubs of the Bermuda type in Antigua, but the term "club" there is a euphemism for a whorehouse, itself a symbol of the mutual exploitation that seems to characterize the tourist-native encounter in many societies.

Nonetheless, the periodic ritualization of a revitalizing cultural synthesis in Antigua and other Caribbean countries bears witness to a native desire to preserve the indigenous heritage rather than surrender it to an overarching foreign presence. The spirit that motivates cultural pride and persistence needs to be better understood as well as the conditions that allow the process of revitalization to evolve on its own terms. Much can be learned from the Bermudian experience.

29. Manning, "Cup Match and Carnival."
30. Gregson Davis and Margo Davis, *Antigua Black* (San Francisco: Scrimshaw, 1973), p. 103.

CHAPTER 12

Paradise Reviewed: Tourism in Bali

Raymond Noronha
CULTURAL ADVISER TO THE BALI
TOURISM DEVELOPMENT BOARD

B ALI OFFERS AN EXCELLENT TESTING GROUND of various hypotheses current in the literature on the social impact of tourism.[1] First, it is an island, and it has been suggested that the impact of tourism is greater on islands than in other destination areas.[2] Second, from 1969 to 1975 tourism in Bali grew at an average of 27.5 percent a year, and it has been hypothesized that the rate of growth of tourism is correlated with its impact on a destination area.[3] Third, most tourists visit Bali because of its culture, a situation that has been thought to "commoditize" and debase culture in the eyes of the local populace because cultural manifestations are given a monetary value and performed on demand for tourists.[4] This paper will examine these hypotheses in order to determine whether tourism will destroy Balinese culture and lead to a "Waikikianization" of Bali, as the fear is commonly expressed.

---

1. Those who know Bali will easily recognize my indebtedness to my intellectual forebears who have written on this subject. Explicit thanks go first to M. J. Prajogo, former director general of tourism in Indonesia, for permitting me to write this while I was still his "employee"; second, to my colleagues at the Bali Tourism Development Board (BTDB) who provided me with much of the data used here; finally, to Philip McKean who kindly gave me his unpublished dissertation and permission to quote from it freely. The footnotes acknowledge, albeit partially, my other debts.
2. R. F. Dasmann, J. P. Milton, and P. H. Freeman, *Ecological Principles for Economic Development* (New York: John Wiley and Sons, 1973).
3. Vijay Joshi and Michael Sharpston, "Tourism and Development: A Study of Antigua," a restricted circulation report, prepared for the World Bank, 1973.
4. Davydd J. Greenwood, "Culture by the Pound: An Anthropological Perspective on Tourism as Cultural Commoditization," in Valene L. Smith, ed., *Hosts and Guests: The Anthropology of Tourism* (Philadelphia: University of Pennsylvania Press, 1977).

An incidental question is whether a nation should pursue tourism, whatever the social and cultural costs, if there is no other strategy for economic development.[5]

Bali is an island of indescribable beauty, situated on the eastern end of Java in the Indonesian archipelago. In 1974 its estimated population of 2.3 million lived in eight administrative districts formed from 558 village complexes. Administrative village boundaries do not coincide with those of the customary village. In the southern half of the island the customary village is smaller than the administrative unit; in the northern half it is just the reverse. To the Balinese villagers (88 percent of the population) the customary village and religious affiliation with village temples are more important than the administrative system. Each customary village and section of it (*bandjar*) has a leader who is skilled in the ways of custom. The bandjar determines with whom its members should associate and how they should behave. Common membership in the bandjar gives rise to numerous voluntary associations for irrigation and other activities such as dance, crafts, and music. Primary loyalty always remains with the customary village. Beyond the village only a common creed is shared: a pragmatic Hinduism. This sharing, however, is not action oriented. It is merely an adaptation to the numerous cultural intrusions on the island and is based on a common heritage and worship of common symbols in a hierarchy of temples.

Till recently, there was neither the need nor the motivation to go outside the village. Population pressures and declining agricultural yields now make it necessary for at least some villagers to seek employment outside. In the nonagricultural sector, government is the biggest employer. In the 1970s tourism offers a new employment opportunity to the Balinese, but the basic problem is whether the Balinese can profit from tourism without loss of their culture. Another question is whether the Balinese can be induced to cooperate with each other when there is no cultural precedent for cooperation beyond the confines of the customary village (except on occasion with neighboring villages on joint irrigation schemes). Furthermore, how can the two parallel systems—the legal-administrative and the customary—coordinate to control tourism and to secure the maximum economic profit from it?

5. C. E. Gearing, W. W. Swart, and T. Var, *Planning for Tourism Development: Quantitative Approaches* (New York: Praeger Publishers, 1976), p. 32.

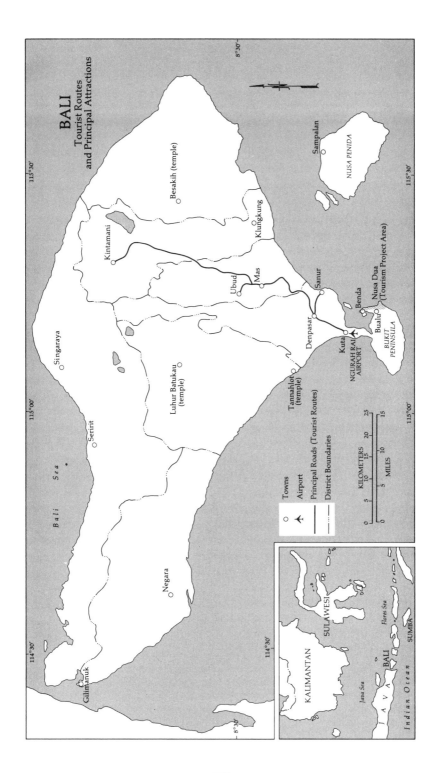

BALI
Tourist Routes
and Principal Attractions

Besakih (temple)

Klungkung

Kintamani

Mas

Ubud

Sanur

Denpasar

Nusa Dua
(Tourism Project Area)

Benda

Bualu

Kuta

NGURAH RAI
AIRPORT

BUKIT
PENINSULA

Singaraya

Luhur Batukau
(temple)

Seririt

Tannahlot
(temple)

Bali Sea

Negara

Gilimanuk

Sampalan

NUSA PENIDA

Towns

Airport

Principal Roads (Tourist Routes)

District Boundaries

KILOMETERS
0   5   10   15   20   25

0   5   10   15
MILES

KALIMANTAN

SULAWESI

Flores Sea

Java Sea

J A V A

BALI

SUMBA

Indian Ocean

8°30'

115°30'

115°30'

115°00'

115°00'

114°30'

114°30'

8°30'

The Tourist

Tourism, which both the central and regional governments believe offers the quickest and surest route for development, is of recent growth. In 1968 the first five-year plan for Indonesia viewed the profits made by neighboring countries from tourism and decided to adopt tourism as a strategy for economic development. This decision was echoed a year later by the regional plan for Bali and the first step toward mass tourism there: Tuban airport (now known as Ngurah Rai International airport) was enlarged to accommodate international flights.

Before 1969 there was a trickle of tourists, most of whom came by steamships, on a four-day stopover. Then, as today, Bali was not a terminal destination but only a port of call. Some visitors, however, came to stay: the painters Spies and Bonnet, the musicologist McPhee, the anthropologists Mead, Bateson, and Bello, the writer Covarrubias. They evoked new styles—the now invariate monkey dance for the tourist, the "young artists school" with its stylized naturalism. They recorded music, otherwise forgotten or likely to be. Though these resident expatriates touched Balinese life and opened avenues for the conversion of everyday expressions of arts and crafts to monetary gain, they remained empathic outsiders.

With the extension of Ngurah Rai airport, the tourist trickle turned into a stream. Over a period of seven years, between 1969 and 1975, the number of tourist arrivals by air grew from nearly 47,000 to more than 202,000, an average growth rate of 27.5 percent a year. If one includes the significant number of tourists who still use the surface route to Bali, the number of tourists visiting the island in 1975 would be about 275,000.[6]

Characteristics of tourists

Today's tourists represent nearly every nation. A recent analysis of some 40,000 passengers departing from Ngurah Rai airport in April, May, August, and December 1975 shows the following com-

---

6. Bali Tourism Development Board (BTDB), April 1975; and Ngurah Rai Airport Administration, February 1976.

position by nationality: Indonesians, 19 percent; Australians, 16 percent; Americans (from the United States), 13 percent; Japanese and English, 7 percent each. European nations together accounted for 35 percent of the visitors surveyed. Nearly half the non-Indonesian tourists visited Bali on a package tour. The median length of stay was four and a half days, and each visitor spent about US$43 a day. More than 70 percent of the tourists showed a clear preference for staying at Sanur, with most of the rest going to Kuta and Denpasar and only a few to Ubud.[7] Sanur, Kuta, and Denpasar (the capital of Bali) are the main resort areas and are situated in Badung district. They have replaced the former Dutch capital, Singaradja, in the north as tourist centers.

Tour routes

Tour routes on the island are the same as they were before the advent of mass tourism: The most frequent tours are to Ubud and Kintamani in the north, via Denpasar and Mas, with carefully planned stops at preselected art shops en route; to Besakih temple in the east, via Klungkung, again with a few preselected stops; and to the Tannahlot temple in the west. Travel agents and airlines play an important role both in the choice of tours and the selection of shops, since they arrange more than 70 percent of the local tours and the agents generally obtain commissions from the art shops. Few hardy souls venture out of the Kintamani-Besakih-Tannahlot triangle, but their number will grow as more tourists rent privately owned motorbikes from enterprising Balinese for US$3 to US$5 a day. Cultural performances for most tourists include the colorful and lively monkey dance, which does not tax the attention span. A smaller percentage watch the barong dance. And nearly every day there is a temple festival on the island graced by processions of festively clothed Balinese. For some, there is the tooth-filing ceremony; for the luckier, a cremation. The clicking of cameras does not disturb the Balinese, who apparently love audiences.

The encounter

Who do the tourists meet and what is the quality of their contact? No detailed analysis is available on this, other than a few remarks

7. BTDB, "Laporan Pendahuluan Survey Wisawatan Melalui Udara Di Bali," November 1976.

by McKean[8] and my own observations. A general conclusion is that the length and purpose of the visit correlate almost directly with the kind of Balinese met and the depth of that contact. At one end of the tourism spectrum is the charter tourist who, to borrow Cohen's colorful terminology, follows a preset migratory trail and views Bali from the environmental bubble of an air-conditioned room.[9] This institutionalized product of modern tourism stays generally at hotels of international standard in Sanur, where the decor is pseudoauthentic Balinese, religious pennants have been secularized and wave gaily at the entrance, and hotel personnel flit around in traditional Balinese costumes with flowers in their ears. These tourists are in formal contact with hotel employees, tour agents, and guides. I have wondered increasingly over the years whether this type of tourist is not more interested in the fellow members of the tour than in the Balinese, since fleeting formal relations seem to suffice for most, and sun and sand occupy a significant percentage of their stay in Bali.

At the other end of the tourism spectrum is the hippie, the "drifter tourist," whom McKean saw in large numbers at Kuta in 1971. Bali was, and still is to a much lesser extent, one of the stopping points in the hippie migratory trails of the 1960s and early 1970s.[10] According to McKean, hippies encountered mainly marginal, lower-income Balinese, but their interaction was flawed. The hippies and Balinese did not comprehend each other's behavioral patterns and goals, and this resulted in mutually incompatible relations and conflict. My observation of Balinese-hippie relations differs from McKean's in several respects: First, I discovered that most of the objections to hippies were voiced by officials and upper-class Balinese who rarely came in contact with them; the ordinary people accepted hippies with the curiosity and tolerance that marks most Balinese. Second, the Balinese adapted to the needs of hippies by inventing the "home-stay" in which tourists could reside with a Balinese family for as little as US$1.50 a day.

8. Philip F. McKean, "Cultural Involution: Tourists, Balinese and the Process of Modernization in an Anthropological Perspective," Ph.D. dissertation, Brown University, 1973.
9. Erik Cohen, "Nomads from Affluence: Notes on the Phenomenon of Drifter-Tourism," *International Journal of Comparative Sociology*, vol. 14 (1973), pp. 89–102.
10. K. Allsop has a perceptive and delightful description of these trails in "Across Europe and Out of Sight, Man," *Punch*, August 2, 1972.

Third, a source of conflict could result from the perception that all tourists are "rich," and hippies seem to counter that perception. Finally, the term "hippie" is loosely used in Bali to include anyone casually dressed by Western standards (jeans and long hair). From the time I first visited Bali in 1973 the number of hippies has been on the decline. Their places at Kuta have been taken by middle-income tourists who are interested in seeing Bali and meeting its people but are unwilling to pay the exorbitant rates that international-standard hotels charge for accommodation and food; nor do they wish to be confined to the rigid schedule of the charter tourist. Like their counterparts on package tours, budget tourists do not necessarily meet Balinese of a higher economic class.

Visitors to the island who stay longer than the average tourist come into contact with a wider section of the Balinese—artists, intellectuals, teachers, doctors, entrepreneurs—depending on the purpose of their stay. In no case, however, is the outsider accepted as a member of the community though the Balinese may establish a relation of respectful equality with him or her.

The Impact

The growth of tourism has had far-reaching social and economic effects on the island of Bali. It has provided new employment opportunities, not only in hotels but also in arts and crafts, in entertainment, and in travel agencies. This prospect of employment is one of the many factors contributing to population growth in the major tourist areas. At the same time, however, the tourist boom has resulted in the rising price of land, land speculation, and the conversion of land from agricultural to nonagricultural uses. More important, mass tourism has introduced organizational changes in Balinese tourism. There has been a transition of ownership out of Balinese hands, and the Balinese response to tourism is being increasingly orchestrated by outsiders—mainly Indonesians from Jakarta and transnational corporations.

Hotels and employment

From 1968 to 1975 the number of tourist accommodations in Bali increased by 300 percent. In April 1975 there were 116 hotels, with a total of 3,072 rooms. Of these, 109 were small hotels, with less than

50 rooms. But with this expansion there has been a gradual shift of ownership out of the hands of the Balinese. Except in the case of hotels like Bali Beach, the Hyatt, and the now defunct Kayu Aya, which were owned from the beginning by the government either entirely or in partnership with transnational corporations, most hotels are not now owned by Balinese.

Most of the small hotels, which were started in anticipation of profits from the tourist boom, are not profitable. They have banded together to form an association called the Bali National Hotels Association to try to compete with the larger establishments. The big hotels (particularly the Hyatt, Bali Beach, and Sanur Beach) not only benefit from economies of scale but also can indulge in price cutting. They have greater resources than do the small hotels to absorb losses when demand is low, links with airlines, and more effective representation abroad. Charter tourists are generally accommodated at these large hotels. The economic woes of the small hotels led the Private Development Finance Corporation of Indonesia to fund a study to investigate whether, for instance, common marketing and other services could make most of these hotels financially viable. The results have not been published.

Hotel employment is the major direct source of income from tourism for the Balinese. Each twin-bedded room averaged 1.5 employees, and in 1974 total employment was estimated at 5,438, of which 4,706 were Balinese.[11] Hotel employment has affected many more persons than this since employee turnover averaged twenty-one months, except at Bali Beach where services can be terminated only through involved and lengthy legal procedures. Average gross monthly salary was Rp13,000 (about US$31). Women accounted for 16 to 17 percent of all workers. Most jobs were obtained through personal application, and 39 percent of the total staff was trained. Although there were nine hotel training schools in Bali with an estimated enrollment of 1,500 pupils, 60 percent of the employers responding to a questionnaire stated that they did not rely on the training schools for their employees. The schools stated that 88 percent of their pupils had found employment, and the average waiting period after qualification was three months.[12] At three hotels in Sanur (Bali Beach, Hyatt, and Sanur Beach) 54 percent of the

11. Udayana University, "The Impact of Tourism on the Socio-economic Development of Bali" (Denpasar, 1974).

12. Government of Indonesia, International Labour Organisation (ILO), and United Nations Development Programme (UNDP), "Manpower Survey for the Hotel

employees were born in Badung district, and of these 16.6 percent were born in Sanur.[13] It should be expected that with a twenty-one-month turnover employees from more distant parts of Bali would migrate in search of employment. In fact, before the Hyatt Hotel opened in 1974 there were 7,000 applicants for 400 jobs, and many of these were from districts other than Badung. Most of the lower level jobs are filled by Balinese; the supervisory, managerial, and administrative posts are generally held by non-Balinese.

Handicrafts and art

The Department of Industry estimated that 4,000 woodcarvers were employed in 1973, most in the districts of Badung and Gianyar. Earnings vary with the size of the carving and according to whether the carver works independently or for an art shop. Udayana University estimated that an independent carver would receive about 40 percent of the sales price, whereas if he were employed by an art shop he would receive only 20 percent. One source estimates that woodcarvings of the value of US$50,000 to US$60,000 were exported in 1971,[14] but this estimate does not take account of carvings bought and personally carried home by tourists.

The independence and earnings of the Balinese woodcarver will, however, be affected by the rising price and growing shortage of wood. Ebony is imported; sawo, a red wood most suitable for carving, is obtained from Bali's forests. The prices of both have more than tripled since 1972 when sawo, for instance, cost Rp42,000 (about US$100) a cubic meter. This means that most woodcarvers can no longer afford to stock their own supplies. They are becoming increasingly dependent on art shops, a trend that will in turn proletarianize the woodcarvers and bring them less income.[15]

---

and Tourism Industry in Indonesia," Project INS/74/020 (Jakarta, 1974); and UNDP and ILO, "Training for Hotel Industry and Tourism: Project Findings and Recommendations," Project INS/72/020 (Geneva, 1975).

13. Checchi and Company, "Transportation for Nusa Dua," a report to the Directorate General of Tourism, Indonesia, and the World Bank (Washington, D.C., December 1974). This survey of areas from which hotel employees at three Sanur hotels had come found that 56 percent of the employees had migrated, 85 percent of them because of jobs.

14. Ruth Daroesman, "An Economic Survey of Bali," *Bulletin of Indonesian Economic Studies*, vol. 9 (1973), pp. 28–61.

15. I Gusti Ngurah Bagus ("The Impact of Tourism upon the Culture of the Balinese People," paper prepared for the Joint UNESCO–World Bank Seminar on the

Travel agents

As with hotels, the number of Balinese-owned travel agencies has decreased with the growth of tourism. Although there were forty-four agencies in Bali in 1975, only one was Balinese-owned, a drop from nine in 1970; most are ostensibly owned by Indonesians. The leading agency today, with an estimated 70 percent of the business, is PACTO, which is linked with the American Express Company. An estimated 1,036 persons were employed in travel agencies in 1974, 992 of them Balinese.[16] The monthly salary averaged Rp18,000 (US$43) but is not the only source of income for the travel agent; commissions from art shops and dance associations are an important component of total earnings.[17]

Entertainment

Dance and art are talents which cater only partly to the tourist demand. Udayana University estimated there were 1,929 entertainers in 1974, most of them part-time only and mainly from Badung district. Here, too, tourism has tended to decrease income from performances and increase competition among the bandjars. The earnings vary with the type of entertainment. In 1971 bandjar Bona earned US$21 a week for its weekly performance of the monkey dance;[18] in 1973 the 110 member troupe of bandjar Bengkel (near Denpasar) received between US$14 and US$17 for the monkey dance at Bali Beach and lower sums for other performances. Bandjars could earn more if they staged their own performances, but this requires extensive publicity and contacts with tourists and runs the risk that the audience may be too small to provide an adequate return. The bandjars therefore prefer to contract with hotels where most of the tourist performances are held. Competition among the bandjars for these contracts results in increasing control by the middlemen, mainly travel agents, even to the extent that the agents dic-

---

Social and Cultural Impacts of Tourism, Washington, D.C., December 8–10, 1976), quotes a 1972 Udayana University estimate that only 45 percent of woodcarvers and handicraft workers are independent. This percentage has probably decreased.

16. Udayana University, "The Impact of Tourism."
17. Bagus, "The Impact of Tourism."
18. McKean, "Cultural Involution."

tate the type and duration of the performance and the dancers' attire.[19] The actual income a bandjar receives depends on its bargaining ability and the commission it is willing to offer. In an effort to break the control of hotels and travel agents over bandjars, the district chief of Badung prohibited performances in hotels in 1975. This effort was unsuccessful, mainly because the bandjars lacked organization, the performances were not publicized, and there was no regular transport to them. The dances were soon resumed in hotels.

Guides

The term "guide" is a euphemism that includes taxi drivers and anyone else who happens to have some idea of a cultural item and answers questions. McKean has examined the role of the guide as a culture broker and has referred particularly to Oka as an ideal.[20] Oka is a rarity whom only a privileged few tourists ever meet, however, and it is Oka who chooses the persons he would guide. The majority must settle for a taxi driver, a partially qualified guide, an unemployed educated Balinese who wants to develop "business" connections with a foreigner, or a Balinese who has a motorcycle for hire or some batik to sell.

But unlicensed guides are not the only ones available. Both the Area Department for Tourism (DIPPARDA) and Udayana University, in conjunction with the Department of Education and Culture, conduct diploma courses for guides. It is not possible, however, to determine the number of successful pupils or their subsequent employment. My enquiries in 1973 and 1974 provided conflicting reports on these matters. The Bali Guide Association loosely estimated in 1974 that more than 120 guides were needed during the peak tourist season but could not estimate how many more. Nor was the association aware of the occupations of guides during the off-season. Estimating the number of trained guides in Bali is a difficult matter, particularly since many travel agents and hotel managers employ their relatives as guides. A good free-lance guide could average about US$70 a month if he worked fifteen days a month, while guides who work for leading travel agencies might earn between US$50 and US$80 a month. These estimates, however, refer

19. Bagus ("The Impact of Tourism") states that "all dance associations (*seka*) have relations with certain travel bureaus."
20. McKean, "Cultural Involution."

to only a small percentage of the guides in Bali. Guides dealing with large groups, or attached to a hotel of international standard, tend to be extremely impersonal. Contact between guide and tourist is formal and does not involve the intimate sharing of knowledge that an Oka can give.

All attempts to regulate guides have proved ineffective. In October 1974 the governor of Bali passed a decree requiring all guides to wear traditional Balinese dress. This decree has not been and cannot be enforced. Not only is there insufficient personnel but the most effective means of enforcement has not been tried: informing arriving passengers at the airport that they should employ only licensed and qualified guides. Thus the Balinese guide is often a person whom the tourist meets by chance and takes a fancy to, without any particular regard to qualifications.

Land

Land prices were relatively stable until speculation began in 1968, the year when it was first decided to foster the development of tourism. The number of sales transactions then increased remarkably in both Sanur and Kuta, and prices jumped accordingly: between 79 and 114 percent in Sanur in one year (1969–70) and between 43 and 100 percent in Kuta in three years (1967–70). Agricultural land was converted to nonagricultural purposes,[21] and although the price of farmland increased 50 percent from 1965 to 1971, reaching Rp12,000 (US$44) an aré, in tourist areas the price rose by 25 percent in one year to Rp50,000 (US$182).[22] Under Indonesian law, land cannot be transferred, except by lease, to non-Indonesians, and most of the land was sold to Indonesians from Jakarta.[23] By 1976 prime land in the Kuta area was as high as Rpl million (US$2,410) an aré.

In January 1970 a decree required all land sales within 200 meters of the sea to be approved by the office of the governor, and the num-

---

21. I Gusti Ngurah Bagus, "Sanur dan Kuta: Masalah Perhobahan social budaya di Daerah Pariwisata" (Denpasar, 1975).

22. McKean, "Cultural Involution," p. 203. An aré is a local measure equal to 81 square meters.

23. SCETO (Société Centrale pour l'Equipement Touristique Outre-mer), "Bali Tourism Study," draft report to the government of Indonesia/UNDP/IBRD, 6 vols. (Paris: United Nations Development Programme, January 1971), vol. 6, p. 60; vol. 2, p. 217.

ber of sales has since dropped. Widespread rumors of purchases under the names of nominees and of speculation in the western outskirts of Denpasar continue, however. The decree does not appear to apply here, and future development is projected.

Population

The Central Bureau of Statistics projected a population growth rate of 2.5 percent a year from 1971 to 1981. Most of this growth is confined to the three areas where tourism is the greatest: Badung, Gianyar, and Klungkung. The growth rate in these three districts has averaged over 5 percent in the past decade. The influx of people into Badung, and particularly the capital city of Denpasar, is owing to people's expectations of jobs, not necessarily the actual availability of jobs. In 1972 Badung reported only 31 percent of its labor force of 130,258 was fully employed, and 67 percent were underemployed. In April 1973, in an effort to stem the immigration of other Indonesians, particularly from Java, the governor of Bali passed a decree that no non-Balinese would be allowed to enter the island unless employment or housing were already provided. This decree exists on paper but is impossible to implement.

Distribution of Benefits

Though the information is inadequate, there are several levels at which the distribution of the benefits of tourism can be examined: national, regional, and local.

National and regional

SCETO reported that in 1969 visitors spent an estimated US$3.5 million, but of this only 35 cents of each dollar remained in Bali. McKean in 1973 quotes an estimate that tourism would constitute between 21 and 28 percent of Bali's gross domestic product in 1979, without taking into account multiplier effects.[24] Neither estimate is based on careful examination of facts. It is true that foreign exchange earnings from tourism in Bali have gradually overtaken

24. McKean, "Cultural Involution," p. 125.

those from other sources, but no study has carefully estimated leakages and how much of the earnings actually remain in Bali or in Indonesia. As the Development Faction report of the Indonesian Parliament pointed out, the tourism master plan accords the government of Bali only a minimal role, and the benefits received by the regional government are all indirect: through local taxes, the development fund, and from building permits. Bali has to rely on the central government for infusions of funds.

In the regional development budget for 1969, 22 percent of a total sum of nearly US$2.6 million was allocated for communications and tourism, while only 16.2 percent was allocated for social expenditure (health, family planning, education, culture, and the like). Details for later years are not available.

District

The impact of tourism at the district level has been uneven, as the regional development plan admits. By far the richest district is Badung, as shown by the fact that there were seventeen candidates for district chief in 1976, whereas poorer districts like Karangasem and Bangli had at most two candidates. Another index of the importance of Badung is the district budget. A 10 percent tax that tourists pay on food and accommodation is a direct contribution to the district, which also collects license fees from hotels, art shops, and restaurants. In 1972–73 Badung's receipts alone totaled US$4.79 million, which was 47 percent greater, for instance, than the receipts of the northernmost district, Buleleng, together with its grant from the regional government. Other districts have repeatedly complained of the inequities of a system that allows Badung to receive the major share of tax receipts by virtue of its location. In December 1972 the governor of Bali cajoled Badung into giving 30 percent of its receipts for distribution among other districts. Subsequent efforts to increase this percentage have not succeeded. There are mutual charges about lack of information as to how these funds are distributed and spent. Badung continues to be the richest district, with more schools and hospitals and better roads than any other.

Bandjar and individuals

At the bandjar level, both McKean and the Udayana University found no uniform procedure for the distribution of income derived mainly from cultural performances for tourists. Sometimes individuals receive a share of the earnings, or each family receives a percentage of the receipts, while the remaining portion is kept for the bandjar as a whole. In other cases the entire proceeds are reserved for the bandjar. Where proceeds are received by or distributed to individuals, no information is available on how they are spent. Personal observation, however, leads me to believe that the largest amounts are for prestigious items such as family ceremonies, family shrines, compound walls, and, more recently, for motorcycles. Where the proceeds, or part of them, are reserved to the bandjar the main expenditures are on bandjar temples, agricultural improvements, schools, new costumes, and gamelans (orchestras).

Personal observation confirms all reports that art shops, hotels, taxi drivers, and tour agents (including guides) increasingly control the distribution of tourism income by determining which groups can perform, whose artifacts will be sold, at what price, and when. The commission for guides, taxi drivers, and tour agents ranges from 10 to 30 percent of the sales price. Hotels choose which group will perform and are in a position to determine what price will be paid. Tour agents and taxi drivers can easily suggest to the freshly arrived tourist (in a land where tourist information services are not the best) which shops should be visited. Because the price is not fixed in most shops (except at the government handicrafts center at Tohpati, north of Denpasar, fortunately on the main tourist route), the money the artist, woodcarver, or basketmaker will receive varies enormously according to the bargaining ability of the purchaser. Tourist trade enterprises and hotels are easily able to dominate individual producers and bandjars on an island where the necessity and motivation for cooperation are found only within the customary village and where individuals and groups from different villages compete with each other. Furthermore the government has no administrative links with the customary units which produce the crafts.

The Balinese Response

The Balinese have responded to the opportunities tourism presents with a resilience that amazes even the most casual observer. They have seized every economic opportunity offered them, adapted styles of art and dance to suit the tourist, created a new kind of tourist accommodation, the home-stay, as an alternative to the staid and costly hotels, introduced the "bemo"—a three- or four-wheeler—and the motorcycle in areas where transport is minimal, and even formed modern bandjars.

In the field of art the Balinese have accepted new styles and forms introduced by foreigners. Bonnet started the young artists school of painting, and in 1932 Spies commissioned the first monkey dance, which has now become a staple for every tourist. Tjakorda Oka originated the tourist barong performance. The kebiyar (an individual mood dance), so rare today, was first perfected by Mario (of whom Covarrubias writes so ecstatically) in the 1920s and 1930s. Rembang was the culture broker who raised Sesetan bandjar to its cultural heights through recognition of tourist needs.

It is true that some of the ancient dances are dying out and that some crafts are being lost.[25] Tortoiseshell work has become less profitable, the *pandes* (a caste of silversmiths) of Celuk are no longer the sole makers of silverware, the manufacture of terracotta figures is left to one old man in Djasi (a village in east Bali), bone carving is a poorly paid art, and horn carving will soon die out. At the same time, batik has been adopted from Java by the Balinese. A new style of furniture is being manufactured at Belega, near Ngurah Rai airport. The market is flooded with woodcarvings and masks. Many of these products may offend the purist (Adrian Snodgrass refers to them as "blancmange nudes"), but this does not mean that excellent art is unavailable or dying out or that the tourist market has affected the quality of arts and crafts manufactured for religious purposes. These flourish, as all careful observers note. Tilem, Ambara, Hardja, and Ida Bagus Made, to mention only a few of the many fine artists, may turn out potboilers, but they never lose their talent for and appreciation of good work.

The influx of visitors has also brought other changes to Bali. New associations have been formed to take advantage of tourism.[26] The

---

25. Dale Keller and Associates (Adrian Snodgrass, research), "A Survey of the Small Industries, Materials, and Cultural Resources of Bali," report prepared for the Directorate General of Tourism, Indonesia (Hong Kong, 1972).

26. Bagus, for instance, reports in "The Impact of Tourism" that in the village of Batubulan, famous for its daily barong performance for tourists, voluntary associations increased 25 percent between 1966 and 1975.

former princes have adapted to the situation, and the upper strata are still in control—whether in the hotel business, as is the former ruling family of Badung with Puri Pemetjutan, or in dance academies such as Asti and Kokar, which train students not merely in traditional dance but also in modern adaptations. The Balinese have lost their insularity and are willing to tour other countries with their superb dance troupes. In Sanur the Beach Market managed by the bandjar reflects Balinese adaptiveness to modern economics, and a new bandjar of hotel workers comprises members of different faiths from different parts of Indonesia.[27] Tourism academies have been started, and hotel schools multiply. In Bukit some of the workers improving roads and building infrastructure have been accommodated by the villagers in their houses. In Bali the number of registered motorcycles rose from 11,988 in 1973 to 15,111 in June 1974, and 64 percent of these were registered in Badung district. In 1968 the total number of vehicles of all types registered was 7,725 as compared with 17,470 in 1973.[28]

There have also been other changes which are not easily measured. Beggars were unknown a few years ago; today, they are common in the marketplace. Beach vendors, each urging the tourist to buy his crudely fashioned wares or visit his beach stall, are legion and a pervasive nuisance. Tourists riding motorbikes on the beaches add another annoyance and foster pollution. Along the tourist routes large signs have mushroomed, mainly advertising beer. Some of the best sawahs (irrigated paddy fields) along the most frequented tourist route from Denpasar to Mas have been replaced by art shops, which hope to profit from the tourist boom, although few do and most are converted into residences. There is as yet no islandwide zoning legislation to control this uncoordinated growth of signs and shops. Even if there were, it is doubtful whether enforcement would be possible. Prostitutes are more evident today, particularly at Kuta, although the Balinese claim that all are immigrants. For some observers these are symptoms of cultural decay that mass tourism is said inevitably to bring; for others, they are mere warts that in no way detract from the greater benefits of tourism in Bali.

27. John S. Lansing, *Evil in the Morning of the World: Phenomenological Approaches to a Balinese Community* (Ann Arbor: University of Michigan Center for South and Southeast Asian Studies, 1974).
28. Checchi and Company, "Transportation for Nusa Dua."

Planning and Organizations

Balinese responses to tourism till 1968 were largely spontaneous, uncoordinated, and dependent on local resources and initiative. In that year the central government of Indonesia decided that if it were to encourage international tourism in Bali, planned development was preferable to further uncontrolled growth. In 1969 a consulting firm, SCETO, was employed to prepare a master plan for Bali financed by the United Nations Development Programme (UNDP) and with the World Bank as executing agency. In effect SCETO was asked to prepare a plan to facilitate the growth of mass tourism in Bali.

The master plan

SCETO's entire approach was "based on the Southeast Asian tourism market and on *quantity rather than quality tourism* because of the fact that the sole acceptable criterion for measuring its success is the return on invested capital."[29] They recognized that this approach would lead to distortions, which they "attempted to take into account but they were not always able to furnish appropriate solutions because of the lack of means to conduct ecological and sociological investigations."[30]

The drafters of the plan estimated that by 1985 nearly 730,000 tourists would visit Bali each year and spend an average of four days in luxury and first-class hotels. Concerned that such a large influx of tourists would destroy Balinese culture, they concluded that 6,950 rooms should be built at Nusa Dua and 2,500 rooms should be distributed among Sanur, Kuta, and Denpasar in the context of an urban development plan.

Nusa Dua lies on the eastern shore of a peninsula connected by a narrow isthmus to the main island of Bali. SCETO felt that because of its distance from most of the tourist attractions and its isolation from the Balinese community contact between tourist and Balinese

29. SCETO, "Bali Tourism Study," report to the government of Indonesia/UNDP/IBRD, 6 vols. (Paris: United Nations Development Programme, April 1971); the emphasis is supplied.
30. SCETO, draft report, January 1971, foreword.

could be regulated. Since the surrounding limestone plateau has hardly any agricultural value, construction there would not inter-fere with crop production, except for some coconut groves which would be removed. Land was easily available at a low price and without disruption of major communities. Furthermore, a large tourism resort at Nusa Dua would offer economies of scale. In con-trast, hotel development at Sanur and Kuta would be difficult. Land there was scarce and speculation had already begun. Sanur and Kuta would eventually form an urban conglomeration with Den-pasar that would present additional problems.

SCETO's concern about the potentially harmful effects of the con-tacts between tourists and Balinese is also seen in the basic premise of the master plan that any changes introduced should "reinforce, not detract from, traditional Balinese social structures."[31] It was recommended that control of excursion routes and proposed tour-ism centers should be in the hands of the village associations; that payments by the tourists should be to the bandjars, not to in-dividuals; that in order to encourage "cultural manifestations" in the villages, the goals of these centers should be greater employment rather than profit; and, finally, that each bandjar at the tourism cen-ters should have a representative in a wider association, then envi-sioned as the Bali Tourism Development Authority.

With hindsight it is easy to question some of SCETO's conclusions. It was aware of increasing land speculation and knew that both land and hotels were passing out of Balinese hands. It was also aware that neither the Balinese nor the regional government had the organizational and financial capability to create tourism centers and manage the proposed authority, and yet SCETO proposed con-trolled tourism, which would have the effect of introducing out-siders as middlemen and controllers. It also should have seen that the tourism resort proposed at Nusa Dua was beyond Balinese capa-bilities and would extend control by outsiders and leakages of tour-ism revenue. Finally, some may question SCETO's view that concen-tration of hotels at Nusa Dua would be preferable to dispersion. Such a concentration would increase the influx of job seekers into Denpasar and create additional problems since hardly any residen-tial facilities exist near Nusa Dua; nor would it contribute to the equitable distribution of revenues among the districts since Badung

31. SCETO, "Bali Tourism Study," April 1971, vol. 1, p. 9.

would again obtain most of the revenues. However, given SCETO's view that the type of tourist at Nusa Dua would be interested largely in beaches and golf and only peripherally in cultural activities, and also that revenue was the most important determinant of its recommendations, the proposed plan was drawn rather carefully.

The considerations mentioned above apparently did not disturb the central government, which adopted the master plan by presidential decree in 1972. There is no evidence that, in the process of formulation and adoption of the plan, the regional government and the Balinese bandjars were consulted. This apparent lack of consultation could possibly have stemmed from the fact that Bali lacked the funds and the capacity to formulate and execute a master plan and therefore had to rely on central intervention. In the four years following the decision to use tourism as a means of economic development and the adoption of the master plan, however, tourism in Bali changed radically, as mentioned earlier, and these changed conditions should have given the central and regional governments some cause for thought.

The Bali tourism project

The Bali master plan is equivalent to a statement of intentions; it can be put into effect only through local legislation and action. The first step in this process was the request of the government of Indonesia for World Bank assistance. The Bank was less optimistic than SCETO about the prospects for tourism development and conservatively estimated the rates of growth between 1978 and 1983 at 14 percent a year. The Bank agreed to support infrastructure construction for a resort area in Nusa Dua, but one that would at first contain only 2,500 rooms (to be built by 1985 at the latest). In both the construction and operation of the hotels it was agreed to offer preferential employment to members of the two villages closest to the proposed site. Infrastructure (roads, electricity, water) was to be improved in these villages and medical services provided by the hotels. The project also includes a demonstration farm to encourage vegetable production to supply hotels and help spread vegetable-growing techniques among Balinese farmers. The project provides for technical assistance to formulate zoning plans, excursion routes, and further execution of the master plan. The use of local materials is encouraged as well as building styles in conformity with Balinese traditional architecture, and an earlier regulation limiting the height of the hotel buildings to no more than fifteen meters is confirmed. Finally, the Balinese are assured continued access to beaches for both ceremonial and economic purposes.

It is realized that, given the scarcity of capital in Bali, hotels built under the project will be owned by non-Balinese and that most of the employees will come from Badung district. In addition, the Bank accepted the superficially attractive theory of regulating contact between tourists and hosts. This was questioned, but since the master plan had already been adopted the matter was not pursued further. To provide for balanced growth and also to ensure a reasonable economic return for Nusa Dua, the government of Indonesia agreed to limit accommodation in international standard hotels to 1,600 rooms outside the Nusa Dua area. The definition of international standard, however, was such that hotels of less than 100 rooms or without air conditioning could continue to be built.

Infrastructure building has already commenced at Nusa Dua. By October 1978, about a year later than originally scheduled, all the access roads were expected to be built, the layout completed, and water and electricity connected. It was also expected that the zoning regulations for Nusa Dua and the Bukit peninsula would be adopted by then. As of June 1977, however, responses from hotel investors were limited, and no firm contract had been entered into for hotel construction. One advantage of this delay is that it offers an opportunity for the central and provincial governments to complete the organizational arrangements that will give the Balinese a greater voice in determining the pace and direction of tourism development.

Organizations

Numerous organizations and agencies, public and private, are concerned with or have the brief to control tourism in Bali, and there is a need for greater coordination and sharing of information among them. Among the most important are the Bali Tourism Development Board (BTDB) and the Bali Tourism Development Corporation (BTDC), which were created to regulate tourism and protect the Balinese way of life; the Area Department for Tourism (DIPPARDA); the Consultative and Promotional Council for Cultural Affairs (LISTIBIYA); and the Hindu Dharma Parishad.

BTDB was constituted by presidential decree in 1972 as a coordinating and integrating body to promote the development of tourism in Bali.[32] One of its most important goals is to link customary organizations with government so that the Balinese can determine both the direction and pace of tourism development. This goal came from the realization that there are no institutionalized links between the legal-administrative and customary organizations in Bali and that therefore tourist trade enterprises could easily exploit the Balinese. But BTDB is not as yet representative of Balinese customary organizations. Its members are government officials and, initially, four of the twelve members were Balinese merely because they happened to be heads of government departments. Retirement has reduced the number of Balinese members.

The second organization, BTDC, was incorporated in 1973 with the Ministry for Tourism and Communications as the sole shareholder for the time being. This corporation is comparable to an executing arm for tourism development under the master plan. It supervises construction of sites and is responsible for their managment and subsequent transfer to an appointed body or organization. BTDC is at present in charge of the Nusa Dua project.

DIPPARDA is the regional tourism office under the governor of Bali. Theoretically it is responsible for the regulation and development of tourism in Bali. It is, however, understaffed and underbudgeted. Furthermore, there is confusion about the scope of its activities under the master plan and since the formation of BTDB.

LISTIBIYA members are leaders of arts and dance in Bali, with the governor of Bali as a nominal chairman. This body is charged, among other matters, with the maintenance of standards in the arts, and it has the power to grant the important certificate of art to groups that want to perform for tourists. Unfortunately, LISTIBIYA's performance has been uneven.

The Hindu Dharma Parishad, a private group, is the premier organization to determine what constitutes correct practice of the Hindu religion in Bali. One of its aims is the codification of Hindu customs, which is in some respects unfortunate since custom should remain flexible and adapt to changing local (in this case, village) circumstances, as it has in the past. Furthermore, the Parishad is a revivalist organization running somewhat counter to the eclectic pragmatism of the Balinese. But it is fairly powerful and is consulted

32. The controversy as to whether BTDB is a board or an authority (as the Bahasa version of the decree has it) is unresolved, although under Indonesian law nomenclature makes a considerable difference.

by the governor. One of its functions is to supervise architectural reconstruction and approve designs such as for rebuilding and expanding the principal temple of Bali, Besakih.

These are not the only organizations concerned with tourism, however, a fact that adds delay and some confusion. To commence business a hotel must first be investigated by DIPPARDA and must thereafter obtain permits from both the office of the governor and the line representatives of the Department of Commerce; the central government also has the independent power to issue hotel licenses. Handicraft shops can be constructed if they obtain a permit from the district chief but can commence business only after obtaining a license from the Department of Handicrafts and Small Industries. Tourism centers require the approval of both the district chief and the Department of Education and Culture, and dance groups are first approved by LISTIBIYA and then granted a license by the district chief.

The major problem is the confusion between the roles of BTDB, a creation of the central government, and DIPPARDA, which is entirely subordinate to the regional government. While some view BTDB as a controlling authority, others see it as mainly an advisory body. Furthermore, at the initial stages its functions overlap those of DIP-PARDA. A review committee appointed by the governor of Bali saw BTDB purely as an advisory body and reported no conflict between the roles of the two organizations. This view was not shared by the central Parliament, however, which in 1975 found no clear guidelines to distinguish the functions of each organization and coordinate their activities.

Planning and tourism development: A retrospect

For several reasons, the number of hotels and tourist facilities (art shops in particular) grew at an uncoordinated and rapid rate between 1968 and 1976, thereby implicitly contradicting the assumptions of the planners. First, the 1968 decision to adopt tourism as a means of economic development of Bali was arrived at without local consultation. There was, and is, little awareness among the Balinese of the five-year plan and the subsequent master plan. It was the elite, mainly Jakarta Indonesians, who were aware of these plans and could take economic advantage of the proposals. Second, the SCETO study was based entirely on forecasts of international arrivals and foreign exchange earnings. Its recommendations neglected the significant percentage of tourists from other islands of Indonesia, most of whom do not stay in hotels of international standard. Third, the type of tourism proposed by the master plan is generally beyond the financial and managerial capacity of most Balinese. They can, however, better afford to construct and manage small hotels and home-stays. Furthermore, the growth of the small hotels was fostered by the limitation on the number of hotel rooms of international standard outside Nusa Dua and the promise of vast profits from the coming tourist boom. Fourth, since no hotels could be built on the Bukit peninsula, which also lacks roads and other facilities, hotel investors tended to overconstruct in well-established tourist areas. The master plan concentrated on Nusa Dua and implicitly encouraged further growth in Sanur, Kuta, and Denpasar by suggesting that these areas could accommodate an additional 2,500 rooms. Tourism should have been viewed in an islandwide context, and further growth in areas other than Nusa Dua should have been regulated.

Fifth, the proposed Nusa Dua resort is geared mainly to the charter tourist. SCETO and the master plan pay insufficient attention to small-scale hotels and to other types of tourists such as families and youths. An increasing number of middle-income tourists are satisfied with a clean room, clean food and water, and a clean bathroom at reasonable rates and do not want to pay the charges of hotels of international standard. Sixth, ordinances and decrees, whether presidential or passed by provincial governors, are statements of intention without teeth—they cannot be enforced. The time lag between an ordinance and its legislative enactment, if that takes place, is long enough to allow the influential and affluent to act with impunity. Thus, for example, although the governor of Bali declared areas contiguous to the tourist route from Denpasar to Ubud a "green belt" on which no construction can take place, this decree has not prevented art shops and billboards from sprouting up and defacing the route. Seventh, there is no islandwide zoning legislation, and even if there were it would be difficult to enforce in the absence of sufficient staff. The most effective means of enforcing ordinances and legislation would be through the bandjars, which have power within their territorial boundaries. This has not yet been tried because of the lack of institutionalized links between the bandjars and the government and the absence of bandjar representation in an islandwide organization. Eighth, there is a continuing lack of coordination and information sharing among government regulatory agencies in the field of tourism. Finally, the master plan underestimates the cultural resilience and adaptiveness of the Balinese. The Balinese want tourism; they also want to be involved in it. Any attempt to regulate contact between the Balinese and tourists is impossible unless voluntarily adopted and controlled by the Balinese themselves through their bandjars.

Some Answers

Most careful observers of Bali maintain that tourism has not destroyed Balinese culture. Why is this so? One possible reason is that customary ties with the bandjar are strong. The Balinese in the city might belong to an "arrtay" (*rukan tangas*—a statutory neighborhood association that forms a self-help unit), but he does not lose his bandjar membership or his ties to it. A second reason could be that tourism routes are well defined, and tourism touches only the fringes of Balinese life through the people directly connected with hotels; most lives continue to be centered in villages. The third and probably the most important reason is one suggested by both McKean and Lansing.[33] Tourism offers the Balinese an opportunity to profit from doing things they always have done: dancing, painting, and carving.

Audiences are always welcome at Balinese ceremonies and the Balinese recognize that tourism benefits them. But the Balinese have learned to distinguish between audiences. A performance has its own meaning for the Balinese, independent of its meaning for tourists. This separation of meanings is not confined to performances but extends to all arts. As Bagus points out, arts such as drama, sculpture, and traditional temple ornaments flourish because of their special meaning for the Balinese, who distinguish them from the souvenir and commercial arts developed for the tourist market. Although at times the dividing line between the two types is thin, the independence of meanings has permitted traditional arts to maintain both their quality and purpose without being radically affected by the advent of tourism.[34] In fact, the income gained from a tourist performance and sale of crafts is channeled

33. McKean, "Cultural Involution"; and Lansing, *Evil in the Morning.*
34. Bagus, "The Impact of Tourism."

back to strengthen the religious and temporal bonds that are the sources of strength for the Balinese: the bandjar and the village temples. Tourism has thus affirmed these most important ties which link the past with the present and the future and which form the boundaries through which no outsider can penetrate, not even Balinese who are not members of the same bandjar.

To respond, then, to some of the questions raised at the beginning of this chapter: Tourism for the Balinese, as for the Cuna Indians of San Blas and the Puerto Vallartans,[35] has served to reinforce cultural traditions and ethnic identity. The fact that Bali is an island has in no way made the impact of tourism more detrimental. The strength of Bali lies in its cultural history and in the fact that although cultural events attract tourists they are not dependent on their presence and can take place without them. Nor has the increase in the number of tourists caused adverse effects, for there is little reluctance to welcome the visitor.

The threat to Balinese culture and way of life comes not from numbers as such but from the way in which tourism in Bali is organized today. Until 1969 Balinese responses to tourism were spontaneous and, though uncoordinated, sprang mainly from local initiative and local resources. The intervening years have seen a qualitative change. Tourism activities are still largely uncoordinated and the hotels at Nusa Dua are as yet unbuilt, but the Balinese response is increasingly determined by outsiders. The Balinese have been relegated to roles of functionaries and employees; they play little part in decisionmaking but are largely executors of decisions made by others. Non-Balinese tourism enterprises grow in strength and in their ability to dictate which routes tourists should follow, which shops tourists should visit, and which Balinese groups should perform for the tourist. These organizations are in a position to play one bandjar off against another and to reduce a bandjar's income in the process. Furthermore, there is a need for better communication of tourism development plans to the Balinese. If the process continues it is possible to envision the gradual loss of control by the bandjars over their members. Once this link is broken tourism in-

---

35. M. Swain, "Cuna Women and Ethnic Tourism," paper presented at the 73d annual meeting of the American Anthropological Association, Mexico, November 24, 1974; and Nancy Evans, "Tourism and Cross-cultural Communication," *Annals of Tourism Research,* vol. 3 (1976), pp. 189–98.

come will cease to be channeled back to strengthen the bandjars and the village temples that give the Balinese their sense of identity and uniqueness.

It might be suggested that the government has intervened too late and, with hindsight, that the proposed Nusa Dua resort development will only shift control of tourism even more to outsiders. Such suggestions neglect the history of tourism development in Bali which, like most other tourism destination areas, proceeded from spontaneous development to governmental intervention. The central government intervened at a stage when further spontaneous development would have resulted in chaotic conditions, and the regional government lacked the resources (particularly managerial resources) to plan and control the growth of tourism. It should also be realized that most Balinese want more tourism, and there are few alternatives for economic development.

It is not true that little can now be done to alter the direction of tourism in Bali. Even the most conservative forecasts indicate that the number of tourists a year will cross the 500,000 mark by 1985. This affords the opportunity to plan further development and to control the growth of tourism. It also means that the Balinese can still be involved in the process. Consultation does not come easily, but unless those most affected by tourism are consulted, tourism itself is in jeopardy. The main reason for constituting the BTDB was to give the Balinese a voice in the development of tourism, but since 1974 it has been increasingly recognized that BTDB's present membership does not fully represent the islanders. The question is what organization would. The answer may lie in a fundamental structural change in the present administrative setup and in welding the customary organization with the legal-administrative.

In practice and apart from surveys that are being conducted, Balinese customary leaders are now being consulted on the formulation of master plans for each area and on zoning ordinances. A program of information and consultation has been initiated to offer each customary village choices with respect to tourism. At the district level repeated attempts have been made to convince Badung to share a greater percentage of its tourist revenues with other districts. Finally, the Directorate General of Tourism for Indonesia, realizing the importance of the social aspects of tourism, has now made it a matter of policy and practice to take these factors into account in the formulation of tourism development plans for other islands.

Should the social aspects and costs of tourism be ignored when there is no other alternative strategy available for economic development, as would seem to be the case in Bali? Two interconnected responses can be made: First, even when tourism appears to be the only path to economic development, its adverse impacts can be minimized by taking social considerations into account and modifying plans so as to achieve the maximum economic gain with minimal disruption. Second, it is for the people to choose what means they will adopt to obtain economic development. In the case of Bali this means that the bandjars must decide, on the basis of their own priorities, what social costs must be borne if they want tourism for development. This also means that bandjars must be linked with the process of decisionmaking. If this takes place then the pessimistic conclusion of the SCETO team that the cultural manifestations of Bali "will probably have disappeared" by 1985 will be disproved.[36] Paradise will not then be lost.

36. SCETO, draft report, January 1971, vol. 2, p. 194.

CHAPTER 13

The Early Effects of
Tourism in the Seychelles

David Wilson
DEPARTMENT OF SOCIAL ANTHROPOLOGY
THE QUEEN'S UNIVERSITY OF BELFAST

THE SEYCHELLES ISLANDS, WHICH LIE IN THE INDIAN OCEAN
north of Madagascar, were a quiet, unfrequented back-
water until the opening of an international airport in 1971.[1] Since
then they have become one of the more fashionable of international
resorts, and tourism now challenges agriculture as the major feature
of the economy. The nature and extent of these recent developments, which have transformed the economic and social life of the
islands, are described in the following sections. They present the
historical background, accounts of the preconstruction period
(1960–69), the construction boom (1969–74), the growth of tourism,
the emergence of a postconstruction stage of development after
1974, and an analysis of the costs and benefits of tourism.

Historical Background

The Seychelles consist of two clusters of islands. The central granitic group of some forty islands and islets is steep and mountainous with a narrow coastal plateau, and the outer coralline group
of forty-three islands is flat and often without water. They cover a
total area of about 107 square miles and contain a rapidly growing
population of some 56,000 inhabitants. The majority of the people
live on Mahé in the granitic group, and most of the remainder on

1. The author undertook fieldwork in Seychelles toward a D.Phil. in social
anthropology over a period of fourteen months between 1972 and 1974. The present
paper deals with events up until 1975 but does not consider the implications of the
rapidly changing situation since then.

205

nearby Praslin, La Digue, and Silhouette. The rest of the islands have either no permanent population or only a handful of plantation workers.

The islands were uninhabited when first settled by the French, who came from Mauritius in 1770, accompanied by their slaves, allegedly in response to rumors that the English were thinking of occupying the group themselves. Land grants were standardized at 112 acres and accorded only to white settlers, who had to be married to whites. Freed slaves were entitled to quarter-size "habitations." By 1826 the population had risen to 743 whites, 407 free coloreds and blacks, and 6,146 slaves.[2] The colonial experience of Seychelles thus parallels that of other islands in the Indian Ocean such as Mauritius or Reunion, as well as that of areas like the Caribbean. In general, these areas are distinguished by a common experience of intense colonization, slavery, indentured labor, plantation agriculture, a small island economy, cultural focus on a distant metropole, and the development of multiracial societies.

In 1814 the islands were ceded to Britain under the Treaty of Paris and remained in British hands until their independence in 1976. Labor difficulties and shortages after emancipation turned planters away from labor-intensive crops such as sugar and cotton, and the islands gradually developed a one-crop economy based on the coconut palm. Cinnamon became an important second crop in the late nineteenth century and is still exploited in feral rather than cultivated stands on the steep mountainsides above the level of the palms. Periodic booms during the twentieth century in commodities such as vanilla and patchouli have also provided occasional financial windfalls for the islanders. The planters in Seychelles never rivaled the extreme wealth of their contemporaries in other plantation colonies, nor did the laborers suffer the extremes of poverty that were the lot of their class elsewhere. Nevertheless, a vast gulf remained between the two groups, and their access to land, wealth, and political power was sharply differentiated.

Widespread miscegenation over the years has dissolved the boundaries between these racial groups, and it is no longer possible to quantify the population on the basis of race, although the majority

---

2. Robert René Kuczynski, *A Demographic Survey of the British Colonial Empire*, 3 vols. (London: Oxford University Press, 1949), vol. 2, p. 909.

are of darker color. The 1960 population census describes the Seychellois as:

> predominantly colored, those of pure French origin being comparatively rare. Unmixed African blood, too, probably no longer exists . . . It must suffice to record that the skin-color and features of "Les Seychellois" run the whole gamut. French, African, Madagascan, English, Indian, Chinese, crews of calling ships, exiles, visitors, all these and more have contributed their genes to a common pool.

Contemporary Seychelles is thus the product of a complicated legacy of French, English, and non-European traditions introduced by the various settlers. Consequently, some aspects of the social structure present a heterogeneous cultural picture, and a local Creole culture has evolved with its own set of values radically different from those of the European-oriented elite and their middle-class emulators. These include a tendency toward consensual as opposed to legal unions, an easygoing attitude toward work and sexual relations, a belief in the efficacy of *gris-gris* (magical practices), and a tolerance of (if not indulgence in) other features of the local life-style such as heavy drinking and petty larceny. Racial differences have become incorporated into a pervasive system of status differentiation based on the idiom of color, in which to be "white" or "whiter" is considered more desirable, and to be "black" or "blacker" is for many islanders a mark of social inferiority and low status. At the same time, all the inhabitants of the islands proudly refer to themselves as "Seychellois," and they share in common such features as the Creole language,[3] the Catholic religion, a cash economy, and universal suffrage, introduced in 1967.

The Preconstruction Period, 1960–69

In 1960 the economy of Seychelles remained based on copra and, to a lesser extent, other export crops (see Table 13.1). The major oc-

---

3. French remains the language of the *grand blanc* (the white land-owning elite) and the Catholic Church, while English is the main language of education, government, and tourism development. In the 1971 census 97.4 percent of the islanders spoke Creole, 37.7 percent English, and 29.4 percent French.

Table 13.1. *Main Domestic Exports in 1960, 1970, and 1973*

	1960		1970		1973	
Commodity	Quantity	Value (rupees)	Quantity	Value (rupees)	Quantity	Value (rupees)
Cinnamon bark (tons)	987	821,842	1,306	3,680,723	1,630	7,174,984
Cinnamon leaf oil (kilograms)	60,694	610,085	17,206	399,106	2,057	74,455
Coconuts (number)	—	—	369,320	76,025	545,900	123,839
Copra (tons)	4,689	4,768,419	4,416	5,074,907	3,337	4,657,494
Guano (tons)	7,100	284,000	6,431	339,647	7,000	446,587
Patchouli oil (kilograms)	435	24,600	541	25,560	—	—
Vanilla (kilograms)	7,575	539,481	829	30,186	4	55

— Negligible or zero.
Sources: Compiled from Annual Trade Reports for 1960, 1970, and 1973.
Note: The most recent vanilla boom ended in 1960; the low price of patchouli made production unprofitable; cinnamon prices rose rapidly around 1970 because war in Vietnam restricted the major southeast Asian supply. The Seychelles rupee is pegged to the pound; in 1975 US$ 1.00 was the equivalent of 6.59 Seychelles rupees.

cupations were agriculture (employing 5,358), fishing (652), domestic services (1,659), and manual labor (2,078). The agricultural census of that year showed that there were 56 estates of more than 250 acres, and that these 56 employers owned no less than 65 percent of the land. Government, with more than 3,000 employees (including 1,600 on temporary relief work), was the second largest employer after agriculture. Thus the large majority of Seychellois (darker colored) were restricted to poorly paid unskilled work and were dependent upon a very few employers. Opportunities for economic—and hence social—advancement were few, job security low, and personal networks the main agency of recruitment. The dominance of the white land-owning elite was unchallenged. Although a patchouli boom in the 1940s and a vanilla boom in the early 1950s had helped alleviate the deteriorating economic position of the islands, by the end of the 1950s these windfalls had come to an end. The main problems were pressure from a rapidly growing population and declining profitability, productivity, and employment on the plantations. This situation was further exacerbated by the return to the islands of 2,000 Seychellois from service overseas in the Royal Pioneer Corps. In spite of considerable temporary government relief work there were still 1,819 people listed as unemployed in the 1960 census. Benedict, writing of the conditions he observed in that year, found that the twin problems of prices rising faster than wages and extensive underemployment and unemployment were producing "not only economic distress, but discouragement and social disorganization which manifests itself in lack of planning, drunkenness, theft, sporadic outbursts of aggression, job jealousies, and an unstable family life."[4]

A report commissioned by the government of Seychelles calculated that the productivity of the plantations reached their peak in 1952 and entered a gradual decline in 1955.[5] This was explained by the senility of a large majority of the palms (many of which were between seventy and ninety years old), losses caused by the melittoma borer, bad husbandry and the neglect of coconut soils by the planters, and the fragmentation of estates under French laws of inheritance still in force. The steady increase in domestic consumption of nuts by the expanding population further reduced export production, and the situation was aggravated by the increasingly unfavorable terms of trade for primary products on the world market. By the end of the 1950s the islands had been forced into the red and Seychelles became a Grant-in-Aid Colony, a situation which prompted the British government to action. The first of a succession of development plans was introduced, all of which advocated heavy expenditure in the public sector and the development of tourism. The government's objective in opting for substantial development of the islands was thus "to enable the Government of Seychelles to balance its budget again . . . [and] advance the welfare and prosperity of the people of Seychelles as a whole."[6]

Since then, a certain amount of debate has centered around the question of whether the plantations were really in decline, thus prompting the development of tourism. Although export production of copra did fall during the 1950s, by the mid-1960s it had nearly regained its former level (see Table 13.2). The extent to which the subsequent dramatic decreases in exports during the construction boom were determined by the natural decline of the copra in-

4. Burton Benedict, *People of the Seychelles* (London: Her Majesty's Stationery Office, 1966), p. 3.

5. F. C. Cooke, "Report on the Coconut Industry in Seychelles" (Victoria, Mahé: Government Printer, 1958).

6. "A Plan for Seychelles" (Victoria, Mahé: Government Printer, 1959), p. 2.

Table 13.2. *Copra: Quantity and Value of Exports*

Year	Exports (tons)	Average f.o.b. value (rupees per ton)[a]
1920	2,729	378
1925	4,874	329
1930	5,922	204
1935	4,311	136
1940	4,716	115
1945	4,028	330
1950	5,974	972
Average		
1951–55	6,185	950
1956–60	5,235	975
1961–65	5,826	904
1966–70	5,409	1,025
1971–75	3,244	1,779

Sources: Compiled from the following Seychelles government publications: Agricultural Census for 1960, Annual Trade Reports for 1960 to 1973, and the *Seychelles Statistical Bulletin* no. 2 (February 1976); also "Information Transmitted to the Secretary-General of the United Nations" (London: British Ministry of Overseas Development, 1974).
Note: Export column excludes increasing quantities of nuts consumed locally as such, crushed locally for cooking oil, and lost because of toddy-tapping of the trees to produce palm wine.
a. US$ 1.00 was equivalent to 6.59 rupees in 1975.

dustry or by the attraction of labor into the better paid construction sector thus remains a moot point.

The preconstruction phase was characterized by a stagnant GNP[7] in spite of gradually broadening opportunities. During this period a land settlement scheme was introduced (1958), the United States Satellite Tracking Station opened (1963), a coir factory was established (1964), a low-cost housing program was started (1964), a new road system was built around Mahé (1960–65), and tea produc-

7. Estimated to be 1.8 percent over the decade 1960–70. United Nations Conference on Trade and Development, *Developing Island Countries* (New York: United Nations, 1974).

tion commenced (1966). The decision to build the airport (announced in 1965) was followed by a speculative property boom, although actual construction work did not begin until 1969. Unfortunately, "figures of the economically active were not available . . . it was not possible to compile even the most rudimentary statistics."[8] It has been estimated, however, that during this period the net annual growth of jobs in the formal sector was 200, while the annual growth in population averaged 1,000.[9] It can thus be assumed that unemployment was not greatly relieved during the 1960s and may even have increased slightly. The situation was not helped by the continuing decline in agricultural employment, a trend that was already well under way in 1960 (see Table 13.3).

This lack of substantial opportunities almost certainly contributed to the small but steady emigration of white Seychellois during the 1960s. For example, 643 Seychellois left for Australia between 1966 and 1970,[10] a figure equal to 1.4 percent of the 1965 population. Many of these migrants were the younger members of better-off Seychellois families.[11] If a similar rate of departure is assumed for the first half of the decade, then between 1960 and 1970 approximately 2.8 percent of the population, mainly white, would have left for Australia alone. Such an exodus represents a significant shift in the racial composition of the island.[12] Consequently, when the economy later began to expand there were considerable opportunities for colored and black Seychellois to move into higher paid positions which would previously have been occupied by whites. In addition, many nonwhite Seychellois sought work abroad throughout the 1960s in East Africa, the British Army, the Royal Fleet Auxiliary, and as plantation workers on the outer coralline islands. Seychellois girls also went abroad in considerable numbers to work as nannies and domestics, especially in the Middle East and Italy.

8. Report of the Labour Department, 1969–70, p. 2.
9. The estimate is by Robert Grandcourt, a Seychellois recently graduated from the University of Sussex, to whom grateful acknowledgment is made for several statistical and other details in this paper.
10. Reports of the Labour Department, 1967–68, p. 19, and 1969–70, p. 17.
11. Richard Ramage, "Report on the Public Service" (Mahé, 1967), p. 6.
12. Interesting confirmation of this shift comes from the censuses of 1960 and 1971. In 1960, 4.7 percent of the Seychellois spoke French as a first language (the *grand blanc*) whereas by 1971 only 1.9 percent used French as the language of the home, a decline of 2.8 percent.

Table 13.3. *Employment in Agriculture and Fishing*

Item	1947	1960	1971	1974
1. Total population	31,834	41,425	52,244	57,373
2. Population of working age				
(estimated)	12,734	17,665	19,518	21,136
3. Employment in agriculture and				
forestry	9,989	5,910	4,295	3,957
4. Employment in fishing[a]	—	652	586	575
(3) as percentage of (2)	78	33.5	22	18.7
(4) as percentage of (2)	—	3.7	3	2.7
(3) plus (4) as percentage of (2)	—	37.2	25	21.4

— Unknown.
Source: "Review of the Economy" (Mahé: Government Printer, November 1975), p. 10.
a. Excludes part-time, casual employment.

The Construction Boom

When work began on the airport in 1969 it touched off an employment boom in the construction industry (see Table 13.4). By 1970 "the supply of labor continued to exceed demand, but artisans and tradesmen in the higher skilled categories were again scarce."[13] This gap was filled by expatriates, usually British, who began arriving in increasing numbers, and also by returning Seychellois (mainly colored) who had been living and working in East Africa but who were being forced out by Africanization programs. Finally, a "number of overseas entrepreneurs arrived in the colony, starting local business agencies and services, and employing local personnel in clerical work."[14] By 1971 a labor shortage was being forecast if the pace of tourism development was not carefully regulated.[15]

In 1972 the first international hotel opened, followed closely by a second one in Victoria, the only town and port in the islands. Between 1972 and 1975 new international hotels were finished at the rate of about one a year. In 1972 a brewery was also founded, along with a large new complex of shops, offices, and a sports stadium on

13. Report of the Labour Department, 1969–70, p. 4.
14. Ibid., p. 5.
15. Report of the Labour Department, 1971, pp. 4–5.

Table 13.4. Estimates of Employment During the Construction Boom

Sector	1969 July	1970 March	1971 May	1973 April	1974 Jan.	1974 Dec.	1975 August
Agriculture	4,468	4,468	4,268	2,511	2,511	2,797	2,853
Mining	50	8	125	81	18	59	59
Manufacturing	495	495	939	553	466	576	572
Electricity			163		132	156	198
Construction	1,000	1,551	4,131	4,164	4,163	2,740	2,753
Distribution			841	622	663	700	671
Restaurants		987	265	181	182	214	246
Hotels	800			1,002	888	1,214	1,569
Transport		297	967	1,331	1,087	1,267	939
Business		104	119	311	289	313	274
Public administration		1,624	594		1,020	1,060	1,060
Social services	3,763	1,893	1,339	4,139	1,512	1,510	1,676
Recreation		105	113		164	246	244
Other services	50	52	—		71	103	276
Total	10,626	11,584	13,864	14,895	13,166	12,955	13,390

— Unknown.

Sources: Because these statistics are sometimes questionable, comparison between the various sources should be made with suitable caution. Report of the Labour Department, 1969–70; "Provisional Census Results" (London: British Ministry of Overseas Development, May 1971), mimeographed; Report of the Labour Department, 1973; "Information Transmitted to the Secretary-General of the United Nations," 1974; Seychelles Statistical Bulletin, no. 2 (January 1976).

Note: The above figures exclude domestic servants (estimated at 1,700 in 1971), agricultural workers on estates of less than twenty acres (estimated at 800 in 1971), casual employees, and self-employed.

an area of reclaimed land in central Victoria. A landing strip and jetty were completed on Praslin. In 1974 a landing strip and hotel opened on Bird, the nearest coral island to the central granitic group, and a new port was opened in Victoria. On-shore facilities included cement and grain storage silos, a new power station, and a cold-storage center.

By 1972 there were "ample employment opportunities for all able-bodied adult males," and only young people living in the rural areas were unable to get jobs. For them "bus fares to Victoria were more than they could hope to earn in the jobs available for them,"[16] a reminder that wages, though rising, were still low for many. The high demand for labor in the construction industry,

16. Report of the Labour Department, 1972, p. 2.

coupled with the relatively high wages to be earned there, was beginning to cause difficulties in other areas of the economy:

> Agricultural employers, especially those on the outer islands, complained that they could not obtain sufficient labourers because of higher wages available in the construction industry. Construction firms were themselves competing with one another for unskilled labour, and they found it necessary to provide transport for their employees between various residential centers and worksites. Such facilities probably contributed to difficulties experienced in the agricultural sector.[17]

The relative rates of pay were 1.30 rupees an hour in construction as a laborer, and between 78 and 88 cents an hour in agriculture (78 cents if working a thirty-hour week, 88 cents if working a forty-five-hour week).[18]

In 1973 the construction industry reached its peak, and the following year employment in that sector declined dramatically from 4,163 in January to 2,740 in December. This trend continued in 1975, signaling the start of a distinct postconstruction development stage as work on the major hotel, port, and airport facilities came to an end. By the end of 1974 it was reported that 1,750 young people had been unable to find employment.[19]

The 1969–74 period was thus characterized by full employment, a slowing down of the number of Seychellois going abroad to work (no mention is made of emigration to Australia during this period, and it is possible that this too fell substantially), a continuing decline in employment in the agricultural sector, and an influx of expatriates into the islands. A reasonable estimate of the number of foreigners working in Seychelles can be made. There were 567 temporary employment passes issued in 1973.[20] Of these, 83 were for managerial work, 151 at the technical and professional level, 57 supervisory, 181 construction artisans, 27 shop assistants, 24 secretaries, and 44 others. In addition there were, at a conservative estimate, 50 resident self-employed expatriates and approximately 200 Americans at the Tracking Station. This gives a rough total of 817

17. Ibid., p. 3.
18. Report of the Labour Department, 1973, p. 24 (£1 = 13.3 rupees).
19. "Information Transmitted to the Secretary-General of the United Nations" (London: British Ministry of Overseas Development, 1974).
20. Report of the Labour Department, 1973, p. 2.

expatriates working in the islands, a figure which represents 5.4 percent of the work force in the formal sector for that year (although see the note to Table 13.4). If it is assumed that 50 percent of these expatriates had a wife and one child, then they made up about 3 percent of the total population in that year and constituted a significant new English-speaking elite in the islands.

The stimulation of demand caused by the construction boom is reflected in imports into Seychelles during this period (see Table 13.5). A comparison of the level of imports in 1963 with that of 1973 reveals that the total value rose more than ninefold. The fastest growing sections were crude materials, machinery and transport equipment, and miscellaneous manufactured items.

The Growth of Tourism: Costs and Benefits

The number of visitors to the islands escalated from 771 in 1967 to 3,175 in 1971 (the year the airport opened), and reached 37,321 in 1975. This remarkable growth was matched by an equally rapid expansion in the number of hotels and beds available for tourists (see Table 13.6). Although no figures have been officially published, it is possible that the gross earnings from tourism surpassed the total visible exports of Seychelles in 1972. On the same set of assumptions, however, it is also likely that by 1974 these earnings were still only about half the value of the goods imported into the islands during that year (see Tables 13.7 and 13.8).

The costs and benefits of tourism are deliberately placed together in this section, for what may well appear as a gain to some will be considered a loss by others. The implicit assumption made throughout all the development plans of the last fifteen years has been that tourism would benefit Seychelles. The government has, however, recently indicated a growing awareness of the dangers of too rapid a growth: "Experience of other countries such as Bali and many of the Caribbean islands has shown that an all-out desire to maximise tourism involving vast expenditure on infrastructure, hotels and amenities too often results in a short burst of activity and prosperity followed by decline and stagnation."[21] In spite of this caution, there will need to be considerable further expansion of

21. "Review of the Economy" (Mahé: Government Printer, November 1975), p. 21.

Table 13.5. *Imports to the Seychelles, 1963–75*
(thousands of rupees)

Commodity	1963	1971	1972	1973ᵃ	1974	1975
Foodᵇ	5,549	15,314	17,851	30,692	41,692	47,050
Beverages and tobaccoᶜ	1,103	8,489	8,581	6,320	6,221	7,780
Crude, inedible material (excluding fuel)	88	959	1,401	1,802	1,627	2,150
Mineral fuelsᵈ	1,257	5,972	6,210	12,391	25,240	36,130
Animal and vegetable oil and fats	71	394	572	991	1,259	1,310
Chemicals	758	4,004	4,993	5,911	7,168	9,950
Manufactured goods	3,001	14,804	27,454	30,403	26,624	25,070
Machinery and transport equipment	1,842	24,906	32,833	30,053	24,873	33,210
Miscellaneous manufactured items	650	8,020	10,624	14,667	15,035	18,630
Postal packages, etc.	312	1,141	1,152	1,890	2,336	2,380
Total	14,631	84,003	111,671	135,120	152,075	183,660

Sources: Trade Reports, 1963, 1971, 1972, 1973 (Mahé: Government Printer). The 1974 figures are from "Information Transmitted to the Secretary-General of the United Nations," 1974. The 1975 figures are from *Seychelles Statistical Bulletin*, no. 2 (February 1976).

Note: In 1975 US$ 1.00 was the equivalent of 6.59 Seychelles rupees.

a. The peak of the construction boom in this year is reflected in highs in imports of manufactured goods and of machinery and transport equipment.

b. Increasing imports of food paralleled growth of tourism. See Table 13.8.

c. Imports of beverages dropped in 1973 following the opening of a local brewery. Imports of tobacco dropped in 1974 when a local cigarette factory started production.

d. Fuel imports rose as more cars were imported, although the rise in the price of gasoline during this period is also reflected. In 1973 the following numbers of vehicles were on the road in Seychelles: private cars, 2,037; taxis, 90; motorcycles, 491; buses, 31; commercial vehicles, 330; public and commercial, 52; and miscellaneous, 172 ("Information Transmitted to the Secretary-General of the United Nations," 1973). In 1974 a further 432 vehicles were registered ("Review of the Economy," [Mahé: Government Printer, November 1975], p. 67).

tourist facilities if the published targets (see Table 13.8) are to be achieved. The fact that no new hotels are currently being built (although a medium-sized one is being planned), coupled with an obvious international reluctance to embark on hotel investment at present, makes further expansion difficult. Thus tourism in Seychelles appears to be at a turning point. On the one hand, the in-

Table 13.6. *Hotel and Bed Availability*

Date	Hotels (number)	Rooms		Beds	
		Number	Average per hotel	Number	Average per hotel
1970	—	—	—	140	—
1971 July	6	94	15.7	163	27.2
1972 January	10	285	28.5	555	55.3
July	12	321	26.8	626	52.2
1973 January	19	450	23.7	899	47.3
July	21	436	20.8	861	41.1
1974 January	22	450	20.5	891	40.5
1975	25	—	—	1,385	55.4

— Unknown.
Sources: 1970 and 1975 from *Seychelles Statistical Bulletin,* no. 2 (February 1976), p. 1; the remainder from "Information Transmitted to the Secretary-General of the United Nations," 1974. The number of hotels for 1975 is my estimate.

Table 13.7. *Trade, 1960–74*
(thousands of rupees)

Item	1960	1969	1971	1972	1973	1974
Imports	9,496	40,000	84,004	111,671	135,122	152,105
Domestic exports	8,166	12,378	7,916	9,525	12,969	—
Re-exports	40	—	1,916	3,752	5,888	—
Total exports	8,206	—	9,832	13,282	18,887	21,000
Transshipments	—	1,591	1,166	183	378	—
Trade deficit	1,290	26,091	74,174	98,391	116,262	131,105
Estimated gross receipts from tourism	—	3,080	9,503	45,728	58,316	72,754

— Unknown.
Sources: Trade Reports for relevant years; 1974 figures from "Information Transmitted to the Secretary-General of the United Nations," 1974.
Note: In 1971 tourism overtook visible exports as the major earner of foreign exchange, and by 1972 tourist receipts were five times higher than domestic exports. Note the relation between growth of tourism and increasing imports. See Table 13.5 on imports and Table 13.8 on the growth of the tourism industry.

Table 13.8. *Growth of Tourism*

Year	Visitors[a]	Average daily tourist population	Estimated gross tourism receipts[b] (thousand rupees)	Estimated net earnings from tourism[c] (thousand pounds)
Actual				
1967	771	28	2,308	87
1968	1,059	40	3,169	118
1969	1,029	40	3,080	116
1970	1,622	50	4,855	182
1971	3,175	90	9,503	354
1972	15,278	400	45,728	1,715
1973	19,484	600	58,316	2,187
1974	24,308	900	72,754	2,729
1975	37,321	1,382	111,702	4,190
Projected				
1976	60,000	1,700	179,580	6,735
1977	75,000	2,000	224,475	8,420
1978	90,000	2,500	269,270	10,104
1979	105,000	2,900	314,265	11,788
1980	120,000	3,300	359,160	13,473
1986	150,000	4,300	448,950	16,840

Sources: Information concerning actual and projected tourist arrivals from "Summary of Development Policies" (Mahé: Government Printer, 1973); and "Seychelles Economic Survey" (London: Barclay's Bank International, 1972).

a. Not taken into account are cruise-ship passengers calling at the islands; for example, there were 1,340 in 1970, 5,965 in 1973, and 3,321 in 1974.

b. Estimates of gross tourism receipts are based on the following figures provided by Robert Grandcourt: an average of 1,700 rupees for a hotel and 1,293 rupees for other expanses (£ = 13.3 rupees; US$ 1.00 = 6.59 rupees) for an average stay of ten days, which gives a total expenditure of 2,993 rupees per visitor.

c. Estimated net earnings assume an import content of 50 percent, a figure borrowed from the Virgin Islands, which does not seem unreasonable for Seychelles. Robert Erbès lists the following representative figures: 50 percent for the Virgin Islands, 45 percent for Hawaii, 43 percent for the Bahamas, 30 percent for Hong Kong, 22 percent for Kenya ("International Tourism and the Economics of Developing Countries" [Paris: Organisation for Economic Cooperation and Development, 1973], mimeographed). Erbès points out that these disparities are partially explained by different methods of estimation.

dustry could stagnate and create little further employment opportunity (especially for men after the construction stage), thus confirming the worst fears of the government. On the other hand, continued large (by local standards) expansion could conceivably increase the density of tourists to levels that would place an intolerable strain on both pubic and social services as well as on the social fabric of local community life.

The labor market

One of the major difficulties facing planners in Seychelles is the extreme sensitivity of the economy to relatively small developments. The start or finish of two major hotel-building projects thus produces a shortage or glut of labor on the market. Two mitigating factors here are: First, because tourism in Seychelles is year-round, hotel employment is permanent rather than seasonal and does not further exacerbate the situation (see Table 13.9). Second, a tradition of "occupational multiplicity"[22] in the islands facilitates the adaptation of the labor market to changes in supply and demand.

Land speculation

The construction boom undoubtedly contributed to the long-term decline of productivity and employment in agriculture, which had begun in the 1950s. Estate owners were tempted to sell their land to the developers, and laborers sought higher paid work in construction. Land prices had escalated rapidly as foreigners and the Seychellois themselves purchased land in expectation of profitable resale to non-Seychellois.[23] Speculation had the triple effect of hindering the acquisition of land for public purposes, limiting the possibility of a wider ownership among the ordinary Seychellois, and shifting a considerable amount of the best agricultural land to expatriates. Although the government owns 27 percent of the total land area in Seychelles, the bulk of it is on the more remote islands or in national parks in the more mountainous areas of Mahé. The 22.3 percent held by foreigners includes much of the best land for development, which also tends to be prime agricultural land on the coastal plateau.[24] The government has recently and perhaps

22. The pursuit of several occupations, either simultaneously or successively, sometimes found in areas where employment opportunities are traditionally limited.
23. "Review of the Economy" (November 1975), p. 2.
24. Ibid., p. 53.

Table 13.9. Seasonality

| Month | Percentage of visitors arriving each month | | | Average 1973–75 |
	1973	1974	1975	
January	9.4	5.9	7.0	7.4
February	8.7	7.3	7.6	7.9
March	9.8	7.9	9.4	9.0
April	9.7	6.0	6.6	7.5
May	6.9	5.4	7.1	6.5
June	7.1	8.1	6.6	7.3
July	9.2	8.6	9.0	8.9
August	10.4	11.7	12.1	11.4
September	6.7	8.6	8.0	7.8
October	7.0	8.7	8.7	8.1
November	7.1	9.0	7.8	8.0
December	7.7	13.0	10.2	10.3

Sources: 1973 figures calculated from the number of visitor arrivals each month given in "Information Transmitted to the Secretary-General of the United Nations," 1974; and 1974–75 figures from the Seychelles Statistical Bulletin, no. 2 (February 1976), p. 3.

belatedly imposed restrictions on the transfer of land to expatriates, and a development program must now be presented to and approved by the government before the transaction can be completed.[25] Unfortunately, this is not an effective measure because it exempts nonnationals who possess a resident's certificate valid for life.

The fishing industry

A serious side effect of the expansion of tourism has been the persistent shortage of fish—the staple protein—since about 1972. Because of the reduced number of fishermen (see Table 13.3) and a growing demand for fish from the tourism sector, fish prices have failed to fall as usual during the northeast monsoon, when fish are more plentiful, and have in general been rising faster than the retail

25. "Summary of Development Policies," p. 4.

price index.[26] This has in turn caused considerable hardship among those who can least afford it, the urban and rural poor, who have not been able to purchase sufficient quantities to dry and salt for a reserve during the southwest monsoon when fish tend to be scarce and prices high.

It is difficult to understand why more people have not been attracted into fishing by the high prices obtainable. Part of the explanation is that the industry has traditionally been conducted on a casual and often part-time basis, with the catch usually for family or local consumption. It is also a low-status occupation and perhaps because of this may be prone to exhibit that development economist's nightmare—a backward sloping supply curve. The more money earned by one fishing crew that I knew, the longer the men would stay on shore (usually in the bar) before going out again. The local Creole attitude toward work is also reflected here, as illustrated in a story recounted by President Mancham:

> A Seychellois fisherman was quietly netting fish from his pirogue and was approached by an inquisitive tourist. The fisherman explained that he caught enough fish for his and his family's needs, then he went home to attend his garden for an hour, and then he sat on the beach and looked at the sea. The tourist was horrified. He patiently explained that if the fisherman caught more fish than he needed he could sell them, buy another boat and have a man working for him, then another and another—and then he would be rich and would hardly have to work at all. He could sit and look out at the sea for most of the day which, of course, the fisherman was quick to point out was precisely what he did already![27]

A more pragmatic explanation as to why, in the short term at least, fishing has failed to respond to increased demand is that there has never been either cold-storage facilities or a rapidly expanding market until the advent of tourism. Seychelles appears to be ideally situated for the establishment of a more highly capitalized fishing

26. Fish prices, indexed at 100 in June 1969, had reached 374.6 by January 1973 and stood at 336.0 in January 1976. The index would have been even higher if prices had been available for June, the time of the southwest monsoon when fish are scarce. The general retail price index (1969 =100), including imported food such as rice, tinned milk, and tinned margarine, stood at 158.3 in 1973 and 264.6 in 1976. "Review of the Economy" (November 1975), p. 60; and *Seychelles Statistical Bulletin*, no. 2 (February 1976).

27. *London Times*, June 24, 1976.

industry geared to expanding markets at home and abroad. Increasing numbers of trawlers from Taiwan, Japan, and Korea are now fishing in the Indian Ocean on the shallow banks around Seychelles and seem to be making healthy catches. The establishment of an island-based fishing industry would clearly make a significant contribution to the country's economy. Fish products could provide the basis for a sizable export trade, and canning and processing factories would create employment. Although the government has frequently stated its intention to stimulate development in this area, little has been achieved so far.

Agricultural production

The increased volume of imports associated with tourism has already been noted. Careful planning is obviously needed in order to tune in the domestic economy to the tourism sector. Increased production of vegetables (the hotels at the moment fly in most of their fresh supplies from Kenya), furniture, construction materials, and the like are needed in order to reduce the import factor in tourism receipts as well as to increase local employment opportunities in the postconstruction period. Seychelles has lagged behind in these areas so far, as can be seen by the massive increases in food imports (Table 13.5) and the continuing fall in agricultural employment (Tables 13.3 and 13.4), although it is perhaps significant that the latter picked up slightly at the end of the construction boom. Without doubt far more could be produced locally than at present, and the work of the Department of Agriculture's Research Station has shown that with a little fertilizer, water, shade, and care it would be possible for the islands to achieve self-sufficiency in many products presently imported. Local growers remain unresponsive, however. Possible explanations for this reluctance to accept new ideas include the export-crop orientation of the larger estates, the conservatism of smaller producers, the shortage of credit for agricultural development, the lack of marketing organizations, fear of the theft of produce, and the general inertia of island life. Equally important is that there is, in a sense, no truly agricultural sector in Seychelles because few people depend solely on the land for their livelihood, and such work is considered demeaning by many.[28] In spite of these obsta-

28. *The People,* the weekly newspaper of the Seychelles Peoples United party, had the following comments to make concerning the status of agricultural labor (October

cles, some progress has been made in the last few years, and the production of poultry and pork products is now sufficient to satisfy local demand. The government's land settlement scheme, which had placed 240 families by 1968 on plots varying in size from three and a half to ten acres, is also partly aimed at establishing a population of small-holding producers.

The dominance of overseas capital

Generous tax concessions have certainly contributed to an influx of foreign investment into Seychelles.[29] Ownership of all the major international hotels is in foreign hands, and many of the smaller hotels are owned by resident nonnationals. So are many of the ancillary tourism businesses such as those which operate tours, game-fishing boats, charter yachts, and car rental agencies. That these companies are, by their very nature, interested in maximizing profits could lead to considerable conflict of interest between the government and the tourism sector. Unfortunately, no figures are available for wage rates in the tourism industry, but the initial construction work was well paid compared with agriculture, and the hotels now provide employment (especially for women) where none existed before. Other objections to international companies generally concern the repatriation of profits and their general reluctance to recruit nationals from the host country for senior management positions, but again no figures are available for Seychelles at present.

Women and employment

The existing balance between male and female employment would appear to be shifting as the tourism industry enters the postconstruction stage. Although no figures are available, there are

---

9, 1974): "In our islands farm work was considered as the lowest, meanest form of activity. In point of fact, only farm workers in the Seychelles are called *laborers.* This label is significant. It bestows no rank. It carries no dignity. In other words, farm workers were treated as little more than beasts of burden." (Translated from the original French.)

29. An investment allowance of 30 percent plus initial allowance of 30 percent, followed by annual allowances of 10 percent for seven years, means an aggregate allowance of 130 percent of capital investment. "Tourism Development in Seychelles" (Mahé: Government Printer, 1970), pp. 5–7.

several positive indicators. The creation of 250 new jobs in July 1975, largely in the hotel industry, compensated somewhat for the decrease in other sectors such as construction, although the new jobs were mostly for women.[30] At a more descriptive level, a recent report has noted:

> In Victoria groups of half-sullen youths, Afro haircuts over T-shirts and jeans, hang about in the little town center, staring with faint aggression at the British, European, and South African tourists bustling happily about the handicraft shops. They have part-time jobs or no jobs at all, while their girlfriends, or the girls to whom they aspire, are waitresses in the hotels, earning as much or more than they do. They are bored and suffer from a feeling that they have been demeaned.[31]

If sustained, this trend could initiate significant changes in social life—an increasingly matriarchal family, for example, and growing resentment of tourists by the displaced Seychellois male. In fact, this resentment was clearly evident during my own stay in the islands and has certainly not been helped by some of the more deplorable publicity given to Seychelles in recent years concerning the alleged sexual availability of young local women.

The younger generation of women are certainly beginning to lead a much less restricted life as a result of the winds of change blowing through the islands. They can now obtain remunerative employment instead of being confined to the home and chaperoned when they go out. If a young girl lands a good job she can earn more money than her father and is better able to dictate her own lifestyle. Hotel jobs are attractive because they bring the girls into contact with Europeans either working in or visiting the islands. Parents often turn a blind eye to their daughters' fraternizing with such people, whereas to associate with Seychellois men in a similar fashion would not be tolerated. In reply to a question about the apparent ease with which foreigners seemed to gain access to local girls, one Seychellois presented me with the following rather stark contrast:

> The mother of a girl is suspicious of all Seychellois men and wants to know everything about their background, family, jobs, and so on. She does everything she can to prevent her daughter's contact with

---

30. *Seychelles Statistical Bulletin*, no. 1 (November 1975).
31. Martin Wollacot, *Manchester Guardian*, October 17, 1975.

Seychellois men. However, all that an American from the Tracking Station has to do is pull up in the road in front of the girl's home in his sports car, toot the horn, and the mother is virtually pushing her daughter out of the door. His nationality is enough.[32]

For parents with an eye to social advancement, there is the prospect of a prestigious wedding to a white foreigner for their daughter. For girls at the lower end of the social scale, there is the rather more basic attraction of being taken to nightclubs, bought drinks, given money and presents, and, at least for a while, taken away from the hard realities of day-to-day life. New arrivals in the islands seem to feel they are taking the local girls by storm. It is not immediately apparent to them that they are being drawn into a system of male-female relations rooted in historical tradition, the prestige of a lighter skin, and the economic exigencies of island life.

Education

Education at the postprimary level has expanded rapidly in recent years, an improvement that can be attributed to the increased demand for literate, educated, and skilled personnel from both the public and private sectors. In 1965 a vocational and technical training center opened and by 1974 had 440 students; a teacher training college that opened in 1970 had 107 student teachers by 1974; and in 1975 a hotel and catering school enrolled its first students. Literacy among adults (those over fifteen) has increased from 46 percent in 1960 to 57.3 percent in 1971.

The rise in the level of education is seen when the proportion of the economically active population engaged in selected occupations in 1960 is compared with that in 1971 (see Table 13.10). Once again, however, the question is who benefits. In certain quarters of Seychelles the educational system is thought to be heavily biased against those who need it most. One political party newspaper carried the following analysis of entrants into the only two academic secondary schools in Seychelles in 1974:[33]

Students admitted to Regina Mundi School for girls:
49 out of 92 leaving Regina Mundi Convent Primary School (tuition charged)

---

32. Unpublished field notes.
33. *The People,* December 28, 1974.

Table 13.10. *Percentage of Economically Active Population in Selected Occupations*

	1960		1971	
Occupation	*Number*	*Percent*	*Number*	*Percent*
Professional, technical, and				
related workers	669	4.2	1,309	7.3
Teachers	333	2.1	652	3.6
Clerical workers	213	1.3	607	3.4
Typists and stenographers	20	0.1	129	0.7
Mechanics and electricians	168	1.0	700	3.9
Masons and carpenters	1,070	6.8	1,813	10.1
Transport and communications	222	1.4	704	3.9
Drivers	118	0.7	417	2.3
Police and fire brigade	139	0.9	370	2.1

Sources: 1960 census and 1971 "Provisional Census Results."

48 out of 804 leaving all other primary schools (free)
Students admitted to the Seychelles College for boys:
62 out of 106 leaving Seychelles College Primary School (tuition charged)
30 out of 674 leaving all other primary schools (free)

Social change, 1960–75

The traditional elite in Seychelles has, historically, included both the native-born, French-speaking *grand blanc* and the metropolitan, British expatriates sent out to govern the colony. With the declining importance of the plantations and the increasing opportunities in both government service and the expatriate-dominated development sector, the *grand blanc* has been eclipsed by the British and English-speaking elite, especially from 1970 to 1975. Between them, however, the two groups still posses a virtual monopoly of the available resources upon which the existing economic order depends—agricultural land, tourism development and ancillary services, and light industry. The exceptions are the import-export and wholesale-retail trades, which are largely in the hands of the small Chinese and Indian communities (in 1960 estimated at 284 and 354 members respectively).

In 1960 members of the elite topped the social, political, economic, and educational hierarchies in Seychelles. By 1975 they undisputedly dominated only the economic sphere. In 1960 access to these hierarchies was based essentially on race. Since then both the emigration of native-born whites and the increasing educational and occupational opportunities open to the rest of the population have lowered—although not completely abolished—the tacit color bar restricting access to higher positions. With the introduction of universal suffrage in 1967 the traditional elite lost control of the political machinery of the islands. A new political elite has emerged, supported by a new set of resources in the form of the popular vote, political power, and patronage. Black politicians are today ministers in the government. In the 1974 general election, however, the standard practice of both major political parties was to balance the slate with both a light and dark-colored candidate in each of the six double-member constituencies.[34] In general, the political elite seems reasonably satisfied (at least before independence and the complete transfer of power) with the continued control of economic resources by the traditional elite. But the political situation is clearly in a transitional stage at present, and further change can be expected in an independent Seychelles.

Additional sociopolitical developments may or may not be precipitated by a new intellectual elite that seems to be emerging in the islands. This group encourages pride in local culture, especially the Creole language, an Afro-Seychelles indentity (instead of the Euro-Seychelles nexus of the traditional elite), and alignment with the Third World. The advocates of this new ideology are characteristically—but by no means entirely—young, university or college educated, and, even if colored, ideologically black Seychellois who are now beginning to return home after gaining their higher education overseas (usually in the United Kingdom).

One of the prime socioeconomic changes that have taken place from 1960 to 1975 is the emergence of a middle class of skilled ar-

---

34. This is not the place for a detailed discussion of politics in Seychelles. Generally speaking, however, the two main parties are not divided on the basis of either color, class, or rural-urban location. The Seychelles Peoples United party (SPUP) lies to the political left of the Seychelles Democratic party (SDP). The SDP governed from 1967 until 1975 when it invited the SPUP to join in a coalition government, which at the time of writing is still extant. In the early 1970s the SDP was in favor of tourism and maintaining links with Britain, whereas the SPUP became increasingly critical of tourism (see below) and was the first to come out in favor of independence. The SDP eventually followed suit and won the 1974 elections on a pro-independence ticket, gaining 52 percent of the vote and 13 out of 15 seats in the Legislative Assembly. The SPUP, with just under 48 percent of the vote, won the remaining two seats.

tisans, traders, civil servants, teachers, and those employed in expanding sectors such as transport. The people in these occupations have perhaps benefited most from the growth of tourism (see Table 13.10). As social mobility increases, achieved indicators of status such as education, occupation, linguistic ability, overseas travel, and dress are beginning to displace the traditional birth-ascribed values of skin color and family pedigree. Seychellois of all colors who are rising in the social hierarchy are likely to adopt modes of behavior appropriate to the higher level to which they aspire. Thus, patterns of church attendance and attitudes toward gris-gris, family organization, work, drinking, and the law are all likely to shift from the Creole toward the European end of the cultural continuum. Some of the far-reaching ramifications of this shift are seen in the patterns of consumption discussed below.

Those gaining least benefit from the developments of the last fifteen years are undoubtedly the urban and rural poor. A household budget survey in 1973 showed that those with incomes between 200 and 600 rupees a month spent 80 percent of their income on food, drink, tobacco, and rent, leaving no more than 20 percent for all other items which contribute to the standard of living.[35] In this sample, 36 percent of the households had monthly incomes in the range of 200 to 600 rupees, another 18 percent had a total income of less than 200 rupees, while at the top of the sample 9 percent had incomes of over 2,000 rupees a month. In sum, low incomes, inflation, soaring fish prices, and rising male unemployment after the end of the construction boom are causing increasing hardship to many islanders at the lower socioeconomic level. Although petty larceny and drunkenness have always been a feature of the Creole life-style, the significant increases in such offenses in recent years, as shown below, would seem to support my observation of a growing feeling of social dislocation among the very poor:

Reported cases of selected crimes	1961	1971	1974
Theft	863	771	1,253
Assault	34	601	687
Disorderly conduct	357	1,028	1,031

35. "Information Transmitted to the Secretary-General of the United Nations," 1974.

Patterns of consumption

Changes in local consumption patterns can exacerbate the economic situation by sucking in more imports. A good example of this in Seychelles is the importation of beer, a large proportion of which goes onto the local market. After the construction boom started and before the airport opened, there was a massive increase in the consumption of beer, accompanied by a decline in the production of traditional alcoholic beverages such as palm toddy and bacca (fermented sugar cane)[36]:

Million liters of beer	1958	1963	1968	1970	1971	1972	1973
Imported	0.25	0.47	0.98	1.70	2.22	1.64	0.22
Manufactured locally	—	—	—	—	—	0.96	2.60
Total	0.25	0.47	0.98	1.70	2.22	2.60	3.80

Since 1968, beer consumption has risen by over 30 percent each year, with the apparent exception of 1972, when the figure may be artificially low. That year importers' stocks were not replenished because the local brewery started production under German management. The amount of bacca sold decreased from 400,000 bottles in 1968 to about 100,000 in 1973, and toddy production also decreased from an estimated 4.20 million liters to 3.29 million liters during the same period. Inasmuch as beer is about five times more expensive than locally produced alternatives, these figures point convincingly to the impact of higher wages linked to changing tastes and expectations.

Although wages have risen considerably in some sectors, status requirements have increased at a similar rate. Seychellois today want clothes that are imported and tailor-made instead of homemade, manufactured beer and spirits instead of toddy or bacca, and English cigarettes instead of local tobacco, all of which leaves the ordinary man as poor as before, with little improvement in essentials such as housing or diet.

The demonstration effect

Ever since the islands were first occupied in 1770, the cultural focus of Seychelles has been Europe, and social advancement has

36. Ibid.

been displayed by the adoption of European attitudes and behavior patterns. With the acquisition of wealth and education an individual's "color" can even become "whiter" in that he may deny to outsiders his relation to members of his family who are perceived as "darker" than himself. The increased consumption of imported commodities discussed above can therefore be interpreted not so much as emulation of tourists—the demonstration effect—but rather as a predictable emphasis on and extension of existing cultural values and priorities. (In any case, the increased imports antedate the actual tourist boom and are more obviously related to the growing incomes of the construction period.) To talk simply of "consumer preferences" rather than "status requirements" would miss the crucial point. Demand is socially motivated, and elevation in the community is traditionally associated with the adoption of European patterns of consumption.

Those who have had no access to the benefits of tourism development may develop a feeling of relative deprivation, or, as I suspect may be the case in Seychelles, such a feeling may be reinforced. As Bryden has pointed out, "the feeling of relative deprivation may be compounded by historical inequalities associated with membership of a racial group."[37] This may be one factor that contributes to an increasing resentment shown toward tourists by many Seychellois. One indication of how visitors to the islands are perceived by the Seychellois themselves is that the word "tourist" has been mistranslated into Creole as *tous riches* (all rich).

Cultural change

Under the so-called "corrosive effect" of tourism, the culture of the host country is commercially exploited and becomes devalued, while the local inhabitants lose their dignity by performing for the benefit of goggling strangers. It could be argued that this is beginning to happen in Seychelles as locals are encouraged to perform traditional dances, such as the sega, contredanse, and moutia, for tourist audiences. It can also be said, however, that the tourists' interest has stimulated local pride in, and enthusiasm for, these products of the Creole culture which were beginning to disappear. There has also been a resurgence in Creole songs and folk music in the last

37. John M. Bryden, *Tourism and Development: A Case Study of the Commonwealth Caribbean* (Cambridge: Cambridge University Press, 1973), p. 93.

few years, which reflects the rapidly growing demand from the
tourism sector for both musicians and records, although local radio
has also helped increase their popularity.[38] Tourism has further
provided an expanding market for locally produced trinkets, such
as shell necklaces, coral artifacts, hats and bags made from vacoa
(palm leaves), raffia work, and coconut-shell ornaments, and has
created overnight a small cottage industry catering to this demand.
Again this may stimulate local appreciation of products such as
vacoa hats and bags that have traditionally been low-status indicators because of their identification with the Creole culture. Unfortunately, no figures are available to indicate the amount of employment being generated in the informal sector.

It must be emphasized again that Seychelles culture has never
been uniform but has always consisted of a series of alternative patterns ranging from the European to the Creole. The general attitude
of the Seychellois toward the Creole culture must be viewed in the
wider context of the overall system of values which Seychelles has
inherited from the slave society. The Creole culture and language
are rooted in slavery, and they suffer from the same general dis-
paragement as do other ethnic characteristics identified with Africa
and the black slave: the prestige accorded to a lighter skin, the
assumed superiority of those with lighter complexions, and the frequently voiced contempt for those of darker color. (Moreover, this
superiority is passively accepted by many darker colored people,
who told me on several occasions, a little wistfully, that *noir content
blanc, mais blanc pas content noir,* "the blacks like the whites but the
whites don't like the blacks.") In recent years, however, pride in
some of the distinctive features of the local culture, especially the
Creole language, has been gradually emerging with a concomitant
reduction in the feelings of inferiority and low status felt by those
who come from that milieu. Children are no longer sent home from
school with the humiliating notice saying "I am a Creole speaker"
pinned on them by their teacher, which happened at one school as
recently as the late 1960s. These new attitudes stem from increasing
social mobility, the advent of universal suffrage, and a growing
social and political awareness. These changes have in turn been
stimulated by economic developments since 1960, especially the

---

38. Radio broadcasts are mainly in English, however, with some French and only
occasional Creole news bulletins and record programs.

growth of tourism in the 1970s and the enthusiasm of many tourists for some of the distinctive products and symbols of local culture. Future years may well see an even greater degree of blending between the two subcultural extremes.

Planning and conservation

In the fields of planning and conservation Seychelles seems to have made considerable effort to profit from the mistakes of other countries and avoid some of the more obvious pitfalls of tourism. As a general rule, new hotels must have no more than two or three stories, about the same height as the surrounding palms. They must also be set back from the beach, to which access is free. Hotel facilities are all open to local residents, who have not been slow to make use of them. Finally, it is unlikely that on the outer granitic and coralline islands anything other than small developments of cabins and lodges will be permitted. The government is also trying to avoid the establishment of hotel complexes on Mahé, although at present about a third of the development is concentrated along one stretch of coast (Beau Vallon Bay). The extensive tourist development on Mahé has already caused a certain amount of interisland migration (see Table 13.11).

Conservation efforts have produced a steady stream of ordinances throughout the 1960s for the protection of wildlife and for

Table 13.11. *Population Density of the Main Islands of Seychelles, 1960–71*

		1960		1971	
Island	Area (square miles)	Population	Density per square mile	Population	Density per square mile
Mahé	58.7	33,478	570	45,420	774
Praslin	17.3	3,886	224	4,244	245
La Digue	5.6	1,842	328	1,985	354
Silhouette	6.3	780	124	417	66
Coralline islands	17.8	1,292	74	527	30

Source: Census 1960; "Provisional Census Results," 1971; and "Review of the Economy" (November 1975). Some of the sources may be slightly incompatible concerning whether small satellite islands are included.

the establishment of nature reserves and marine parks in which shelling is forbidden. Spear-fishing is outlawed (visitors arriving in the islands with spear guns have them impounded), and the killing of green turtles—an endangered species—is also banned (although, perhaps understandably, turtle meat continues to provide an occasional source of protein for the poorer people in rural areas). The cropping of seabird eggs on the outer islands is also carefully controlled. All these measures have helped build up an international reputation for conservation in the islands of which they can be proud. Considerable publicity by the local media has given the Seychellois a strong appreciation of the many unique species found in the islands (especially the inedible ones!) and a native of La Digue, for example, will now proudly point out to the visitor a paradise flycatcher, of which only some thirty breeding pairs exist and only on this island. Tourists are increasingly being made aware of the unique botanical and zoological assets of Seychelles, which, if properly handled, should become one of the islands' greatest attractions as well as a secure national heritage.

Summary

Whether the traditional economy of 1960 could have been prolonged or improved is hotly debated among both expatriates and Seychellois alike. It seems clear, though, that pressure from the increasing population meant that more jobs and wealth had somehow to be created if the islanders were not to suffer a considerable decline in their already low standard of living. To engender more wealth in a country where land is scarce and mountainous, mineral wealth nonexistent, and agricultural productivity, employment, and profitability falling was the problem facing government planners who proclaimed tourism the answer.

Since then, Seychelles has increasingly pinned its economic future on tourism. Initially, no one questioned the assumption that this could only benefit the islands, although the minority Seychelles Peoples United party gradually came to see these developments as directly responsible for many of the problems facing the islands: soaring land prices, rapid inflation, sudden shortages of staple commodities such as fish and vegetables, increasing volumes of imports, domination by expatriates and foreign capital, increasing poverty and malnutrition, the neglect of agriculture, the failure to exploit the potential for a deep-sea fishing industry, and the Seychellois being turned into a "nation of waiters." In the words of the party newspaper:

> As a whole, the development plan concentrated only on the economic aspects and totally neglected the human side . . . A division has been created between those who possess everything and those who possess nothing . . . Decent education remains the domain of only those who can afford to pay, which means that the majority remain in their dungeon of ignorance and apathy . . . Inequalities are rampant in employments where an expatriate or son of a rich man gets higher wages and better opportunities than a poor Seychellois, even though he has managed to obtain the same qualifications . . .No effort was made to encourage a sense of responsibility in our people . . . or to encourage cooperation among individuals and various communities. On the contrary, there was a mad scramble to exploit one another.[39]

The governing Seychelles Democratic party, however, points to such positive results of its policies as the eradication of unemployment, the high wages in the development sector, the creation of opportunities outside the traditional plantation-oriented system, new possibilities for advancement at all social levels, the prospect of establishing the islands as an important international financial center, the benefits of improved transport and communications facilities, the end of Seychelles' long isolation from the outside world, and the high local demand for such symbols of twentieth-century sophistication as radios, records, and imported clothes and drinks. President Mancham delivered the following reply to his critics when questioned on local radio about the rising cost of living caused by the tourism development:

> I think it is wrong for people to continually speak about the rising cost of living without taking into account the great rise in the standard of living of the average Seychellois. Twenty years ago a Seychellois laborer found it difficult to find money even to buy a bottle of toddy. Today he is a big drinker of beer . . . A few years ago Mrs. Mazerieux was almost the only shop who sold good quality materials as only a few high-class ladies could afford them. Today expensive dress materials are sold in all shops, and hundreds of Seychellois women are wearing them. Take another example, not

39. *The People,* April 26, 1975.

many years ago a young Seychellois would have considered himself lucky if he had long khaki trousers to wear on Sundays. Today you will not see him in less than a gaberdine . . . When fish is dear at the market they should not just rush to criticise the government, because this is the very government which has worked to give them better working opportunities, their transistor radios, their shoes, and their gaberdine.[40]

Without doubt the reality of the situation lies somewhere between these two party views of the impact of tourism in the islands, but development is still in a state of considerable flux as the islands adjust to the postconstruction phase.

Before tourism development, agriculture and fishing were low-status and unprofitable occupations, mainly providing for family and local consumption. When better paid, higher status opportunities arose, there was understandably a drift away from such pursuits into construction and hotel work. It is hoped, however, that this will prove to be a transitional stage and that sooner or later some Seychellois will be drawn back into agriculture and fishing by the realization that considerable money can be made in these occupations, a fact which may also revise the prevailing attitude toward such work. Alternatively, increasing male unemployment may force many Seychellois back to the land. Clearly the government has an important role to play here in stimulating projects to develop both fishing and agriculture. What appears at present as a serious conflict between tourism and agriculture may well evaporate over the next few years with an increase in agricultural productivity, a concomitant reduction in the need for food imports to sustain the tourism industry and the local population, and the establishment of a more healthy equilibrium between these two sectors of the economy.

Quantifiable economic changes are of course easier to document than the qualitative social changes which often accompany them and which in Seychelles have been considerable. It could be said that tourism has acted as a sort of social catalyst in the islands, stimulating the development of sociopolitical awareness and change. Increasing social mobility, the erosion of the position of the traditional elite, and a blending of the European and Creole subcultures are further encouraging, as well as merely reflecting, this process. Tour-

40. Interview with James Mancham on Radio Seychelles, December 13, 1972.

ism has certainly gone a long way toward solving the economic problems faced by the planners in Seychelles at the end of the 1950s, but there is a danger of creating a further set of problems which may not be so easy to solve. It remains to be seen how successfully the leaders of the new republic can adapt the islands to the conditions of the postconstruction period and realize that vision of an Indian Ocean paradise cherished by Seychellois, tourist, and anthropologist alike.

CHAPTER 14

Tourism in Cyprus

Antonios Andronicou
CYPRUS TOURISM ORGANIZATION

T HIS PAPER EXPLORES THE DEVELOPMENT OF TOURISM in Cyprus between 1960, when the island gained its independence, and July 20, 1974, when the republic was invaded by Turkey. This invasion underscored the fragility of the tourism industry and its sensitivity to political events. In 1975 tourist traffic dropped to 57,000 from 264,000 in 1973, and the foreign exchange earnings fell to around £6 million (US$15 million) from £23.8 million (US$59.3 million) in 1973, which was a huge blow to the Cyprus economy. In 1974 the Turks gained control of 40 percent of the territory of the island, including 82 percent of the tourist accommodations, 96 percent of the new hotels under construction, and the major tourist center of Famagusta. This situation gives dramatic emphasis to the well-known principle that economic development should not be concentrated in only one sector of the economy and that planning for tourism should ensure the proper regional distribution of hotel accommodation and general infrastructure.

Although tourism was not the only sector of the economy to be hurt by the invasion, the revitalization of the tourism industry has proved a herculean task, mainly because the creation of the necessary infrastructure required more time than the redevelopment of, say, agriculture or manufacturing. With the opening of a new international airport in Lanarca and the construction of new hotels, about 180,000 tourists visited the Greek Cypriot half of the island in 1976, and the future looks bright. This discussion of the cultural and social impacts of tourism, however, relies on observations made during the period up to July 1974.

The Setting

Situated at the crossroads of three continents—Europe, Asia, and Africa—Cyprus is the third largest island in the Mediterranean with an area of 3,572 square miles. It is 140 miles from east to west and 60 miles across at its widest part. The total length of its coastline is about 486 miles. One of the sunniest islands in the Mediterranean, Cyprus offers an infinite variety of landscape. A central plain is bounded on the north and the south by two mountain ranges running from east to west; the Kyrenia or Pendadaktylos mountains to the north reach as high as 2,700 feet, and in the Troodos mountains to the south, of volcanic origin, the highest peak is Mount Olympus at 6,400 feet. There are long unspoiled beaches and hundreds of small coves with unpolluted waters. The greatest part of the island is still untouched.

Cyprus has one of the healthiest climates in the world, as evidenced by its very low mortality rate, the high expectation of life, and the fact that there are no prevalent endemic diseases. Winters (December to February) are mild and rainy in the plains, cold and snowy in the Troodos mountains; the summers are long, hot, and dry—around 30 degrees Celsius in Nicosia, the capital—much cooler on the coast, and fresh in the mountains.

In mid-1974 the de jure population of Cyprus was estimated at 639,000 compared with 634,000 in the previous year; that is, there was an increase of 0.79 percent. The ethnic distribution has probably not changed significantly since the 1960 census: 78 percent Greeks, 18 percent Turks, and 4 percent of other national origin—Maronites, Armenians, and British. The average annual rate of population growth between 1946 and 1960 was 1.7 percent, compared with a growth rate of 0.7 percent from 1960 to 1974.

Like most other developing countries, Cyprus is witnessing rapid urbanization and the creation of new urban centers. In 1974, 42 percent of the total population was urban. From 1960 to 1974 the urban population increased by 31.0 percent, whereas the rural population increased by only 0.4 percent. The Cyprus Social Research Centre, in a 1974 report entitled "Nicosia and Limassol—Urbanization and Social Change," revealed that, although the immigrants from villages to towns present certain distinctive features, there are no indications of dislocation or disorganization. Migrants to cities are more religious, less likely to be members of athletic or political associations, and have larger families than city dwellers.

Economic Activity

Cyprus attained its independence from British colonial rule in August 1960. A very cursory glance at the most important sectors of the economy at that time (see Table 14.1) reveals that agriculture was the largest industry on the island, as it still is. Although it provided employment for more than half of all the workers, it produced less than 25 percent of the gross domestic product. The average per capita income of those engaged in agriculture was estimated at £67, which is unusually low compared with the average of £160 per capita for the nonagricultural population. Manufacturing contributed only about 10 percent of the gross national product, a very low percentage indeed, even for nonindustrial countries. Virtually no real manufactured goods were exported. Minerals constituted 50 percent of all exports, and mining contributed between 10 and 12 percent of the gross national product. The mining industry was on the decline, however, because of the depletion of mineral resources. Foreign trade and the balance of payments presented a desperate situation. Cyprus imports were equal to 50 percent of the gross national product. Tourism, an important potential source of foreign exchange, was in a state of complete decline. Tourist traffic was reduced to a mere trickle (around 21,000 actual arrivals) because of political uncertainty brought about by the struggle against colonial rule from 1955 to 1959.

The government of the newly established republic was faced with the immense and serious task of restructuring the economy and placing it on a sound basis. Fortunately, there was no need to grapple with such serious problems as starvation, extreme poverty, high mortality, massive illiteracy, and negative social attitudes (for example, resistance to change and the pressures of the extended family) which sometimes constitute real barriers and constraints to economic development. Social conditions in Cyprus compared favorably with those in other developing countries in Europe.

After independence the government of the newly born Republic of Cyprus launched its first five-year Economic and Social Development Plan for 1961–66 and two subsequent five-year plans for 1961–71 and 1972–76. The basic objectives of these plans were full utilization of the productive resources of the island, rapid and balanced economic growth, a sound balance of payments, full employment and improved social services and standard of living, and balanced regional development.

As Table 14.1 indicates, spectacular economic growth was achieved from 1960 to 1973. Gross domestic product at factor cost rose from £82 million in 1960 to £309.5 million in 1973, an annual compound rate of growth of 11 percent, and the per capita income rose from £162 in 1960 to £547.3 in 1973, an annual rate of growth of 10 percent. (One Cyprus pound equals about US$2.50.)

Table 14.1. *Industrial Origin of Gross Domestic Product at Current Factor Cost, GNP at Current Market Prices, and per Capita GNP, 1959–73*
(millions of Cyprus pounds)[a]

Sector	1959	1960	1961	1962	1963
Agriculture, forestry, fishing, and hunting	16.8	14.6	19.4	21.7	20.4
Mining and quarrying	8.4	7.0	6.0	5.6	6.1
Manufacturing	8.4	9.5	10.7	11.1	12.1
Construction	3.2	4.8	6.2	7.4	7.9
Electricity, gas, and water	2.0	1.7	1.9	2.0	2.2
Transportation, storage, and communication	4.8	7.4	8.3	9.3	10.1
Wholesale and retail trade	8.0	9.9	12.0	13.8	15.6
Banking, insurance, and real estate	1.7	2.2	2.4	2.8	3.5
Ownership of dwellings	5.8	10.8	11.1	14.2	13.9
Public administration and defense	12.0	7.2	5.7	6.5	6.9
Services	5.0	6.9	7.8	8.3	8.5
GDP at factor cost	76.6	82.0	91.5	102.7	107.2
GNP at current market prices	—	94.7	104.7	117.1	122.3
Per capita GNP (Cyprus pounds)	—	162.1	180.8	203.2	210.1

— Unknown.
Source: Ministry of Finance, Statistics and Research Department, Economic Reports, 1959–73.
a. One Cyprus pound equals about US$2.50.

Development of the Tourism Sector

Developing countries embarking on development programs are more often than not confronted with mounting requirements for foreign exchange. For countries facing such a constraint on their economic development, it is argued that tourism offers a major opportunity. It stimulates investments, provides a means of earning foreign exchange, and is at the same time a source of employment. Under proper planning conditions tourism may also provide an impetus to social change—directly through education and training to meet the needs of a service industry and indirectly by introducing different social habits and patterns.

In the case of Cyprus, the planners saw tourism as a means of ensuring diversification, restructuring the economy, and earning badly needed foreign exchange. Thus tourism was accorded a high degree of priority in the development effort. The economic impor-

1964	1965	1966	1967	1968	1969	1970	1971	1972	1973
17.8	28.0	26.5	34.2	32.3	39.2	35.6	46.1	48.7	40.5
5.1	8.1	9.2	9.7	10.2	12.4	12.6	10.7	9.4	11.6
12.2	14.0	15.5	17.3	19.1	22.2	25.5	29.9	37.9	43.3
6.2	7.1	8.9	10.4	12.2	14.5	16.9	19.8	23.0	28.7
2.3	2.4	2.6	3.1	3.3	3.6	4.3	4.6	5.2	5.6
9.9	11.7	12.9	13.9	15.2	17.4	19.8	23.2	25.4	32.3
13.4	19.0	20.5	22.9	26.2	30.6	31.9	36.6	42.2	49.3
3.4	3.9	5.6	6.8	7.3	8.3	11.1	11.8	13.2	17.4
14.1	14.2	14.7	15.2	15.8	16.5	17.7	19.7	21.3	23.2
6.3	7.4	8.0	8.4	9.3	11.0	11.4	12.9	15.7	19.0
8.1	9.4	10.9	14.0	17.2	19.0	21.7	25.9	31.9	38.6
98.8	125.2	135.3	155.9	168.1	194.7	208.5	241.2	273.9	309.5
113.8	142.2	152.1	172.6	188.1	211.9	234.4	270.1	306.5	347.0
193.8	240.6	255.6	289.2	310.9	358.2	381.1	435.6	489.6	547.3

tance of the sector was thought to rest in the size of its contribution to foreign exchange earnings (a factor of great importance because of the decline in the contribution of some of the traditional sources of foreign exchange earnings—for example, minerals and foreign bases), national income, regional development, productive utilization of the natural beauties of the island, and employment opportunities which could be provided directly and indirectly.

Two important indicators of the size and direction of the demand for tourist services are the number of tourist arrivals and gross foreign exchange earnings realized. Table 14.2 shows the evolution of tourist arrivals and foreign exchange earnings from 1960 to 1973. The actual annual average rate of growth in tourist arrivals during the period was of the order of 19 percent, a very high rate indeed, compared with international tourist traffic. Similarly, the annual rate of growth in foreign exchange earnings over the fourteen-year period was about 19 percent.

Table 14.2. *Tourist Arrivals, 1960–73*

	Arrivals				Growth rate (percent)			
Item	*1960*	*1966*	*1971*	*1973*	*1960–66*	*1966–71*	*1971–73*	*1960–73*
Tourists	25,700	54,100	178,600	264,066	14	27	21	19
Excursionists[a]	60,900	88,500	129,300	168,770	8	8	14	8
Foreign exchange earnings (millions of Cyprus pounds)	2.3	3.6	13.6	23.8	8	30	32	19

Source: Five-Year Plan for Economic Development, Planning Bureau; and Cyprus Tourism Organization, Annual Reports.
a. Visitors staying less than twenty-four hours.

Some of the basic characteristics of tourism in Cyprus were:

—Tourist policy was aimed at attracting visitors from the high- and middle-income groups to the exclusion of mass tourism.

—About 90 percent of all arrivals were by air because of the general development of air services and the fact that Cyprus is an island far from its main tourist markets.

—The most important countries of origin were the United Kingdom, Germany, the Scandinavian countries, United States, and Greece.

—The Cyprus tourist season is much longer than in most other tourist countries, lasting for nine months (March to October and December). It is characterized by three peak periods—April, July to September, and December—which correspond to the Easter, summer, and Christmas holiday seasons respectively. Thirty percent of the total tourist traffic arrives between July and September.

—Between 1963 and 1969 over 80 percent of all visitors came to Cyprus for a vacation, and between 1970 and 1973 this percentage increased to over 90 percent.

—The average length of stay throughout the period fluctuated between 9.2 and 13 days, which is one of the reasons for the comparatively high revenue earned per tourist.

Two characteristics of tourist demand in Cyprus are relevant to the purposes of this paper. The first is that the bulk of the additional tourist traffic attracted to Cyprus between 1969 and 1973 concentrated mainly in Famagusta and Kyrenia (45 and 18 percent respectively). As a result, a huge hotel construction program was mounted in the Famagusta area with consequences that are analyzed below. The second and far more important characteristic was that the great majority of the additional tourists between 1969 and 1973 chose to stay mainly in hotels of the higher categories (three to five stars). This development was in line with the basic tourist policy adopted by the government to attract tourists from the upper- and middle-income groups. An analysis of hotel capacity by category, region, and occupancy rates for 1971, 1972, and 1973 (see Table 14.3) reveals that over two-thirds of the bed capacity was in the three- to five-star category (1971, 66 percent; 1972, 71 percent; 1973, 73 percent); about 45 percent of the three- to five-star hotels were in the Famagusta and Kyrenia districts; and the highest occupancy rates were usually recorded in these hotels.

Cyprus Society and Culture

Before examining the impact of tourism on Cyprus society and culture, it is relevant to analyze that culture in some detail. Before the Turkish invasion in July 1974, the Greeks and Turks of Cyprus had lived side by side for almost four hundred years. Although the Turkish Cypriot culture differs from the Greek Cypriot culture, there was some fusion between the two communities, and Greek and Turkish Cypriots describe themselves in very similar ways. This section of the paper refers primarily to Greek Cypriot society although much of it may also apply to the Turkish community.

Alex Inkeles defines culture in his book *What Is Sociology?* as: "The grand total of all the objects, ideas, knowledge, ways of doing things, habits, values and attitudes which each generation in a society passes on to the next." He goes on to say that

> the transmission of culture is man's substitute for the instincts whereby most other living creatures are equipped with the means for coping with their environment and relating to one another. Yet it is more flexible than instinct, and can grow: that is, it can store new information infinitely more rapidly than the process of mutation

Table 14.3. *Number of Beds and Bed Occupancy in One- to Five-Star Hotels, 1971–73*

Region	Five stars Number of beds	Five stars Rate of occupancy	Four stars Number of beds	Four stars Rate of occupancy	Three stars Number of beds	Three stars Rate of occupan
1971						
Nicosia	620	47.1	—	—	537	34.1
Limassol	300	20.6	244	33.8	170	47.5
Famagusta	—	—	1,425	48.0	486	47.0
Larnaca	—	—	—	—	65	41.9
Paphos	—	—	—	—	—	—
Kyrenia	—	—	300	60.6	360	48.2
Hill resorts[a]	—	—	140	31.2	60	14.0
Total	920	42.6	2,109	47.4	1,678	42.6
1972						
Nicosia	620	48.3	—	—	578	40.8
Limassol	300	32.4	226	36.0	165	29.9
Famagusta	—	—	2,048	54.1	1,078	51.1
Larnaca	—	—	—	—	56	42.1
Paphos	—	—	—	—	—	—
Kyrenia	—	—	305	70.6	419	51.6
Hill resorts[a]	—	—	130	36.1	59	18.0
Total	920	43.1	2,709	54.1	2,356	45.9
1973						
Nicosia	620	46.3	—	—	589	42.2
Limassol	300	38.7	569	19.5	165	25.5
Famagusta	—	—	2,791	47.5	1,344	45.6
Larnaca	—	—	226	2.0	57	30.0
Paphos	—	—	214	18.7	—	—
Kyrenia	—	—	305	66.6	466	50.1
Hill resorts[a]	—	—	150	27.9	111	18.4
Total	920	43.8	4,255	44.1	2,732	43.3

n.a. Not available.
— No hotels of that category.
Source: Cyprus Tourism Organization, Annual Reports, 1971, 1972, 1973.
a. Assumed to be in operation 180 days.

and biological evolution can enrich the instinctual storehouse of any other species.[1]

1. Alex Inkeles, *What Is Sociology?* (Englewood Cliffs, N.J.: Prentice-Hall, 1964), p. 66.

Two stars		One star		Total		
Number of beds	Rate of occupancy	Number of beds	Rate of occupancy	Number of beds	Rate of occupancy	Region
						1971
224	34.2	215	26.8	1,611	38.0	Nicosia
99	40.7	77	26.4	890	35.8	Limassol
249	50.6	115	38.4	2,275	47.6	Famagusta
—	—	26	n.a.	91	41.9	Larnaca
45	41.3	—	—	45	41.3	Paphos
149	36.9	294	36.2	1,103	48.5	Kyrenia
214	22.4	718	17.1	1,132	20.9	Hill resorts[a]
980	39.5	1,445	27.0	7,147	41.4	Total
						1972
285	27.3	181	25.5	1,664	39.4	Nicosia
103	30.4	76	20.4	870	31.9	Limassol
291	46.3	115	45.6	3,533	53.2	Famagusta
—	—	—	—	56	42.1	Larnaca
45	45.8	—	—	45	45.8	Paphos
184	44.7	342	27.4	1,250	50.5	Kyrenia
278	26.8	535	16.4	1,002	22.2	Hill resorts[a]
1,186	37.3	1,249	25.4	8,420	44.9	Total
						1973
343	31.8	183	19.5	1,735	39.4	Nicosia
137	31.1	41	29.9	1,212	28.2	Limassol
611	45.6	113	26.3	4,859	46.2	Famagusta
—	—	25	6.0	283	16.0	Larnaca
45	31.9	21	n.a.	280	22.6	Paphos
308	49.7	290	33.8	1,369	50.6	Kyrenia
226	19.7	571	23.3	1,058	24.8	Hill resorts[a]
1,670	39.4	1,223	26.1	10,796	41.4	Total

A glance at Cyprus reveals a society of very hard-working people prepared to save and make temporary sacrifices for the wealth to improve their status. The ideology and value system attach great importance to individual achievement and are generally responsive to innovations, new ideas, and opportunities. Education, both secondary and higher, is viewed as the vehicle of advancement, and Cyprus has one of the highest literacy rates in the world. Because there is no university there, however, all students have to go to universities abroad, mainly in Greece, Turkey, the United Kingdom, France, Germany, and other European countries, and the United States. After they return to Cyprus these educated people often hold positions of importance and exercise great influence in society, affecting both attitudes and values. Although Cyprus is not a completely meritocratic society, family background is no obstacle to reaching the top of the hierarchy in the civil service or the management of industry, and there is a high degree of social and geographical mobility. The cabinet, the parliament, the judiciary, the upper echelons of the civil service, and top management in industry, trade, and other sectors of the economy are largely composed of people from poor or middle-income families who have climbed to the top of the ladder through hard work, proven ability, and education. Entrepreneurial talent is widely dispersed among the upper and middle classes, the latter being a substantial proportion of the whole population, although economic power is not evenly distributed but concentrated mainly in the upper or upper-middle class.

The Greek Cypriot culture may thus be described as competitive and individualistic. A competitive spirit is encouraged at an early age, and upward socioeconomic striving is highly valued.[2] According to custom, for example, the professional and social potential of the bridegroom is supported by a dowry, a gift of money or property from the bride's parents. The Turkish Cypriot culture differs in not attaching such great importance to achievement and wealth, and the Turkish community was therefore relatively less well represented in the business and economic life of the island.

Rural people are less cosmopolitan, less progressive, less forward-looking in their attitudes, and much warmer in their relations than are those in urban (tourist) areas. Furthermore, family ties are stronger in rural than in urban communities. Hospitality forms an integral part of Cyprus culture. On the whole, Cypriots are characterized by sincere and spontaneous feelings toward foreigners. In

2. Perhaps one example of this spirit is seen in the fact that, despite Turkish control of 70 percent of all natural resources on the island since 1974, the Greek Cypriots were able to increase their exports from £26.9 million (US$67.3 million) in the first six months of 1975 to £49.1 million (US$122.8 million) in the same period of 1976.

fact, the Greek word *xenos,* "foreigner," means guest-friend, who is looked upon as a sacred person.

The political leadership is fully committed to Western values. Fundamental decisions are made on rational grounds through deliberative process and democratic institutions. Various organizations and special interest groups are able to influence to a good extent the decisionmaking process. The planning function is organized to permit the participation in the planning process of the trade unions, the employers' federation, Chambers of Commerce and Industry, experts from the private sector, and representatives of local authorities. The ideological orientation and the sociopolitical structure lean heavily toward individualism, free enterprise, and capitalism. In the economic development of Cyprus the approach was not toward intensified state control of economic activity but toward liberating and encouraging the energies and initiative of the private sector. The government used economic weapons to provide incentives and disincentives that would direct the economy along the desired paths. Only where private enterprise failed to respond did the government interfere. In the five-year plans for economic development prepared and implemented since independence only 25 to 35 percent of total investment was envisaged and carried out by the state, and the balance was contributed by the private sector. Private initiative thus played an important and leading role in the island's economic development.

Cyprus appears to possess some of the characteristics of Apter's "reconciliation model" under which "the government's efforts take the form of stimulating non-governmental or local entrepreneurship. This may be done through private sources of trade for promoting entrepreneurship, through expanding the possibility of joint government and private enterprise, through industrial development corporations and similar projects and through encouraging outside investment." Although all of Apter's conclusions about countries of this type are not applicable to Cyprus, at least one point appears to be relevant: "the pace of growth is never more dramatic than that which the public is prepared to accept since policy must agree with public desires . . . coercive techniques remain at a minimum."[3]

3. D. E. Apter, "Systems, Process and the Politics of Economic Development," in *Industrialization and Society,* B. F. Hoselitz and W. E. Moore, eds. (Paris and The Hague: Unesco and Moulton, 1963).

Impact of Tourism on Values and Attitudes: Creation of Conflict

Government policy after independence was consistently aimed at attracting high- and middle-income tourists, and marketing programs were geared toward these social groups. The influx of tourists did not have serious adverse effects on the social values or attitudes of Cyprus because, among other reasons, the tourist was not considered as an "invader" or an "unwanted" person whose behavior was a demonstration of financial superiority. There is no positive evidence at all that the "demonstration effect" of tourism was detrimental. Indeed, the impact of this phenomenon was marginal compared with the more important and wider effects of the mass media such as radio and television.

Still, the influx of large numbers of tourists, especially in the area of Famagusta where about 45 percent of the tourist traffic was concentrated, did have some influence on social behavior and values. The total population of Famagusta city in 1973 was around 40,000, and tourist arrivals in Cyprus in the peak month of July amounted to 38,000. Therefore, about 17,000 foreign tourists visited Famagusta in a single month, and since Famagusta also attracted local tourists from Nicosia, the ratio of foreign tourists to the local population was not more than 1:3.5. In sheer numbers the proportion of foreigners to Cypriots was not overwhelming, even during this peak month, but the intermingling of a great number of foreign people with the local residents did have some effect. The Cypriots who came into close contact with the tourists were, apart from hotel staff and people in the catering professions, young males, who made friends and enjoyed themselves with the tourists—especially with unaccompanied females—in the evenings at bars, restaurants, and nightclubs. The close and continuous contact of Cypriot youth with foreigners made them adopt a sense of values in such matters as sex, morality, and type of dress slightly different from the prevailing traditional views held by their parents. This state of affairs caused some concern because Cypriot parents attach great importance to sexual modesty. I would not, however, allege that the impact on the behavior of the youth was detrimental or that it created any irreparable strain on the relations between youths and their parents. Most parents eventually accepted the view that entertainment, night life, different modes of dress, and tolerance in sexual matters were not necessarily evil. It can thus be argued that the so-called demonstration effect in this particular case helped the older generation to acquire an open-mindedness, a greater tolerance, and a broader overall view of social behavior—attitudes prevalent in the developed industrial countries from which the tourists emanated. Cyprus culture was able to absorb these different patterns of behavior and attitudes without any disrupting effects, and to the extent that it assimilated these differences the culture was perhaps enriched.

There is also little doubt that the development of tourism created new jobs. Women in particular were hired not only for the low-paid jobs of cleaning and washing but also as receptionists, managers, and tourist guides. The improved financial status of females did not create conflicts between parents and children or husbands and wives, nor did it challenge the authority of the parents or husbands. The ambition of every parent in Cyprus is to offer his children a good education and secure for them jobs which will establish them as decent citizens. The financial benefits accruing from tourism in fact enabled family members to share these financial burdens and encouraged savings that are used by the children to create their own homes and to live more comfortably. The redefinition of the role of females as a social group started in Cyprus in the early 1960s. It was accentuated by the development of tourism but nonetheless was a natural social change brought about by general economic development. Under the Cyprus constitution women have equal rights, which they claim and exercise with no animosity on the part of the males. In fact, women hold responsible positions side by side with men in all spheres of activity in Cyprus society, although admittedly in much smaller numbers.

Illegitimate births, abortions, or prostitution were not observed in Cyprus as a result of tourism development. The annual reports of the Medical Department reveal that the incidence of venereal disease was lower in Famagusta and Kyrenia, the main tourist regions, than in Nicosia and other urban centers.[4]

4. J. G. Peristiany, "Honour and Shame in a Cypriot Highland Village," in *Honour and Shame: The Values of Mediterranean Society*, J. G. Peristiany, ed. (Worcester and London: Ebenezer Baylis and Son Ltd., Trinity Press, 1965), describes the strict code that traditionally governs the conduct of Cypriot women and regards overt sexual behavior as a reflection on the family honor.

One negative effect of tourism was seen in the occasional disappointment of Cypriots from inland areas, especially Nicosia, who during the summer visited Famagusta to spend a day with their family at the seaside. They were apt to find a shortage of services and facilities (mainly parking space and a free stretch of beach) along a popular but limited section of the Famagusta shore. Because of overcrowding the town could not meet the needs of local tourism. These disappointments were directed not against the foreign visitors, however, but against the municipal authorities for improper planning and inadequate provision of infrastructure in the peak months of July and August, when the greatest number of tourists flooded the area.

The Encounter

Cyprus is not an industrial society, and personal relations are informal and close. The Cypriot is psychologically capable of adjusting to change; culturally and educationally he does not object to the encounter with tourists. In fact, most people seem to regard it as a pleasant event. Communication is no problem because the majority of the Cypriots speak at least one foreign language—English. Cypriots tend to be enthusiastic and warm, and many of them welcome visitors not solely for profitmaking but with spontaneous hospitality. Except in the case of Cypriots working in hotels and restaurants, the encounter between residents and tourists is usually seen not as a cash-generating activity, but as an opportunity for genuine human rapport, toward which the whole philosophy of tourism (cultural exchange) is geared. A French journalist who recently visited Cyprus villages has described this friendly type of encounter:

> My arrival in a rented car with red license plates—which signifies that I am a foreigner—never goes unnoticed. Someone always comes to greet me and I always wind up at one of the tables. I am spoken to in English, sometimes French. If I am invited to someone's table it is not, as in other Mediterranean countries, to make me spend my money. Quite the contrary. When the check comes they all sing out in unison, "No, Steve" (one becomes friends very quickly) "a visitor never pays in Cyprus!" A waiter in a cafe once even ran after me to return the tip I had left. What a culture shock![5]

5. Steve Walsh, *La Généraliste,* June 26, 1976 (translated from the original French).

There are many other examples of reciprocation betwen tourist and Cypriot because of compatibility, mutual interests, and respect, factors which sometimes create lasting friendships. Many Cypriot families invite tourists to their own homes and offer them hospitality or show them around in their private cars for the sake of making new acquaintances. I can cite hundreds of cases of Cypriot families from Famagusta and Kyrenia, including hoteliers, who after the invasion received letters from tourists who not only expressed sympathy but also offered to help in various positive ways.

The Cyprus Tourism Organization controls the profession of tourist guides. No one is allowed to enter the profession except Cypriot nationals, who must have the appropriate educational background, be of decent character, and have graduated from the school for guides, which teaches Cyprus history, archaeology, art, and culture. The foreign guide who acts as intermediary or cultural interpreter is nonexistent. Foreign guides may be allowed to accompany tourists, but only to act as translators for Cypriot guides. A tourist on a conducted tour will be given an objective and accurate description of the archaeological site, historical place, or ancient monument and will have all his queries answered by the local guide conducting the tour. The role of these guides is considered of vital importance, which is why their professional requirements are high.

With one exception all hotels belong to Cypriots; there is no foreign hotel chain in Cyprus. Foreign tour operators who promote and sell Cyprus tourism abroad have offices on the island, but they are usually manned by local Cypriots. Brochures, guidebooks, leaflets, and other promotional material issued by the tour operators or travel agents are based on material provided by the Cyprus Tourism Organization. These arrangements rule out the misrepresentation of Cyprus history or culture by people alien to the situation. Similarly, advertisements by tour operators and travel agents are usually produced in close cooperation with the Cyprus Tourism Organization. In addition, because the bulk of tourist traffic to Cyprus was flown by the national carrier, Cyprus Airways, the role of foreign intermediaries was further minimized.

My own conclusion drawn from the Cyprus experience is that the cultural costs of tourist development may have been exaggerated in some cases. I do not think that social systems must of necessity be integral wholes so that if there are changes in one section the whole system must either collapse or degenerate. Is it not possible for some people to hold modern values while others have a completely different set of values? Or might people apply modern commercial values in one sector of their lives but have a completely different set of values in another sector? Is it not a false distinction to make a clear-cut division between traditional culture on the one hand and Western or modern culture on the other? Sociological research might shed some light on these questions and indicate the directions to be followed by developing countries to minimize the cultural costs of tourism development. There is no doubt that in tourism planning it is vital to protect the essential and unique elements of a country's culture. To gain affluence at the expense of national identity and personality is undesirable and should be ruled out. There must be changes, however, and those which are essential and probably not harmful should be encouraged and accepted.

Impact of Tourism on Cultural Manifestations

The development of tourism in Cyprus gradually created a demand for traditional handicrafts and gave an impetus toward revitalizing some of the crafts which were moribund. There is little doubt that without tourism development some of these would have become completely extinct. Pottery, for example, is a centuries-old art that has been handed down to the present artisans over the generations. It is now practiced in a few villages which attract tourists who come to admire the artisans' skill and their dexterity in using the old tools. Another traditional craft is the weaving of curtains, tablecloths, scarves, and the like. This craft, practiced mainly by women, has also brought tourists to distant villages to buy the products and to watch them being made. Embroidery is another traditional art requiring patience, elegance, and excellence of performance. Basketry makes use of stalks, canes, reeds, and wild grass—materials of no other economic value. Jewelry, wood carving, and leather making are some of the other crafts that have been revitalized and reestablished by the influx of tourists and represent a new utilization of resources.

Tourism development has not only provided employment for the people (about 2,000 in 1972) engaged in these crafts but also enriched their lives and made them more worthwhile. Mass production has not been introduced to the craft industry, and with one exception—a machine-printed scarf that imitates foreign style—the products have not been commercialized or cheapened. Most of the goods are handmade products of real craftsmanship. To encourage the revitalization of ancient crafts the government set up training programs and apprenticeship schemes. Youths, mainly from families traditionally engaged in the crafts, were given intensive instruction in both design and technique. Support and encouragement were also given by the government to the school for the deaf and the reform school, which do excellent weaving and wood carving.

There is room for further development of local crafts and handicrafts. The design of products for sale to tourists should not derive solely from existing models and traditional patterns but could be inspired by the country's recent history and its struggle for independence. This creative effort must spring from a deeper knowledge of traditional forms, and designers with the proper skills and imagination must prove their ingenuity by adapting these traditional forms to conditions of modern living. There is also room for development in the field of traditional costume and dress. Finally, there is the question of commercialization of the products. To avoid exploitation by middlemen some communities have formed local cooperatives to market the products and protect the interests of the producers. There are, however, many cases where exploitation by middlemen is taking place.

The cultural services of the Ministry of Education encouraged and supported drama, flower shows, art festivals, folkloric dances, and other performances related to the history and culture of the island. The influx of tourists created a new demand for these spectacles, which expanded and flourished considerably in recent years and are now a common part of the national scene, enjoyed by both residents and tourists. The folkloric dances are especially significant in that they combine the artistic expression of the performers with a revitalization of national costumes and the development of Cyprus music. The artists start their training at the secondary level of education and are chosen because of their aptitude, grace, and dancing ability. At a later stage they join local clubs and associations for the perpetuation of local folklore, encouraged and financed by the Ministry of Education and the Cyprus Tourism Organization. Here too, however, there is room for further development. For instance, a national ballet might be established, with choreography inspired by the history and national life of Cyprus.

Impact of Tourism on the Welfare of the People

Because of its intersectoral nature, the development of tourism encompasses practically all fields of economic activity. It offers employment not only in the tourism industry proper—hotels, restaurants, travel agencies, bars and nightclubs, handicrafts, and retail trades—but also in transport and construction, and even in agriculture and fishing (through tourist demand for fruit, vegetables, meat, and fish). It can thus be argued that the development of tourism affects a large section of the population. Table 14.4 indicates the number of people engaged in hotels and restaurants from 1964 to 1973. Although these are by no means all the jobs created by the development of the tourism industry, they accounted for 3.5 percent of the economically active population. If employment in tourist services (see Table 14.5) is added in, the total number of people employed in tourism was around 16,500, or 5.5 percent of the economically active population. Employment generated in the construction sector (buildings, roads, ports, and airport), in remaining services (architects, engineers, planners), and in the retail trades could easily more than double this number, without taking indirect employment in agriculture into consideration.

An attempt was made (see Table 14.6) to find out the cost per job created in the hotel industry compared with the cost per job in manufacturing and utilities (electricity, gas, and water). The estimated cost per job in hotels was £8,740 in 1972-73. This figure does

Table 14.4. *Direct Employment in Tourism*

	Number of people employed		Percent of economically active population	
Year	Hotels, hotel apartments, and guest houses	Restaurants, cafes, and taverns	Hotels, hotel apartments, and guest houses	Restaurants, cafes, and taverns
1964	890	5,511	0.4	2.1
1965	962	5,598	0.4	2.3
1966	1,069	5,585	0.4	2.2
1967	1,402	5,508	0.5	2.1
1968	1,398	5,618	0.5	2.2
1969	1,457	5,730	0.5	2.2
1970	1,638	5,845	0.6	2.2
1971	2,206	5,962	0.8	2.2
1972	2,649	6,181	1.0	2.3
1973	3,296	6,304	1.2	2.3

Source: Ministry of Finance, Statistics and Research Department, Services Survey.

Table 14.5. *Employment in Tourist Services, 1972*

Service	Number of establishments	Number employed
Tourist agencies	132	674
Car rental services	55	116
Tourist guides	n.a.	75
Crafts and handicrafts	276	2,944
Airline offices	12	324
Speed boats and other sea facilities	n.a.	50
Cyprus Tourism Organization	n.a.	50
Subtotal		4,233
Airport staff	n.a.	350
Taxi services	336	1,500
Bus, transport	730	1,530
Total		7,622

n.a. Not applicable.
Source: Cottage Industry Survey, 1972; and Ministry of Finance, Statistics and Research Department, Registration of Establishments Survey, 1972.

not include employment created in subsectors like travel agencies, car-rental services, and the like, or even employment created in the actual construction of the hotels. Thus the cost per job must in fact be much lower. In contrast, it was estimated that the cost per job in manufacturing was £11,920. These figures must be read with great caution, but they give an approximate indication.

Table 14.7 compares the increase in wages of people engaged in the hotel industry proper with those in other sectors of the economy, using 1967 as the base year. It is obvious that wages from 1967 onward increased much more rapidly in the hotel industry than in other sectors. Table 14.8 gives the actual salaries in agriculture, manufacturing, and hotels and restaurants. Salaries in the hotel and restaurant trades, especially for females, are usually higher than those in the other sectors. Not included in the comparative figures are additional benefits to hotel staff, such as meals and accommodation.

The development of tourism created a sudden demand for trained labor, which necessitated the establishment of a number of hotel schools where training was offered at all levels and in all specializations. One such was the Hotel and Catering Institute established with the cooperation of the International Labour Organisation. Its quality of instruction, facilities, and environment are among the best for schools of this kind. Initially, a number of lecturers from abroad taught at the school and trained Cypriot counterparts. The school now admits students from other developing countries as a manifestation of international cooperation in the field of tourism.

The development of tourism in Cyprus has benefited the economy as a whole as well as a substantial number of individuals engaged in both the tourism industry proper and other sectors. These people and their families have undoubtedly improved their

Table 14.6. *Cost per Job in Manufacturing, Utilities, and Tourism*

Sector	Unit
Manufacturing[a]	
Capital formation	
1972	£7.5 million
1973	£8.0 million
Total	£15.5 million
Additional jobs created, 1972–73	1,300
Capital formation/additional job	£11,920
Utilities (electricity, gas, water)[a]	
Capital formation	
1972	£3.9 million
1973	£5.2 million
Total	£9.1 million
Additional jobs created, 1972–73	1,300
Capital formation/additional job	£7,000
Tourism (hotel industry)[b]	
Beds created, 1972–73, in one- to five-star hotels	3,650
Average cost per bed	£2,000[c]
Estimated total cost	£7,300,000
Additional jobs created, 1972–73	835
Estimated cost per job	£8,740

Note: One Cyprus pound equals about US$2.50.

a. Data from Economic Report, 1974; and Ministry of Finance, Statistics and Research Department, Statistical Abstract, 1974.

b. Data from Cyprus Tourism Organization, Annual Reports; and Ministry of Finance, Statistics and Research Department, Services Survey, 1973.

c. Estimate of Cyprus Tourism Organization for four-star hotels.

Table 14.7. *Index of Average Annual Wage Rates in Tourism Compared with That in Other Sectors of the Economy, 1965–72*

Sector	1965	1966	1967	1968	1969	1970	1971	1972
Agriculture	92	98	100	109	118	128	149	168
Mining and quarrying	95	99	100	105	123	133	145	159
Manufacturing	91	95	100	104	114	122	136	158
Construction	94	96	100	109	120	145	165	189
Electricity, gas, and water	97	98	100	127	135	142	153	178
Trade	90	93	100	104	108	115	124	154
Banks	93	95	100	110	112	121	132	152
Insurance	98	99	100	107	125	136	145	170
Transport and communication	92	96	100	102	123	135	150	178
Government	95	96	100	108	127	128	142	166
Municipalities	96	98	100	105	123	129	144	159
Services	91	95	100	103	117	120	145	163
All activities	93	96	100	107	120	130	146	169
Tourism (hotel industry)	70	76	100	116	133	145	162	193

Source: Ministry of Finance, Statistics and Research Department, Economic Reports and Services Surveys.

financial position and standard of living, life-style and nutrition, life chances and general welfare. Because the technical know-how and educational level of Cypriots are high, there was no need to import foreign labor for any of the administrative or managerial posts in the hotel industry, in engineering, or elsewhere. In fact, the employment policy followed by the government prohibited the importation of foreign labor. Many women were thus brought into the tourism sector, as well as underemployed agricultural workers, all of whom derived financial benefit from the development of tourism; at the same time, the underemployment of agricultural labor was ameliorated. With a nine-month tourist season in Cyprus, seasonal employment is somewhat of a problem but not so acute as in other countries.

The more crucial questions are: Has the impact of tourism development been the same on all social groups of Cyprus society? Has it benefited everyone equally? Has the accruing welfare enriched a few at the expense of others? Has there been any foreign exploitation?

Table 14.8. *Normal Average Monthly Salaries
of Selected Occupations by Industry, 1971–73*
(Cyprus pounds)

	Agriculture			Manufacturing Food		
Occupation	1971	1972	1973	1971	1972	1973
Managers	n.a.	166	173	n.a.	157	197
Department heads	n.a.	n.a.	n.a.	n.a.	106	140
Foremen and housekeepers	81	96	95	72	70	87
Clerks (females)	34	36	33	36	36	41
Laborers and chambermaids	23	26	29	28	29	33

n.a. Not available.
Source: Ministry of Finance, Statistics and Research Department, Statistics of Wages, Salaries and Hours of Work.
Note: Salaries include overtime and service charges. One Cyprus pound equals about US$2.50.
a. Females.

Under Cyprus legislation foreign investment must involve local participation of capital, which is usually, but not always, in the majority. As stated earlier, out of all the existing hotel accommodation in Cyprus, only one complex of about 1,000 beds belongs to a foreign firm. In this case, too, there is local participation of capital. The same is true of travel agencies, which by law must employ local staff except when the required skills are not available in the Cyprus market, which rarely happens. It can therefore be stated without any reservation that rarely was there any exploitation of local people by foreigners.

It is true, however, that the benefits resulting from tourism were not distributed equally among all social groups. In a capitalist system this is always the case. The hotel owner benefits much more than the charwoman, and the tour operator must have a reasonably high margin of profit, probably higher than that of the hotel owners, in order to promote a tourist destination. If the available hotel capacity exceeds expected demand for tourist accommodation, hoteliers may be forced to lower their prices, and the resulting benefits will be derived by the tour operators alone. But it cannot be seriously alleged that there was any overexploitation by the tour operators, since the market mechanisms were operating more or less satisfactorily.

| Manufacturing | | | | | | Hotels and restaurants | | |
| Beverages | | | Textiles | | | | | |
1971	1972	1973	1971	1972	1973	1971	1972	1973
n.a.	193	221	n.a.	141	196	122	186	250
n.a.	136	151	n.a.	104	152	n.a.	78	173
80	103	116	73	85	74	n.a.	70[a]	98
52	57	67	38	35	43	56	63	72
n.a.	34	34	n.a.	32	37	42	48	54

Land Development

In land development there was more serious exploitation in one particular case. As previously indicated, from 1969 almost 45 percent of the tourist traffic was concentrated in the Famagusta region, particularly in an area about five miles long and three-quarters of a mile wide. Table 14.9 shows that the rate of growth of all types of hotel accommodation in Famagusta since 1969 ranged between 14 and 67 percent a year as against an annual average rate of growth of 13 percent in the whole country. Over and above hotel construction there was a huge building program to meet the great demand for residential housing and commercial buildings. This unprecedented growth in construction created the usual problems of high density, such as increased traffic, inadequate parking space, and very tall buildings. The small section of the Famagusta beach, henceforth referred to as the problem area, reached saturation point, and the demand for tourist accommodation pushed land values very high. Table 14.10 indicates the evolution of land prices of various categories of land in three different towns: Paphos, the least developed in all ways; Famagusta, the area under discussion; and Limassol, a region moderately developed for tourism and more highly developed then Famagusta for industrial and commercial use. A comparison of Tables 14.9 and 14.10 reveals a close relation between the increase in land values and the increase in hotel accommodation in Famagusta. About 60 percent of the total of 7,573 beds in hotels and hotel apartments in the Famagusta district were concentrated in the problem area. Note the great difference between the value of tourist seaside land in Paphos and Limassol and that in Famagusta. In the problem area the market value of one donum (about a third of an acre) on the shore in 1973 was around £150,000, while similar land in Paphos was £5,000 and in Limassol around £50,000. Agricultural land, however, had more or less the same value in all regions. Prices of commercial land in Famagusta were almost the same as those in Limassol, with only marginal differences; in Paphos the value of commercial land is of course much lower because it is a small town with little commercial activity. Thus the annual rise in land values in the problem area between 1960 and 1965 is estimated to be roughly around 20 percent, between 1965 and 1970 around 40 per-

Table 14.9. *Development of Hotel and Apartment Accommodation in Famagusta and the Whole of Cyprus*

	Famagusta			Cyprus	
Year	Hotel beds	Percent of total	Annual rate of growth	Hotel beds	Annual rate of growth
1961	457	11.4	—	4,003	—
1962	519	11.9	13.6	4,370	9.2
1963	545	11.8	5.0	4,602	5.3
1964	589	11.1	8.1	5,288	14.9
1965	589	11.1	0.0	5,288	0.0
1966	850	14.6	45.8	5,880	11.2
1967	862	13.9	0.3	6,211	5.6
1968	1,156[a]	16.8	34.1	6,865[a]	10.5
1969	1,932[a]	25.2	67.1	7,677[a]	11.8
1970	2,214[a]	26.6	14.6	8,338[a]	8.6
1971	3,645[a]	36.6	64.6	9,963[a]	19.5
1972	5,444[a]	43.3	49.4	12,576[a]	26.2
1973	7,573[a]	48.2	39.1	15,719[a]	25.0
Average			26.0		13.0

Sources: Planning Bureau, Five-Year Plans for Economic Development; Cyprus Tourism Organization, Annual Reports and Records.
a. Includes capacity of hotel apartments.

Table 14.10. *Evolution of Land Values*
in Three Areas of Cyprus
(Cyprus pounds per donum)[a]

Region	Tourist seaside land	Commercial land	Agricultural land for dry-farming
Paphos			
1960	500	2,500	80
1965	1,000	3,200	105
1970	2,300	4,700	140
1973	5,000	8,000	160
Famagusta			
1960	1,600	3,000	80
1965	4,000	5,300	105
1970	21,500	16,200	140
1973	150,000	70,000	170
Limassol			
1960	1,500	3,000	80
1965	3,000	5,000	105
1970	11,200	18,000	140
1973	50,000	75,000	170

Source: Compiled by Antonios Andronicou from data supplied by the Department of Lands and Surveys. Figures may have in some cases a margin of error of 10 to 15 percent.

a. A donum is about a third of an acre; one Cyprus pound equals US$2.50.

cent, and between 1970 and 1973 over 90 percent, with an average annual increase of over 40 percent between 1960 and 1973. During the same period, tourist seaside land increased in value at the average annual rate of 30 percent in Limassol and 20 percent in Paphos.

Before 1960 the land in the problem area was either for agricultural use or composed of sand dunes. The average size of each plot ranged from seven to ten donums and the income therefrom was low. Who then derived the benefits accruing from the rise in land values? In some cases the bulk of the monetary benefits went into the pockets of a small number of developers and speculators who bought the land in the open market, at prices admittedly much higher than those in other areas of Cyprus but lower than the developers' final selling price for the building sites. Fortunately, there were few such cases of exploitation because the original owners of the land often realized the value of their property and either engaged in the hotel industry, developed the land themselves for commercial use, or held onto it in the expectation of higher prices. There is no doubt, however, that the rapid development brought about by the demand for tourist services led to the parceling of land and to the exploitation of a few landowners by a handful of developers who amassed considerable wealth. Worst of all, this rapid development placed an enormous strain on the existing infrastructure and adversely affected the environment. The government took steps to counteract these harmful effects, but the pace of development was so rapid that the remedial measures (such as limiting the height of buildings and density of construction) did not prove completely effective. Under existing institutional arrangements the local municipal authority was responsible for issuing building permits, constructing roads, creating parking places and recreational grounds, and so forth, but the municipal authority was not technically or professionally equipped to tackle effectively the innumerable problems created, nor were their legislative powers adequate to deal effectively with the new situation. Because of the high price of land the municipality did not have the financial resources needed to create recreation areas and public amenities. Nor could the municipality easily resist the pressures from certain groups of citizens who would accuse the authorities of retarding the development of their town if they imposed strict controls and restrictions. The mistake of the overdevelopment of the Famagusta area served as a warning, however, and the government immediately drew up an Island Plan, enacted regulations, and defined land-use zones, under which the volume, density, and height of buildings were controlled in the remaining areas of Cyprus, that is, Kyrenia, Paphos, Larnaca, and most parts of Limassol.

The conclusions to be drawn from this analysis are that the great demand created by rapid tourism development outstripped the available facilities; the rise in land values enabled a few people to amass wealth at the expense of others and made problematic the creation of facilities for use by the general public; and the existing legal and institutional arrangements were proven inadequate to cope with the changing situation and urgently needed to be strengthened and enforced.

Measures which could prevent similar situations are: (1) a master plan for physical planning of the island, providing for all aspects of development by defining zones for shipping centers, recreational services, and tourism development; (2) detailed zoning regulations to limit the use of land and the height, volume, and density of buildings; (3) a land development tax, a betterment charge, or a value-added land tax. Some of these measures were in fact taken. The last is still to be applied and will probably be tested in the courts. It should go a long way toward alleviating or minimizing the undesirable effects of the increase in land values created partly through public investment in infrastructure and similar projects. Above all it is designed to limit land speculation, and it is hoped that public revenues and eventually society as a whole will get some of the benefits accruing from large increases in land values.

Control of Decisions and Significant Events

My analysis has, I believe, indicated that in a free enterprise economy like that of Cyprus, final decisions regarding the development of tourism rest with private initiative and generally with the entrepreneurial class. These decisions are largely influenced by government policy, and the existence of adequate controls is of vital importance, especially in those cases where the decisions of the private sector have far-reaching consequences that affect the society as a whole or have repercussions in other sections of the economy or the environment.

In Cyprus the government's five-year plans for economic and social development involved:

— The advancement of loans at low interest rates for the construction of hotels. Specific criteria were laid down by the Council of Ministers — the apex of authority in the administration — on the recommendations of the Economic Planning Commission and the Cyprus Tourism Organization.

— A huge investment program in infrastructure, again approved by the Council of Ministers, providing for the improvement of transport facilities (air services, construction of airports, roads, harbors, marinas), embellishment of existing archaeological sites and monuments, restoration of ancient theaters, and the encouragement of arts and crafts. This program was prepared by the appropriate authorities in the central government, and the views of local authorities were always taken into consideration before its final approval.

—Establishment of hotel training schools and a school for guides.

—A marketing program to promote Cyprus as a tourist destination, recommended by the Cyprus Tourism Organization and
approved by the Council of Ministers.

—An Island Plan for Physical Planning, the enactment of regulations, and the definition of zones for the control of development, approved by the Council of Ministers. The Island Plan
was based on the recommendation of the Economic Planning
Commission, the Town Planning Department, and the Tourism
Organization, and again the views of local authorities were
taken into consideration.

In all the above cases there were adequate controls at the national
level, and local authorities performed their functions under the
supervision of the central government. For instance, although planning regulations were administered by local and regional authorities, the Department of Town Planning supervised the actual implementation.

This paper has noted various policy measures of national importance: restrictions on foreign labor, the regulation of foreign investments, and the professional control of guides and travel agents. In
all these cases regulations were enforced by the appropriate central
authorities whose powers emanated from specific legislation. This
legislation contains provisions for adequate checks and controls,
and there is no question of any misuse of power. In all cases where
control proved inadequate—except in Famagusta's problem
area—the main decisions and their implementation presented no
insuperable problems, because under the existing institutional and
administrative set-up there existed adequate checks and balances.
In cases where loopholes and weaknesses were discovered, efforts
were made to put things right either by administrative decisions on
the part of the executive power, by legal provisions through the
legislative powers, or even by judicial action through the courts.

CHAPTER 15

Tourism in Malta

Jeremy Boissevain
CENTER FOR EUROPEAN AND MEDITERRANEAN STUDIES,
UNIVERSITY OF AMSTERDAM

Peter Serracino Inglott
DEPARTMENT OF PHILOSOPHY,
ROYAL UNIVERSITY, MALTA

T HE DEVELOPMENT OF TOURISM in Malta mirrors the explosive growth of the industry in the Mediterranean. Arrivals in Malta increased from just under 20,000 in 1960 to well over 300,000 by 1975, with most of the spectacular growth coming since 1965. Now, after the first decade of mass tourism, it is useful to take stock of the way in which the industry has grown and is affecting the lives of the people of this small developing country between Europe and Africa.[1]

Background

Malta is composed of three islands, Malta, Gozo, and Comino, covering a total of 120 square miles. With just under 318,000 inhabitants and 2,600 persons a square mile, Malta is one of the smallest and most densely populated countries in the world. Its history has been greatly influenced by its small size and strategic location in the center of the Mediterranean.

For centuries it was run as an island fortress, first by the Knights of St. John (1532–1798), then by France (1798–1800), and finally by Britain, from whom the country received its independence in 1964.

1. We are particularly grateful for help in many ways from May Bezzina, Gemma Cachia, Annabel Hill, Hannie Hoekstra, Joan Killick, Tony Macelli, Paul Sant Cassia, Victoria Vitale, and from John Pollacco and Paul Galea of the Malta Government Tourist Board.

Under these circumstances self-government was necessarily limited, and the islands were ruled by a civil-military administration highly centralized in Valletta, Malta's capital. Following World War I, modified self-government was introduced and a national parliament elected. Thus a highly centralized form of government continued following independence. There are no mayors or town councils. After a closely contested election in 1971, the working-class Malta Labour party replaced the Nationalist party, traditionally the party of landowners, traders, civil servants, and established professionals. The MLP returned to office again in 1976.

Malta's economy was based on furnishing services and goods to the military and naval garrisons of its rulers. Under Britain, growing numbers of Maltese were also directly employed in the garrison, the naval dockyard, and the civil service. The number of professionals and businessmen increased as entrepot commerce flourished following the opening of the Suez Canal in the nineteenth century.

The balance of power in the Mediterranean gradually passed from British hands. By the late 1950s this was reflected in the drastic decline of the defense establishments in Malta. Teams of advisers finally began to look for alternative economic possibilities. Foremost among these were plans to convert the overstaffed naval dockyard to a viable commercial enterprise. Attempts were also made to attract manufacturing, which Britain had systematically kept away to safeguard its monopoly of local skilled labor for the dockyard and the military. The first steps were also taken to encourage tourism.

In the late 1960s there was an economic boom sparked by the arrival of new industries and mass tourism. Since 1970, boom conditions have been replaced by a slower but still vigorous growth. A large number of foreign firms, attracted by various incentives, established themselves in Malta, increasing domestic exports between 1964 and 1974 eightfold. During the same period annual imports also grew, but much more slowly.

Malta was able to capture an important portion of the wave of tourists which in the 1960s began cascading into the sunny Mediterranean from gray industrial centers in northern Europe. British currency restrictions for nonsterling areas accelerated this influx. Thousands of British discovered in Malta a sterling island in the sun. The expansion of industry and tourism raised the gross domestic product from £M47.4 million in 1964 to more than £M100 million by 1975. (The Maltese pound was worth about US$2.85 in 1975.)

This increase was reflected in a considerable rise in the level of prosperity. During this period, for example, car ownership increased from 19,500 to 45,000, from one car for every eighteen persons to one for every seven.

The benefits of economic prosperity were not, however, evenly distributed. Wage rates of white-collar workers and industrial employees lagged far behind those in tourism and building, creating considerable tension. Newly prosperous industrial managers, real estate speculators, and building contractors began to rival the traditional elite of professionals, higher civil servants, and traders. The new textile and electronics industries hired mainly women, who generally were more ready than men to accept low wages and poor working conditions. This increased relative male unemployment. Perhaps the most critical development was the severe housing shortage created by the exploding demand for tourist accommodation. Unemployment, care for socially handicapped, and the housing shortage together with economic independence became the issues in the 1971 elections. They continued to furnish themes for the speeches of Labour Prime Minister Dom Mintoff during the 1976 election campaign as well.

Government and Tourism

In 1946 a British financial adviser declared that it was quite improbable that Malta could derive much from tourism.[2] Nonetheless, the Government Public Relations Office had a Tourist Bureau attached to it, and in 1955 the bureau was made an independent office. Between 1955 and 1959, £M76,122 was spent on tourism. Although later economic advisers were more encouraging about the prospects for tourism, they noted such difficulties as distance from the United Kingdom and the lack of hotels and entertainment facil-

---

2. W. Woods, *Report on the Finances of the Government of Malta* (London: His Majesty's Stationery Office, 1946). Much of this section is based on Anna Portelli, "The Tourist Industry in Malta: A Marketing Approach," B.A. (Hons.) dissertation, Department of Economics, University of Malta, 1976.

ities.[3] Little was done. But in spite of pessimistic predictions and innumerable problems, tourist arrivals have grown at a rate of 22 percent a year since 1960.

The Maltese themselves began to take a serious interest in tourism when it became clear that Britain was going to relinquish Malta as a military base sooner than expected and grant the islands their independence. In November 1958 a Government Tourist Board was statutorily established to devise and execute a program of tourist development. The following year, while the country was still under the British colonial regime, a first five-year development plan appeared which categorically stated that tourism was to have an indispensable role in the diversification of the economy (in lieu of dependence on British Services operations), together with industrial and agricultural development programs.[4]

Out of an estimated £M32.2 million capital investment provided in the plan, only £M545,000 was directly budgeted for tourism, although part of the sum allocated for industrial development was also available for hotel building and other tourist resort projects. £M125,000 was to be spent on advertising in the first two years, after which it was hoped that private enterprise would be doing enough so that government support would not be needed. The rest of the allocation was almost exclusively for beach development.

The plan was reviewed in 1961. The allocation for tourism was increased fourfold to £M2.2 million: £M1 million for hotels, another million for resort sites, and the rest for advertising and other promotional activities. Under the colonial administration less than £M1 million was actually spent, however, since tourism was not being pushed according to plan.

In the second development plan for 1964–69, out of a capital expenditure of £M38.4 million, tourism was allocated £M3.6 million distributed on lines similar to those in the previous plan. This time,

---

3. T. Balogh and Dudley Seers, *The Economic Problems of Malta: An Interim Report* (Malta: Government Printing Press, 1955).
4. The official development plans referred to in this section are: *First Development Plan for the Maltese Islands, 1959–64* (Malta: Department of Information, 1959); *Review of the Development Plan for the Maltese Islands, 1959–64* (Malta: Department of Information, 1961); *Second Development Plan for the Maltese Islands, 1964–69* (Malta: Department of Information, 1964); *Third Development Plan for the Maltese Islands, 1969–74*, revised October 1970 (Malta: Office of the Prime Minister, 1970); *Development Plan for Malta, 1973–80* (Malta: Office of the Prime Minister, 1974).

however, the money began to be spent. Between 1964 and 1968, seventeen new grant-aided hotels began business and six other large hotels were under construction. Tourist arrivals increased from 37,879 in 1964 to 136,995 in 1968. Employment in hotels rose in the same period from 766 to 2,473.

In the third development plan for 1969–74, £M4.6 million was allocated to tourism with about £M2 million for hotels, £M2 million for resort sites, including a yachting center, and the rest for promotional activities. This plan was superseded by the fourth development plan for 1973–80. By that time only two-thirds of the expenditure for the period had been spent, and the fourth plan attributed the slowdown to the "failure to diversify sources of origin." Most tourists came from Britain because of a lack of promotional activities elsewhere, it was said. The average rate of annual growth of tourist arrivals between 1969 and 1973 was 3 percent as compared with 64 percent between 1964 and 1968. The boom of the 1960s was over.

The fourth plan stressed hotel-accommodated tourism and diversification of the market. It aimed at an average annual growth rate of 10 percent over the 211,200 arrivals in 1973; gross foreign earnings of £M22.6 million in 1979; and 10,500 beds in hotels.

In 1975 tourist arrivals were 334,519—26 percent higher than estimated; gross foreign earnings were calculated at about £M30 million; and there were 9,724 beds with an additional estimated 15,000 beds in holiday flats and villas. Everything seemed to have worked faster than was planned. But by 1976 there were symptoms that the pace was not being kept up and a critical point had been reached.

Tourist Types

Tourists who come to Malta may be divided into three categories, based on length of stay, which in turn largely determines the impact the tourist has on the host culture. The first group includes cruise passengers (49,219 in 1975) who spend an average of four hours in Malta, long enough only to visit Valletta, some archaeological sites, and souvenir shops. In the second group are holiday tourists (334,519 in 1975) who in 1975 spent an average of 13.95 guest nights in Malta. This category forms the basis of the tourism industry (see Table 15.1).

The third type is composed of foreign residents, or settlers, as they are called in Malta (3,162 in 1975), who live for all or most of

Table 15.1. *Categories of Tourists*

Year	Cruise passengers (arrivals)	Holiday tourists (arrivals)	Settlers (currently resident)
1960	8,676	19,689	n.a.
1965	16,937	47,804	n.a.
1970	64,998	170,853	5,534
1975	49,219	334,519	3,162

n.a. Not available.
Source: Malta Tourist Board and Government Gazette.

the year in Malta. The increase of settlers almost exactly parallels that of temporary tourists. Most are retired British who were attracted to Malta by the climate, the widespread knowledge of English, and the modest cost of living. But perhaps the most significant attraction was the low income tax rates the government applied to settlers in the expectation that their presence would stimulate the economy. The financial role of these "permanent tourists" has, in fact, proved to be extremely important, as has their cultural and social impact.

In 1971 permanent tourists paid an estimated £M1.5 million in taxes (about 7.7 percent of government revenue from the relevant taxes, though permanent tourists form only about 1.7 percent of the total population). Although in 1970 expenditure by settlers was greater than by temporary tourists, because of the higher import content of the settlers' purchases, tourists yielded more foreign exchange. Another effect of the settlers was on domestic service: Wages increased notably, but not the number of maids.[5]

The present government has sought to curb the settlers' impact on the grossly inflated property market by raising taxes and limiting the property they can purchase in Malta to the house they occupy. Thus in 1972 the income tax for new settlers was increased from sixpence on the pound to the normal high rates applicable to Maltese, and the income they were obliged to bring in was raised from £M1,400 to £M4,000 a year. Largely as a result of these measures

5. For further information on the impact of foreign settlers, see Joe Libreri, "Foreign Settlers in Malta: An Economic Analysis," B.A. (Hons.) dissertation, Department of Economics, University of Malta, 1971.

the number of settlers has decreased somewhat during the past few years.

Balance of Payments

The most striking impact of tourism is its substantial contribution to the balance of payments. In 1975 the gross income from tourism was £M27.7 million, or one-fifth of the total export of goods and services. Although no sound studies exist of the import content of the income from tourism, the Malta government calculates that roughly half of every tourist pound is spent on imported goods and services. In 1975 the import content of the £M27.7 million was estimated to be £M13.4 million. This is probably rather optimistic, since at present no difference appears to be made between the import content of local and tourist consumption, and little is known about the role of foreign capital and hence about repatriation of profits.[6] But even at a lower figure the tourist-derived income is of great importance to a country largely devoid of natural resources other than sun and sea. In large part thanks to tourism, Malta has had a surplus in its balance of payments since 1960, although the amount has fluctuated widely.

Employment

The influence of tourism on employment, especially in the hotel industry, has increased steadily. Employment in hotels rose from 503 in 1960 to 3,833 in 1975, and its share of the labor market increased from 0.6 percent to 3.5 percent (see Table 15.2). Hotel employment, along with the more traditional domestic service and the new industries, has provided an important new source of

---

6. Other studies have concluded, by rough and ready methods, that the import content is between 35 and 50 percent. See Lino Spiteri, "The Development of Tourism in Malta" (Malta: Joint Consultative Council, Malta Chamber of Commerce, Federation of Malta Industries, Malta Employers Association, 1968); and Rita Ghigo, "The Contribution of the Tourist Industry to Malta's Balance of Payments: A Preliminary Appraisal," B.A. (Econ.) dissertation, Department of Economics, University of Malta, 1975.

Table 15.2. *Hotel Employment*

Year	Beds	Employees	Total labor force	Percentage
1960	1,388	503	84,539	0.59
1965	2,380	819	88,120	0.93
1970	7,935	2,723	96,099	2.83
1975	9,724	3,833	107,814	3.56

Source: Malta Tourist Board and Annual Abstract of Statistics.

employment for women. Nonetheless, women hold the most marginal jobs and hence are affected more severely than men when economic difficulties loom. This is evident from Table 15.3. During the momentary slump in tourist arrivals in 1972, following the protracted confrontation between the Malta government and the British government over the military bases in Malta, 25 percent of the female labor force of the hotels were discharged, while only 15 percent of the men were let go. Since 1971 the Labour government has specifically encouraged male employment to offset the growing male unemployment. In 1974 a bill was passed which made it mandatory to employ males rather than females wherever possible.

Furthermore, in September 1975 the government published minimum staffing requirements for the top five classes of hotels. These ranged from one employee for every 1.3 beds at the deluxe level to one for every four beds. These ratios are applicable only when a certain percentage of occupancy is reached. If during the hotelier year—which ends October 31—the overall occupancy rate falls

Table 15.3. *Hotel Employment by Sex*

Year	Arrivals	Employees		Total	Percentage of females
		Male	Female		
1970	170,853	1,679	1,044	2,723	38.2
1971	178,704	2,159	1,156	3,315	34.9
1972	149,913	1,820	866	2,695	32.1
1973	211,196	1,965	925	2,890	32.0
1974	272,516	2,292	1,090	3,382	32.2
1975	334,519	2,622	1,211	3,833	31.6

Source: Malta Tourist Board.

below 49 percent, then a hotel may apply the ratio for the class immediately below it.

Through its multiplier effect, tourism has stimulated growth in other economic activities besides hotel keeping. For example, there were no more than a dozen restaurants in 1960; in 1975 there were 79, employing some 558 (males 383) full-time and 163 (males 114) part-time workers. The number of cars for hire has also increased sharply from 549 in 1965 to 2,177 in 1975, an increase of almost 400 percent in ten years. A range of other service establishments benefit from tourism, including shops near the tourist areas which sell everything from fruit, through suntan lotions, to water-sport articles. Even doctors, nursing homes, and undertakers benefit, for 13 percent of the holiday tourists and most of the settlers are over sixty years old and are increasingly in need of medical care.

Housing and Welfare

Tourism has also benefited the construction and real estate businesses and those who serve them, such as lawyers and, particularly, notaries. Many of them became extremely wealthy during the property boom of the 1960s.

Between 1960 and 1965 the construction industry in Malta suffered a recession, and over 1,000 construction workers emigrated. In 1964 advisers predicted a 25 percent fall in employment between 1961 and 1969.[7] But the situation changed in 1964 with the beginning of a construction boom, very largely sparked by the Santa Maria project.

The Santa Maria project, initiated by the privately owned Malta Developments at Mellieha in the north of Malta, was begun in 1963. A thousand acres of farmland belonging to the church was bought for a total annual ground rent of £M5,000 for development into an isolated, first-class garden estate with chalets and villas for settlers. By 1970 the annual ground rents were estimated to be worth £M30,000 to the developers. The project, which is thought to have kicked off the property boom, was imitated by many others. Mean-

---

7. W. F. Stolper, R. R. Hellberg, and S. O. Callander, *Economic Adaptation and Development in Malta* (New York: United Nations, Department of Economic and Social Affairs, 1964).

while there were protests from the farmers who lost the land they had been cultivating. They were offered alternative jobs in the project, but few actually worked full time on their Santa Maria lands and hence could not take up this offer without also giving up their other land.

Settlers were the key element in the boom. They spent £M3 million yearly on housing from 1965 to 1970. A labor bottleneck occurred and costs rose. In 1968 the minimum legal wage rate for a construction worker was raised by 17 percent, but actual wages were usually twice as high as the minimum. Prices of houses in the 1960s rose alarmingly.[8]

Many examples of astronomical increases in land values indicate the boom's dimensions: A piece of land in Gozo, bought at £M600, realized a price of £M4,000 a few years later; a small villa, built at a cost of £M3,500, was sold for £M9,000; within a year a flat bought for £M4,000 changed hands twice and was sold a third time for £M10,000. Ground rents increased equally spectacularly. A plot of land with an original ground rent in 1962 of £M250, in 1967 yielded £M6,500 a year.[9]

By the middle of 1969 sales of luxury residential buildings declined, and the following year they stagnated at a low level. Many projects—some already initiated—were suspended. Talk of a proposed betterment levy and land gains tax may have contributed to the drop, although the tax was never introduced.

The housing boom during the 1960s seriously aggravated the already acute housing shortage in three ways. First, the foreigners' luxurious villas introduced a new style of housing that the Maltese wished to emulate. After visiting these sumptuously equipped, roomy villas set in their own gardens, the Maltese were no longer satisfied with their terraced town houses and flats. Second, real estate speculators began snapping up old houses in the villages and countryside and marketing them to foreigners for many times the purchase price as "old houses of character." Wealthy settlers and increasing numbers of nonresident foreigners in search of investment opportunities competed directly with Maltese from the poorest

8. Carmel Pisani, "An Economic Assessment of the Construction Industry and the Recent Property Boom," B.A. (Hons.) dissertation, Department of Economics, University of Malta, 1972.

9. Examples produced by Albert Missi, president of the Federation of Malta Developers and Estate Agents, in a talk at the University of Malta, June 6, 1967.

classes, those who normally lived in the "old houses of character," for the same property. Third, because of the soaring cost of construction materials and the shortage of labor, construction of public housing was severely restricted.

Thus, for various reasons, the housing shortage became acute in the late 1960s, especially for engaged couples, searching for a place to live so that they could marry. Housing became one of the important political issues during the 1971 elections. The Malta Labour party's promise to do something about it undoubtedly contributed to its victory at that time, just as its excellent record in building new housing and introducing measures to curb land speculation—such as imposing a sizable tax on property transfers and limiting foreign ownership to one owner-occupied house—helped it win the 1976 election campaign.

Family

It is felt that tourism loosens the traditional bonds of many closely knit Maltese families, although no systematic research has been done in this field. First, tourism has certainly stimulated the growth of discotheques and other centers of leisure activities which draw sons and daughters, if not occasionally their fathers too, out of the family circle. Second, tourism-generated employment opportunities remove unmarried women from the traditional, mother-controlled housebound existence. Employment also provides an economic basis which further reinforces a new measure of independence. This weakens family ties based in large measure upon the jealous, authoritarian control of the children by their parents, particularly the father. Finally, increased contact with foreigners and persons from other parts of the country has widened the marriage market considerably. When Maltese have married foreigners, as they increasingly have, the extended family bonds are weakened by cultural differences and distance as newly married couples settle abroad.

Community Integration

How has the growth of tourism in Malta affected the island's integration as a whole? In contrast to developments in some places, tourism in Malta has had only a marginal effect on aggravating intergroup conflict. In fact, there is some evidence that tourism has furthered greater solidarity among Maltese.

As already indicated, the tourism-induced building boom and consequent housing shortage had political repercussions and was one of the issues on which the Malta Labour party successfully attacked its Nationalist opponents in the 1971 election campaign. Although this is no longer an issue, the building boom did create in the space of a few years a truly wealthy class. Private fortunes skyrocketed—to £M30 million in the extreme case of the Pace family Bical enterprise, now in liquidation.

The wealthiest classes are also favored by the income tax laws, for the maximum tax of 60 percent is applied annually to all incomes over £M2,500! Tourism will thus continue to favor wealthy entrepreneurs who have committed assets to it. Since prominent members of the two major political parties, as well as the politically important General Workers Union, are heavily involved in tourist-related activities, however, it is not likely that tourism will ferment class-based political conflict in the foreseeable future.

Neither has there been much tension between Maltese and tourist. But there are two exceptions. One was the ill feeling generated by the exclusive Santa Maria estate. Local farmers who lost access to valuable agricultural land when the church sold the Santa Maria land to developers were furious. Many other Maltese from all walks of life resented the "Maltese not welcome" character of the estate that was symbolized by the red and white striped booms that barred the entrance. The booms have since been raised and a few Maltese now live on the estate. Other developments have not had the exclusive character of the Santa Maria and have not caused friction. The other, less overt exception is the resentment many young Maltese women feel toward tourist girls, who tend to monopolize the attention of young and not so young men during the summer.

Maltese like foreigners and, by and large, are hospitable. This friendliness, in conjunction with the sea and sun, is one of Malta's most important tourist resources. It is, however, possible that with the growth of lower-middle-class mass tourism and the increasing popularity of holiday flats and villas, certain points of friction will develop. The middle- and working-class tourist competes more directly with the average Maltese citizen for goods and services, since his income is nearly commensurate. The luxury-class tourist confines much of his shopping and swimming to the air-conditioned boutiques and private pools and beaches of his hotel. If he travels, he does so by hired car. The middle- and working-class tourist, in contrast, shops in local stores, often swims in the overcrowded public beaches, and travels by bus. In short, he adds visibly to the overcrowding of these densely populated islands. Renters of holiday villas and flats also compete directly for goods in the shops. There is considerable grumbling among local housewives that the tourists have driven up the price of fresh fruit and vegetables, even though this is not always true. A case in point was the scarcity of cauliflowers in the spring of 1976. The shortage was due, according to the farmers, to excessive rain, but the public blamed tourists and settlers. This type of friction is limited at present both in scope and in impact, although it may well increase. Generally tourists are liked and consequently feel welcome and come back. Well over half of all British tourists who visited Malta in 1975 came because they visited the islands previously or had friends who had.[10]

The increase of long- and short-term tourists also generated a certain self-confidence and even pride among Maltese. As an outpost of empire to which military personnel and their dependents were *sent,* the Maltese had long regarded everyone and everything from northern Europe as better. Their colonial masters did nothing to disturb this mass inferiority complex. Now foreigners of all classes are *choosing* to come for what Malta has to offer. This has led to a new awareness of Malta's long-neglected natural and cultural environment. The intrusion of a numerous and interested "they" category in a tight little island community also crystallized a more pronounced "we" category. It has obliged the Maltese to formulate more clearly for themselves what they are and what they stand for—to think more consistently about their own culture instead of merely taking it for granted or imitating foreign tastes. Much of the renaissance of Maltese culture which was so evident in the 1960s was influenced by the excitement of developing a national identity after more than four centuries of colonial rule. Nonetheless, tourism was of critical importance in developing this identity; it provided an immediate audience and wealthy patrons for those actually furthering Malta's cultural independence.

10. Government Tourist Board.

Decisionmaking

Malta's government, already highly centralized, became even more so following independence. The tempo of centralization was further accelerated after 1971 by the modified state capitalism of the Labour government. Thus decisions, whether political or economic, which affect tourism, are increasingly made by the central government. This reflects not only the ideological orientation of the government but also a growing awareness that tourism cannot be allowed to develop without controls if the country is to derive maximum benefit. Government decisions that affect the tourism industry are made largely by the Office of the Prime Minister, generally on advice of the economic planning unit and, to a lesser extent, the Tourist Board, which is concerned with increasing and monitoring the volume of visitors. The goals of the present government regarding tourism were set out in the fourth development plan: to seek more tourists outside Britain, to concentrate on the relatively high spenders, to increase hotel capacity, to improve transportation to Malta, and to raise the quality of tourist services available.

These goals were virtually attained by 1975, although heavy dependence on United Kingdom tourists remained. Concrete measures taken by the government to realize its aims include:

—establishment of a national air carrier, Air Malta
—enlargement and improvement of the airport and runways
—measures to restrict charter flights on nonnational carriers
—greater promotion on the continent
—elimination of subsidies for hotel building and a slowdown on issuing building permits
—a tax on fresh-water swimming pools (£M150 for private pools, and from £M250 to £M500 a year for hotels, depending on pool capacity)
—a sharp increase in the price of fresh water consumed by hotels (up from £M0.137 to £M2.00 for 1,000 gallons)
—classification of hotels and regulation of minimum staffing
—an increase in the airport passenger service charge (up from £M0.50 to £M1 a head)
—a program of road building and landscaping.

Besides participating in the tourism industry as an airline operator, the government has become a hotel operator. It recently transformed a former military installation into a holiday camp and turned it, along with leases to other important properties, over to Air Malta management.

These measures obviously were not received with enthusiasm by all sections of the tourism industry. Medium and small hotel owners in particular resented the hotel classification, the increase in water charges, and minimum staffing requirements. But protest against government measures has generally been ineffective. An exception was the successful public protest initiated in the late 1960s by the historical and cultural preservation society, Din L-Art Helwa, to restrict the height of a hotel that threatened Valletta's historical skyline. Protests to implement tighter and more imaginative planning legislation and reinforce existing measures to control building and clean up beaches and other public recreation areas have met with little response from the government in power.

The lack of success in influencing government policy (or its enforcement) is due largely to the extraordinary centralization and power of government. There are no organized protest groups—potential members fear victimization if they criticize government. In a small country run by a powerful government there is basis for such fear. Protest is thus neither open nor sustained. Unless a political party takes up an issue—such as "Malta is being sold to foreigners," the cry of the present government when in opposition—most protest is limited to private grumbling and anonymous letters to the editors of the major newspapers. As a result there is virtually no public debate on tourism and its consequences.

How much foreign capital participates in the Malta tourism industry is not known, nor is the degree to which foreign interests are able to influence decisions affecting the industry. There is some evidence, however, that foreign investment in the tone-setting deluxe hotels is increasing. More research in this area is badly needed. Nonetheless, the slump in tourist arrivals in spring and summer of 1976, caused by the worldwide economic recession, indicates that decisions essential to Malta are made outside the country. Some foreign tour operators dropped Malta from their tour offerings, while individual tourists chose to go elsewhere or stayed home. More serious, however, was the collapse of three British tour agencies that had been active in promoting Malta.

Owing to the absence of a critical public, the government must also monitor the impact of tourism. The 1973 development plan noted perceptively that "the influx of uncontrolled numbers of tourists can disrupt the social fabric. There are therefore social constraints which bear directly on Malta's ability to accept tourists." As yet there is no evidence that the government is attempting to evaluate the impact of tourism or to study the very real potential problem of tourist saturation.

Tourist-Host Encounter

The contacts the tourist has with his hosts are structured by his aims in visiting the country. Tourists visiting Malta, with but few exceptions, do not seek an exotic culture and life-style, as do those visiting Italy, Bali, or North Africa, for example. Sun and sea, with some relaxing night life, are the main attractions; local culture, in the form of prehistoric temples, Valletta's bastions, or a parish *festa*, is secondary and may be sought if the tourist has the interest, energy, and time.

Most of the Tourist Board brochures promote the seaside image of Malta. Local culture is mentioned only to assure the sun lover that Malta has a genuinely European way of life. The privately run advertising agencies and tourist guidebooks sometimes touch on local color, though this is not emphasized. In other words, the literature equips the tourist to visit the island and its monuments, not its people.

Such promotion and presentation tends to become self-fulfilling. Maltese whom the tourist usually meets are those connected with tour operators, airlines, hotels, swimming establishments, monuments, shops, restaurants, and means of transport. Encounters with taxi drivers, tourist guides, hotel receptionists, and others who serve him may be unique for the tourist, but for the Maltese such interaction merely replicates countless experiences. These interactions, though friendly, thus remain essentially perfunctory and pragmatic. Direct encounters between tourist and host outside this service relation is limited to chance meetings at beaches, restaurants, or festas. Those between tourist girls and increasingly more forward Maltese boys are probably the most common.

An exception to the usual type of tourist encounter is found among the thousand-odd students who visit Malta annually via the National Student Travel Service to attend courses in English, Mediterranean studies, and sailing. They often stay with Maltese families and thus associate widely with local people outside the tourism sector, as do members of the few cultural and artistic tours. Normally, however, the tourist returns home having absorbed a superficial knowledge of Malta as a tourist resort with a number of interesting monuments, but visitors remain relatively ignorant about the customs, life-style, political aspirations, and social problems of their hosts. The tourist sees only what he has been led to expect.

Impact on Cultural Manifestations

Tourists have had considerable influence on local cultural manifestations—art, theater, crafts, music, and even food. The genuine admiration of tourists has helped the Maltese appreciate their own cultural heritage and added another dimension to their search for a national identity.

There is a major difference between the patronage of temporary tourists and that of permanent tourists, or settlers. Few temporary tourists patronize the local theater, which presents plays in English; in contrast, the local repertory company lists 700 settlers as members out of a total of 800 who subscribe to a season ticket for performances.

Temporary tourists buy folkloric or historical paintings of local scenes, especially sea battles, but few works by authentic artists. Permanent settlers, however, have been the principal patrons of the best local artists, none of whom could survive on their art alone before tourism began. Now at least one does, and all have increased their sales in Malta and established contacts abroad through a few permanent settlers who are noted art critics or have other connections with galleries and art journals. Victor Passmore, an established artist who has settled in Malta, has had even more far-reaching effects. Not only is his own work influenced by the local milieu, but he has himself more or less influenced almost all the local artists in a manner only paralleled by the sojourn of Caravaggio on the island in the seventeenth century. Passmore has also helped these local artists to become internationally known.

Foreign literary figures resident in Malta such as Nigel Dennis and Nicholas Monsarrat have published works with strong Maltese color, but on the whole they have not mixed well with local creative writers. There is no doubt, however, that their frequent presence on the island helps to stimulate local cultural life. As with other tourists, there is a big difference in cultural impact between the artist who stays for a length of time and one who just passes through. Since the advent of tourism a flourishing handicraft industry has come into being. Using Maltese materials and motifs, both Maltese and foreign craftsmen are making products which range from beautifully styled knitwear, woven textiles, wrought iron, and blown glass to entire suits of tinny armor and kitschy trinkets. Both tourists and Maltese buy these products, and some of the better quality ones are exported. The government has actively encouraged the industry by making available for use as studios and workshops some old quonset huts formerly used by the military.

There has also been a growing demand by restaurant owners and organizers of folklore groups for guitarists and singers of traditional music. Tourists assume—mistakenly in Malta's case—that all Mediterranean restaurants have traditionally served folk music and dance with the food. Their assumptions become self-fulfilling. A modest folk music industry now provides after-hours work for a few authentic singers and guitarists and many young dancers who perform "traditional" folk dances, most of which are only a year or two old. The tourist demand for folk music has unquestionably helped preserve the limited traditional instrumental and vocal music that existed. It has also helped to make this music acceptable to some young educated Maltese who might otherwise have copied the middle-class disdain with which their parents regarded this "peasant" music. Patriotism doubtlessly has also played a role, for the music has provided an authentic item of local culture to a newly independent country in search of its identity after four centuries of heavy-handed foreign rule.

Although tourism was largely responsible for the way in which the government shifted the carnival celebration from winter to spring, it has as yet had little noticeable impact on other traditional rituals. Participants in the colorful religious ceremonies and processions make no distinction between the flashbulbs and cinecameras of locals and holidaying Maltese emigrants, who are intensely proud of the pageantry, and those of north European tourists, who are astounded by it. If the parochial festa celebrations and Good Friday processions are growing more elaborate, this is due chiefly to parochialism and internal tourism rather than international tourism. The more spectators there are, the more the participants enjoy it.

Conclusion: Values and Attitudes

International tourism has had considerable impact on Malta, which is not surprising in view of the smallness of the country and the rapid growth of the new industry. Under the influence of both temporary tourists and settlers Maltese have changed their attitudes toward many things. There is a greater awareness and appreciation of things Maltese, not only historical monuments but also arts, crafts, and even locally produced wine. These, in turn, have also been influenced by tourist tastes and expectations. The Maltese concept of the good life has also felt the influence of tourism. This is reflected not only in house styles but also in the increased popularity, especially among the slightly better off Maltese, of such leisure activities as visits to restaurants and nightclubs and sailing.

The presence of large numbers of free-spending foreigners has almost unavoidably led many Maltese in the tourism industry to adjust their prices upward, in spite of government controls. The once-only anonymous visitor is thus often overcharged or short-changed by taxi driver, shopkeeper, and bus conductor. The we-they distinction in commercial ethics also has its counterpart in boy-girl relations. In the past few years Maltese young men have become considerably more forthright toward unaccompanied female tourists, many of whom admittedly hold more permissive moral standards than do Maltese girls. Youths now often behave in ways that would be quite unthinkable toward Maltese girls, although their behavior is still timid by other standards. Unquestionably, too, the permanent holiday atmosphere and the presence of affluent foreigners bent on a good time has helped accelerate the erosion among young Maltese women of traditional Catholic moral values of modesty in dress and behavior.

The Maltese idea of the foreigner has also changed. Twenty years ago all foreigners were "English" (service personnel); outsiders are now "tourists." The brief, repeated exposure to a variety of nationalities in their pleasure-seeking holiday roles, divorced from the social control of their habitual workday social environment, has inevitably led to stereotyping. For most Maltese, Swedes are seen as misers who order a bottle of soft drink and share it with several straws; French and, especially, Italians are excessively demanding, impossible to satisfy; Libyans are unreliable women chasers; Germans are earnest and affluent; and British are courteous and undemanding. It is not known what impressions tourists form of Malta and the Maltese during their brief visits. Nor is it known what the long-term impact of such stereotyping will be. It is not unthinkable that such image-forming becomes self-fulfilling and may even have political repercussions. It is another area in which further research is badly needed.

CHAPTER 16

The Sociocultural Effects
of Tourism in Tunisia:
A Case Study of Sousse

Groupe Huit
FRENCH CONSULTING FIRM

S OUSSE, THE LARGEST CITY in the Sahel region of north-
eastern Tunisia, offers a unique opportunity to study
the sociocultural impact of tourism on the local population of a developing country. Unlike other large urban centers in Tunisia,
Sousse has both a rapidly growing tourism sector and an infant industry newly emerging as a result of recent government policies.
The interaction of the problems posed by both these sectors in a
large city surrounded by a highly integrated agricultural area is well
worth attention.

Tourism and industry are undoubtedly the two major sectors on
which present-day Tunisia is depending to help get its economy
"off the ground." Both these sectors have undergone a series of important changes since the 1960s. Their sociocultural impacts on
Tunisia cannot ever be fully assessed on the basis of a single example, but it is in Sousse that the two phenomena are the most concentrated and their impacts the most profound.

The recent increase in accommodation facilities in Sousse as well
as its growth targets for the next several years are among the highest in Tunisia.[1] The amount of employment generated in the Sahel
as a result of the 1972 law on the promotion of the export industry is
exceptionally high (close to a third of the total for the country as a

---

1. Nearly 20 percent of all accommodations built in Tunisia between 1969 and
1975 were in Sousse and along its northern coast.

whole and similar to the rate of increase recorded for Tunis). The environment in which these phenomena occurred is particularly complex and extremely interesting. It consists of a large population with old traditions governing patterns of social behavior; a production-oriented economy; and a large city on which a major tourist area has been grafted, encircled by a traditional agricultural system.

What were the reactions of the local population to the sudden transformations in the job market, to an invasion of behavior patterns, life-styles, and material, intellectual, and moral values totally alien to its social traditions? How did the people perceive these changes? Did these changes lead to a willingness or unwillingness on the part of the local inhabitants to establish relations with the tourists? And did it lead to conflict between natives and foreigners or among the different segments of the local population itself?

Development of Tourism in Tunisia

In most countries such as Tunisia that are more than 2,000 kilometers from the major tourist-generating areas, tourism is a relatively recent phenomenon. By 1958 Tunisia still had no more than a few hotels concentrated in Tunis, the capital, and some others scattered among other large cities throughout the country. Not until 1962 did the Tunisian government decide to develop this sector as part of an integrated development plan to diversify economic growth. The intent was to develop agriculture and industry, to reduce disequilibriums in the balance of payments, and to limit foreign debt, together with the equally compelling desire to promote human progress through better schooling, employment opportunities, and more equal distribution of income. All this required a substantial financial effort, and tourism was considered one of the means to get the necessary finance.[2]

With the promotion of "mass tourism in search of sea and sun," the tourist phenomenon began to expand by leaps and bounds. The

2. "It is, therefore, highly essential to consider investments in tourism as a means to expand the country's economy and to use the benefits derived from this sector to create and consolidate the foundations of a new Tunisian economy, while remaining totally optimistic as to the possibilities for growth in this sector." (Ahmed Ben Salah, Conference on the Development of Southern Tunisia, Zarzis, May 2–5, 1967.)

growth rate in the hotel sector has been on average more than 24 percent a year—one of the highest anywhere in the world—and has been particularly significant in a country the size of Tunisia: from one bed per thousand inhabitants in 1960 to twelve beds per thousand inhabitants by 1975.

Tourism to Tunisia is genuinely a mass phenomenon, with 80 percent of all Tunisia's visitors coming in groups. As a result, the emphasis has come to be on gigantic, highly integrated tourist hotels, providing accommodation, food services, and recreational and entertainment facilities. The figures recorded for 1975 showed an average of 237 beds per unit for Tunisia as a whole and 341 for Sousse in particular.

The tourism sector initially grew in the country's marginal areas (the east coast of Jerba, Dkhila between Sousse and Monastir, southwest of Hammamet, and provincial capitals), which are primarily coastal. The construction of tourist hotels in these areas further accentuated the coastal concentration of cities, infrastructure, industry, intensive agriculture, better educated inhabitants with a higher employment rate, and political and economic power.

In places such as Jerba and Zarzis, where there is no urban infrastructure, and also in Tunis, the Hammamet-Nabeul area, and the coastal zone between Sousse and Monastir, the resort hotels were constructed outside the large urban centers. In Sousse, however, the hotels cling to the city, which is the third largest in the country (with a population in 1975 of 80,000 in the city itself and 180,000 for the metropolitan area as a whole) and the seat of government for a well-organized region.

The expansion of tourism has been more or less regular, but there has been a shift in the control of the sector. At first it was dominated by the government, which was responsible for 40 percent of all accommodation facilities constructed between 1960 and 1965.[3] Then the private sector began to move in, and private investors are responsible for almost all the new units built since the end of the 1960s. In Sousse, soon after the municipality opened a first-class hotel, a dozen more units were constructed whose financing was ensured at the time by private investors seeking an outlet for their capital. Contrary to what occurred in other areas, the local middle

---

3. Government intervention concentrated in Monastir-Skanes where three hotels were opened, one of which was formerly a palace, and an international airport was constructed.

class played an active role in both the financing and construction of hotels.

Development of Industry

After independence in 1956 the industrial sector got off to a slow start. A development strategy was implemented under which industry was regarded as a prime vehicle for the country's economic development as well as for its eventual regionalization. At the end of the 1960s the Growth Consolidation Plan called for a definite change toward greater private investment and a high priority for the processing industry. The 1972 law on the export industry marked the true turning point: Tunisia's new industries were to be oriented primarily toward the foreign, private market. The approach of the fifth plan confirms this trend.

Thus the objectives of both tourism and industry seem to have been designed along parallel lines. They define the development of foreign-oriented, mass tourism concentrated in coastal zones, increasingly bound by the rules of private business, and a manufacturing industry also geared to foreign markets and financed by private investors.

Tourism and Industry in Sousse

Sousse includes an Arab quarter and a European city which hug the port and in which all services and activities are centralized. To the west a radial-concentric pattern of homes, infrastructure, and services follows the road system, intersected at right angles by a checkerboard of farming areas. The residential zone is linear, with industry to the south and tourism to the north (see map).

Tourism has drawn the residential zone northward. Fourteen major hotels line the oceanfront; behind them are modern-style private homes owned by middle-class Tunisians. The outlying towns and villages of Hammam Sousse, Akouda, Kalaa Kebira, and Kalaa Sghira are becoming more and more integrated into Sousse proper as a result of the expanding tourism sector (26 percent of Sousse's hotel employees come from these neighboring towns and villages). Tourism has not only been the guiding force in the creation of the residential zone north of Sousse but has also penetrated into both

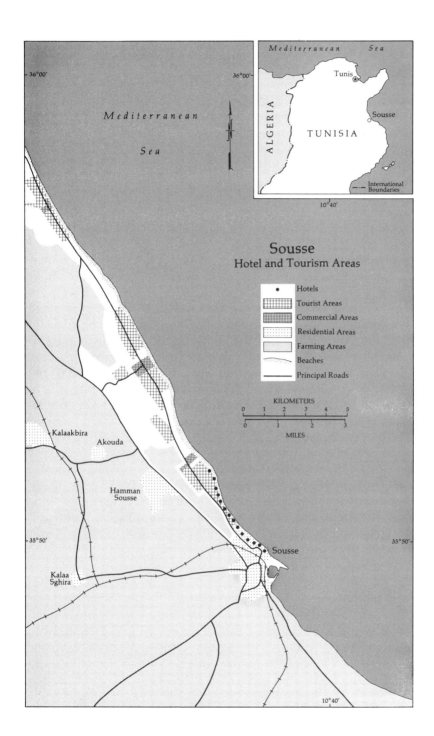

Sousse
Hotel and Tourism Areas

- Hotels
- Tourist Areas
- Commercial Areas
- Residential Areas
- Farming Areas
- Beaches
- Principal Roads

KILOMETERS

MILES

Mediterranean Sea

Sea

Mediterranean Sea

Tunis

Sousse

ALGERIA

TUNISIA

International
Boundaries

Kalaakbira

Akouda

Hamman
Sousse

Kalaa
Sghira

Sousse

the modern city and the old Arab quarter. It has completely altered the businesses and the atmosphere of Avenue Bourguiba, Rue Ibn Oualid, and the Place Farhat Hached. Small shops and displays of crafts aimed at the tourist trade line the major thoroughfare of the Arab quarter up to the Kasbah and the museum. The marketplace along the Sfax road, southwest of the city, is also visited by foreigners.

The economic situation in the Sahel in the 1960s was not especially promising. Cheap imported goods were competing with the textiles produced by local craftsmen, industry was limited to a few brickworks, the port was short-circuited by more rapid modes of travel to Tunis, a single-crop economy was based on the cultivation of olives, and there was a high rate of population growth. Since that time, however, industry has become a highly important sector of activity. Vehicle assembly plants, factories that manufacture spare parts for automobiles, textile mills, engineering, and food-processing plants have made Sousse the fourth largest city in the country in terms of volume of industry and the fifth city in terms of value added and industrial employment (including mining). In 1967 the city had only 4,290 workers in industry. By 1973 the figure rose to 6,813, and in 1974 and 1975 a total of 2,757 new jobs were created.

Between 1967 and 1975 the average annual growth rate of employment in tourism (20.9 percent) remained well above the comparable rate for industry (10.6 percent). In the last two years of that period, however, jobs grew faster in industry (18.5 percent a year) than in tourism (13.8 percent a year). This example clearly demonstrates the receptive attitude of the people of the Sahel to industrialization and contradicts the generalization made by J. Heyten that the Tunisian people despise working in industry and are much more attracted by glamorous jobs in hotels.[4]

Employment: A Basic Concern

Although one of the most basic concerns of every Tunisian is finding a job, motivations and reactions with regard to employment

---

4. J. Heyten, "The Impact of Tourism on the Developing Countries: Economic, Financial and Social Implications," *Cahier du Tourisme*, no. 26 (Aix-en-Provence: Centre des Hautes Etudes Touristiques, 1974), p. 25.

vary widely according to age and sex. What may be desirable for the head of a household is not necessarily or easily acceptable for either his wife or his daughter.

Whatever the case may be, a new tourist hotel or industrial plant is generally regarded, above all, as a symbol of the national policy aimed at creating employment opportunities and fighting unemployment. Even the smallest industrial or tourist unit will mean the immediate employment of at least a temporary contingent of workers at the building site.[5] These employment opportunities are especially meaningful for the poorer segments of the city's population living in districts such as Souassi and Chorbana. For others such as tradesmen, transport workers, government officials, manufacturers, hotel owners, and farmers, an increase in local job opportunities will mean an expanding market for their goods and services.

The continuing expansion of tourism occurred when the labor market was already being strained by the creation of new employment opportunities in the tourism sector itself, in supporting services, in government, and in industry. One result of this was an exodus of workers from agriculture and fishing because work in both the factory and the hotel is less back-breaking and offers the advantage of a fixed income. A typical example can be found in the irrigated perimeters of Chott Meriem, slightly north of Sousse, where there is a gradual replacement of local agricultural workers by a colony of Jendoubis. The repercussion of a phenomenon such as this on the agricultural economy is obvious. The people of Jendouba may be good farmers in their own native region, but they have neither the ancestral knowledge of an extremely unusual type of agriculture nor the attachment—the motivation of those who were actually born on the land—to farm successfully in the Sahel.

Another aspect of this expansion of employment opportunities was related to the need of the hotel industry as a whole for a range of supporting and ancillary services. These jobs are difficult to quantify. Although the number of such establishments has grown considerably, many of them did not survive; the nature of their business is seasonal and nonpermanent; and, finally, these services are not only for tourists and tourism but also for local inhabitants of

---

5. Nearly 1,600 construction jobs in Sousse alone.

Sousse and of the Sahel in general. We have estimated that in Sousse jobs in the ancillary services now number about 3,500.[6]

Both tourism and industry have large and relatively comparable wage bills. The total pay packet distributed by hotels was calculated in 1975 at 1.8 million dinars a year; the global pay packet of industrial workers is 3 million dinars a year.[7] The average annual salary per employee is 527 dinars in tourism and 468 dinars in the industrial sector.

The swelling of job opportunities in tourism, industry, and the service sector encourages both intra- and inter-regional migration. The recruitment efforts of hotels in Sousse reach well beyond the city itself and penetrate throughout the metropolitan area and the Sahel as well.[8] These hotel workers are extremely young on the average. Fifty-one percent are less than thirty years old and a significant proportion (30 percent) are women and young girls.

Tourism, like the textile industry, uses large numbers of female employees and is therefore an important element of social change.[9] But the portion of young girls' earnings that is kept and used by them personally should not be overestimated. Many fathers appropriate almost the entire salary of their daughters and are totally against allowing a hotel owner to open a bank account or post office account in the name of the girl. They keep well informed, through multiple cross-checks, of their daughters' basic salaries. These young female employees are therefore able to keep only that portion of their take-home pay derived from tips.

In more general terms, however, the assurance of a steady job and of regularity in the overall number of working hours (if not in the actual work schedule[10]) is an important element of social change for the residents of Sousse. This change is especially evident for those attracted to Sousse from surrounding areas, where their horizon was determined by the extent of their land, and farming was the only way of spending their time.

6. Groupe Huit, "Cities and Development" (Tunis: Ministry of Economics, Office of Regional Development, 1973).

7. One Tunisian dinar equals approximately US$2.30. Calculations of pay packets were based on an unpublished survey by J. M. Miossec prepared for Groupe Huit (1975).

8. J. M. Miossec, unpublished survey.

9. Textile mills employ a third of all industrial workers in Sousse.

10. Female employees do not generally remain in hotels after dark.

Economic Change and Upheaval of Cultural Values

The transition from a partially self-sufficient economy to a totally monetized one was both an economic and a social shock for the inhabitants of Sousse, whether or not they were directly involved in the new industrial and tourist economy.

The traditional products of local craftsmen were speedily replaced by new articles, some of which were imported from other regions of the country and from abroad. The quality and the fact of possession of these goods (such as transistor radios, mattresses, electrical appliances, television sets), like the quality of a bride's trousseau, became elements of prestige. Radio, TV, schools, newspapers, and magazines conveyed "modern" ways of thinking that served to underscore materialistic values. Traditional values were shaken to a degree that varied according to the social and economic level of the individual and the family. The demonstration effect of foreign visitors was significant, but, among the poor, opportunities for satisfying their new desires were rare and the result was a disturbing sense of frustration. Among the rich two opposing attitudes are found: either total and aggressive rejection of these modern values or a tendency toward typical nouveau riche behavior and values.

The positive material effects of tourism

Tourism injects a total of 5.5 dinars (US$12.80) per night's lodging directly into Sousse's hotel industry (averaging out good and bad years), 19 percent of which is for accommodation, 50 percent for food, and slightly under one-third for recreation and entertainment sponsored by the hotels.[11]

The effects of tourism also carry over into the agricultural and manufacturing sectors of the country's economy. For example, the Société Avicole du Sahel (Sahel Poultry Company), with thirty employees, supplies most of the eggs and chickens required by the

---

11. J. M. Miossec, unpublished survey (remittances abroad have been taken into account).

city's major hotels. The irrigated perimeters of Chott Meriem and Bekalta furnish, either directly or through the marketplaces in Bekalta and Sousse, most of the fruits and vegetables consumed by tourists. Moreover, independent local fishermen regularly sell their entire catch at good prices to hotels. Hotel owners obtain their fish from ports as far away as Mahdia, while their sources of meat and other food products extend beyond the Sahel into Tunis and the northwest.

For furnishings and basic equipment, hotel owners enjoy privileged treatment as the major customers of the Skanes furniture factory (with 600 employees) and the Tunisia ceramics works (located in Bizerte and employing 200 workers). The tourism sector is also the major consumer of the products of local rural and urban craftsmen (tapestries, bedspreads, leather goods, wood carvings, and the like).

Even more important, the services and infrastructure, originally designed to serve foreign visitors exclusively, today benefit Sousse as a whole, particularly its recently created industrial plants. The existence of an international airport, high quality administrative and financial services, rapid links by rail and by road with the capital, and good recreational and entertainment facilities all explain, to a large extent, the recent choices of building sites in Sousse by both Tunisian and foreign industrialists, as well as their reluctance to construct in other cities farther inland.

The negative material effects of tourism

One negative aspect of tourism that is not unique to Sousse (or to Tunisia, for that matter) is the seasonal swelling in demand and an inflationary trend during the summer months when tourist traffic is at its peak (see Figures 1 and 2).[12]

Of perhaps greater importance is the effect of tourism on the competition for water, a problem found exclusively in semi-arid countries. The difficulty of ensuring an adequate water supply for Sousse's resort areas and the ensuing conflicts with other consumers cause social repercussions that are in some cases highly significant. Ever since the beginning of the century various areas in the Sahel without water supplies of their own have been obtaining

---

12. René Baretje, *Tourist Demand* (Aix-en-Provence: Centre des Hautes Etudes Touristiques, 1968), pp. 281 and 532.

Figure 1. *Seasonal Flow of Traffic in Tunisia, 1974*

Tourists and passengers (thousands)

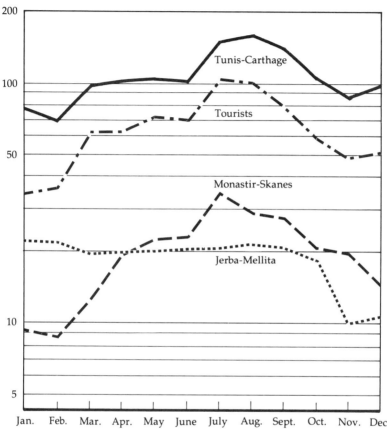

Source: Office National du Tourisme et Thermalisme, Office des Ports Aériens de Tunisie.

water from the Haffouz basin west of Kairouan. Conflicts here did not display the savagery experienced in other regions, but the development plan for the irrigated perimeters of the Kairouan region is unlikely to be carried out without encountering problems.[13] In

13. A little farther north, wells were sunk in an area of irrigation agriculture at Jilma in an effort to supply water for Sfax, but the wells were destroyed by the farmers. In the Hammamet-Nabeul area open conflict between citrus growers and hotel owners led the government in 1973 to finance a large-scale project to pipe water from the Mejerda to safeguard the citrus fruits of Cap Bon peninsula.

Figure 2. *Seasonal Expenditures in Goods and Merchandise of a Hotel in Sousse*

Tunisian dinars (millions)

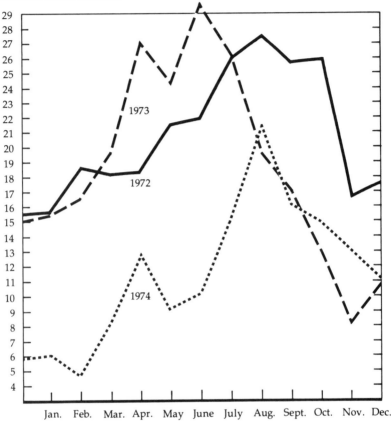

Source: J. M. Miossec, unpublished survey prepared for Groupe Huit (1975).

1970 a dam was constructed on the Nabhana river for an irrigation project north of Sousse, but as late as 1973 a portion of the water from this dam was still being diverted to the city to help satisfy the rapid rise in demand generated by tourism.

Intracity competition among consumers is best illustrated by two figures: The average per capita consumption in Sousse is approximately 60 liters a day and the average consumption per tourist is 300 liters a day. When local inhabitants see hotel owners watering their magnificent gardens or filling up their swimming pools while water continues to be cut off sporadically in other parts of the city, tensions are bound to rise.

A suggestion for the future might be pilot programs for desalination of sea water, implemented especially for tourists and financed by these tourists. The cost per head would be small compared with the significant strain it would place on the budget of the average Soussian. In any case, tourism could help finance research in desalinization—a field where possibilities are far from exhausted.

Artistic value and the national heritage

The positive and negative effects of tourism on local art and, in particular, on the products of local craftsmen are by no means peculiar to Sousse. The purchasing potential of the tourist can be used to revive traditional crafts of great value, such as ceramics, pottery, embroidery work, tapestries and rugs, leather goods, and silver plate. The National Crafts Office is seeking to preserve the high standards of ancient crafts while at the same time helping them to penetrate modern distribution channels. Moreover, the evolution of a new form of tourism based on discovery and multiple destination circuits (as opposed to the mass tourist resort areas on the beach) enables the country to preserve certain habitats already in danger of disappearing altogether, such as the Ksar troglodyte caves in Chenini and Hadada, the old quarters of Tunisian cities such as Medenine, and the Marhalas of Houmt Souk, Nefta, and Kairouan.

It is nevertheless uncertain how the local population will respond to such renovation efforts. How will they react when they see the fortified towers of Ksar Tatahouine converted into hotel rooms? How will they treat the tourist buying old pottery which, for them, is not nearly as practical as the new-fangled plastic containers? What will they think when tapestries made to lie directly on the ground or at the entrances to their homes are bought as decorations for a city apartment and turned into objects without a soul? And how will they respond to their camel muzzles being used as women's handbags, their olive-pressing sacks being converted into bedspreads, their looms being called upon to furnish the latest fashion in women's clothing? What will they think of their large and beautiful cloaks being turned into garb for tourists with a yen for the exotic? The beauty of these products has always been intimately related to their function, and the change in their end use confuses rather than amuses their manufacturers and traditional users. Finally, it needs to be pointed out that such a change in function often results in a deterioration in the articles themselves. The Gafsa tapestries, for example, have suffered from modifications of their design and color to suit the tastes of the new clientele.

The architecture of Sousse has also been affected by tourism, and new aesthetic values are changing the face of the city. The first hotels, the Bou Jaffar and Sousse Palace, were constructed on Avenue Bourguiba. Both are extremely well integrated into the surrounding urban environment, although the architectural style of the latter hotel shows certain traces of modernism. Then the oceanfront began to expand in leaps and bounds. The natural barrier between the city and the sea was replaced by a broad asphalt bank, which formed an obstacle to the city's road network. One-way streets became common and perpendicular cross-streets were blocked off.

The hotels built along the ocean turn their backs on the city and seem grafted onto it with no continuity even among themselves. No attempt has been made at integration. The sole concern of the contractors appears to have been an easily recognizable similarity with the "modern" international style of architecture such as that found along the Seine waterfront in Paris, the "marine" of Cannes and Nice, and at Miami Beach.

Unfortunately these large tourist cages are, in the eyes of the local people who have no other basis for comparison, true symbols of the life-style of the highly industrialized, developed countries. Thus they regard as "most beautiful" the hotel that is the most conspicuous, the tallest, and the most monstrous of all.[14] For instance, the Sahara Palace in Nefta, relatively well integrated into the surrounding landscape, is often considered less beautiful than the hideous Dar Jerba Hotel in Jerba; the discreetly elegant Yasmina Hotel in Hammamet is considered shabby compared with the gaudy Phenicia a few doors away. Houses shooting up in the shadow of these large, barracks-like buildings in residential neighborhoods, financed primarily by the salaries of the city's hotel employees, have abandoned local architecture in favor of this new, imported style.

---

14. Questionnaires handed out in high schools and universities attempted to analyze the students' perceptions of their spatial environment. They were asked to rank, in order of importance, five well-known buildings or structures. The students invariably placed airports and hotels at the top of their lists (generally the Sousse Palace, which is the tallest hotel in the city), rating them above examples of indigenous architecture.

Contacts and Conflicts Between Residents and Tourists in Sousse

Paradoxically, mass tourism results in infrequent contact with the inhabitants of the host country. A recent survey of tourists visiting Sousse gives some idea of the kinds of contact and types of relations that are possible.[15] The average stay of those tourists was somewhere around nine days, too short a time to permit anything more than a superficial contact with residents. The exigencies of mass tourism also inhibit contact with the local people. Tourists are recruited en masse by travel agencies, shuttled over on charter flights, transferred in a group by motor coach from the airport, and then left in their hotel where they spend an average of twenty-two hours out of each day. This includes four hours on the beach, three hours at the pool, and fifteen hours within the actual hotel. Sousse is visited on an average for only two hours a day, and 65 percent of the tourists do not visit it at all!

Most visitors to Tunisia, and to Sousse in particular, are middle-income tourists, many of whom cannot afford to make excursions inland, or even to lay out the fares to go from their hotel to the center of town.[16] Their opportunities for contact with the local population are therefore limited from the start.

Like other new, peripheral tourist resorts that are great distances from traditional tourist-generating countries, Tunisia is virtually unknown to many tourists, who come with a distorted picture of

15. J. M. Miossec, an unpublished survey of hotel clientele prepared for Groupe Huit. Sixty-seven tourists were interviewed in Sousse in July and August 1975; most were staying in Sousse but some were staying in Skanes, Monastir, or elsewhere. These interviews were extracted from a survey of several hundred tourists throughout Tunisia, and the results for Sousse are comparable with those for the entire sample.

16. "Here in Sousse we frequently deal with middle-income tourists from European countries. These people do not have a large sum of money to purchase a great deal of Tunisian merchandise. These tourists are frequently forced to sell their cameras or other belongings. They then come down to the police station and file a statement to the effect that the articles were either lost or stolen so that they can later be reimbursed by their insurance companies for the value of the articles they sold. Once reimbursed in this manner, they end up by having enjoyed a vacation almost free of charge." (Statement by a police officer in Sousse, August 1975.)

what to expect. And, like other host countries, Tunisia leaves the tasks of recruiting, transporting, educating, and distracting its visitors in the hands of travel agencies. The caricatures and stereotypes used by their advertising departments—pictures of the sea, the blue sky, the fine sand, and tanned bodies—do nothing to educate tourists about their destination and leave them with narrowly limited expectations that offer the key to the understanding of their behavior. Tourists expect their visit to confirm, in concrete form, the mental images and daydreams they had prior to departure, which of course vary according to social class, nationality, cultural and educational level, and motivation.

How do visitors see Sousse? What do they expect from the city? In the earlier mentioned survey, their answers to the first question reflected a limited level of knowledge. They tended to confuse Sousse with Tunisia and with other "sun and sea" countries (75 percent of the responses). Their perception was global in form (gestalt). Sousse was either chosen or imposed on them as a destination for one of several reasons, but they might just as well have been in any other region within Tunisia or in another country.

Tourist responses to the second question also reflected their basic ignorance of the society of their host country. They listed as the country's attractions its natural resources such as sun, vegetation, and landscape (djebels). The sea and the beach were cited by 89 percent of the respondents. In contrast, Tunisia's civilization, history, people, present society, development problems, and the like were cited in all by only 11 percent of the tourists surveyed. Undoubtedly these impressions represent a certain type of tourist and a certain phase in the history of the development of international and Tunisian tourism.

Of all tourists interviewed, 39 percent stated that they had actually met Tunisians. This is, in reality, a rather low percentage, given the natural open-heartedness of the Mediterranean cultures. Initial contact is relatively easy and is often provoked by the Tunisian himself. But aside from contacts with guides and hotel employees, tourists remain within their own groups. Friends coming to Tunisia to relax tend to remain together. Intertourist relationships are apparently more important than relations with native Soussians (58 percent of the responses). Another factor is the low rate of tourist return to Tunisia. Less than 5 percent of all visitors return to Sousse, and therefore their contacts with Tunisian society remain rather superficial.

Contact between tourists and Tunisian women are extremely rare. Only 6 percent of the tourists interviewed stated that they had met a Tunisian woman during their stay. While some male Tunisians do mix with tourists on hotel beaches, in bars, or in nightclubs, it is a rare occurrence for a Tunisian woman to be seen in any of these places.[17] In town or in areas surrounding the hotels it is difficult, even considered improper, to speak to a Tunisian girl or young woman. They do not like to be seen with tourists, especially with male foreigners. None of the tourists interviewed mentioned having any type of relation, even if brief, with hotel maids. This can easily be explained by the rare opportunities for contact; the fact that maids clean the rooms after the occupants have left; the language barriers between clients and maids, who are either extremely young (39 percent are less than twenty years old) or, at the opposite end of the scale, middle-aged women (many of them widows); and by the close surveillance generally kept by an old woman from the girls' native village.

Some tourists who flee from the "solitude of crowds" are searching for a certain form of communication, understanding, affection. This search for companionship and for play is sometimes reflected in an erotic quest. Several couple profiles have already become stereotypes and are easily recognized: for instance, the foreign, middle-aged woman and the young Tunisian male, the homosexual couple, or the young European girl provoking a sensation with her new Tunisian "friends."

Any attempt to count the number of participants in this process is complicated by the fact that these relationships are between European women and Tunisian men (rarely between European men and Tunisian women), and in interviews female tourists show a great reluctance to talk. In the opinion of several hotel managers, approximately 5 percent of their hotel's total clientele are homosexuals (easily discernible). In any case, there has emerged a local market of a few hundred young gigolos, who gravitate around hotels and other spots frequented by tourists and proposition them. There is a clear-cut hierarchy, from the peeping Toms who observe rather than participate in the tourist milieu, through the small-time procurer or pimp and the amateur or neophyte who takes his chances,

---

17. Some Tunisian families do stay in hotels as tourists, but such cases are extremely rare.

on up to those rare individuals who operate out of a rigidly defined territory on the beach, in a bar, or at a public meeting place. These relations are formalized through the exchange of a few dinars. To profit from this line of work, however, a Tunisian must first acquire a certain expertise in spoken English or German.

Another self-seeking relationship, much more sophisticated than those described above (and which may or may not be sexual) is the acquaintance formed by Tunisian males for the sole objective of obtaining from tourists assistance in getting employment with an European firm. This type of contact has, however, become less frequent since the slowing down of immigration to Europe in 1973.

Tourist-resident relations are not all as superficial or as corrupt as those described above. Some tourists are truly interested in the world surrounding them and in their hosts. Six percent of the tourists interviewed had actually gone to a Turkish bath—the major meeting place in Tunisia—while 21 percent had visited the home of a Tunisian family, and 24 percent had met the family of a Tunisian woman or man with whom they took a stroll or a short excursion (15 percent). The Sousse museum and fortress had 65,000 and 25,000 visitors respectively in 1974, although in view of the low admission charge these are extremely small numbers for a city which has more than 300,000 tourists passing through each year.

The Soussian and Tunisian View of Tourism

At the time the first hotels were being constructed and the country's tourism strategy was first being launched, there were frequent references to a "tourism industry." Tourism and its symbols, such as the jumbo jet and luxury hotels, elicited an image of studied modernity and of much sought-after development. The inaccuracy of equating tourism with industry, and industry with development, led to equating tourism with development, implying not only economic growth and the generation of employment but also significant psychological factors such as prestige.

In the eyes of the Soussians tourism has permitted the entire region to diversify its economy; in addition, the international airport and the express trains providing links with the capital have put Sousse on the map, so to speak. Tunisians in general regard the regions along the country's eastern coast as "rich" in both an economic and a social sense, and tourism serves to accentuate this disequilibrium.

A fair segment of the population is now freed at last from basic material wants and needs and able to find jobs and housing, to educate their children, and to eat properly. There is beginning to be an interest in leisure activities other than the Tunisian family's traditional forms of entertainment such as festivals, visits to friends and relatives, and vacations in the houses of their birth. For the people of Sousse, the hotel has become a place for amusement or diversion where alcohol may be freely consumed. The upper classes are even beginning to celebrate marriages there. The hotel holds a strong attraction for the young and not-so-young alike because of the more liberal forms of behavior which it condones.

Conclusion

The situation in Sousse is unique in that the demands, constraints, risks, and potentials of a fragile agricultural environment, a large urban nucleus, an emerging industrial sector, and mass tourism are meeting head on. There are serious dangers involved, and in some instances the danger points have already been overstepped.

The first danger lies in the spatial expansion of Sousse to the north, west, and south. Tourism is rapidly developing along the coast north of the city, while industry is developing along parallel lines in planned industrial zones to the south. But the chaotic expansion of small subcontracting firms is spawning industrial units north of the city along the Tunis road as well. A residential area composed of land-devouring private homes is also stretching northward, drawn by the proximity of the resort hotels. This situation can only lead to further conflict and holds the threat of total chaos.

The second danger is socioeconomic. Giving priority to tourism, which might seem to be a government strategy, could exert an adverse effect on other sectors of the economy, particularly agriculture, and give rise to serious conflict. Those who criticize what they consider to be the country's present policy—a gradual evolution from a productive or manufacturing economy to a service-centered economy—could become increasingly hostile. If this new service economy proves to be oriented to serving foreigners, people will resent their dependence on foreign countries and their hostility will grow, especially since Tunisia has only recently succeeded in getting rid of the restrictions of colonialism. Can this infant tourism industry which emerged as a result of the basic directives of the law of 1972—an industry which has shown itself increasingly manipulated by foreigners and oriented toward markets in the rich, industrialized countries—do anything at all to help change this dependent relationship?

The third danger is crucial to any arid country. It concerns the distribution of water. The tourism sector seems to be enjoying special privileges in the allocation of water, to the detriment of basic agricultural production in the irrigated perimeters of the area.

Circumstances in Sousse could deteriorate rapidly, primarily because these problems and concerns are coming to a head in an enclosed environment. It is therefore a perfect example of a situation that requires the immediate implementation of an integrated development plan in which due consideration is given to agriculture, the city, its industry, and tourism.

CHAPTER 17

The Dynamics of Tourism Development in Puerto Vallarta

Nancy H. Evans
DEPARTMENT OF SOCIAL SCIENCES
CALIFORNIA STATE POLYTECHNIC UNIVERSITY

A LTHOUGH SOCIOCULTURAL RESEARCH ON TOURISM is comparatively recent, it has pinpointed specific topics—tourist types, the various stages of tourism development, the impact of tourism on the host country, planned versus "spontaneous" tourism—that invite more intensive study. Thus far, it appears that developing tourism not only produces a local dependency on the world market but also increases the rate of change in an impacted area. As the modernization process accelerates, so does the need for understanding and coping with it on both local and national levels.

The typology most frequently noted for tourism studies concerns change through time, specifically a three-stage form of development.[1] The following stages and their characteristics, following Noronha's review of the literature, appear to describe generally the impact of tourism at certain points in time and coincide with my observations in Puerto Vallarta in the state of Jalisco, Mexico.

1. Organic. Both exploring and wandering tourists visit with a minimum of disruption to the area. The nature and extent of tourism's impact is dependent upon the population density of the area and its resources.
2. Organic. Tourism is serviced and controlled through local institutions and decisions. It is influenced by local entrepreneurs and characterized by increased employment, a differentiation of occupations, new ideas, and a higher standard of living.

---

1. Raymond Noronha, *Social and Cultural Dimensions of Tourism: A Review of the Literature in English*, draft report to the World Bank, 1977.

3. Institutionalized. Individual and mass tourism are present. Decisionmaking for growth and development is taken over by outsiders. There follows an increased demand for goods and services, population growth, changes in social stratification, increased educational opportunities, and a host of social changes toward modernization.

The decisionmaking, social interaction, and events that influence individuals to extend their range of adaptability and change their behavior can be observed as new allocations of time and resources.[2] In this process of change, decisionmaking activity is particularly crucial to social adjustment and adaptation.

This study concentrates on the changes and the nature of continuity in the decisionmaking process in one Mexican community affected by tourism development. It focuses on the processes and events over a ten-year transition period, 1965–75, as institutionalization grew out of organic tourism, and considers the following questions:

— Who participates in decisionmaking? What kinds of decisions do they make?
— Is there continuity of decisionmaking, or do new roles develop?
— How do these decisions affect the working class?

National attitudes and policies are of great importance in the local community affected by tourism. Many governments today believe in the economic benefits of tourism and actively study, support, and allocate funds for its development. But few have experimented with innovative plans on such a wide scale as has Mexico. Since 1969 Mexico's attack on rural poverty and urban congestion has featured the creation of regional tourism centers, sometimes referred to as "America's new Rivieras." The Mexican government has set up agencies responsible for the general infrastructure development of whole areas; in Puerto Vallarta, Jalisco, and coastal Nayarit the agency is the Fideicomiso. Industrial parks in the rural highlands and tourism centers along the coasts are designed to create rural employment and stem the migration that threatens major cities.

How the national tourism policy affects a particular area is seen in the case of Puerto Vallarta. As a tourist destination already inter-

---

2. Fredrik Barth, "The Study of Social Change," *American Anthropologist*, vol. 69 (1967), pp. 661–69.

nationally known, it was selected in accordance with a federal plan to build on natural growth in an otherwise predominately agricultural region. Puerto Vallarta is envisioned as the center of a coastal ribbon of tourist resorts stretching along the west coast of Mexico through Nayarit and Jalisco.

Background

Although old-timers remember a tiny local hotel in 1910, tourism in Puerto Vallarta began in the late 1940s with a few American visitors. This small port was the county seat for the isolated Banderas valley and the hillside and mountain pueblos nearby. Coastal freighters carrying produce and passengers to Baja and Alta California connected Puerto Vallarta with the United States, while a small private airline and a rough, seasonal dirt road were all that connected it with central Mexico until the early 1960s. By the post-World War II period, several small local hotels housed regular visitors from America and Mexico. Word of mouth spread Vallarta's reputation for mild tropical climate, beautiful beaches, and relaxed hospitality, but only during Easter Week were there large numbers of strangers in town.

During Mexico's accelerated land reform program, some 600 small farmers in Puerto Vallarta had received—as ejidatarios[3]—around 9,000 hectares of land. But most of the land immediately surrounding Puerto Vallarta was too steep, swampy, or saline to work commercially, and members of the ejido turned to fishing or to agricultural employment on the United Fruit hacienda in the Banderas valley. Vallartans were too removed from centralized authority to be concerned with federal regulations governing ejidos, and newcomers were continually welcomed to live, if need be, on ejido land. A parcel of land was available for a nominal sum and a signed promise to build a house, live on the land, and con-

---

3. The ejidos, a form of land grant, are the core of Mexico's land reform program, rooted in the ideals of the Mexican Revolution of 1910–21. Although there were both collective and individual grants, those in Vallarta were distributed individually; first in 1929 with 2,808 hectares for 468 members (male heads of families), again in 1937 with an additional 2,046 hectares for 84 members, and finally in 1968 with 4,297 hectares for 75 more members. Ejido members received only the right to use the land; they could not sell it, and the right to be an ejidatario could be transferred only by inheritance.

tribute an occupation for the communal good. By 1975 only 184 ejidatarios could claim original rights and were farming at least part-time, although several thousand other families were also living on ejido land.

The small port grew slowly at first as the surrounding rural area contributed its excess population. Many individuals migrated on to Guadalajara and Mexico City where a wider variety of opportunities existed, and the United States attracted others. Some of the entrepreneurs who initiated tourist businesses in the 1960s are men who acquired their capital, skills, and English-language ability while employed in the United States.

Modernization progressed more rapidly after a federal agency installed electricity in 1958. Although mayors traditionally donated commemorative park benches, streetlights, and trees for the plaza and boardwalk of the town, their election depended more and more on their ability to appeal to state and federal agencies for financial support for major projects, such as a sewage system, hospitals, schools, and a potable water supply. Private citizens also initiated projects and contributed financial assistance. One wealthy townsman, for example, was responsible for several primary schools, a trade and secondary school, an auditorium, sports field, and amphitheater. A retired American couple started a free English-language night school, and the wife of an American hotel owner spearheaded a drive to collect local prehistoric artifacts and create a local museum. Entrepreneurial activity, civic cooperation, and limited state and federal funds provided these facilities.

A number of regular American visitors were encouraged to invest in homes and businesses in Puerto Vallarta, despite the fact that it was illegal for foreigners to own coastal property in Mexico. Two different legal procedures were employed. A few Americans acquired their property through an expensive but quasi-legal process of incorporation under the auspices of a Mexican bank, but most investors used a *presta-nombre* (borrowed name) whereby the property was purchased in the name of a trusted Mexican friend or lawyer. This was standard practice in many parts of Mexico, as described in several American-authored guidebooks on retirement. By 1965 there were in Vallarta several hundred American-owned homes and apartments, a few hotels, and an unknown amount of private American money invested in tourism businesses. In most cases, these investors were advised that the federal government would eventually take measures to regulate land tenure, but they decided that the immediate and probable future profits of tourism were worth the risks.[4]

By 1970 Vallarta had nurtured a middle sector of skilled workers, merchants, white-collar employees, and professionals who embraced an ideology of modernization similar to that of Mexicans in industrializing communities in the highlands.[5] Encouraged in their ideals by American residents who acted as role models and as friends, business partners, and employers, middle-class Vallartans shared a strong sense of nationalism, a belief in the need for economic and social development, and a commitment to education as a means to both personal and community advancement. They bought electrical appliances, especially radios and refrigerators, supported a weekly newspaper, attended two movie theaters, and young people in particular rapidly adopted modern casual clothing. Primary school was considered mandatory for children, secondary school enrollment increased, and one private school prepared those who wished to enter a university. New businesses included recreational and entertainment centers such as photography stores, a scuba-diving shop, a discotheque, and several nightclubs and restaurants. In general, the increasingly tourist-oriented economy was viewed as a means of local modernization, individual and family advancement, and a major vehicle to attract state and federal money to the community and the region. Tourism was considered the major factor responsible for the government-built paved highway, the jet airport and terminal completed by 1970, and the federal plans for a marina and deep-water pier.

Tourism

The traditional tourist season in Puerto Vallarta lasts four and a half months, December 15 through the end of April, including Christmas vacation and Easter Week. At least 25 percent of any an-

---

4. According to a state-published brochure, *Viva Puerto Vallarta* (Mexico D.F.: Informes, 1974), investors in Puerto Vallarta numbered 40,259, more than 25 percent of which (11,895) were foreigners. Local officials, however, consider this estimate far too high.

5. Frank C. Miller, *Old Villages and a New Town: Industrialization in Mexico* (Menlo Park, Cal.: Cummings Publishing Co., 1973), p. 120.

nual tourist count are Mexican vacationers at Easter, who outnumber the townspeople and camp everywhere. Hotels are full, it is said, to 125 percent capacity.

American visitors in the decades before 1960 made their own travel arrangements and apparently adapted to Vallarta's informal and less than luxurious hotels. By 1965, following a burst of construction, Vallarta could boast of 500 hotel rooms among approximately fifteen privately owned hotels, only one of which was a luxurious, first-class type. Although all hotel owners trained their employees, this large hotel held classes before opening, provided some English-language training, and rapidly advanced local employees to managerial positions. Despite its location several kilometers outside of town, it was considered an excellent place to work and a source of pride to townspeople. Waiters, exclusively men, earned an excellent income, because of tips, compared with the average wage in town. Other employment in tourism was provided by seventy-five taxis, thirty charter fishing boats, guided jungle tours, and several curio shops.

The production of a major American movie, serious promotion by a Mexican airline, and a 1968 prize-winning documentary film about Puerto Vallarta which circulated among travel agencies in the United States brought Vallarta to the attention of the tourist world. American, Italian, and Canadian cruise ships began making one-day stops in the winter months. By 1970, with the completion of the international airport, twenty-six international flights arrived weekly at Puerto Vallarta. During this same year, an all-weather paved road opened, connecting with the major west-coast highway, and a second motel was built to accommodate travel trailers and mobile homes. More and more outsiders found employment in Vallarta, and the 1970 census registered 23,843 inhabitants in Puerto Vallarta, compared with 12,000 in 1965. The 50,000 tourists for Easter 1970 were even more visible since their previous open camping areas were gone.

The number of hotels has more than doubled since 1965, primarily along the hotel strip north of town. These latest resort hotels provide a complete vacation center, making it unnecessary for wealthy tourists to visit town, but the main tourist beach continues to be crowded as the "in" place to meet. Parachute towing and horseback riding are available there, and vendors sell food and curios from all over Mexico. Many young Americans are highly visible, and local Vallartans comment unfavorably on their "hippy" dress, behavior, and attitudes toward drugs. Some middle-class families send their teen-age children to Guadalajara for high school because of the extensive use of marijuana in Puerto Vallarta.

Many former American residents have died, returned to the United States, or moved to outlying areas away from the bustling growth. Impersonal packaged and group tours have increased, with emphasis on the two-to-five-day Mexico-Guadalajara-Puerto Vallarta circuit. Canadian tourism has also increased. Car ferry services between Cabo San Lucas and Puerto Vallarta began in 1974, but it is estimated that 70 percent of the tourists still arrive by air, 23 percent by road, and 3 percent by sea. Seven international flights are scheduled daily plus the charter flights during the winter months. With the completion of the deep-water pier in 1974, cruise ships no longer anchor in front of the main tourist beach and ferry their passengers to the little pier. From the small harbor it is a long, expensive taxi ride into town, and many passengers do not bother to go—an economic blow to the curio and restaurant business. The problem is increased since cruise directors have created an attitude of fear toward eating in Mexican restaurants. Nonetheless, 350,437 visitors (176,599 foreigners and 173,838 nationals) registered in first- and second-class hotels in 1974.[6] Government employees' paid vacations and low-cost union-organized tours increased the number of Mexican tourists in Vallarta, especially in the summertime when business is usually poor.

As of 1975 there were 42 first- and second-class hotels in Vallarta, and the number of beds increased to 5,000. Hotel owners, comparing their business with that of previous years, complained of a slump, and the tourist department reported an increase of only 3.8 percent in business with an estimated 70,000 visitors at Easter. There is no doubt that business is beginning to level off, but it is no longer so seasonal. Two new types of tourists are steadily increasing: condominium owners and summer tourists. There are four condominiums, all partially empty, containing approximately 500 apartments. Three of them are several kilometers south of town, and while the occupants appear to have had little impact thus far, the townspeople do resent their possession of previously public beaches.

---

6. *Aqui: Vallarta* (the local newspaper of Puerto Vallarta), February 5, 1975, p. 4.

The hot, humid summer months that discouraged earlier travelers have seen a steady increase in foreign tourism. More and more schoolteachers, students, and vehicle travelers find Vallarta reasonable and tend to stay for several weeks. These summer tourists are welcomed, it is said, with the hospitality more characteristic of previous years.

Federal Involvement

Between 1965 and 1970 the federal government financed two major projects of significance to tourism in Vallarta: a paved road connecting with the west-coast international highway, and an international jet airport. Before their opening, local and out-of-town land developers recognized Vallarta's potential, and land sales and speculation flourished. Tourism was booming and Vallarta more than doubled its population in five years. The electricity frequently failed, potable water was a problem, and the sewage plant completed in 1969 was considered by many to be obsolete before it began to function.

Local, state, and national officials in Vallarta recognized three serious problems: The growth rate and rapid expansion of the tourist trade necessitated modern and expensive infrastructure; foreigners were illegally buying and speculating on Vallarta land; and urban corporations were investing in ejido land and individual enterprises unrestricted by local control. The latter was referred to as "internal neocolonialism"—an urban form of paternalism. Federal studies confirmed the importance of these and similar problems elsewhere, and federal policymakers proceeded to generate plans to deal with them.

During the six-year term of President Echeverria (1970–76) two presidential decrees were particularly crucial for the development of tourism. The first provided for foreign acquisition of coastal land for private residences (and commercial use through rentals) through a ten-year lease. The lease would be held in trust by a bank under the control of the national credit institution. The foreign leaseholder would have options for two ten-year renewals, and at the end of the thirty-year period the property must be sold at market value. The second decree announced the expropriation of 5,161 hectares of ejido land in coastal Nayarit and Jalisco, 1,026 hectares of which were the property of the ejido of Puerto Vallarta. A Fideicomiso, a government agency, was established to regulate land tenure and supervise the development of the coastal region. Shortly thereafter, another decree separated Puerto Vallarta from the Nayarit coast and created another Fideicomiso for the town. With the creation of this agency, the institutionalization of tourism, the third stage, began in Puerto Vallarta.

Fideicomiso Puerto Vallarta

In 1973 the Fideicomiso Puerto Vallarta began operation with the following objectives: (1) to receive 1,026 hectares of expropriated ejido land to be regularized or sold as private property, that is, to legalize land tenure; (2) to regularize foreign-"owned" (presta-nombre) property on ejido land and permit new aliens to lease coastal property; (3) to develop and put into operation a master plan for the necessary infrastructure to support a tourism sector; and (4) to be the instrument and drive for regional development.

Its legal structure is complex and not well understood by many local people, particularly the poor and uneducated. The Fideicomiso is composed of three bodies: the grantor, which is the federal government represented by the secretary of finance and public credit; the fiduciary or trustee, a local branch of the newly created department of the National Bank; and the beneficiaries or fideicomisarios, the members of the Puerto Vallarta ejido who will receive compensation for the expropriated land. A technical committee approves the direction and operation of the plan, and consists of representatives of several federal, state, and local organizations.[7]

The profits generated by the regularization and sale of land go to finance and maintain the new infrastructure, to create enterprises that aid the farmers in becoming businessmen, and to pay the indemnification fees to the ejido members. A small percentage is allot-

---

7. Fideicomiso Puerto Vallarta, "Twenty-three Questions and Answers about the Fideicomiso Puerto Vallarta" (Mexico, D.F.: Talleres Gráficos de México, 1973), lists the membership of the technical committee as follows: Departamento de Asuntos Agrarios y Colonización, Secretaría de Hacienda y Crédito Público, Secretaría de la Presidencia, Departamento de Turismo, Secretaría del Patrimonio Nacional, Banco Nacional de Obras y Servicios Públicos, S.A., Gobierno Constitucional del Estado de Jalisco, Fondo Nacional de Fomento Ejidal, Confederación Nacional Campesino, Ayuntamiento de Puerto Vallarta, and Ejidatarios del Ejido Puerto Vallarta.

ted to the national association of ejido development, Fondo Nacional de Fomento Ejidal (FONAFE), but the profits must also support the local Fideicomiso itself.

The Fideicomiso work has not progressed smoothly. The land survey, evaluation, price setting, and zoning are complex operations involving more than 8,000 lots (300 American owned) in eleven *colonias* (neighborhoods) with thirty-three different price zones. The Fideicomiso introduced many limitations on individual rights and prerogatives in land use and ownership, and public opinion has strongly opposed the prices set. An expensive campaign to gain community cooperation encompassed many methods: speeches and participation in all civic functions, regular newspaper advertising and articles, daily radio programs with entertainment and free public announcements, and the sponsoring of charities and civic projects.

The Fideicomiso began construction of a bypass, a second bridge, a sewage system and treatment plant, and a complex in town that contains a museum, curio shop, playground, and restaurant. The first three projects are both wanted and needed but as yet are unfinished. The complex, while beautiful, is considered an impractical, expensive business venture. The most visible efforts are in the tourist zones—hotel condominiums and expensive residential areas which restrict public access to the beach and appear to benefit no one but affluent nationals and foreigners. One such project became the target for public ridicule when heavy summer rains washed tons of relocated topsoil across the highway.

Today public opinion of the Fideicomiso varies. Considered a necessary evil by businessmen and a taxing agency by the uneducated, it has been the scapegoat for every problem, including the weather! Ejidatarios and property owners have made it the target of organized opposition and question its legal authority and, more importantly, its excessive valuation of the land. Some critics claim that expropriated ejido land in other parts of Mexico (Baja California is often cited) is valued at prices as much as 70 percent lower and is therefore in the price range of its former possessors. Many individuals and several colonias still refuse to pay the assessed prices although they registered their property. The Union de Colonos, formed as an opposition group to the Fideicomiso, continues to be a viable organization even though there is no visible evidence that it has won concessions from the Fideicomiso. The union serves as a decisionmaking group for the local property owners who attempt to have local input into the Fideicomiso.

Some middle-class businessmen blame municipal officials for not protecting town interests, claiming that although local officials are part of the decisionmaking body of the Fideicomiso, they are too intimidated by the power, status, and presumed expertise of outside officials to be forceful in presenting their views. Opinions expressed both inside and outside the Fideicomiso suggest that its officials are neither efficient nor well qualified for their responsibilities, and many Vallartans are hoping the newly elected president will either remove the agency from town or replace its staff, the latter possibility being most likely.

Although the Fideicomiso acts as a clearinghouse, controls planning and development, and probably in the long run will prove to be the major influence for local development, it is not the only decisionmaking body. The opportunity and necessity for decisionmaking proliferates on every level as townspeople and newcomers press for additional infrastructure and increased tourism. The pressures of rapid population growth alone—from 10,000 in the early 1960s to a conservative estimate of 50,000 in 1975—create new problems daily. As one prominent Vallartan lawyer expressed it recently, "We live in a constant state of emergency!"

Decisionmaking Today

Institutionalized agencies are welcome additions to a community grown too big for individuals and groups to provide the necessary goods and services. Individual initiative is still important but restricted largely to educational and cultural affairs. The services introduced into the community in recent years have somewhat improved the lot of the poor, but it is difficult to assess the effects with any accuracy.

Who participates in decisionmaking? What kinds
of decisions are made?

Since tourism is primarily a service industry, its growth created a huge service population. These workers, plus those in the secondary support businesses, now require additional services themselves.

The Fideicomiso, in its role of providing infrastructure, has facilitated the introduction of several new government agencies in Puerto Vallarta. These agencies are attempting to meet some of the growing needs of the area.

The Seguro Social (Social Services) has made the most significant addition to the community: a hospital, complete with ambulance, clinics, and specialists. Previously, those eligible (federal and state employees) traveled to Guadalajara for serious illnesses because the local hospital is considered inadequate and used primarily by the poor. Union members whose employers pay into Seguro Social are now eligible for free or minimal-charge aid, and all large restaurants, hotels, taxi drivers, construction workers, and the like are unionized. Since the cost of private medical care and pharmaceutical products is rising rapidly, the Seguro Social provides an additional choice of medical services for many.

Another addition is Aramara, a Vallarta suburb of government-built low-cost housing for the working class. Four hundred units recently completed will house approximately 2,000 people in a small, attractive community complete with swimming pool, clubhouse for classes, and locations for a market and several small neighborhood businesses. Because the available housing does not begin to take care of those both qualified and wanting it, weekly drawings are held to select from among those eligible. A minimum-wage employee (currently US$4.59 daily) pays $6,400 for a three-bedroom house at 4 percent interest. Payments are met by withholding 18 percent from the monthly paycheck. Since the maximum payment for a house is $10,000, comparable housing in Vallarta would rent for almost double the maximum monthly payment in Aramara. As with most government agencies in Mexico, the housing authority requires long and sometimes complicated paperwork which discourages anyone with little education from applying.

Goods, particularly modern manufactured items, have long been scarce and expensive in Puerto Vallarta. Buying trips to Tepic or Guadalajara are cooperative, and many individuals bring back items to sell. Although a government-subsidized basic commodities market has had a branch in Vallarta for many years, it is poorly stocked and its prices are generally not below the local markets. But a new store for government employees sells basic commodities and appliances for half the local prices and will be a major boon to many townspeople.

None of the decisions resulting in the above facilities were made in the community, but they are locally considered a positive result of the rapid population growth that attracted federal attention. The growth, in turn, has resulted from the increased economic opportunities that attracted migrants to the developing tourist resort. Vallartans cannot be said to have relinquished control since the government has always been responsible for providing modern public facilities.

Is there continuity of decisionmaking or do new roles develop?

At the local level, decisions have not changed radically in the last few years. There is a long tradition of active local participation—even by newcomers—in providing medical, educational, and cultural facilities, and these same concerns take only slightly new forms today. One Fideicomiso official made it his personal project, with the backing of an international hotel, to coordinate with the state fine-arts program to bring free concerts to Puerto Vallarta once a month. Among service-oriented businessmen, there is an eagerness to provide the community with facilities and services comparable to those in the larger urban centers and the United States. The Lions and Rotary clubs have each raised money to build two primary schools in recent years and are currently supporting some promising students through higher education. Civic-minded individuals constitute the newly formed Sister City program, which arranges for exchange students, coordinates the Eyes-International Program, and holds round-table discussions on civic projects. A women's group is building a child-care center, having just completed a children's clinic.

The municipal government has just completed a Sister City monument, a small decorative building filled with commemorative plaques and pictures. Although this is in keeping with the mayor's traditional role, many citizens today complain that the municipal funds should be spent only for practical necessities, that the mayor should have more "vision." His job, once part-time but now very busy and heavily scheduled, is filled with officiating at many tourism and civic functions.

Middle-class businessmen and professionals, drawn together primarily by the tourism industry, have formed a variety of new organizations based on their professional and business interests. The Hotel and Restaurant Association, which meets frequently with the head of tourism, is composed of local hotel and restaurant owners, managers, and those from other tourist towns. During the 1976 winter season, when tourism decreased by more than 10 percent, they discussed ways of combating the trend. In particular, they are trying to standardize services and lower costs and prices. They are also lobbying to force the government to eliminate the 15 percent entertainment tax, having succeeded in removing it for foreigners with tourist cards. Concerned that Vallarta is getting a reputation for being expensive, they are considering different strategies, including the Holiday Inn's type of budget packages. In these new roles, decisionmaking is still individual, but the new organizations represent an information level and cooperative strength never before possible.

Problems which require follow-up and maintenance remain unsolved. The constant repair needed to keep cobblestone streets in good order, the antirabies campaign required every two years, the supervision necessary to maintain standardized hospital services, the clean-up necessary after Easter Week—all these problems and a myriad more go with rapid modernization. Under conditions of rapid change many individuals in Vallarta are innovative, experimental, and eager to solve new problems, but behind them there is no local system of taxation providing the revenue necessary for the maintenance and repair that are taken for granted in developed countries. Middle-class criticism, particularly among well-educated local businessmen, is focused on the local government but few practical solutions are offered.

How do decisions affect the working class?

There is a great difference of opinion about what constitutes poverty in Vallarta. Older community members, some quite affluent today, can remember the tiny palm-thatched and nonelectrified homes of their youth; younger people today view the *palapas* (houses made of wattle) as totally inadequate and deplorable. In neighborhoods along the coast north of town and in the hills and along the river to the east, the majority of homes belong to newcomers and are in transitional states. Brick or adobe rooms have been attached to the original palapa house, and some construction materials lie nearby. Water trucks wend their way along streets hardly more than trails, and electrical service does not extend to the total area. Families continually build on cheap or free ejido land which, in years to come, will undoubtedly be expropriated. Even there, Vallarta's radio station blares out over transistor radios announcing free innoculations, school registration, and free concerts and lectures.

Recent migrants to Vallarta say they have many more advantages than they had in their villages and give two reasons for their move. That "there is work here!" is most commonly heard, and laborers quote the difference between the wages and variety of jobs available in Vallarta and those in the village or rancho from which they came. They have followed relatives or friends and usually live with them until they can afford to rent or buy a place of their own.

The second reason for moving to Vallarta is the opportunity for their children's education. Although class size is large by U.S. standards and school construction does not keep up with population growth, Vallarta's reputation for educational opportunity and excellence continues. Almost every child in Vallarta finishes primary school (sixth grade). Some local educators feel that the availability of unskilled jobs in tourism keeps many from continuing their schooling, but it is more likely that the family cannot afford to support them any longer. Although less than 50 percent go on to secondary school, some choose to attend private schools for practical skills while working part-time or full-time. Night school is now available for illiterate adults, literacy being a requisite for many union-controlled jobs in tourism today.

The single most important skill beyond literacy in Vallarta today is the ability to speak English. It almost certainly guarantees an excellent job. Large hotels, banks, and government agencies give their employees crash courses. There has recently been an influx of English-speaking migrants from border towns and the United States, and these people found jobs as taxi drivers, tour guides, and hotel help quite easily. Many Vallartans make an attempt to attain this skill. Upward of 500 students of all ages begin the free Holt English-language school every fall, although less than half complete the year. It is impossible to ascertain the number taking private lessons, but American residents are besieged with requests to give them. Currently, there is a Mexican engineer serving a jail sentence who not only translates for the police but gives English lessons to private citizens from his cell!

Whether the Vallartan poor can be said to have more options than elsewhere depends largely on individual experience and perception of the new situation. Street begging is not allowed, but the church has a food program and a free pharmacy, and the Sister City program and individual Americans contribute gifts and food to the schools at Christmas. Many believe the Vallarta myth, frequently heard both seriously and in jest, that a family or child may be "adopted" by an American tourist and taken to the United States. In the last twenty years it has happened frequently enough to keep the myth alive. Another, more realistic possibility is slipping across the border into the United States. The many familial networks between Vallarta and the United States make this quite simple.

Summary

Although the rate of change and growth of a town is not strictly measurable, it can be observed in the concrete events, activities, behavior, and decisions over a period of time. It is possible to observe the ten-year sequence of behavior and events that changed Puerto Vallarta. The impact of tourism and rapid growth following the introduction of modern forms of transportation created both the necessity for and the availability of new forms of decisionmaking at more complex and institutional levels. Individual and local-group decisions still focus on educational, medical, and cultural services, but infrastructure demands finances and expertise not generally available at the local level.

During the organic growth of tourism, Vallartans tried to get state and federal support. When it appeared that tourism could support local and regional development, the federal government recognized it as an economic solution to rural unemployment in the coastal area and stepped in. At present, many Vallartans feel that they got rather more than they bargained for and, with organized resistance, hope to see changes in the Fideicomiso and government policies. But they are also conscious that they have changed, that they have made new allocations of their time and resources, and have taken definite and irrevocable steps toward modernization.

CHAPTER 18

Tourism for Discovery: A Project in Lower Casamance, Senegal

Christian Saglio
TECHNICAL ADVISER,
SENEGAL DEPARTMENT OF TOURISM

T RADITIONAL INVESTMENT PROGRAMS for the development of tourism in Africa virtually exclude projects that would enable tourists to discover what lies beyond the beach and come into contact with the real Africa. True encounters between tourists and their hosts are rare and limited. The lack of understanding between them is strongly conditioned, on the tourists' side, by three interacting elements: the promotional literature he sees, the length of his visit, and the type of accommodation available.

Promotion is often left to tour operators and agencies, beyond the control of tourism officials in the countries of destination. The result is apt to be a distorted image of wild, darkest Africa, a land of deserted beaches, tom-toms, lions, witch doctors, and bare breasts. This caricature, tailored to the Westerner hankering after exoticism, is designed to give the illusion of adventure—but one that is carefully prepared, always controlled, and experienced with the assurance of undisturbed comfort.

Most of the tourist literature thus merely accentuates stereotypes and preconceptions in order to make a sale. It does nothing to change the tourist's notion of the African world, which may be based on the Colonial Exposition of 1930 or his childhood reading of Tarzan. Hampered by this preconception, tourists on organized group excursions are carefully scheduled and allowed no real contact with the African people. The brevity of the visit and the desire to see as much as possible often merely reinforce the superficial picture which the visitors bring with them.

For the local people, the repetitive nature of mass tourism means a high degree of saturation and a degradation of human relationships. In Senegal, Cayar and Fadiout are among the most popular destinations sold by travel agencies during the last fifteen years. There has been a great deal of tension between visitors and local residents in these two towns, the tourist not wishing to be seen as a mere spender of money and the villager refusing to be treated as another object to be photographed. The magazine of the Touring Club of France tells of the brief stay in Casamance of a journalist "disguised as a tourist" who observed such deplorable things as candy littering the sand, a few coins given to a little girl to take off her loincloth and dance for the camera, an old man who was asked to climb up and tap palm wine for a photograph, and ceremonies performed on request.

A significant degree of segregation and isolation marks the tourist's accommodation: air-conditioned hotels, concentrated for the most part in easily accessible areas—capital cities and beaches—in an artificial world completely divorced from the reality of the country. Even when the tourist ventures out, most of his impressions are filtered through the windows of an air-conditioned car or the time-worn harangue of a hired guide. Spontaneous contact with his hosts is thus extremely difficult. Furthermore, the host encountered is often a hotel employee trained to serve the tourist in the Western manner to which he is accustomed; even the cuisine is international, which is not the least of the paradoxes.

This absence of spontaneous contact between visitors and local residents contributes to a mutual lack of understanding, which is manifested in a number of ways. The local people face the problem of conforming to the expectations of the tourist and are in danger of being exploited as part of the exotic setting offered by the package tour. Because their life-style is unfamiliar to tourists, the local people may feel they are being "looked at," much as a zoological specimen, and may suffer feelings of alienation. Their social structures may suddenly be perceived as archaic and valueless; ritual ceremonies are organized as entertainment or even held on request; spuriously "typical" houses are constructed with every comfort, including inside plumbing, which give the tourist a false impression; craftsmen produce trinkets exclusively for the tourist market—mass-produced objects without ethnographic value, masks that are meaningless caricatures.

Tourism of this kind can also have a significant demonstration effect, leading to the abandonment of certain traditional values, especially among young people. The proletarianization of the rural Diola in Casamance, with the creation of new jobs at the Cap Skirring Club Méditerranée, has severely shaken social structures that had been stable for centuries despite the upheavals of history and colonization. A new hierarchy of values has developed that gives importance to money. Socioeconomic relations have become monetized, and young people are now able to break out of the traditional restraints and achieve a new status. New needs have arisen, often unrelated to the environment, and morals and life-styles have been affected.

Tourism for Discovery Project

To counteract these negative aspects of tourism, a new form of integrated village tourism was developed in Senegal. After two years as an ethnologist in the field, I was recruited in November 1971 by the Agency for Cultural and Technical Cooperation to draw up a project called Tourism for Discovery. This project, involving four countries (Benin, Mali, Niger, Senegal), soon had to be adapted to the actual conditions in each, but in Senegal I was able to keep it more or less within the broad lines originally sketched out.

The model called for simple lodgings to be built, managed, and operated by local people. They would offer only minimal comforts to small groups of tourists, but there would be opportunity for real contact between guests and hosts. In contrast to the sedentary type of tourism at beaches or in large cities, a genuine voyage of discovery would be possible via traditional modes of transport (canoes) and natural communication routes (waterways). The guest houses were to be constructed along the tour routes, using traditional materials and methods. They thus mitigated the contrast between the quality of facilities usually provided for tourists and the living standards of the local people. Moreover, only a small investment was required.

According to the plan, the management of the lodgings was to be left entirely to the villagers. Cooperatives were therefore organized and made responsible for the operation of the camps as well as the allocation of profits at the end of the year. The same concern for integration was shown in planning meals around local products and traditional cuisine and arranging activities for tourists.

The new projects were designed to enable each village involved to combat the exodus to the cities after the rainy season by offering young people a wide range of new jobs. The plan also called for action at the point of sale by replacing the old tourism advertising literature with original material stripped of clichés. It was a modest effort in terms of outlay, but original in its determination to get off the beaten paths in design, implementation, management, and promotion.

Implementation

After many reconnaissance missions to look at possible sites for the experimental program in Senegal, the final choice was Lower Casamance. This region lies between The Gambia and the southern border of Senegal and includes the Casamance River and its tributaries (see map).

Distances are short, the environment and the climate are agreeable, and the area is well populated. The traveler arriving from Dakar or The Gambia has a plethora of choices among different excursions and types of lodging. The regional capital, Ziguinchor, offers traditional, comfortable hotel facilities, and will offer even better ones in the near future. Because of the attraction of its many inlets, the coast already provides first-class beach resort facilities, especially at the Cap Skirring Club Méditerranée and La Paillotte. A number of other tourist facilities are planned along the coast from Cap Roxo to Diembering, particularly at Boukot and Kabrousse.

The initial project was not completed until 1976, after some major modifications of the original design. The facilities have not been conceived to comprise an integrated circuit such as those being organized in Mali or Niger, but they are rather a network of individual and distinctive complexes located within a limited area and surrounded by a variety of other tourist attractions.

Four camps have been established and are now operating at Elinkine, Enampore, Baïla, and Thionck Essyl. Together they offer more than 100 beds, at a total cost of about CFAF10 million (US$40,000). This sum includes the cost of construction, technical assistance, travel expenses for survey teams and coordinators, a truck to transport materials, repair and maintenance of the truck, and the driver's wages. Not included is my own salary for time spent on the project as part of my activities with the Department of Tourism (approximately one seven-day mission in the field each month once the project got under way). Nor does this total include

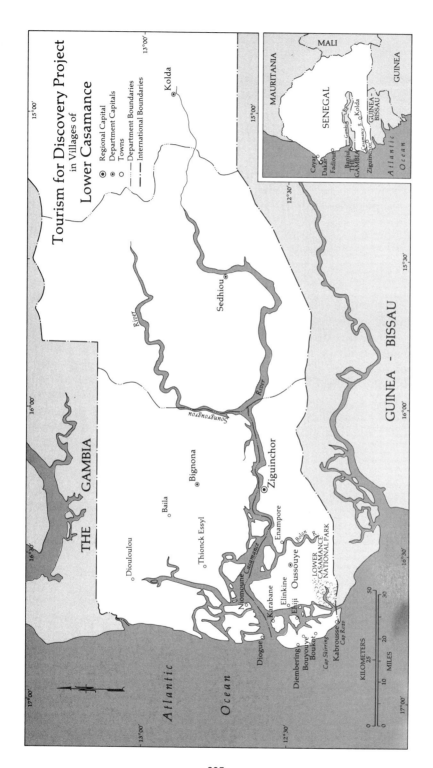

Tourism for Discovery Project
in Villages of
Lower Casamance

⊙ Regional Capital
⊙ Department Capitals
○ Towns
----- Department Boundaries
-··-··- International Boundaries

expenses for Adama Goudiaby, director of the Ziguinchor crafts center and regional coordinator for tourism, who has been closely associated with the project, supervising operations, taking part in all meetings, and encouraging the villagers by many visits. He also helps run a valuable in-service training program for the management teams. The material resources available to Goudiaby, hitherto extremely limited, have been substantially increased through assistance from CUSO (Canadian University Service Overseas), which now provides supplementary salary, an all-terrain vehicle, and travel expenses.

General Problems

In the 1972 rainy season less than 700 millimeters of rain fell in the Oussouye region (against an average of 1,400 millimeters). As a result of this drought many people had left the villages of Casamance, and there was a shortage of labor. The workers who remained were so preoccupied with the critical problem of the drought that it was difficult to interest them in the project and train teams for construction and operation. Furthermore, the hardness of the soil and the drying up of the wells made it arduous to work the clay for building.

A second series of problems revolved around the major effort required to inform people about the new project and elicit their cooperation. The administrative authorities, accustomed to large-scale projects such as the vacation villages of Neckermann or Club Méditerranée, were often suspicious or even hostile to our project. They criticized the small amount of the investment, feared upheavals and problems in the villages, and doubted the desire of tourists to live in clay houses. There was also a deep-seated reluctance to show visitors some of the traditional ways of life, which many of the elite tend to hold in contempt under cover of an official attitude of overvaluation.

I was frequently reproached, at least at the beginning, for not including glass windows, numbered doors, electricity, and even air-conditioning. Many highly placed individuals had to be convinced of the importance of preserving the integrity and quality of the traditional architecture. Even the villagers themselves would have preferred to build in cement block with sheet metal roofs because it "looks better and cleaner for tourists." Many meetings were necessary to gain the understanding and full support of the administrative, political, and village authorities, but this educational process was essential to the success of the project.

The choice of site was often difficult because of rivalries among village leaders, especially between the village head recognized by the administration and the various traditional chiefs, whose role is highly important among the Diolas. These disagreements could be resolved only through numerous meetings and lengthy discussions (twenty-three for the village of Enampore alone), which often lasted an entire day. Each person expressed his opinion in turn, with the remarkable respect for democracy shown in these village societies.

Once the site was chosen it was absolutely necessary to drill wells, because those existing were almost dried up. A number of problems impeded this operation, including landslides, procurement of iron and cement for pipes, and the choice of well drillers. When completed, however, the wells often won additional support for the project among villagers who had depended on the old drying wells.

One purpose of the project was to restore the value of the traditional Diola dwelling by reproducing it as faithfully as possible. Construction of these houses required a collective effort of a type that until then had never involved a monetary transaction, and no standard existed for estimating costs. Many meetings were held with the villagers to take account of such elements as the price of palm slats, the rate for cutting and clearing, the price of roof straw, and average village income. Thus the actual cost of construction for each camp was determined in agreement with the people.

The sites selected for the Tourism for Discovery project are located, by definition, away from major tourist routes, and their inaccessibility caused additional problems and delays. Ferries often broke down or ran aground; trails were frequently impassable, especially during the rainy season. For months on end I was totally dependent on Serer fishermen at Elinkine for transportation (the Diola canoes were neither equipped with motors nor designed for long trips). Their prices were often very high and involved tiresome bargaining. After a canoe was assigned to the operation, I had more freedom of movement, but canoes are subject to such hazards as running aground, motor breakdowns, and capsizing in high winds. Furthermore, because communication among villages is mainly by river or sea, there were many problems of procurement and delivery of construction materials.

Elinkine

The village of Elinkine is made up of Diola farmers, Serer fishermen, and a few Mandingo families, about 1,000 inhabitants in all. It was selected mainly because of its location: fifteen kilometers from Oussouye by a fairly good trail and fifty kilometers via ferry from both Ziguinchor, the regional capital east on the river, and Cap Skirring on the coast to the west. Situated on the bank of a major inlet, Elinkine has long been used by fishermen and travelers as a crossing and an easy starting point for a whole range of canoe excursions to Karabane, Diogue, Niomoune, Ehiji, Diembering, Bouyouye, and Boukot. An existing telephone line makes it possible to give notice of the arrival of tourists.

The camp was built a short distance from the village on open land with an extensive view of islands and waterways. Three traditional rectangular houses were constructed, the third one financed by the villagers themselves from the profits of the first year of operation. Each house contains four rooms with two beds each (that is, a total of twenty-four beds for the camp), a large central lobby with wicker chairs and mats, a toilet with septic tank, a bathroom with shower and washstand. A smaller building between the others serves as a kitchen and storage area. Other facilities include a water tower and well connected by a Japy pump, a gas refrigerator, an open dining structure, roofed with broad palm fronds, on the bank of the waterway, a small wooden dock, two canoes, and a twenty-horsepower motor.

Although construction began in early 1973, high winds struck the complex in the rainy season and destroyed one of the huts. The traditional foundations therefore had to be strengthened with shell material and a cement slab, always a prudent precaution when building on soil that has not been stabilized. It also reduces the risk of the clay walls being tunneled by termites. Thus, it was not until just before Christmas 1973 that the Elinkine camp could offer meals to its first visitors, and not until December 1, 1974, that it could be regarded as operational and able to accommodate overnight guests. During these two years the villagers were able to organize themselves for this collective undertaking and to assess both the difficulties and the advantages of the project.

Today Elinkine offers the traveler a modest but gracious facility, authentically African with the addition of the basic comforts. Mats replace doors and windows. The locally made beds have good mattresses covered with locally dyed counterpanes. A few hammocks hung between the mangroves allow the guest a pleasant waterside siesta. Construction and materials for buildings, improvements, and operation cost a total of about CFAF2 million (US$8,000).

Enampore

The village of Enampore, about twenty kilometers from Ziguinchor, is less open to the outside world and more traditionalist than Elinkine. Its 1,500 inhabitants are farmers whose religion is largely animistic. The village was chosen because of the unusual architecture of its impluvium houses.

Unique in Africa (although also found in New Guinea), the impluvium house is a large circular building with clay walls and a distinctive two-layered roof of palm thatch. One layer forms a funnel to collect rainwater, which is stored by the community against the dry season; a central opening performs the dual function of reservoir and light source. Because of its size and plan, each building resembles a traditional village. A central courtyard is encircled by an interior gallery where communal activities take place, such as spinning cotton, plaiting palm fibers, cooking, and conversing while drinking *bounouk*. About fifty persons normally would live in the largest house, with all their livestock and necessary provisions.

Although the impluvium design is well adapted to the traditional social organization and climatic conditions of Enampore, none had been built there for a long time. It was not until December 1973, after a year of difficult psychological preparation, that work on the tourist facility was begun.

Today the Enampore camp consists of a beautiful traditional house built by the villagers using the methods of the past. It can accommodate some thirty tourists in small rooms, rather dark but cool, arranged in a ring around the central courtyard. Two of the rooms are equipped as bathrooms, each with two showers, a washstand, and a toilet, separated by partitions. The sanitary facilities, the water tower, and the outside kitchen are identical to those at Elinkine, as are the furnishings and equipment.

More than a simple hostel, the Enampore camp is a living museum of the Casamance dwelling and crafts. All around the large circular gallery everyday objects are hung in the Diola fashion: farm tools such as the large *kadyendo* for rice cultivation, the *daba* (a type of hoe), plaited baskets, gourds, earthenware pots, weapons, cloth, pottery, musical instruments (the *bougheur* and other drums, flutes, and horns). The visitor is thus made to feel part of a different environment and civilization.

The total cost of works and improvements was CFAF2.5 million (US$10,000). This was CFAF500,000 more than for Elinkine because of the large dimensions of the hut and the effects of inflation.

Baïla and Thionck Essyl

Thionck Essyl, with a population of 8,000 Diola Bouloufs, is the largest village in the region. Its Muslim inhabitants depend mostly on farming for their living, though there is some fishing as well. Baïla contains about 2,500 Diola Fogny people, again mostly farmers of the Muslim faith. New camps in these villages, both north of the Casamance River, were completed in June 1976, funded by a credit of CFAF5 million (US$20,000) from the Agency for Cultural and Technical Cooperation. The facilities are similar to those at Elinkine and Enampore, with thirty beds in each camp, and the same methods of construction were used. Only the architecture is different. The first groups of young people from the Rivages and Africa Tour agencies stayed there during the 1976 rainy season. It should be noted that the villagers took a much greater part in the construction of these two camps, contributing their labor free and often materials as well.

Management and Operation

Under the authority of the village chief, the work of serving visitors is assigned to young people of the village. A management committee supervises the three operating units of two persons each in charge of meals, accommodation, and excursions. Prices are set by agreement, as is the remuneration for each worker and the share allocated to the cooperative. The members are paid after each visit according to the number of tourists and the services rendered. This method of payment avoids the risk of establishing a small bureaucracy that a system of regular wages might entail.

In the typical case of fifteen tourists spending two nights, with four meals and two excursions, the camp cooperative would receive a total of CFAF24,000 (about US$10) after those in charge of the various units were paid. The details are given in Table 18.1. At present, the excursions unit is the least profitable because of large and frequent outlays to repair the outboard motors, but it is essential to offer recreational activities at the camps.

Accounts carefully maintained by the villagers show that profits realized during the 1974–75 tourist season totaled CFAF1,200,000,

Table 18.1. *Earnings from a Typical Stay at a Tourist Camp*

Income and expenses	CFAF
Meals (CFAF 500 each)	
Total paid by tourists (500 × 15 × 4)	30,000
Less expenses	18,000
Supplies (150 × 15 × 4)	9,000
Wages to unit chief (75 × 15 × 4)	4,500
Wages to assistant (75 × 15 × 4)	4,500
Balance to cooperative	12,000
Accommodation (CFAF 500 per person)	
Total paid by tourists (500 × 15 × 2)	15,000
Less expenses	4,500
Supplies (50 × 15 × 2)	1,500
Wages to unit chief (75 × 15 × 2)	2,250
Wages to assistant (75 × 15 × 2)	2,250
Balance to cooperative	9,000
Excursions (CFAF 5,000 each)	
Total paid by tourists (5,000 × 2)	10,000
Less expenses	7,000
Operating expenses (2,000 × 2)	4,000
Wages to first boatman (750 × 2)	1,500
Wages to second boatman (750 × 2)	1,500
Balance to cooperative	3,000

Note: The figures given here are for a typical visit of fifteen tourists, who spend two nights in camp, are served four meals, and go on two excursions. CFAF500 is the equivalent of about US$2.

that is, close to US$5,000, for the village of Elinkine alone. The substantial operating balance is distributed at the end of the year by a board, whose members are appointed by the village and are often community leaders such as the chief, teacher, or nurse. The profits, used prudently, have permitted the coordinated development of village activities and the integration of the tourism operation in the local economy. Furthermore, operating and amortization costs are very small. Every two or three years it will be necessary to rethatch the straw roof or to reinforce the clay walls, but neither the generating unit nor the electric pump requires large outlays or frequent repairs. Thus, it has been possible to utilize the profits immediately for other activities such as vegetable farming, raising livestock, fishing, and crafts. This has in turn enabled many young people to find jobs locally and has effectively deterred migration to the cities. Another part of the profits has been allocated to improving community facilities such as health and maternity clinics, youth centers, and classrooms.

Despite the financial success of the camps, the development of tourism in the villages has not been without problems. Arguments have inevitably arisen, and an adjustment period has been necessary to integrate the cooperatives into the general pattern of village life. In some cases, villagers who had emigrated to Dakar or Ziguinchor returned, expressing more or less openly their desire to join the cooperative. Often the management committee became envious of the operating units and demanded to be paid as well. In sum, money always creates problems, and the new influx of cash initially disturbed the balance of an economy based primarily on self-sufficiency. Adjustment to the phenomenon of tourism has, however, been more or less successful, depending on the village. The future of the tourism cooperatives will be determined in conjunction with both national and regional authorities on the basis of practical experience. Whatever form they eventually take, however, it is essential that the villagers themselves continue to exercise their own initiative and share in the profits.

Success with Tourists

One advantage of the Casamance experiment was that the reactions of foreign visitors could be tested immediately. It is now evident that tourists will respond eagerly to an opportunity for contact with the traditional African way of life. Since early 1974, tourists from the Club Méditerranée vacation village at Cap Skirring have abandoned the comfortable stay at a hotel in Ziguinchor in favor of the rustic camps of Elinkine and Enampore. Three times a week, fifteen tourists go there for a canoe outing to Karabane, an evening meal, and an overnight stop. Whereas a few years ago barely 20 to 25 percent of those staying at resorts made any excursions at all, today the proportion is approaching 40 to 45 percent.

To diversify the clientele as much as possible, and not depend on a single organization, the Department of Tourism has approached various travel agencies to sell tours that start from Dakar and include the traditional village camps as well as other nearby tourist attractions, such as national parks and beaches. It is difficult, however, to make the agencies aware of the economic and social rules that guarantee the successful operation of the camps. Surprisingly, it is easier for tourists to discover and understand a different way of life and social traditions than it is for the professionals in the field, who remain strongly attached to their own way of doing things.

The best contacts have been made with travel agencies specializing in youth groups that visit the camps during the winter season for three-week stays. The most dynamic of the agencies are Rivages, FMVJ Travel, Jumbo, Africa Tours, and Grandes Vacances. It is expected that Anglo-Saxon and Scandinavian tourists, who now come from The Gambia to visit hotels at Ziguinchor, will be equally interested.

With popularity comes the potential for new problems and pressure to increase capacity to meet the growing demand. To avoid risk of saturation, camps are located in villages with at least 1,000 inhabitants, and accommodations are limited to twenty to thirty beds in each. As more facilities are required, the existing camps will not be expanded, but new ones will be built in other locations. In all cases the villagers will be prepared for the coming of tourists as a regular event through meetings and the educational process described above for the Casamance project. Care in the selection of travel agencies is expected to give some measure of control over the type of clientele—with emphasis on the young and adventurous, who are easily assimilated into the community.

Aftermath of the Casamance Operation

The Casamance project has elicited an interest that is proportionately much greater than the physical results achieved. In this connection Elinkine and Enampore have proved valuable as models to demonstrate the purposes and procedures of the project, and officials and future managers have visited the camps to study their operation. The national authorities, who have vigorously and tenaciously supported Tourism for Discovery, regard this not as an imported project but as their own, and they fully intend to continue and extend it. The response has been identical at the regional level. The governor of Casamance and the prefects of Ziguinchor and Oussouye are personally and directly involved. They have given their full support to the project, despite the many demands on their time, and are continuing to encourage and supervise it. As for the local people—in other places often indifferent to tourism, which they experience without participating in it—here they are totally involved in the construction, management, and operation of the tourist facilities.

Another significant result of the Casamance project is the interest it has stimulated among private investors. Attracted by the modest capital outlay, rapidity of construction, and promptness of return, several small-scale regional promoters have emulated the Elinkine and Enampore models by building similar tourist facilities with traditional architecture and local management. Among these privately financed camps are those of Albert Sambou at Diembering, Malang Badji at Karabane, Soukouna and Ndjaye at Ziguinchor, Abdoulaye Mbaye at Boukot, Pathe Seck at Kabrousse, and Salif Diallo at Kolda. In all cases they have benefited from our experience and advice, and some of these camps (those at Diembering and Karabane) are already effectively complementing those of the Tourism for Discovery project in an integrated program. In addition, government-run camps have been established or are being remodeled, such as Santiaba Mandjak in Lower Casamance National Park and Kaffoutine on a beach west of Bignona, twenty kilometers from Diouloulou.

Other African countries have also shown a keen interest in Senegal's rural tourism and have asked for documentation and assistance. Although the Diolas—because of the quality of their domestic architecture and the beauty of their environmental setting—were uniquely suited to initiate Tourism for Discovery, the success in adapting the project to other regions of Senegal with differing social, economic, and political conditions indicates that the formula is equally applicable to other countries and other social and political structures. The major prerequisite is the ability to develop the interest of the people themselves so that the project benefits from their broad participation and becomes an integral part of the community.

Although the government also plans to develop beach resort, business, and convention tourism, Moustapha Fall, director of tourism, has stated that discovery tours hold enormous potential and will make their mark on tourism in Senegal in a few years. To be sure, the impact of the energy crisis is difficult to predict, but it is believed that because of Senegal's proximity to Europe and the Americas, it will be less affected than other African countries. To offset the increase in the cost of air travel it will be necessary to hold down the costs of construction and services. In this connection Fall points out: "The development of tours off the beaten path, with accommodations within the reach of every purse, will complement the traditional facilities ... and offer a most valuable itinerary for the discovery of our cultural and artistic heritage and the beginning of a true meeting of cultures."

The Department of Tourism believes it necessary to continue extending the Tourism for Discovery operation to other regions of Senegal such as Middle and Upper Casamance, Bétanti Islands (Saloum), Eastern Senegal, and Fleuve. The financing needed for these new projects still poses serious problems, following the withdrawal of the Agency for Cultural and Technical Cooperation. Other sources of funds are being sought, and a major contribution will be required from the villagers to finance and build new camps. Future activities will increasingly concentrate on overall organization or specific problems such as sanitary equipment, allocation of profits, management training, and promotion.

The new phase of the project will profit from the four years of experience in Casamance, where tourism was developed by trial and error without upsetting local customs and sensitivities. Prudence and respect for tradition are the keys to the success of the operation and its integration in the social and economic life of the community. As a celebrated Wolof proverb says, *Ndank ndank moy tyapu golo tyi Niayes,* "By treading softly you can catch the monkey in the Niayes" (a region of dunes and palm trees). This illustrates very well the African wisdom that underlies the whole approach of Tourism for Discovery.

Appendixes

Policy Recommendations Adopted by the Seminar

Conclusions on Distribution, Planning, and Participation

1. Tourism can make a substantial contribution to the economic and social development of many countries.

2. Tourism development should be undertaken consciously and methodically, and carefully planned as part of the national development effort.

3. Care should be taken to identify the precise tourism product, or products, which the country wishes to develop. The product includes not only facilities within the destination, but also the way in which they will be marketed and the way in which tourists will be transported to the destination.

a. Tourism should capitalize on the unique features of the country in order to make maximum use of local resources, to ensure a marketable product, and to reduce risk of competition from other destinations.

b. These unique assets include the cultural and natural patrimony of the country. In being partly based on such cultural and natural attractions, tourism may also play a role in preserving and developing them.

c. Countries should recognize that there are choices in the type of tourism to be developed, since various types of tourism may have different distributional and social consequences. Among the choices which may exist are those regarding the balance between individual tourism and mass organized tourism, and between pleasure-motivated activities (for example, beaches) and "exploration" or "education" activities (for example, tours of historic monuments).

d. Countries should develop recreational and touristic assets to satisfy demands by their own residents, although such assets should not be subsidized if they will be accessible mainly to the wealthier elements in the society.

e. For social as well as economic reasons countries should seek to encourage tourists from several different social, regional, and national origins.

f. Countries should attempt to seek markets with different seasonal patterns so as to smooth out the level of tourism activity in the year in order to increase the economic returns from tourism investments, as well as to reduce the social disruptions inherent in seasonal fluctuations in employment.

g. The characteristics of the "life cycle" of the product influence its impacts. It may take many years until the target market is thoroughly penetrated. It is also probable that new competitive products will be developed later in other destinations, which may require costly measures such as renovations, price cutting, and extra promotion to maintain market share and hence employment.

h. In regions in which many small countries compete in the tourism market, mechanisms of consultation and coordination should be developed to avoid the possible negative economic and social effects of unrestrained attempts to increase market shares.

4. As a general principle, countries should attempt to develop tourism and tourism projects on a *scale*, at a *rate of growth*, and in *locations*, which are consistent with making maximum use of national and local resources, which do not place undue strain on such resources, and which avoid serious adverse social, cultural, or environmental impacts. More precise recommendations to achieve these principles would include the following:

a. Countries should plan tourism on an integrated basis with other sectors, taking account of social, economic, and environmental objectives and constraints.

b. Plans should, where appropriate, deal with preservation and development of the cultural and natural heritage.

c. Planning should be interdisciplinary and include persons trained in the social sciences.

d. The profits (to firms) and budget surpluses (to governments) arising from tourism should not necessarily be plowed back into further tourism investment. They should be used, together with other investable funds, to secure a sectorally, regionally, and socially balanced pattern of investment and development.

e. Countries should avoid, where feasible, overdependence on tourism as a source of foreign exchange.

f. Large projects, which have widespread economic and social effects (for example, through creating more indirect employment in backward linkage industries) may be advantageous in large, diversified economies. But, in general, caution and gradualism are preferable. In all cases, governments should establish as a matter of course for each tourist area maximum acceptable rates of growth of tourism and of population, as well as a ceiling level of tourism, and should control construction of hotel rooms (and other accommodation capacity) accordingly. "Tourism carrying capacity" is a useful term to evoke the fact that there can be too much tourism and that it can be developed too rapidly in particular situations. In practice, however, too little is known about precise magnitudes, and this deserves further research.

g. The general advantages of gradualism and small scale must, of course, be weighed against the existence of minimum thresholds of development necessary to launch new products successfully (minimum levels of effective publicity expenditures, minimum flows to justify opening up new transport routes).

h. The desirability of using existing infrastructural networks will often argue in favor of placing new tourism developments near existing urban centers, rather than in remote areas. But there are, of course, cases in which the location of the basic physical or cultural assets of the country indicates the desirability of "greenfield" tourism development.

i. Special efforts should be made to ensure that tourism-induced demands for foodstuffs and for handicrafts be supplied, to the extent possible, by poorer rural families. This may imply the inclusion in tourism projects of extensive technical assistance, cooperatives, and credit schemes.

j. Governments should, as a matter of course, carry out thorough social and cultural impact studies of tourism projects before approving them.

5. Planning of new tourism projects in particular areas should be integrated with the planning of additional local services and facilities, including infrastructure, housing, health, and education, for the existing local population and for the additional people attracted by new opportunities in the tourism development area. The housing needs of different income groups should be taken into account.

There may be a case for subsidizing some of these services to local residents, through levying higher taxes and charges on hotels and tourism firms. Certainly, the subsidy should not go the other way.

6. There are a number of related areas in which policy measures could attempt to ensure that tourism development brings the greatest possible benefits to the local economy and society:

a. Wherever use must be made of foreign investors or transnational organizations to assist with management of enterprises in the destination country, every effort should be made to ensure that such enterprises make maximum use of local inputs and personnel. Furthermore, there should be the most careful attention paid to the terms on which transnationals manage tourism firms in destination countries.

b. Governments (or aid agencies) might provide technical and financial assistance for coordinating arrangements for publicity and promotion, reservations, and the like, for small local hotels and other tourism enterprises. This could enable them to compete more effectively with the large national and transnational groups in attracting tourists.

c. There is scope for the promotion of small-scale local entrepreneurship—in shops, local travel services, restaurants and cafes, and locally developed tourist attractions—through the provision of training courses and technical assistance and credit facilities. Moreover, it may be possible to develop incentives to encourage large tourism establishments to subcontract certain services to small businesses, or even to require new large-scale tourism projects to provide for the participation of local entrepreneurs. This could be an issue in negotiations over the terms of new projects.

d. A careful assessment should be made of the staffing needs of new projects and the extent to which these can be met by people from the locality or from elsewhere in the country. In general, preference should be given to residents of the project area. Special attention should be paid to ensuring access to employment opportunities for disadvantaged groups.

e. In most circumstances, specific training courses will be required, whether in formal training institutions or elsewhere, for local hotel and tourism staff. Existing tourism firms, as well as new ones, should be required to support training activities, since the whole industry stands to benefit from a better trained labor force. The scope and content of training programs should be worked out by representatives of the industry, of the workers, and of the authorities, to ensure that the training provides skills relevant to the needs of the industry. Training institutions may play a role in providing knowledge about local, regional, and national culture and should aim to instill in tourism staff pride in their work. The cost of such training should be borne at least in part directly by the tourism industry. Training should be monitored as to its relevance and whether the trainees are indeed being employed in suitable jobs in the industry.

7. Governments should ensure that all resources, such as beaches, parks, and historical monuments, remain in the public domain and that their use for tourism should not unduly alienate these resources from the people of the country.

8. Although this phenomenon is not exclusive to tourism, tourism development can, and apparently usually does, lead to unexpected and undesirable distributional effects—especially through the operation of the real estate market and the rise in the value of properties. The authorities need to use such mechanisms as are available to them (land and betterment taxes, taxes on unimproved land, income tax, community corporate ownership, zoning controls, building controls) to avoid an excessively unequal distribution of the benefits of tourism.

9. Effort should be devoted to building up local competence in planning. Moreover, host populations should be actively consulted and involved in tourism plans for their areas and have a voice in determining if they should have tourism, the rate of tourism growth, the types of tourists and investors to be encouraged, and, concomitantly, the type of overall development suitable for the community. This implies the creation or encouragement and strengthening of local and community groups. It also requires effective local education in the problems and benefits of tourism and cultural encounters. Although such local participation may seem to delay development, it can result in much sounder ultimate outcomes for the local community, the nation, and also for tourists. Resources should be provided to local authorities and other groups to assist them in these roles. Such resources might include financial support, technical assistance, or organizational support. Where local authorities are weak in instituting and implementing planning controls, firm central government action may be required at least initially to make up for the weakness.

10. There needs to be substantial coordination among different agencies (including those responsible for culture) to ensure formula-

tion and implementation of sound tourism plans. It is, of course, undesirable for the tourism authorities to attempt to take over direct planning and management of all infrastructure, social services, investments in tourism superstructures, preservation of cultural and natural heritage, and development of artistic creation necessary to tourism development.

Conclusions on the Encounter and on Cultural Aspects of Tourism

1. General considerations:
a. In assessing the impact of a tourism project on the local and regional population, three broad categories of people should be considered separately: those employed in tourism sector activities; those living in the vicinity of a tourism project and having occasional contact with tourists; and those who never have any contact with tourists.
b. Measures for improving the encounter between tourist and host should take account of the fact that many tourists during their vacations desire to be free from many constraints they encounter in their everyday lives.
c. The attitudes of the local population and the tourists toward each other depend upon such factors as the size of the country, the prevailing socioeconomic and cultural conditions, the speed and type of tourism development, and the nature of the tourists concerned. Those elements and the social-psychological aspects of the tourism-carrying capacity of the local population should be taken explicitly into account in planning tourism projects and form the basis for deciding the pattern as well as the scale of tourism development. Among the alternative patterns available are: enclave development, under which tourists and members of the destination country population are carefully separated; the "semipermeable" pattern, under which mixing is confined to carefully selected groups of the local population such as the elites of the destination country and tourists; and open patterns, where interactions between tourists and destination country populations are maximized through the physical placement of tourism facilities, pricing policies, and the like.
d. The impacts of the encounter depend largely on the type and

intensity of tourist-host contacts, and any measure designed to influence the encounter should take both factors into account.

2. Tourists should be presented with an adequate and not a one-sided image of the country and its people. To this end, national tourist offices should:

a. produce good, effective, honest and informative publicity material

b. give incentives to tour operators and travel agencies to distribute such material with their marketing material, at least to those tourists visiting the country

c. consult with tour operators to try to ensure the production of marketing material which is more satisfactory from the host country point of view

d. be prepared to spend a percentage of their promotional budgets for this purpose

e. widen the methods of distribution of informational material.

3. Tourists should be better prepared for their travel abroad, in order to avoid undesirable unintended consequences of their behavior, by:

a. "awareness" programs, which should not appear to be imposed upon the tourist and should if possible be organized by the authorities in the tourists' own countries. They would inform tourists of the specific social, cultural, and religious environment they will encounter at their destination. In particular, the programs should sensitize tourists to the problems that might arise in their interaction with the lower level tourism sector employees (such as waiters, taxi drivers, and porters), since local resentment most easily arises as a result of this interaction.

b. informational brochures, prepared in tourism-generating or destination countries and distributed through agencies, on flights, or at airports. They should provide practical guidelines to tourists, for instance on the restricted use of beachwear and on appropriate levels for tipping, as well as some basic expressions in the local language.

c. films, shown during travel to the destination.

Appropriate training along similar lines should also be given to employees of intermediary organizations, such as tour operators, travel agencies, and airlines.

4. The local population should be assisted with the tourist contact by educational programs in schools and through the media, de-

signed to strengthen both appreciation of their own culture and respect for other cultures.

5. Local officials, entrepreneurs, and employees who come into contact with tourists (for example, customs officials, taxi drivers, waiters, hotel service personnel, tour guides, shop owners, police) should be assisted with the tourist contact by training. In addition, recognition should be given to the social usefulness of the functions performed by employees in the tourism sector.

6. Guides should:

a. possess a sufficient educational background so that they can absorb the necessary training, particularly on the history, culture, and geography of the destination country. Such training could be undertaken with the assistance of local universities, aid donors, or international agencies.

b. not be largely dependent on commission payments, since narrow commercial considerations could divert them from doing their job properly.

7. Activities in which both the tourist and local population can participate should be organized, such as special festivals of art and music, cultural exhibitions, sports events, sociocultural, cultural-historical, or environmental activities, which could form "modules" for tour packages.

Measures to Encourage the Local Culture for the Benefit of the Population and the Tourist Alike

1. Governments should render accessible to everyone the country's cultural and natural heritage, either *in situ* or in well-conceived museums, and should at the same time respect the visitor-carrying capacity of such sites and museums. In addition, the contemporary culture of a country may be an important asset in attracting tourists. Due consideration in planning tourism should therefore be given to all manifestations of culture, not only those regarded as exceptional but also the less spectacular.

2. Specialized publications and studies (by educational institutions, historical and cultural associations, and public tourism development bodies) may stimulate interest in and respect for these assets on the part of the people and foreign visitors. Publications and studies of this kind would provide basic information for preparing good

publicity and training material; they could also be used by tourism marketing organizations.

3. All national and foreign publicity material should be regularly reviewed by a panel of art historians, archaeologists, architects, sociologists, and representatives of the tourism authorities so that depiction is satisfactory from the host country point of view.

4. In the development of arts and crafts:

a. The production of high quality products should be encouraged.

b. Technical assistance should be provided, where appropriate, through cooperatives to provide craftsmen with materials and equipment needed for their production and to market and transport products more efficiently.

c. Arts and crafts should be stimulated by the organization of associations and meetings of craftsmen and artists, as well as by exhibitions. Due attention needs to be paid to the improvement of technical skills through training schemes.

5. Local material culture should be used for tourist purposes by:

a. greater use of art and handicraft objects in tourist facilities and by their display in public establishments. This would create greater appreciation for the local culture by autochthonous and tourist populations alike.

b. the use of historic buildings as hotels, restaurants, and shops (which should contribute to their preservation).

c. the use of traditional architecture in building tourist facilities.

Participants in the Seminar

David Maybury-Lewis, *United States*
  Chairman, Department of Anthropology, Harvard University

DISCUSSANTS
Alex Inkeles, *United States*
  Professor of Social Psychology, Department of Sociology and
  Education, Stanford University
Luis Lumbreras, *Peru*
  Director, Museum of Anthropology and Archaeology, Lima
Anjani Mehta, *India*
  Joint Director General, Government of India
  Tourism Department
Josef Nowicki, *Poland*
  Director, Research Institute for Developing Countries, Central
  School of Planning and Statistics, Warsaw

PARTICIPANTS
Antonios Andronicou, *Cyprus*
  Director General, Cyprus Tourism Organization
Gusti Ngurah Bagus, *Indonesia*
  Chairman, Department of Anthropology,
  Udayana University, Bali
René Baretje, *France*
  Director, Centre des Hautes Etudes Touristiques,
  Aix-en-Provence
Francis Byabato, *Tanzania*
  General Manager, Tanzania Tourism Development Corporation
Emanuel de Kadt, *Netherlands*
  Institute of Development Studies, University of Sussex
Mario Gaviria, *Spain*
  Sociologist, University of Madrid
Stephen Geissler, *France*
  Deputy Director, Club Méditerranée

Stephen Halsey, *United States*
  Senior Vice-President, International Operations,
  American Express Company
Somchai Hiranyakit, *Thailand*
  Director General, Tourism Organization of Thailand
Jost Krippendorf, *Switzerland*
  Institut de Recherches Touristiques, University of Berne
Hamed Abdel Meguid, *Egypt*
  Undersecretary, Ministry of Tourism and Civil Aviation
Dusan Nejkov, *Yugoslavia*
  Undersecretary, Federal Committee for Tourism
Lothar Nettekoven, *Federal Republic of Germany*
  Sociologist, Africa-Asia Bureau, Society for Development Plan-
  ning, Köln
William D. Patterson, *United States*
  Travel Consultant
Agustin Reynoso y Valle, *Mexico*
  Head of Community Development Services
  (FONATUR), Zihuatanejo, Mexico
Karl-Ferdinand Schädler, *Federal Republic of Germany*
  Economist and Master Craftsman, Expert on Small-Scale Industry
Rustum J. Sethna, *Pakistan*
  Research Scholar, Caribbean Tourism Research Center, Barbados
Ahmed Smaoui, *Tunisia*
  Deputy Director, National Tourist Office
Glaucio Ary Dillon Soares, *Brazil*
  Head, Department of Social Studies, University of Brasilia
Jose J. Villamil, *United States*
  Director, Institute for Social and Economic Research, University
  of Puerto Rico

Papers Submitted to the Seminar
in addition to those in this volume

Gusti Ngurah Bagus, "The Impact of Tourism upon the Culture of the Balinese People"

Abdelwahab Bouhdiba, "The Impact of Tourism on Traditional Values and Beliefs in Tunisia"

Walter Elkan, "The Impact of Tourism on Employment"

Eduardo J. Ellis, "Tourism and the Unity of the Sociocultural Environment"

Mario Gaviria, "The Mass Tourism Industry in Spain"

Davydd J. Greenwood, "Tourism and Employment and the Local Community"

David C. McClelland, "Developing Local Business in the Promotion of Tourism"

Philip F. McKean, "The Culture Brokers of Bali"

Jose Villamil, "Tourism in the Caribbean"

Index

Acapulco [Mexico], 111, 112, 117-18, 132

Africa: agriculture locally important in, 39; airlines of, 88, 90; airport construction in, 85, 97n; dependence on foreign firms in, 81, 87, 88-92, 99; distribution of income in, 81, 83; East, 7, 36, 39, 50, 84, 87, 97n, 154; employment affected by tourism in, 36, 84-85, 87; foreign exchange earnings, 80, 81, 82-84, 87, 98, 99; imports receiving tax concessions, 83; infrastructure cost in, 84; North, 39, 84, 87; planning of tourism development in, 89-90; promotional literature on, 321, 324; religions in, 151-53; resource allocation for tourism in, 45, 80, 86; West, 39, 72-73, 83, 84, 87, 150, 154-55

African arts and crafts: aid to, 72, 151, 154; centers for production and sale of, 74, 150-51, 154; degeneration of, 70-71; economic effect of, 150; as entertainment, 153-54, 155; European aesthetics in, 147-49; marketing of, 150-51; museums for, 154-55; preservation of, 69, 154-55; quality of, 146, 147, 148-49, 151; religious effect on, 149-50, 151-54, 155-56; for tourist consumption, 147-49, 150

Agriculture: conversion of land from, 183, 188; economic dependence on, 205, 206, 239, 290; employment in, 38-40, 104, 105, 178, 208, 214, 222-23, 233, 235, 239, 254, 257, 291, 307-08; exports, 3, 39, 206, 207-09; imports, 39, 235, 294; outflow of labor from, 11, 22, 44, 159

Aid: for arts and crafts, 15, 28-29, 72-73, 146, 154, 155, 252-53, 297, 341, 347; for tourism development, 24-25, 26, 31, 32, 46, 53, 76, 109, 342; for urban preservation, 76

Airlines: national, 28, 88, 90, 251, 278; role in tourism industry, 11, 90, 141-42, 181, 310

Airports: effect of development on, 41, 85, 97n, 114, 131, 159, 160, 180, 205, 212, 215, 237, 310; planning considerations in construction of, 27

Albania, 18

Algeria, 19, 80, 100

Angola, 100, 155

Andronicou, Antonios, 20, 21, 23, 27, 29, 36, 37, 44, 49, 53, 56-57, 62, 66, 69, 72, 74, 237-66

Antigua, 63n, 161n, 176

Antilles, 165

Apter, D. E., 247

Area Department for Tourism (DIPPARDA) [Bali], 187, 197-99

Arts and crafts, 102, 185, 192, 252-53; centers for production and sale of, 73, 74, 191; degeneration of, 14-15, 70-71; export of, 72, 185, 282; marketing of, 15, 40, 72-75, 253; revitalization of, 14-15, 69-76, 145; uses of, 14, 15, 72n 146, 149-50, 341, 347. *See also* Aid (for arts and crafts); *individual countries*

Avecindados, 119-22

Bagus, I Gusti Ngurah, 73n, 185n, 186n, 187n, 188n, 192n, 201

Badung district [Bali], 181, 185, 186, 187, 189, 190, 193, 195, 197, 203

Bahamas: GNP per capita in, 161n

Baïla [Senegal], 324, 330

Bali, 7, 215; arts and crafts affected by tourism, 71, 73-74, 167-68, 185, 192, 198, 201-02; agriculture in, 178, 183, 188; attitudes toward foreigners in, 180, 183, 201-02; commercialization of traditions in, 61-62, 68-69, 70, 71, 180, 182, 186-87; dance troupes in, 193 (*see also* Monkey dance); distribution of income from tourism in, 189-91; employment affected by tourism, 36, 43, 178, 183, 184, 186, 187-88, 195, 196; encounter of tourist and host in,

The full range of World Bank publications, both free and for sale, is described in the *Catalog of World Bank Publications,* and of the continuing research program of the World Bank, in *World Bank Research Program: Abstracts of Current Studies.* The most recent edition of each is available without charge from:

PUBLICATIONS UNIT
THE WORLD BANK
1818 H STREET, N.W.
WASHINGTON, D.C. 20433
U.S.A.